THE FUTURE OF
THE INTERNATIONAL NUCLEAR NON-PROLIFERATION REGIME

NIJHOFF LAW SPECIALS

D. Campbell, Abortion Law and Public Policy. 1984.
ISBN 90-247-3107-0

J. Pictet, Development and Principles of International Humanitarian Law. 1985.
ISBN 90-247-3199-2

J. van Houtte, Sociology of Law and Legal Anthropology in Dutch-speaking Countries. 1985.
ISBN 90-247-3175-5

C.D. De Fouloy, Glossary of NAFTA Terms. 1994.
ISBN 0-7923-2719-5

H.L. Zielinski, Health and Humanitarian Concerns. Principles and Ethics. 1994
ISBN 0-7923-2963-5

K.S. Foster and D.C. Alexander, Prospects of a US-Chile Free Trade Agreement. 1994
ISBN 0-7923-2885-X

F.J.M. Feldbrugge (ed.), Russian Federation Legislative Survey. June 1990-December 1992. 1995
ISBN 0-7923-3243-1

R. Platzöder (ed.), The 1994 United Nations Convention on the Law of the Sea. Basic Documents with an Introduction. 1995
ISBN 0-7923-3271-7

D. Warner (ed.), New Dimensions of Peacekeeping. 1995
ISBN 0-7923-3301-2

M. van Leeuwen (ed.), The Future of the International Nuclear Non-Proliferation Regime. 1995
ISBN 0-7923-3433-7

Netherlands Institute of International Relations
"Clingendael"

The Future of
the International Nuclear
Non-Proliferation Regime

Edited by

Marianne van Leeuwen

Research Department,
Netherlands Institute of International Relations "Clingendael"

MARTINUS NIJHOFF PUBLISHERS
DORDRECHT / BOSTON / LONDON

A C.I.P. Catalogue record for this book is available from the Library of Congress.

ISBN 0-7923-3433-7

Published by Martinus Nijhoff Publishers,
P.O. Box 163, 3300 AD Dordrecht, The Netherlands.

Sold and distributed in the U.S.A. and Canada
by Kluwer Academic Publishers,
101 Philip Drive, Norwell, MA 02061, U.S.A.

In all other countries, sold and distributed
by Kluwer Academic Publishers Group,
P.O. Box 322, 3300 AH Dordrecht, The Netherlands.

Rebecca Solheim, Linguistic Editing
Birgit Leiteritz, Lay-out

Printed on acid-free paper

Contents

1   Introduction: The Future of the International Nuclear Non-Proliferation Regime

Marianne van Leeuwen

In 1968, a treaty was drafted which aimed to stop the proliferation of nuclear weapons and to stimulate the dismantlement of existing nuclear arsenals. In 1970, this Nuclear Non-Proliferation Treaty (NPT) entered into force for its initial term of twenty-five years. Consequently, a conference is to be convened in 1995 "to decide whether the Treaty shall continue in force indefinitely, or shall be extended for an additional fixed period or periods."[1]

The importance of the extension decision cannot easily be overrated as, during the past twenty-five years, the NPT has proved to be the main normative pillar of the international nuclear non-proliferation regime. It has been ratified by more than 160 countries, including all "officially recognized" nuclear-weapon states, and although for a long time a small number of so-called threshold-states - states striving to achieve a military nuclear option without openly admitting it - stayed outside of the Treaty, even among them, the NPT has made converts. In 1992 South Africa ratified the NPT as a non-nuclear weapon state after dismantling its military nuclear capability, and Argentina followed this example in 1994. Yet the decision to extend the Treaty is not expected to be made on the nod.

The NPT Criticized: Nuclear-Weapon States and Arms Reductions

The NPT has always been criticized as discriminatory, even by many of its parties. The Treaty distinguishes between nuclear-weapon states[2] and non-

---

1. NPT Article X.
2. The United States, Russia (as successor to the Soviet Union), the United Kingdom, France, and the People's Republic of China fall under the NPT definition of a nuclear-weapon state. NPT Article IX.3 "... For the purposes of this Treaty, a nuclear-weapon State is one which has manufactured and exploded a nuclear weapon or other nuclear explosive device prior to

1

M. van Leeuwen (ed.), The Future of the International Nuclear Non-Proliferation Regime, 1-13.
© 1995 *Kluwer Academic Publishers. Printed in the Netherlands.*

nuclear-weapon states. The general perception is that it is the latter that have to carry most of the Treaty's burdens. Non-nuclear-weapon states have to promise to abstain from trying to obtain nuclear weapons (Article II). They have to accept full-scope safeguards (Article III) to be executed by the International Atomic Energy Agency (IAEA). Meanwhile, the nuclear-weapon states do not have to submit to safeguards on any of their fissile material.[3] According to Article I, nuclear-weapon states are not allowed to help non-nuclear-weapon states obtain a military nuclear capability (hardly a taxing commitment) and, according to Article VI, they have to negotiate "in good faith" to achieve an expedient end to the nuclear arms race and, eventually, full disarmament. However, for a long time after 1970, the nuclear arsenals of the recognized nuclear-weapon states only grew in size and precision. Only since the second half of the 1980s have important steps been taken with regard to arms reductions, and the present number of nuclear warheads still far exceeds that of the NPT's early years.

During past NPT review conferences, held every five years, failure to conclude a Comprehensive Test Ban Treaty (CTBT) has always been at the center of arguments about arms control and arms reduction.[4] Until recently, Western nuclear-weapon states in particular resisted a comprehensive ban, as they wanted to check and modernize their nuclear arsenals. The United States was the most prominent protagonist of continued testing, and as a consequence, it was the main target for criticism on this score at review conferences. Mexico traditionally acted as the leading critic, with the sympathy of many developing countries, but some industrialized countries were also in agreement. Even at the 1990 review conference, when the United States and the Soviet Union could already point to impressive progress in arms reductions, Mexico stressed the CTBT issue with such inflexibility that it impeded acceptance of a final statement based on consensus.

A second issue frequently raised at review conferences is that of security guarantees, for having renounced a nuclear capability of their own, many non-nuclear-weapon states demand security guarantees in return. In the United Nations Security Council, as early as 1968, three of the five officially recognized nuclear-

---

January 1, 1967."

3. All recognized nuclear-weapon states have now accepted, on a voluntary basis, IAEA safeguards on part of the fissile material in their civilian nuclear cycle. The importance of these safeguards is largely symbolic.

4. Although a comprehensive test ban is recommended in the preamble of the NPT, the Treaty's formal commitments do not mention it.

weapon states had committed themselves to taking appropriate action if a non-nuclear-weapon state that was party to the NPT was attacked, or under threat of being attacked, by nuclear weapons.[5] The resolution in question placed responsibility for collective protective action mainly with the Security Council. But it would be naive to expect the five permanent members to cooperate smoothly in the case of a nuclear crisis. If one of them was involved in an offensive role, the Security Council would not be able to act as a conflict-restraining force. Not surprisingly, then, the Council's resolution posed that states *are* allowed to extend immediate help to non-nuclear-weapon states attacked, or under threat of attack, by nuclear forces, basing its position on relevant articles in the UN Charter. It also emphasized that members of the United Nations have the right to defend themselves unilaterally or in cooperation with others when they are attacked, until the Security Council has taken action to restore international peace and security.

In the past, however, the fiercest debates have focused on negative security guarantees, with non-nuclear-weapon states demanding a commitment by the nuclear five not to use or threaten to use military nuclear force against them. Most nuclear-weapon states have provided such an assurance unilaterally, but have refused to subscribe to a collective and general promise. The United States, for instance, attached great value to the strategy of nuclear deterrence against the Warsaw Pact countries as a whole, in view of their conventional advantage over the countries of the North Atlantic Alliance. Meanwhile, only the People's Republic of China has committed itself unilaterally to a policy of no-first-use, but China until 1992 was not a party to the NPT and its policies received relatively little attention during past review conferences.

The lack of solid results from negotiations on arms reductions has also been frequently attacked at the five-yearly meetings of the NPT's member states, although the criticism lost intensity after the United States and the Soviet Union started to dismantle important parts of their nuclear arsenal. Full nuclear disarmament, however, will obviously not be reached in 1995, if ever.

---

5. Security Council Resolution 255, June 19, 1968. Ten votes in favor, no votes against. Algeria, Brazil, France, India and Pakistan abstained.

The NPT Criticized: Impediments to the Development of Civil-Use Programs

During review conferences, non-nuclear-weapon states have also at times showed great irritation at the impediments to their attempts at building a civil nuclear infrastructure. Article IV of the NPT had, after all, confirmed their right to develop and use nuclear power for civilian purposes "without discrimination." By the end of the 1970s, however, developing countries concluded that a small number of technologically advanced states were undermining Article IV by strictly regulating their nuclear exports. They were particularly incensed by the 1977 Guidelines of the Nuclear Suppliers Group (NSG) and the US Nuclear Non-Proliferation Act of 1978.

The NSG was first convened after India's "peaceful" nuclear explosion of 1974, and the United States and the Soviet Union were among its initiators. The members of this informal group wanted to strengthen the international non-proliferation regime without damaging their economic interests, so the Guidelines were intended to prevent both proliferation and "unfair" competition among the members of the NSG. The suppliers demanded, for instance, that their clients accept certain safeguards (although not, as a rule, full-scope safeguards), so consequently the trade in nuclear items with non-members of the NPT was made subject to some control at least. The suppliers also agreed to treat the potential sale of certain sensitive goods and technologies with restraint, and both non-members and members of the NPT would be confronted with this rule if they wanted to buy sensitive items.

The national non-proliferation policies of the United States went further still: the US demanded full-scope safeguards as a condition for all its nuclear exports, and tried to prevent the spread of sensitive materials, products and technologies as much as possible. At the 1980 NPT review conference, many developing countries particularly protested against the export restrictions, as violations of the Treaty's rulings and intentions.[6]

---

6. NPT Article IV states that "all the Parties undertake to *facilitate*, and have the right to *participate* in, the fullest possible exchange of equipment, materials, and scientific and technological information for the peaceful uses of nuclear energy" (author's emphasis).

Recent Developments

At the beginning of the 1990s, a comprehensive test ban seemed finally to become feasible. As the United States and the Soviet Union/Russia were preparing by mutual arrangement to demolish large parts of their nuclear arsenals, it was hard to see why they should continue to invest in modernizing their military nuclear capabilities. The only remaining justification for nuclear tests was the need to verify the safety and reliability of existing warheads. In the United States, particularly, proponents of a comprehensive ban gained ground rapidly and influenced decision-making, and in 1994, after a unanimous UN decision, the Conference on Disarmament in Geneva revived negotiations on a nuclear test ban. The United States had already installed what amounted to a testing moratorium, to become a full ban after 1996, pending the cessation of nuclear tests by other powers, and most other nuclear-weapon states followed the American example, be it with varying degrees of enthusiasm. Meanwhile, the Chinese, in contrast, felt that they lagged behind in nuclear capability and engaged in a "catch-up" testing program. They are on record as supporting the principle of a comprehensive ban, but during recent negotiations at the Conference on Disarmament they tried to keep alive the option of explosions for "peaceful" purposes and advocated that a CTBT be linked to a declaration of no-first-use by all nuclear-weapon states. These proposals were interpreted as delaying tactics.

All in all, there is a risk that the five nuclear-weapon states will continue to wait for each other to take the formal decision to permanently abandon all nuclear testing. Therefore, although the auspices seem less bleak than they did some five years ago, it remains unlikely that a Comprehensive Test Ban Treaty will be concluded in 1995, at least before the NPT Conference.

Now that all nuclear-weapon states have ratified the NPT and Cold War confrontations between the two opposing nuclear-armed alliances seem a thing of the past, arguments against binding collective security guarantees have also arguably lost their persuasiveness. Commitments on this score are best made through Security Council resolutions. Nuclear-weapon states, however, still have doubts, and in addition, negative security guarantees would not rule out the possibility of a threshold country attacking or threatening an enemy with nuclear weapons. Only positive guarantees could be effective in that context.

Since the 1990 review conference, the United States and the Soviet Union (and Russia since 1992) have made more substantial progress in nuclear arms reductions. In 1991 Washington and Moscow concluded a treaty concerning balanced reductions in their strategic nuclear weapons (Strategic Arms Reduction Treaty, START 1). However, after the collapse of the Soviet Union the relevant systems became spread among four states - Russia, Belarus, Kazakhstan and Ukraine - yet despite this, in May 1992, American representatives managed to obtain commitments from all four governments to live up to the START 1 agreement. Belarus, Kazakhstan and Ukraine also promised to ratify the NPT as non-nuclear-weapon states "as soon as possible." Belarus and Kazakhstan did so in 1993, but Ukraine still demurred.

Meanwhile, the legislative bodies of the United States, Russia, Belarus, Kazakhstan and Ukraine agreed in principle to ratification of the START 1 treaty. The Russian parliament, however, made the formal activation of START 1 conditional on the ratification of the NPT by all successor states, whereas the Ukrainian parliament attached thirteen conditions to ratification, mainly concerning security guarantees and financial support and compensation, and stated that it would only consider ratifying the NPT when its conditions concerning START 1 had been met. The Ukrainian government tried to break the deadlock created by its legislature. In January 1994, the Presidents of the United States, the Russian Federation and Ukraine made a Trilateral Statement in which the thirteen conditions were basically met, at least according to the Ukrainian President. The parliament in Kiev, while not explicitly embracing this interpretation, agreed to proceed with the ratification of START 1 and reconfirmed that Ukraine would ratify the NPT as a non-nuclear weapon state as soon as possible. It finally became an NPT member on December 5, 1994, unlocking the formal implementation of the START agreements.

Early in 1993, Washington and Moscow also agreed upon a follow-up treaty on the reduction of strategic nuclear systems, START 2. According to this agreement, shortly after the year 2000 the United States and Russia will each possess no more than 3,500 strategic nuclear warheads. This ceiling still falls dramatically short of total nuclear disarmament, but even so, impressive technical and financial efforts will have to be made to reach this goal. Heavy involvement by the United States administration will be needed, both at home and in the Soviet successor states.

After years of slumber, the Nuclear Suppliers Group was recently reactivated, spurred on by the shocking findings concerning Iraq's nuclear-weapons' program. It had become apparent that many Western countries had contributed to Iraq's nuclear option by selling it dual-use technology and materials, so in April 1992 the NSG states published new Guidelines, which they have all undertaken to implement at a national level. They are now demanding full-scope safeguards as a condition for nuclear-related sales. In addition, they have drawn up a new trigger list of dual-use items; these goods may only be exported under certain controls. Apart from this new strengthening of the export regime, some countries individually tightened their export laws still further. This was especially the case with Germany.

These policies would have caused an outcry fifteen years ago. After the sobering revelations concerning Iraq's nuclear program, however, criticism of strengthening export controls seems to have subsided. The way in which controls are molded may remain controversial, however, especially if the supplier states emphasize restrictions and denial rather than strict verifications.

Following the findings on Iraq, IAEA safeguards, too, were critically evaluated and improvements suggested. To a large extent, the suggestions focused on activating existing but unused possibilities for control, especially of inspections at undeclared sites and at short notice (so-called special inspections). The IAEA Secretariat and Board of Governors decided that such inspections should only be held after specific information on a nation's intention to proliferate had been provided to the Agency. The implementation of special inspections is bound to be difficult and controversial, however. First, the decision to go ahead has to be approved by the IAEA's Board of Governors, which is likely to disagree and cause delay by its deliberations. Second, intelligence gathering is entirely dependent on the cooperation of IAEA member states. Until Iraq's invasion of Kuwait, for instance, the United States had refused to provide intelligence data for fear of the information ending up in the wrong hands. A small IAEA intelligence evaluation team has now been proposed, which should report directly to the Director General, but a fully satisfactory solution to these problems has yet to be found. The IAEA, meanwhile, deviating from earlier policy, requires notification of construction plans for relevant buildings before construction starts and is preparing several other measures to produce greater safeguards' transparency and effectiveness. In addition, much work has recently been done on technical improvements, for instance on environmental monitoring.

Even though the traditional nuclear exporters have become more responsible, there is still serious concern that proliferation may be stimulated by nuclear and related trade. This is caused by the rise of new nuclear-exporting countries which have not joined the existing international regime, or, if they have done so, are not living up to their commitments. The People's Republic of China and North Korea are the most prominent in this category. Fears are also fed by the fluid situation in the states of the former Soviet Union and some former Eastern Bloc countries: in some instances the political transition has undermined the legal basis for export controls. Major overhauls of safeguards became necessary after the Soviet Union fell apart: increasing amounts of fissile material from the dismantlement of nuclear weapons have to be protected against theft; proper implementation of existing controls has become questionable; proof is accumulating that unscrupulous individuals or, perhaps, organizations are trying to sell sensitive materials abroad for a good price with total disregard for existing export rules. The need for hard currency is pressing in this part of the world, and the living conditions of the former Soviet Union's nuclear elite and weapon technicians have badly deteriorated. Western countries have made plans to prevent nuclear scholars and technicians from putting their knowledge at the service of less desirable regimes by offering them properly paid, relevant work in their own country. This approach, however, while sensible, is based on voluntary participation and obviously cannot be watertight.

Other Recent Developments: Denuclearization, and Proliferation outside the NPT

Outside the former Soviet empire, too, recent developments have shed a special light on the effectiveness and credibility of the Non-Proliferation Treaty. The most important are briefly discussed here.

In Latin America, Argentina and Brazil buried the hatchet of their nuclear rivalry. In 1991 they promised to use their nuclear programs for civilian purposes only. In order to reinforce their mutual commitment, they agreed on reciprocal bilateral safeguards to be implemented in cooperation with the IAEA. Brazil has been making preparatory steps to ratify the Treaty of Tlatelolco which aims make Latin America a nuclear-weapon-free zone. Meanwhile, Argentina ratified the NPT in 1994. All in all, concerns about proliferation dangers in this part of the world have diminished substantially.

South Africa has gone through enormous social and political changes, the end of which are not yet in sight. Its leaders are now striving for domestic democratization, and at the same time, perceptions about outside threats to South Africa's security have changed strongly. South Africa is trying to regain a normal place in the international community and shake off the long isolation caused by its apartheid policies. One part of this policy has been the demolition of its military nuclear option and its accession to the NPT as a non-nuclear-weapon state. This first example of denuclearization has illustrated how a country wishing to prove its "decency" to the world, among other things, can do so by joining the Non-Proliferation Treaty.

Not everywhere, however, have proliferation risks been on the decrease so unequivocally. In the Middle East Iraq's program has been defused and largely demolished, but the mere fact that this country, a member of the NPT community, could have made such progress on the road to a military option is worrying enough. Elsewhere in the Middle East, moreover, work on military options is continuing. Israel, to all intents and purposes, has been a nuclear-weapon state for more than twenty years now, and may be adding steadily to its nuclear capabilities. Perhaps peace agreements and the normalization of relationships with its neighbors will induce Israel to freeze and eventually to reduce its nuclear arsenal. For the time being, however, the country is likely to stick by its undeclared nuclear capability to compensate for the quantitative conventional superiority and the unconventional arms programs of its enemies. Libya's nuclear ambitions have probably not lessened during recent years, and it may be counting on attracting knowledge and hardware from the former Soviet Union. The United States, in particular, has expressed fears that Iran is seeking a nuclear option, while unsubstantiated concerns have been expressed about Algeria, Syria and Saudi Arabia.

The situation is at least as dangerous in South Asia. During the second half of the 1980s, Pakistan crossed the nuclear threshold. This made potential escalation of the conflicts between Pakistan and India even more ominous. According to a journalistic source, Pakistan in 1990 actually took steps to use nuclear means in its confrontation with India over Kashmir - a dispute that has not yet been resolved.[7] A complicating factor is the troubled and frequently very violent character of domestic politics in both India and Pakistan, causing many to have grave doubts about the ability of either to restrain the use of nuclear options in times of crisis. For the time being, however, neither India nor Pakistan plan to go public with their nuclear capabilities or to integrate the use of nuclear weapons into their military strategies. Moreover, some progress has been made through bilateral agreements to limit the risk of nuclearization of conflicts. At the same time, relations between India and its powerful, nuclear-armed neighbor, the People's

---

7. Seymour M. Hersh, "On the nuclear edge," *The New Yorker*, March 29, 1993, pp. 56-73.

Republic of China, have become somewhat more relaxed. It would be foolish, however, to hope that India and Pakistan will follow the South African example in the foreseeable future. The security problems in the region are far too pressing and intractable.

Israel, India and Pakistan have always stayed away from the NPT and are expected to continue this policy for some time.

Proliferation within the NPT

During the past decade, however, it has also been demonstrated that the Non-Proliferation Treaty can be threatened from within, by non-nuclear-weapon states which have ratified and used the Treaty as a cover to obtain a military nuclear option.

In spite of the fact that Iraq acceded to the NPT at a very early stage and had, at first sight, cooperated quite readily and smoothly with the IAEA's inspections of its fissile material, Iraq's nuclear program has been under suspicion for a long time. In June 1981 Israel took unilateral action against Iraq's growing capability by destroying its main research reactor which was about to go critical. Iraq's plans were delayed by this spectacular strike, but not annulled. Just how inventive and effective Iraq's acquisition and construction team had been in continuing the illegal weapons' program only became known outside the country during 1991 and 1992. In the summer of 1990, Iraq's political leadership miscalculated international reactions by conquering Kuwait and thus provoked international military counteraction. Baghdad lost the second Gulf War, and had to allow the United Nations to defuse and demolish its non-conventional arms' programs. Such a policy of forced denuclearization, however, is financially and politically tremendously expensive and can only be employed rarely, after an "offender" has been defeated in war.

In the meantime, another case, that of North Korea, has been capturing the headlines. Unlike Iraq, North Korea has not even tried to keep up the appearance of living by its NPT commitments. In 1985 it ratified the Treaty as a non-nuclear-weapon state, but ever since, despite increasing international pressure, it has refused to cooperate properly with the full-scope safeguards' obligations that are inherent in the Treaty. Its political leadership tried to link acceptance of comprehensive safeguards to US and South Korean concessions such as stopping annual joint exercises and withdrawing nuclear weapons from the peninsula. At the same time, it was producing a military nuclear option, mainly under its own steam, and in the recurring negotiations with the United States, the incipient option was used to obtain further concessions. In March 1993, North Korea threatened to leave the NPT, referring to Article X.1, which allows member states to secede from the Treaty under certain conditions. As secession was widely seen as a precedent to be prevented at almost any cost, the United States made an extra effort to make the North Korean leadership change its mind. North Korea suspended its secession, but did not withdraw it until it reached an agreement with the United States in October 1994. Although this agreement reconfirmed North Korea's duty to allow full-scope IAEA safeguards, it remains questionable whether it will effectively guarantee foolproof verification opportunities. And even if it really proves to provide such guarantees, the agreement, as it contains major financial and diplomatic benefits to Pyongyang, arguably offers an example of how bad behavior by a non-nuclear-weapon state that is party to the NPT may be rewarded rather than punished.

Extension of the NPT: Procedures and Scenarios

In December 1992, the General Assembly of the United Nations decided to convene a conference in the spring of 1995 with the aim of reviewing implementation of the NPT over the previous five years, and deciding upon its extension. According to NPT Article X.2, after the first 25 years a choice has to be made between indefinite extension or extension for "an additional fixed period or periods." The article does *not* cite immediate expiration of the Treaty as an option, and a decision to extend must be made by a majority of the Treaty's parties.

Indefinite extension seems to be the most straightforward alternative. The choice of this option implies the belief that the NPT in its present form will be sufficiently effective in the future, or at least that extension for a fixed period of time would place a time-bomb under the Treaty and the entire international non-proliferation regime, and that an imperfect Treaty is better than no Treaty at all. Most Western countries favor indefinite extension, and with the exception of the People's Republic of China, which had not yet publicized its point of view at the time of writing, all nuclear-weapon states are also on record as being in favor of indefinite extension. It is unlikely, however, that this group of countries will be able to control voting at the 1995 conference. Many non-aligned states want to force the nuclear-weapon states to implement their part of the bargain. Indefinite extension deprives them of an important opportunity to exert pressure.

Extension by one fixed period would mean that the Treaty would automatically expire after that period. All parties would then be released from their obligations, and negotiations would be needed to provide the world with a successor treaty. This would obviously entail a number of grave risks - risks that many developing countries are not likely to want to run. Another version of this option, extension for a defined number of fixed periods, is problematic for the same reasons.

The third alternative is extension for an indefinite series of fixed periods. At the end of each period, it would be *possible* for parties to start procedures to end the NPT. If they did not take such action, the Treaty would automatically continue in force. This option would meet the wishes of those desiring to keep a check on the nuclear-weapon states. Under it, however, the Treaty may be terminated relatively easily. If the periods in the indefinite series were kept short, the latter possibility might even very quickly become reality.

Conclusion: Introducing the Project

The NPT review and extension conference of 1995 marks a crucial stage in the evolution of the international nuclear non-proliferation regime. Its results may well dictate the success of future attempts to control and reduce the spread of nuclear weapons - matters of great concern to the world.

This is why the Netherlands Institute of International Relations "Clingendael" felt that it should join the international debate on nuclear proliferation and its prevention, and invite an international team of experts to contribute their views on specific issues within the larger question of nuclear proliferation.

In dealing with the subject, a two-pronged approach has been chosen, one focusing on pressing cases of proliferation in their regional context, and the other on existing and potential global aids and instruments against the spread of nuclear weapons. Within this framework, both political and technical issues have been addressed. A debate on the future of the Non-Proliferation Treaty and the international non-proliferation regime completes the study.

Although the regional case studies all have their specific aspects and problems, they also share important characteristics, or at least lend themselves to relevant comparisons. All regional contributions, therefore, while not ignoring idiosyncracies, address the relationship between political leadership and security issues on the one hand, and nuclear policies on the other, and raise the question of whether changes in the political or security realms facilitating denuclearization are feasible in the foreseeable future. They also look at whether proliferation in each case could still be stopped or impeded by technical means, including, most importantly, by refusal of nuclear or nuclear-related sales. As, arguably, proliferation dangers have recently been and for the time being still are most acute in South-east and South Asia, the chapters on North Korea, and India and Pakistan occupy a large part of this section.

A separate chapter focuses on the problem of dealing with sensitive nuclear exports and irresponsible exporters, an issue that was highlighted by revelations concerning Pakistan and Iraq which over the years managed to shop, steal and knock together viable or virtually viable nuclear options. Particular attention is paid in this connection to a few newly exporting countries which are not bound by existing regulatory guidelines like those of the Nuclear Suppliers Group.

Under the heading of global non-proliferation aids and instruments, the safeguards' system of the International Atomic Energy Agency is first of all evaluated in the light of recent events, especially Iraq's illegal nuclear program and the worrisome illegal exports from the former Soviet Union and the former Eastern Bloc. The value and likely effectiveness of a Comprehensive Test Ban as a non-proliferation tool is then looked into. Third, the role of the UN Security Council as the guarantor of international peace, and the increasingly relevant issue of security guarantees as a non-proliferation tool, are discussed. Finally, the NPT's role in the international non-proliferation regime and issues concerning the Treaty's extension are broached.[8]

---

8. Chapters were finalized in October 1994, after a workshop attended by authors and "non-writing" experts in September of that year. The editor gratefully acknowledges the intellectual contributions of the authors, and of F. van Beuningen, H.J. van der Graaf, P. van Ham, P. de Klerk, K. Knip, D.A. Leurdijk, G.C. de Nooy, J.G. Siccama, P. Rusman, R. Serry and H. Swarttouw.

This book was produced under the auspices of the Netherlands Institute of International Relations "Clingendael" and sponsored by the Netherlands Ministry of Foreign Affairs.

2   Nuclear End-Game on the Korean Peninsula

Andrew Mack

Introduction

"They are giving up a nuclear program that posed an enormous risk to South Korea, to Japan, to North-East Asia and to the international non-proliferation regime."

> US Ambassador at Large, Robert Galluci, on the North Koreans and the October 1994 US/DPRK settlement.[1]

On October 21, 1994, after some five years of controversy, and 18 months of on-again-off-again negotiations, an agreement was signed between the US and North Korea which in principle resolves the Korean nuclear crisis. The agreement, which is analyzed in detail below, involves the immediate freezing and ultimate destruction of the most worrying elements of the Democratic People's Republic of Korea's (DPRK) nuclear program. In exchange, the North will receive a number of political, economic and security "rewards."

For the non-proliferation community, the need to stop Pyongyang's drive to acquire nuclear weapons seemed self-evident. Within the Asia-Pacific region, a nuclear-armed North Korea would create strong, possibly irresistible, pressures for South Korea to follow suit. (In 1991, Republic of Korea (ROK) government officials allegedly drafted plans for a South Korean nuclear weapons' program.)[2]

A nuclearized Korean peninsula would in turn tilt the political balance in Japan towards the "nuclear Gaullists" who believe that ultimately Japan cannot

---

1.   Speech at Foreign Press Center, Washington DC, October 19, 1994.
2.   This was revealed by the secretary to the Director of the South Korean National Security Agency. See Paul Shin, "US said to stop South Korea's nuke bomb plans," *Washington Times*, March 29, 1994.

M. van Leeuwen (ed.), The Future of the International Nuclear Non-Proliferation Regime, 15-56.
© *1995 Kluwer Academic Publishers. Printed in the Netherlands.*

rely on the US and should therefore acquire its own independent nuclear deterrent.[3] This was not the only proliferation risk. The plutonium output of North Korea's two new reactors would, when operational, have provided Pyongyang with enough nuclear weapons not only for its own arsenal, but also a surplus for export.

If the October agreement is successfully implemented, the risk of regional proliferation will be dramatically reduced, while that of plutonium exports to so-called "pariah states" will be eradicated completely. There remains within the region, however, great skepticism that the North will honor the agreement. Some of the reasons for this skepticism are analyzed later.

The Run Up to the "Agreed Framework"

BACKGROUND

North Korea's interest in nuclear issues can be traced back to the 1950s. In 1956 and 1959 the DPRK signed nuclear cooperation agreements with the USSR; in 1959 it signed a nuclear accord with China.[4] A very small Soviet-supplied IRT research reactor was commissioned in 1965.[5] The Soviets also supplied "hot cells," which the North has admitted using to reprocess "gram amounts" of plutonium from the IRT reactor in the mid-1970s. The IRT reactor was placed under IAEA safeguards in 1977. The 1960s' vintage facilities are of very low capacity and are not a proliferation issue.

---

3. This risk should not be exaggerated. As long as the US is seen by the Japanese security community as a reliable ally, a nuclearized Korean peninsula is unlikely to tilt the political balance sufficiently to shift Japan from its traditional anti-nuclear position. A major proliferation risk *would* arise, however, if Tokyo, for whatever reason, began to have serious doubts about US commitment to Japan's security. In this context, it is worth pointing out that many regional states doubt that the US will sustain its commitment to Asia in the long term given that the traditional rationale for the forward deployment of US forces disappeared with the collapse of the Soviet Union.

4. Leonard S. Spector with Jacqueline R. Smith, *Nuclear ambitions: the spread of nuclear weapons 1989-1990* (Boulder, CO: Westview Press, 1990), p. 121.

5. John Fialka, "North Korea may be developing ability to build nuclear weapons," *Wall Street Journal*, July 19, 1989. The reactor was 4 MW, later upgraded to 8 MW.

The main focus of recent concern is a 30 megawatt (thermal)[6] research reactor at the nuclear complex at Yongbyon, some 100 km north of the North Korean capital of Pyongyang. The reactor, which became operational in 1987,[7] is said to be a "virtual replica" of Britain's first magnox reactor which has in turn been described as a "very efficient military plutonium producer."[8] The British reactor's design is declassified and could have been used to guide construction at Yongbyon.[9] The reactor can produce enough weapons-grade plutonium a year for approximately one nuclear weapon.

The reactor on its own did not cause great concern, especially since the North had, under Soviet pressure, joined the Nuclear Non-Proliferation Treaty in 1985. But years of delay by Pyongyang in signing a safeguards's agreement with the International Atomic Energy Agency, and evidence made public in 1989 that the North was building what appeared to be a large reprocessing plant at Yongbyon to separate plutonium from spent reactor fuel, caused growing alarm. The North Koreans maintain that the plant is a "radiochemical laboratory" - a claim which has met with near universal skepticism.

In late 1991, perhaps in response to its growing international isolation, North Korea signed a historic Joint Declaration on Denuclearization with South Korea. This reiterated a number of NPT obligations, to which both sides were already committed. Of far greater importance was the mutual commitment not to produce fissile material in either country, and to a special *bilateral* nuclear inspection regime which was, in principle, more intrusive than that of the IAEA. Shortly after signing the Joint Declaration with the South, the North finally agreed to sign an IAEA safeguards' agreement - much to the relief of Washington and Seoul.

---

6. This is equivalent to 5 MW (electrical). The thermal measure has been preferred since there is no evidence that the North intended to use this reactor to generate electricity.
7. See "Status of North Korean nuclear facilities," *Arms control reporter*, July 1990, p. 457, B. 38.
8. John Simpson, *Independent nuclear state*, 2nd ed. (London: Macmillan, 1986), pp. 108-9. It has also been claimed that this reactor is essentially a copy of "the French G-1 model ... used by the French in the early 1960s for the development of nuclear weapons." See Song Yong Son, "North Korea's nuclear development," *Singdon-A*, cited in FBIS-EAS-90-174, p. 32.
9. Ann MacLachlan, "US prods IAEA about safeguards for North Korean nuclear plants," *Nuclear fuel*, April 3, 1989, p. 5. See also Joseph S. Bermudez Jr, "North Korea - set to join the 'nuclear club'," *Jane's defence weekly*, September 23, 1990, p. 594.

The commitment not to reprocess spent fuel, if implemented, meant that the North could not create fissile material for nuclear weapons; the IAEA's inspections would ensure that the North did not renege on its commitments. Five *ad hoc* IAEA inspections took place that year (for a chronology of IAEA inspections see Appendix I).

By the end of 1992, however, the early optimism had largely vanished. The North-South talks had made no progress, with DPRK resistance to intrusive inspections being the critical stumbling block. The IAEA had meanwhile become increasingly concerned about two undeclared facilities at Yongbyon. US satellite intelligence data had indicated that at least one of these sites was a nuclear-waste storage facility - probably containing waste from an undeclared reprocessing campaign. In February 1993, the IAEA formally demanded that the North open the two suspect sites for inspection. The North refused this unprecedented "special inspection" demand as emphatically as it had refused the many less formal requests that the UN agency had previously made. Pyongyang reiterated its claim that the disguised sites were military facilities and as such were not to be subjected to inspection. It warned that any attempt to impose sanctions would lead to war, and, on March 12, announced that it was withdrawing from the NPT.

The announcement caused near-panic in Washington. Once out of the NPT, the North would be legally free to make as many nuclear weapons as it wished - and to export them. A rapid flurry of informal behind-the-scenes contacts led in June 1993 to talks at the UN between US Assistant Secretary of Political and Military Affairs, Robert Galluci, and DPRK Deputy Foreign Minister Kang Sok-ju. The talks produced a joint statement in which both parties committed them-selves to: the non-use of force to resolve differences; a denuclearized Korean peninsula; non-interference in each other's affairs; and support for the peaceful reunification of the two Koreas.

All of this represented a considerable success for the DPRK's nuclear diplomacy. The North had prevented the issue of its nuclear program from being taken to the UN Security Council, it had achieved its long-held goal of negotiating directly with the US on the nuclear issue rather than with Seoul or the IAEA, and it had still not agreed to submit its two suspect facilities to inspection. Pyongyang did, however, undertake to "suspend" its withdrawal from the NPT, to submit to an "impartial application of full-scope safeguards" of its declared nuclear facili-ties, and to re-engage in the long-stalled talks with South Korea to implement the terms of the 1991 agreement to denuclearize the Korean peninsula.

The US congratulated itself on the progress which had been made. In fact, the North had promised no more than it had already committed itself to more than two years previously when it first agreed to IAEA inspections and to North/South talks on the nuclear issue. Washington was far more forthcoming. At the second round of high-level talks in Geneva in July, and subsequent working-level meetings in New York, American officials canvassed a range of significant concessions with the North. These included:

— permanent cancellation of the huge and (so the North felt) provocative annual US-ROK "Team Spirit" exercise;
— a so-called "negative security guarantee" for Pyongyang, meaning a US undertaking not to use nuclear weapons against the North;
— a formal US/DPRK non-aggression agreement;
— US support for the introduction into the North of modern light-water reactors (LWRs) to replace the existing graphite-moderated research reactors;
— the possibility of US diplomatic recognition of North Korea;
— and the possibility of a formal peace treaty ending the Korean war.

Optimists in Washington argued that the range of concessions on offer was now sufficiently tempting to persuade the North to "play the nuclear card" - that is to provide credible assurances that it had given up its nuclear program in exchange for the package of proffered "carrots." They were wrong. The North continued to refuse access to the two suspect nuclear facilities at Yongbyon. The IAEA's demand to inspect these facilities was, claimed Pyongyang, based on information provided by "partial" US intelligence agencies. Since the North had only agreed to "impartial" inspections, it was under no obligation to accept the IAEA's demand. Attempts to revive the North-South talks - and thus discussion of an inspection regime which was potentially even more intrusive than that of the IAEA - also failed.

By September 1993, the US and South Korea were back in pessimistic mode. Washington cancelled the planned third round of high-level talks and the North cancelled its planned bilateral discussions on safeguards with the IAEA. By October, batteries and film in the IAEA's on-site monitoring cameras at the Yongbyon nuclear complex had reportedly run out, raising the worrying prospect that the North could divert nuclear materials to bomb production without being detected.

The overriding US concern at this time was, first, to get IAEA inspectors back into North Korea to check on possible diversion of nuclear materials at Yongbyon, and, second, to dissuade the North from carrying out its threat to quit the NPT. Washington was now waving the "stick" of possible economic sanctions at the North, while simultaneously proffering the "carrot" of resuming high-level talks which the North had demanded.

On February 15, 1994, following intensive behind-the-scenes discussions, the North agreed to allow IAEA inspectors back to Yongbyon to conduct inspections of the seven declared nuclear sites there. The issue of inspecting the two suspect undeclared sites at Yongbyon was put into the too-hard basket to be dealt with later.

The inspections took place in March. Agency inspectors found nothing suspicious at six of the sites, but in the critically important nuclear fuel reprocessing plant they found a deliberately broken seal and were prevented from taking radioactive samples. The inspectors also found evidence that a second plutonium production line had been set up in the plant. This was particularly worrying. With a second and much larger gas-graphite reactor due to come on stream in 1995/6 and a third being built, the international community was being forced to contemplate the bleak prospect that in a very few years the North would be able to produce and reprocess enough plutonium for a dozen or more nuclear weapons a year.

All of this was too much for the IAEA, whose Board of Governors convened and issued yet another futile demand that the North abandon its resistance to inspections. The issue was then referred to the UN Security Council, but here Chinese opposition prevented any strong condemnation of the North. The Council simply reiterated the demand that the North accept its international obligations. Pyongyang refused, claiming that its "unique status" of having only temporarily suspended its withdrawal from the NPT meant that it did not have to submit to inspections by the IAEA at all.[10] It hinted that any attempts to pressure it on this issue would leave it no option but to carry through its threat to quit the NPT. It also threatened to quit the 1991 North/South Denuclearization Agreement.

The next mini-crisis came in May and June 1994 when the North prevented IAEA inspectors from effectively monitoring the withdrawal of spent fuel rods from the Yongbyon reactor. During the following weeks, the United States and its

---

10. KCNA news agency, Pyongyang, in English, March 31, 1994.

allies started again to look at the possibility of imposing sanctions on the North. In the words of US Defense Secretary William Perry, the US "shifted [its] strategy towards coercive diplomacy."[11] In Op-Ed columns in the United States, the "military option" was again being canvassed - sometimes by former senior US officials.

SANCTIONS

The sanctions' option was problematic for a number of reasons. UN sanctions were most unlikely to receive Chinese support, and by 1994, China was supplying the North with much of its oil and a considerable amount of food. It might, however, have been possible to create an effective sanctions' regime without China's support. Indeed, as Larry Niksch has pointed out, "Japan and South Korea provide North Korea with about $2 billion in foreign exchange annually, which appears to finance all of North Korea's imports."[12] Denial of these resources by Tokyo and Seoul would have accelerated the economic crisis in the North. But, notwithstanding its tough talk in late 1994, South Korea was deeply ambivalent about sanctions, fearing that they could lead to the precipitate collapse of the regime in Pyongyang - which in turn could lead to civil strife, massive floods of refugees (a concern shared by China), and the huge economic burden of "reunification by absorption," for which the South was unready. Successive Japanese governments have shown little enthusiasm for sanctions, since implementing a sanctions' regime would require the government to take on the pro-Pyongyang Japanese Korean community, Chongryun, which provides much of the DPRK's foreign currency. Such a confrontation risked political violence and the prospect of deeply embarrassing exposures of the corrupt practices linking Chongryun and Japanese politicians. Moreover, in practice it would be extremely difficult to prevent money being transferred from Japan to North Korea via third countries.

A major problem with imposing sanctions on authoritarian regimes is that the greatest pain is imposed on those who have least power; those who have most power are the least affected. Saddam Hussein's continued refusal to comply with UN resolutions, despite being subjected to four years of the toughest sanctions'

---

11. William Perry, speech, *4th Annual Fortune 500 Forum*, Philadelphia, November 3, 1994.
12. Larry Niksch, "Negotiations with North Korea," *Korea and world affairs*, summer 1994, p. 270.

regime in modern history *and* a humiliating military defeat, suggests that, at best, sanctions directed against authoritarian governments are a strategy for the long term.

Also of concern was Pyongyang's likely response to sanctions. The North had warned repeatedly that sanctions could lead to war. This may have been an empty threat, since there was little reason for the North to start a war it would certainly lose, but many policy-makers doubted that the North could be counted on to act rationally. Sanctions would also almost certainly have led Pyongyang to quit the NPT and the 1991 Denuclearization Agreement. Outside these agreements Pyongyang would have been able, perfectly legally, to proceed at full speed with its nuclear weapons' program. In such a context, the legal case for persisting with sanctions would have been highly questionable. The only ground on which the Security Council could have acted against the North had it quit the NPT, would have been that Pyongyang's activities somehow constituted a threat to international peace and security. Yet clearly the intent to acquire nuclear weapons is not, *in itself*, necessarily a threat to peace - after all, the UN did nothing to prevent India, Pakistan or Israel acquiring nuclear weapons. Moreover, while it might have been plausible to argue that the acts of international terrorism for which Pyongyang had become notorious in the 1980s constituted a threat to international peace, there had been no such acts in the 1990s.

THE MILITARY OPTION: DESTROYING THE NORTH'S NUCLEAR FACILITIES WITH "SURGICAL" STRIKES

This option had almost no official support in Washington or Seoul - with good reason. First, military strikes would have been a gross violation of international law without the legal sanction of a UN Security Council resolution - which China would have been certain to veto. Second, such strikes, far from being limited and "surgical" in their effect, would probably have triggered a major war on the peninsula causing hundreds of thousands of casualties. Third, even if there were no North-South war, destruction of the operational Yongbyon gas-graphite reactor could have caused dangerous radioactive contamination. Fourth, military strikes could not have destroyed any plutonium which has already been reprocessed - and hidden.

DIPLOMACY REVIVED

In June 1994, hopes that diplomacy might still work were revived by the visit of former US President Jimmy Carter to Pyongyang. Carter had intensive discussions with "Great Leader," Kim Il Sung, and the meeting led to the North agreeing to "freeze" its nuclear program in exchange for a US agreement to hold the long-delayed third round of high-level talks. The talks started in Geneva in early July but had to be postponed almost immediately following the death of Kim Il Sung.

Reconvened in early August 1994, the talks ended on the August 13 with an agreed statement in which the North committed itself to freeze construction on its new gas-graphite reactors in exchange for provision of modern light-water reactors. Two more months of tough negotiations led to the October 21 "Agreed Framework" for resolving the nuclear crisis, which is analyzed later.

North Korea's Nuclear Program

This, then, is the background to the DPRK nuclear controversy. The sections which follow examine some of the more controversial questions surrounding the DPRK program, including the extent of the North's nuclear stockpile, DPRK motives for acquiring nuclear weapons, and the extent of its dependence on external material, scientific and technical assistance. The concluding sections critically analyze the October 1994 US/North Korean "Agreed Framework" and consider possible future developments.

THE DPRK FISSILE STOCKPILE

Estimating just how much fissile material the DPRK may have acquired is extraordinarily difficult.

As noted earlier, the North has admitted to separating a "tiny amount" of plutonium from the small Soviet-supplied IRT reactor in 1975 and, in 1990, some 100 grams of plutonium from allegedly damaged fuel rods removed from the 30MW (thermal) reactor in 1989. However, IAEA chemical analysis of samples from the Yongbyon facilities has revealed that the North had lied about the number of times it had produced plutonium. It had in fact reprocessed spent fuel in 1989, 1991 and 1992, as well as the 1975 and 1990 reprocessing programs which it had already admitted to.

What the Agency still does not know is *how much* spent fuel has been reprocessed. The quantity issue is critical: if the lowest estimates are correct, the North does not have enough fissile material for even one bomb; if the consensus view is correct, there is enough plutonium for one or possibly two nuclear bombs; and if the extreme (South Korean Institute for Defense Analysis) estimate is correct, the North could have some 40 kg - enough for as many as five or six nuclear weapons.[13]

The consensus estimate assumes that the North did not simply remove a few damaged fuel rods from the 30MW reactor in 1989 as it claimed, but actually refuelled it. David Albright suggests that the spent fuel thus acquired could have provided the North with 11-14 kg of fissile material. Making various estimates for possible losses in the separation process and in bomb manufacture, Albright suggests that "the North might therefore have enough separated plutonium for one and perhaps two nuclear weapons."[14]

A recent South Korean report suggests that more plutonium may have been extracted than was previously estimated. In August 1994, a South Korean official stated that the South had evidence that the operation of the 30MW (thermal) reactor had been stopped for 71 days in 1989, a month in 1990, and 50 days in 1991. Based on this information, the South estimated that the DPRK had extracted between 21.8 and 27.2 kg of plutonium - enough for three or perhaps four nuclear weapons.[15]

When the fuel rods were removed from the 30MW (thermal) reactor in June 1994, the IAEA was prevented from effectively monitoring the defueling process, thus making the task of detecting the amount of past diversion far more difficult. Albright estimates that some 25 kg of unseparated plutonium are contained in the removed fuel rods, which, once separated, would be enough to make three or

---

13. No other analysts see the Korean Institute's estimate as plausible.
14. David Albright, "North Korean plutonium production," *INESAP Bulletin*, no. 2, July 1994, p. 6. The actual amount of plutonium required to make a nuclear weapon varies according to the make-up of the plutonium itself and the degree of sophistication of the weaponization process. It is customarily assumed that the North will require 7-8 kg to make a nuclear device, although, given the right technology, much smaller amounts will suffice.
15. "Report: North Korea has enough plutonium for bombs," *New Straits Times*, August 8, 1994.

perhaps four weapons. This would be in addition to whatever plutonium may have been extracted prior to the June 1994 refueling.

The North's weapon-making potential would have increased rapidly if the 200 and 700MW (thermal) reactors then being built had become operational; construction of both has been halted under the terms of the October 1994 "Agreed Framework." These gas-graphite reactors could, by the year 2000, conceivably have produced some 355 kg of plutonium; 1,705 kg by 2010.[16] This would have provided the North not only with a sizeable nuclear deterrent of its own, but also a surplus of fissile material, or bombs, to export. 1,705 kg of plutonium would be enough for more than 200 nuclear weapons.

OVERSEAS TRAINING OF DPRK SCIENTISTS AND TECHNOLOGISTS

The DPRK nuclear program has been run as far as possible on *juche* principles. But although *juche*, which translates roughly as self-reliance, has been its guiding philosophy, the DPRK regime has had no choice but to rely on external assistance to train its nuclear scientists and technologists. Large numbers of North Koreans have received training in the Soviet Union, Eastern Europe and, to a lesser extent, China.

There have been many accounts of the training of DPRK scientists overseas, some have been contradictory and certainly not all are reliable. Some come from defectors to the South who often tell their hosts what they think they may wish to hear.

According to one South Korean defense analyst, some 3,000 DPRK personnel were trained in the former Soviet Union between 1961 and 1967 alone.[17] *Nucleonics week* has claimed that "several hundred DPRK experts have been trained in plutonium separation in China and the USSR since the 1960s."[18] CIA officials have stated, however, that North Korean scientists have not been trained in nuclear weaponization technologies - as against civilian nuclear technologies.[19] This would certainly be consistent with past Soviet/Russian practice. According to

---

16. Albright, "North Korean plutonium production," p. 8.
17. See Song Yong-Sun, "North Korea's potential to develop nuclear weapons," *Vantage point*, August 1991.
18. Mark Hibbs, "No US agency consensus on DPRK nuclear progress," *Nucleonics week*, June 1, 1994, pp. 8-9.
19. Albright, "North Korean plutonium production," p. 6.

Russian sources, Soviet nuclear specialists also worked *in* the DPRK.[20] A North Korean defector has claimed that DPRK scientists visited French nuclear installations and that nuclear technology was obtained from France and Austria.[21] In February 1992, a Seoul newspaper reported that East German nuclear scientists had trained North Korean scientists in the DPRK, and that in 1989 a nuclear technology transfer agreement had been signed between the former GDR and North Korea.[22]

As the Cold War began to wind down and suspicions grew that the North was embarked on a nuclear weapons' program, DPRK access to *official* technical assistance and technology transfer was increasingly restricted in China and Russia. According to the major South Korean newspaper, *Choson Ilbo*, China stopped all transfers of nuclear technology and withdrew technicians working in the DPRK in 1987.[23] The former Soviet Union also terminated supplies of nuclear fuel (presumably enriched uranium for the very small IRT reactor at Yongbyon) and equipment to the DPRK in 1991.[24]

The end of the Cold War has, however, created new opportunities for the DPRK to get nuclear technology and know-how from the former Soviet Union by clandestine means. During the past few years there has been growing international concern that increasingly impoverished Russian nuclear weapon and missile scientists may be tempted by high salaries to defect to North Korea. There is little doubt that this is a real danger. In September 1993, for example, some 36 Russian missile scientists and technologists were physically prevented from flying to Pyongyang by Russian security forces. The United States says that it has no *evidence* that either nuclear scientists or weapons technology have actually ended up in the DPRK, but this does not mean that this has not happened. A recent account in the Japanese daily, *Shuban Bunshun*, of what is purported to be an official 1993 Russian government assessment of the Russian nuclear brain drain,

---

20. "Nuclear expertise, materials exports feared," *Proliferation issues*, May 3, 1993.
21. "Defector on North's nuclear development," *Proliferation issues*, November 7, 1991, p. 8. The same source also claimed that the North was operating a clandestine underground reactor.
22. "GDR said to give nuclear technology to North," *Proliferation issues*, February 14, 1992, pp. 6-7.
23. Cited in "Nuclear aid to DPRK reportedly halted in 1987," *Proliferation issues*, September 9, 1992, p. 4.
24. Mark Hibbs, "North thought to have separated Pu in 1970s with Soviet help," *Nuclear fuel*, June 22, 1992, pp. 15-16.

stated that 160 Russian specialists had participated in the North Korean nuclear weapons' and ballistic missiles' programs and that *nine nuclear weapon scientists and seventeen missile engineers are currently taking part in them.*[25] The Russian Defense Ministry has denied that the report was accurate.

DPRK DEPENDENCE ON FOREIGN TECHNOLOGY AND EQUIPMENT AND RAW MATERIALS

The type of research reactor the North has built at Yongbyon is perfectly in line with *juche* principles in that it can be fueled by natural (unenriched) uranium moderated by graphite. North Korea has ample indigenous reserves of both. In 1964, the North reportedly received Chinese exploration assistance which led to the discovery of some 4 million tonnes of commercial grade uranium. In the late 1980s and early 1990s, the North received technical assistance from the IAEA for its uranium mining program.[26] Total uranium reserves are estimated at some 26 million tonnes, but only a relatively small percentage of these are recoverable. (See Table I for list of DPRK nuclear facilities.)

Light-water reactors, by contrast, use enriched uranium as fuel and, as far as is known, the North does not have any enrichment facilities. Operating LWRs would be contrary to *juche* ideology since the North would either be dependent on foreign sources of enriched uranium, or would have to import foreign technology to enrich its own uranium.[27]

The *Juche* principle, however, would not have precluded the North from opportunistically seeking to acquire nuclear material where possible. For example, in 1992, a Russian media report claimed that some 56 kg of plutonium -

---

25. See Dunbar Lockwood, "The status of US, Russian and Chinese nuclear forces in North-East Asia," *Arms control association*, June 30, 1994. The Japanese weekly in question was *Shukan Bunshun* and its story was reported by Steven Zaloga in his "Russian military readiness nosedives," *Armed forces journal*, May 1994, p. 55.

26. See Joseph S. Bermudez, "North Korea's nuclear program," *Jane's intelligence review*, September 1991, for a description of DPRK nuclear fuel supplies.

27. "Paper says Pyongyang close to nuclear capability," *Nuclear developments*, June 28, 1990, pp. 6-7. In 1990, the *South China morning post* cited Soviet officials as claiming that East Germany and Romania had sold enriched uranium to the DPRK. This claim, like many others, has never been substantiated and appears highly dubious since East Germany had no enrichment capability and, as far as is known, the DPRK would have had no use for low-enriched uranium.

enough for seven or eight nuclear weapons - had been smuggled into the DPRK from Russia in a trainload of scrap metal.[28] This report has never been confirmed. It is, however, interesting to note that, although there was general skepticism in the South Korean and US security communities about the claims of a high-level DPRK defector in 1994 to the effect that the North had already acquired five nuclear weapons, this skepticism was based on estimations of the amount of plutonium which the North could have produced at its 30MW Yongbyon reactor. But, as an IAEA official noted at the time, five bombs could have been made from *other* sources of fissile material. Smuggled plutonium is one possibility; a clandestine underground reactor is another (see below).

Notwithstanding its commitment to *juche*, the North could not have produced nuclear weapons without access to some foreign technologies and materials. There is no doubt that the DPRK, sometimes using Korean-Japanese "front" organizations, sought to acquire nuclear-related equipment overseas. Unlike Iraq, however, the North did not have large reserves of "hard" currency, nor did it constitute a major market for Western goods. Its ability to entice sellers of nuclear-related technology was thus almost certainly less than that of Iraq.

Relatively little is known of North Korea's procurement network of dual-use equipment. In 1990 *Nucleonics Week* noted that "Swiss and German firms, such as Degussa AG, Magg AG, Siemens AG, Berthiez SA, and Leybold-Heraeus GmbH, supplied North Korea with some dual-use equipment in the 1980s." Degussa, for example, was fined $800,000 for re-exporting beryllium and zirconium of US origin to the DPRK.[29] In November 1990, a DPRK agent was caught trying to obtain detonation capacitors, which can be used in a nuclear implosion, from the US firm EG&G via Singapore.[30] Other reports have claimed that the DPRK may have acquired uranium melting technology and furnaces from Germany and Pakistan.[31]

Japan, Russia and China have been the major sources of foreign technology for the DPRK. In the 1980s, "22 per cent of the $350 million in Japanese exports

---

28. "Radio reports smuggling of radioactive material," *Proliferation issues*, April 22, 1992, p. 15.
29. "Commerce imposes $800,000 fine on W. German firm for alleged re-exports," *US Department of Commerce news,* March 28, 1990, pp. 1-2.
30. Hibbs, "No US agency consensus."
31. Hibbs, "North Korea thought to have separated Pu."

to North Korea involved 'machinery', while machine tools composed 30 per cent of the USSR's $500 million exports to the DPRK."[32]

The most important source of North Korean hard currency and access to high technology is the 247,000-strong Chongryun organization in Japan,[33] which is estimated to funnel between US$0.6 and $1.0 plus billion to North Korea every year. Front companies for Chongryun in Japan - and probably elsewhere - "purchase equipment considered necessary for Pyongyang's nuclear and missile programs."[34] In 1987, according to the Japanese journal *Shokun*, a large group of Japanese scientists and technicians, many with nuclear expertise, visited North Korea. 21,000 scientific documents were allegedly also sent from Japan to North Korea that year. In September 1988, an attempt by North Korea to smuggle 1,300 pieces of equipment, including semi-conductors and computers from Japan, was foiled.[35]

In early 1994, the Japanese media reported that spectrum analyzers, which could be used to improve the accuracy of guidance systems in the new DPRK Rodong missiles, had been exported from Japan to North Korea via China in 1989.[36] North Korea denied receiving the devices. It has also been reported that Japanese-made Global Positioning System (GPS) satellite navigation systems were being fitted to the Rodong-1 as part of its guidance system. GPS systems could, in principle, provide positioning accuracy approximately ten times more precise than the current generation of DPRK missiles.[37]

DELIVERY SYSTEMS

Delivering nuclear weapons unscathed to their intended targets is not easy. According to the CIA, the North's current missiles (derivatives of the Russian SCUD series of missiles) do not have the payload capability to carry a first

---

32. *Ibid.*
33. The pro-DPRK Koreans in Japan account for about 40 per cent of the total Japanese Korean community.
34. "Kim Il Sung's money pipeline," *Time*, April 4, 1994, p. 27.
35. Cited in "Pyongyang reportedly smuggling nuclear know-how," *Nuclear developments*, April 29, 1990, p. 5.
36. "Japan: Anritsu spectrum analyzers under suspicion of being illegally exported to North Korea," Reuters, January 18, 1994.
37. Teruaki Uneo, "Japan: North Korea denies buying Japanese missile device," Reuters, January 19, 1994.

generation DPRK nuclear weapon.[38] First generation weapons could, however, be carried on the new Rodong-I missile which was flight-tested in early 1993 and has an estimated range of more than 1,000 km. Twelve to eighteen of these missiles may already have been deployed, according to South Korean sources. A follow-on missile, the Rodong-II, will have a range of between 1,500 and 2,000 km. According to South Korean sources, development of the Rodong-II, a new generation solid-fueled missile, may be completed by the end of 1995.[39] A third generation of two-stage missiles is being developed which could have a range in excess of 3,500 km. To meet the missile threat (which will almost certainly include SCUDs with chemical warheads), South Korea is deploying a Patriot-based anti-missile system. Using strike aircraft as delivery systems (the North has MIG-29s) would be highly risk-prone since US/ROK air defenses are highly effective. The North has no ship- or submarine-borne launch systems which could deliver nuclear weapons against the South, although US analysts claim that the Rodong-I could be submarine-launched if modified. North Korea has been negotiating to buy obsolete Golf II missile-firing submarines from Russia, ostensibly to scrap.

One mode of "delivery" which would be suited to first-generation nuclear weapons and which would be impossible for South Korea to counter, would involve placing nuclear devices (they would not have to be deliverable nuclear *weapons*) in a tunnel under the demilitarized zone. A threat to detonate such weapons, which would be very "dirty" in the sense of causing massive fallout, could be a powerful deterrent to US/ROK attacks on the North's nuclear facilities.

DPRK MOTIVATION FOR ACQUIRING NUCLEAR WEAPONS

This is an issue of some controversy. Many analysts believe that the North has used international concern about its nuclear program to extract a range of political and economic concessions from the US, Japan and South Korea. These analysts point to the crisis in the North's economy - which has been declining at an increasingly rapid rate since the beginning of the 1990s. They argue that this decline can only be reversed with external economic assistance, that the North

---

38. David Albright, "North Korean plutonium production," p. 6. The North is claimed to be able to produce between 100 and 150 SCUD-Bs and SCUD-Cs a year.
39. "North Korea: Seoul reports Pyongyang SCUD missile and chemical weapons production," *Yonghap* (in English), September 26, 1994.

recognizes this and that it is using "the nuclear card" to try and extract the best possible assistance deal.

The problem with this argument is that if the North had been *simply* playing a bargaining game, one would have expected it to have named the rewards it wanted in return for playing the "nuclear card." It would also have had to indicate an in-principle willingness to produce the information about its nuclear history which the IAEA has sought for so long. Yet while the North made many demands on the United States, until October 1994 it never indicated a specific package of concessions in exchange for which it would have been prepared to submit to "special" inspections. On the contrary, it rejected all demands for "special inspections" repeatedly - and emphatically.

One obvious explanation for Pyongyang's intransigence was that it believed that acquisition of nuclear weapons was a vital national security interest. North Koreans perceived themselves to be threatened both by US nuclear weapons and the growing conventional military power of South Korea. They also - correctly - saw themselves as having effectively been abandoned by their major ally, Russia. Nuclear weapons offered a countervailing deterrent against American nuclear threats, a "strategic equalizer" against the growing perceived conventional threat from South Korea, and compensation for the effective loss of allies. Nuclear weapons, from this perspective, are something to be bargained away only in the most extreme circumstances.

1994: The October "Agreed Framework"

Why, after years of stalling, did the North agree in October 1994 to a plan which could - if implemented - resolve the nuclear crisis and destroy its ability to make nuclear weapons?

The agreement of October 21 does not answer this question directly. It does, however, suggest a number of possible responses. The "Agreed Framework" (reproduced in Appendix II) was far more specific than the August 13 "Agreed Statement" which preceded it. It has been hailed as a solution to the nuclear crisis. Pessimists among North Korea watchers noted, however, that similar optimism had been expressed when the 1991 North/South Joint Declaration of Denuclearization had been signed *and* following the signing of the 1992 IAEA safeguards' agreement. Neither was implemented, primarily due to DPRK intransigence.

Essentially the October agreement requires the North to give up its existing nuclear program in exchange for a substitute nuclear energy program based on light water reactors. In addition, the United States undertakes to upgrade its diplomatic relations with the DPRK to ambassadorial level - subject to satisfactory progress in the nuclear deal. The US also undertakes not to use or threaten to use nuclear weapons against the DPRK providing the latter remains a member of the NPT.

Washington's official optimism about the "Agreed Framework" was evident in the State Department's explanation of its text:

This agreement serves the interests of our allies, South Korea and Japan, as well as the United States. It will bring greater security to this dangerous part of the world and contribute to our efforts to end nuclear proliferation globally. Here are its principal features:

First, it will bring the DPRK into full compliance with its non-proliferation obligations under the Non-Proliferation Treaty (NPT). The DPRK affirms its NPT member status, commits to complying with its IAEA safeguards' agreement, and states willingness to implement the South-North Denuclearization Declaration.

Second, it terminates the existing DPRK nuclear program. Activity at the DPRK's nuclear facilities (5 MW reactor, reprocessing facility, and 50 and 200 MW reactors now under construction)[40] will remain frozen, under the supervision of IAEA inspectors. When light-water reactors are nearing completion, North Korea will dismantle those facilities.

Third, it ensures safe disposition of the spent fuel now in North Korea. The DPRK will forego reprocessing, and instead will safely store and eventually ship the spent fuel out of the country.

Fourth, it addresses the question of the past. The DPRK will accept special inspections or other steps deemed necessary by the IAEA before it receives any nuclear components for a light-water reactor.

Lastly, this agreement will draw North Korea out of its dangerous isolation. It will help integrate Pyongyang into the economic and political mainstream of East Asia.

Our part of the bargain is straightforward. We will lead an international consortium which will oversee construction of two 1,000 MW light-water reactors of proliferation-resistant design in the DPRK over the next decade.

---

40. These are MW *electrical* measures and correspond to 25, 200 and 700 MW (thermal).

Funding will chiefly come from South Korea; Japan will also make a major contribution.

We and the DPRK will establish liaison offices in each other's capitals - something that will help us oversee the implementation of this agreement and open a channel to deal with other issues that concern us.

We plan to reduce economic and financial restrictions selectively on US citizens' dealings with the DPRK, in close consultation with the Congress.

We will provide a "negative security assurance." It would pledge us not to use nuclear weapons against North Korea as long as it remains a member in good standing of the NPT regime. (We have provided similar assurances to other signatories of the NPT.)

To compensate the DPRK for loss of energy production from further operation of its 5 MW reactor and from abandoning 50 and 200 MW reactors under construction, the consortium will provide the North with 500,000 tonnes of heavy fuel oil annually for use in a specific power plant (50,000 tonnes in the first three months, and 150,000 tonnes in the first year of the agreement).

This agreement attains all our goals, including the North's commitment to pursue South-North dialog, without which there can be no permanent resolution of questions of peace and security on the Korean peninsula.

We consulted our allies, Japan and South Korea, at every stage of this arduous negotiation, including frequent conversations between the President and President Kim Young Sam. Korea's and Japan's strong support has been essential to the success of the talks with North Korea. They are fully on board, and doubtless will have more to say themselves.

This is a statement designed, understandably, to put the best possible gloss on an agreement which retains a number of worrying elements. In reality, the October 1994 "Agreed Framework" may be no more than a "freeze" or "capping" deal. Its strong point is that, if implemented, it will preclude Pyongyang from continuing with the program which would have radically expanded its fissile material stockpile and raised the specter of North Korean exports of nuclear weapons or fissile material to so-called "pariah" states in the Middle East. It achieves this desirable end without recourse to either a sanctions' program, which could have led to the North quitting the NPT permanently, or to military strikes, which could have plunged the whole peninsula into a disastrous war.

The downside of the deal from a non-proliferation point of view is that its inspection provisions do not have to be carried out for five or more years and that in the meantime there is little to stop the North from completing the "weaponization" of any plutonium which has already been diverted. It is essentially for this reason that the deal has been condemned by hardliners in the United States and South Korea as a "sell-out." One South Korean newspaper even compared it to Munich.

Dissecting the 1994 "Agreed Framework"

The United States is clearly correct in suggesting that the agreement is better than the alternative of unrestrained production of fissile material by the North, but given the sad history of past agreements, critics are also correct in cautioning against undue optimism. In what follows, I examine some of the more important issues raised by the "Agreed Framework."

PROVISION OF LIGHT-WATER REACTORS

The North first expressed interest in LWRs in discussions with IAEA Director Hans Blix in June 1992. The issue came up in the two rounds of high-level talks between the United States and DPRK in June and July 1993, and the United States indicated that it would in principle support the replacement of gas-graphite reactors with less proliferation-prone LWRs.[41]

The $4 billion cost of constructing the reactors is to be met by a consortium of states, of which the most important donors would be South Korea and Japan.[42] North Korean officials have suggested that their willingness to replace their gas-graphite reactors with LWRs proved that they did not want nuclear weapons.

---

41. The October LWR deal is remarkably similar to a mid-1980s' agreement between the former Soviet Union and North Korea to provide the North with reactors which would have produced 1,920MW(e). The deal fell through because of DPRK foot-dragging on its NPT commitments. In the 1994 US and DPRK high-level talks, the North and the Russians were pushing hard to have the Russians supply the reactors. The South Koreans rejected the idea, arguing that Russian reactors, which they would inherit after reunification, were unsafe, and noting that the Bonn government closed down all the Russian VVER LWRs when East Germany was absorbed into the FRG. At the time of writing, the Russians were again talking with the DPRK about the possibility of Russian reactors replacing the North's gas-graphite nuclear plants.

42. The South Koreans are expected to provide around 55-60 per cent; Japan about 20 per cent; with the balance being provided by other states.

In terms of energy production this is an extraordinarily good deal for the North. The two gas-graphite reactors under construction in the North had an estimated capacity of 250MW(e). In giving them up, the North is receiving two LWRs with a combined output of *2,000 MW(e)*. This is not all. The LWR completion target date is not until 2003. In the interim, the North will be provided with heavy fuel oil as compensation for the 25MW(e) capacity which it foregoes by not proceeding with its gas-graphite reactors. The amount of free oil provided will rise to 500,000 tonnes a year. The significance of this amount may be gauged by the fact that it is equivalent to approximately one-third of Pyongyang's total oil imports in 1992 (1,520,000 tonnes).[43] The free 500,000 tonnes is almost certainly a much greater percentage of the DPRK's 1994 oil consumption, since the ability of China to provide the North with oil is declining as rapid economic growth pushes domestic consumption above domestic production. Chinese exports of oil to the DPRK were only 879,000 tonnes in 1993, down from 1,200,000 tonnes the previous year, according to one estimate,[44] and China provides the DPRK with most of its oil.

But do LWRs in fact make sense in terms of energy production for the North - and are they free of proliferation risk? Peter Hayes has argued that nuclear power is neither a timely, nor a cost-effective, solution to the North's undoubtedly serious energy shortage problem.[45] It is, of course, true that the North will not be paying for the LWRs and will be receiving free heavy oil from the consortium. In this sense, cost may not be an issue. But the $4 billion in question would have enhanced the DPRK's energy capacity far more effectively if it had been spent on efficient new coal-fired thermal power plants, or relative simple conservation measures.

What of the proliferation potential of LWRS? Contrary to the uninformed claims of some, plutonium suitable for making nuclear weapons *can* be extracted

---

43. Seung-Yul Oh, "Economic reform in North Korea: is China's model relevant to North Korea?," *Korean journal of national unification*, vol. 2, 1993, p. 128. The figure cited is a Bank of Korea estimate.

44. See Yong-Sup Han, "China's leverages over North Korea," *Korea and world affairs*, vol. 18, no. 4, summer 1994, p. 246.

45. Peter Hayes, "Should the United States supply light water reactors to Pyongyang?," *Nautilus Pacific research*, November 16, 1993.

from LWR spent fuel, although the yield is unpredictable and the actual repro-cessing more dangerous.[46]

But what does make LWRs attractive from a non-proliferation point of view is that they would make the DPRK dependent on external supplies of reactor fuel. LWRs are fueled with enriched uranium and North Korea not only lacks indige-nous enrichment capabilities but is prohibited from acquiring them by the 1991 North/South denuclearization agreement. The North will therefore have to rely on imported enriched uranium to run its LWRs, whereas its current operational reactor, and the two which were under construction, can be fueled by locally supplied unenriched uranium moderated by locally supplied graphite. Non-proliferation objectives would be assured if the international community were to emulate Soviet/Russian practice and rent fuel rods to Pyongyang. The North would own the energy which could be derived from the rods, but not the rods themselves, which would have to be returned to the supplier when the reactor was defueled. There is no indication in the public domain that this possibility has been discussed in official circles, but renting fuel rods would remove almost all concern about the proliferation potential of North Korean LWRs.

DISPOSITION OF SPENT FUEL

The issue of what to do with the spent fuel from the operational gas-graphite reactor at Yongbyon was not resolved in the August 13, 1994 agreement. Prior to August, the North had argued that it would have to start reprocessing the 8,000 odd spent fuel rods by September 1994 before they corroded to dangerous levels. US officials conceded that corrosion of the fuel rods in their cooling ponds was a potentially serious problem, but rejected the North's contention that the best solution to the problem was to reprocess the fuel rods at Yongbyon. So doing would have given the DPRK enough fissile material for about four or five nuclear weapons. The United States counter-proposed that the rods be sent overseas (China was a likely location) and reprocessed there - an idea the North rejected. In place of reprocessing, the North suggested "dry storage" - that is, that the rods be

---

46. To produce plutonium suitable for making nuclear weapons the reactor would have to be operated so that fuel is irradiated to a much lower burn-up (around 600-800 MWd/T) than in the case when a LWR is operated for maximum power production. In the former case the reactor core would need to be removed more often and this operation would be detectable.

removed and encased in concrete.[47] This would make the task of extracting the plutonium they contained difficult, though not impossible - and could still be dangerous according to US experts. In the short term the rods can be left *in situ* and a range of technical measures - including the filtering and purification of the contaminated pond water - taken to reduce the corrosion risk.[48]

The October 1994 "Agreed Framework" states that "The US and the DPRK will cooperate in finding a method to store safely the spent fuel from the 5MW (electrical) experimental reactor during the construction of the LWR project, and to dispose of the fuel in a safe manner that does not involve reprocessing in the DPRK."[49] The United States has interpreted this to mean that the material will eventually be disposed of overseas. The published text does not stipulate this, but the unpublished accompanying text may do so. Clearly, the North will wish to retain control over the spent fuel as long as possible, since it is of value both as a bargaining lever and - if the agreement fails - as material for four to five nuclear weapons. Equally clearly, the United States will want the spent fuel exported as soon as possible. According to Galluci, "The fuel must be completely shipped out of North Korea by the time the first reactor is completed."[50]

INSPECTIONS

The issue of inspections remains critical. The text of the "Agreed Framework" (see Appendix II) states that when:

> ... a *significant proportion* of the LWR is completed, but before delivery of *key nuclear components*, the DPRK will come into full compliance with its safeguards' agreement with the IAEA (INFCIRC/403), *including taking all steps that may be deemed necessary by the IAEA*, following consultations with the Agency with regard to verifying the accuracy and completeness of the DPRK's initial report on all nuclear material in the DPRK (italics added).

---

47. There are other means of dry storage.
48. For a concise account of the problems of fuel rod corrosion and how to deal with them, see David Albright, "North Korea's corroding fuel," *Nautilus Pacific*, Berkeley, August 3, 1994.
49. "Agreed Framework between the United States of America and the Democratic People's Republic of Korea," Geneva, October 21, 1994.
50. Robert Galluci, speech to Foreign Press Club, Washington DC, October 19, 1994.

This means that there will be no "special inspections" of the two controversial undeclared sites at Yongbyon until the new LWRs are well on the way to completion - perhaps as long as five years.[51] According to Australian safeguards' specialists, access to, and analysis of, the wastes held at these sites will help enable the IAEA to determine whether or not the North has already reprocessed enough nuclear material for nuclear weapons. For the United States, the five-year-plus delay is an acceptable price for the immediate freeze on development of the North's two new gas-graphite reactors and operation of the existing nuclear facilities.

Given the history of past negotiations, Pyongyang's insistence that these critical inspections be delayed for such a long period was bound to generate suspicion. But the regime's reasons for seeking such a delay are not necessarily sinister. The United States, the IAEA and South Korea all see inspections of the two suspect sites and other "transparency" measures as essential to a satisfactory long-term resolution of the nuclear issue. The strong US/IAEA/ROK interest in inspections is the North's guarantee that work on the LWRs will proceed as promised.

US leverage over Pyongyang, on the other hand, is predicated on the assumption that the North has a clear interest in seeing the LWR project through to completion and will thus eventually agree to the demands (including "special inspections" by another name) which the IAEA makes.

DISMANTLING OF NUCLEAR FACILITIES

The "Agreed Statement" states that "Dismantlement of the DPRK's graphite-moderated reactors and related facilities will be completed when the LWR project

---

51. Note that the term "special inspection" is not used in the text of the October Agreement. The North find the term "special inspection" deeply offensive - not least because no other state in the history of the NPT has been required to submit to one. Since the North has refused "special inspections" so adamantly and so many times, publicly accepting a "special inspection" would have meant serious loss of face. The United States clearly believes that it has an understanding with the North that the two suspect facilities *will* be inspected. Pessimists will note that similar "understandings" in the past have not been fulfilled in practice. The North can, of course, avoid "special inspections" (under whatever name) by coming clean about the operating history of its reactor and producing any plutonium which has been diverted. To save face it could claim that the program had been unauthorized and hidden from the leadership.

is completed" - that is, by 2003, if the target date is met. The Agreement does not state when dismantlement must start. In securing agreement to delay destruction of its nuclear facilities, the North has again ensured that it retains leverage over the United States. If it believes that the United States is not fulfilling its part of the bargain, Pyongyang can threaten *at any time* during the next nine to ten years (that is, until the LWR project is finished) to restart its nuclear weapons' program at very short notice. US leverage over Pyongyang at this stage is again predicated on the assumption that the North really wants to see the LWR project through to completion, and thus has a clear interest in fulfilling *its* obligations.

NEGATIVE SECURITY GUARANTEE

The "Agreed Framework" contains an undertaking by the United States not to use or threaten to use nuclear weapons against the North. In the State Department's explanation of the Agreement, this undertaking is said to be conditional on the North remaining party to the NPT. While meeting a longtime DPRK demand, this "negative security guarantee" means that South Korea will lose its "nuclear umbrella."[52] However, since the military balance has been moving inexorably against the North over the past decade, and since Pyongyang knows it cannot count on Russian or Chinese assistance if it starts a war, the loss of its "nuclear umbrella" is of little real security consequence for the South which can rely on continued conventional military support from its ally.

Ongoing Concerns

The October Agreement has much to recommend it, but it does embody risks and uncertainties and what may be worrying precedents. These include:

HIDING CRITICAL EVIDENCE

Although the United States seems confident that the DPRK will eventually permit inspections of suspect undeclared facilities at Yongbyon, this confidence is certainly not shared by ordinary South Koreans, less than one-quarter of whom

---

52. In principle, the "umbrella" will still provide protection from Russia and China.

think that the North can be trusted to keep to its side of the bargain.[53] Skeptics have suggested that the North could seek to remove and hide any high-level wastes located at the two suspect undeclared sites at Yongbyon prior to their inspection. Its ability to do this without being detected would depend on satellite surveillance and the extent of on-site inspection by IAEA inspectors - details of which have not been revealed, although there will apparently be a permanent IAEA presence at Yongbyon. The fact that waste at one of the sites is apparently buried and capped in concrete would make removal difficult, but not necessarily impossible. Moreover, it would be almost impossible to move nuclear waste without leaving some trace.

A STRATEGY OF DENIAL

An alternative strategy for Pyongyang would be to permit inspections and then dispute any resulting findings which tended to incriminate it. There is already a precedent for this in the North's denial of the conclusions of analyses commissioned by the IAEA, which revealed that spent fuel had been reprocessed more frequently than the North had admitted. The North may well believe that the US/IAEA interest in maintaining the freeze on the DPRK program is too important to be put at risk by a controversy over relatively small amounts of plutonium produced in earlier reprocessing campaigns.[54] If such a strategy was to succeed, the North would have gained political, security and economic concessions from the US *and* kept sufficient fissile material for a minimal nuclear deterrent.

---

53. "South Korea: South Koreans suspicious over North Korean nuclear deal - poll," Reuters, October 20, 1994.
54. There was already a precedent for Washington to act this way - in the case of Pakistan. The United States originally sought to prevent Pakistan acquiring nuclear weapons, but once it became clear that Pakistan had already acquired a small nuclear arsenal and there was little the United States could do about it, Washington's policy changed. The US goal was no longer one of pressuring Pakistan into giving up its capability - which was seen as desirable but unrealistic - but to get it to "freeze" the program at current levels. The idea of a least-worst policy of "freezing" or "capping" North Korea's program had been discussed in Washington in 1994 - as the North must have known.

THE ROLE OF THE IAEA

Not least among the ironies of the October Agreement is that, although welcomed as a victory for the cause of non-proliferation, it gives some currency to long-standing DPRK complaints that the IAEA is a creature of the United States. Washington brokered the deal with North Korea, which has important consequences for the IAEA, without at any time consulting the IAEA's Board of Governors to ascertain whether or not this was acceptable. The Agency indicated shortly after the Agreement had been signed that it was calling a special meeting to examine its terms - suggesting that it did not know what they were.

The United States was not given a mandate by the IAEA Board to act on its behalf, and it was Washington, not the Agency, which agreed that the North would not be required to submit to IAEA "special inspections" for five years or more - despite the fact that the IAEA had recently referred the matter to the UN Security Council as being a matter requiring urgent attention.

Moreover, in announcing the October Agreement, the United States did not suggest that it was conditional on acceptance by the IAEA's governing body. The deal has subsequently been endorsed by the UN Security Council and the IAEA's Board of Governors, and it is likely that IAEA officials were kept informed during the talks, but that is not really the point. If the IAEA is perceived as being a creature of the United States, it risks undermining its international credibility. IAEA officials have already expressed their concern that the critical inspections take place before the 1995 NPT renewal conference is held in April 1995. This is most unlikely. Agency plans to push for tough new safeguards' provisions will not be helped by the DPRK inspection debacle.

This said, it is clear that the IAEA has also been unfairly attacked by some of its more ignorant critics during the long-drawn Korean nuclear crisis. The task of the Agency is to monitor compliance with safeguards' agreements, not to enforce them - the latter is the task of the UN Security Council. The Agency *was* successful in its verification role - it *did* detect unauthorized DPRK activities - much to Pyongyang's surprise. In so doing, it helped alert the international community to the DPRK's nuclear ambitions. It was in no sense Vienna's fault that the UN Security Council failed to play an effective role in the crisis.

A DANGEROUS PRECEDENT?

The commonest and perhaps most telling criticism of the October agreement is that it rewards behavior which is antithetical to the letter and spirit of the NPT. North Korea has threatened to quit the NPT, repeatedly reneged on its legal commitments to allow IAEA inspections, yet will now receive diplomatic recognition, negative security assurances and $4 billion worth of assistance for doing what it was legally obliged to do anyway. This, critics argue, is a dangerously destabilizing precedent. And if North Korea can avoid inspections of undeclared nuclear facilities for more than five years, why should this dispensation not be accorded to other states as well? Concern has already been expressed that Iran may emulate the North and threaten to quit the NPT in the hope that it too will be bribed to return to the non-proliferation fold.

But while the precedent is undoubtedly unfortunate, too much should not be made of it. First, the North has committed itself to do far more than simply honor its NPT commitments - it is also dismantling its gas-graphite reactor and reprocessing facilities, neither of which are prohibited under the NPT. Second, it is difficult to think of other cases where one would find states like South Korea willing to pay billions of dollars to bribe would-be proliferators to give up their nuclear options. South Korea was in a unique situation. It is prepared to pay because it believes that reunification is inevitable and sees the LWR project as an investment in its *own* future. Third, there is no evidence to suggest that the North's nuclear program was built for economic ends. Indeed, the opportunity costs created by the nuclear crisis in terms of foregone trade and investment, Japanese reparations, and access to international financial institutions, far exceed the $4 billion over some nine years which the October Agreement guarantees.

DIALOG WITH SOUTH KOREA

South Korea watched the progress of the 1994 US/DPRK high-level talks with obvious - and understandable - anxiety. Pyongyang had, after all, achieved a long-held goal of cutting both South Korea and the IAEA out of the nuclear dialog. Seoul was worried that its interests could be sacrificed by the United States. In the event, the South Korean government praised the final Agreement, but not without misgivings, or a great deal of domestic criticism.

A major failing of the Agreement from South Korea's point of view is that, although the DPRK is required to "consistently take steps to implement the North-

South Joint Declaration on the Denuclearization of the Korean Peninsula" and "to engage in North-South dialog," neither undertaking has to be fulfilled within any particular time frame. Worse still, from the South's point of view, is the fact that none of the proffered "rewards" for the North is made conditional on progress being made in North-South dialog, or on progress towards implementation of the 1991 Denuclearization Agreement. This means that the North can stall and blame any lack of progress in either area on the South, as it has done on so many occasions in the past, without standing to lose anything.

If Pyongyang's intransigence is again perceived in the South as blocking progress in North Korean-South Korean relations, and *if* the North persists with its campaign of hostile rhetoric against the South (which did not cease following the October Agreement), the Seoul government will be in an extraordinarily difficult position. It will still be expected to pay the largest share[55] of the $4 billion cost of the LWR program, yet would receive none of the anticipated political pay-off in terms of improved North-South Korean relations. In such a context the continuation of the North's deeply offensive campaign of vilification simply adds insult to injury.

This issue must be of particular concern to Seoul given the assurance provided by President Clinton to Kim Jong Il on October 20, 1994.[56] Mr Clinton stated that if, through no fault of the North Koreans, construction of the reactors "fails," he "will exert all his powers to have them finished by the US." The North, of course, bitterly resisted the idea that the reactors be constructed by South Korea in the first place. The Clinton assurance may thus provide the North with an incentive to provoke the South into reneging on its LWR commitments.

---

55. At the time of writing there continues to be a considerable amount of disputation about which countries should pay what percentage of the estimated $4 to $4.5 billion for the LWR project. South Korea's Foreign Minister has, in addition, stated that South Korea expects to be repaid in electricity or raw materials by the North for its assistance in the LWR project. This demand, which is not covered in the text of the October Agreement, seems certain to be rejected by the North and is likely to create serious problems in any future North-South dialog if the South insists on pursuing it.

56. See Department of State, "Statement about, and text of, President Clinton's letter to Kim Jong Il," November 1, 1994.

OTHER SOURCES OF FISSILE MATERIAL?

The North's longstanding rejection of the IAEA "special inspections" and to possibly more intrusive North-South inspections under the terms of the 1991 Joint Denuclearization Agreement may, as some analysts have suggested, arise from fears that such inspections would be used to spy on DPRK military capabilities. An alternative explanation is that the North has had something to hide - not just the two suspect undeclared sites at Yongbyon, but at other undeclared nuclear facilities. (It is perhaps worth remembering in this context that Iraq's nuclear weapons' program was almost totally clandestine.)

During the past five years there have been repeated, although never confirmed, defectors' reports that the DPRK has a clandestine underground reactor (or reactors) and speculation that there may also be a clandestine underground pilot reprocessing plant. Many analysts are skeptical about such claims, noting, for example, that the construction of tunnels for underground reactors requires large amounts of earth to be moved which could be detected by satellite surveillance, and that operation of the reactors themselves creates a heat signal which can also be detected (by infra-red-sensing satellites). Moreover, reprocessing plants emit krypton gas, tiny traces of which can be detected remotely. The United States has ship-borne krypton detectors expressly to detect any such emissions from DPRK reprocessing campaigns.

But if reactors are built under a major city, the evacuation of tunnels may go undetected among other construction activities. Alternatively, pre-existing tunnels - of which there are tens of thousands in North Korea - could be used to house nuclear facilities. Reactor heat signatures can be disguised by locating the reactor beneath an overground source of thermal emissions, such as thermal power plants, foundries, etc. The problem with krypton emissions is that the United States can only detect them if the wind happens to be blowing in the right direction. Detection is further complicated by the fact that krypton traces detected downwind of North Korea may have originated in China.

THE POLITICAL IMPLICATIONS OF THE ECONOMIC CRISIS

During the 1990s, North Korea has confronted an increasingly acute dilemma. On the one hand, its need for external economic assistance has grown as its economy has inexorably declined. On the other hand, the effective loss of its allies and the shift in the military balance in favor of South Korea have sharpened its sense of insecurity. The dilemma arises because pursuit of the nuclear option addresses the insecurity issue, but precludes access to external economic assistance. Pyongyang confronted an unpalatable choice between insecurity and insolvency.

It is possible that the change in leadership will incline the regime to place economic security above military security. The October Agreement was signed very shortly after the younger Kim took power, and it has been suggested that he is more reform-minded and pragmatic that his father.[57] At the time of writing, this remained an issue for conjecture. Kim Jong Il had only been seen twice in public since his father's death and there has been much speculation about his health.

The seriousness of the economic crisis is not in doubt - although the reliability of the statistics used is often questionable. According to estimates by the Bank of Korea in Seoul, in 1990 the economy declined by 3.7 per cent; in 1991 by 5.2 per cent; in 1992 by 7.6 per cent; and in 1993 by 4.3 per cent.[58] Industrial plants in the North are reportedly running at only 30-40 per cent capacity. Foreign trade nearly halved (from $4.7 billion to $2.7 billion) between 1990 and 1992. In the first half of 1994 trade with China, Japan and Russia all declined sharply according to the ROK Unification Ministry.[59] Foreign debt has risen to $8-10 billion. Grain production in 1993 had slumped to 3.88 million metric tonnes - little more than half the amount needed. In 1993, China provided 1 million tonnes of the shortfall,[60] but serious food shortages persist. The regime has called on North Koreans to "skip meals" one day a month and, in some areas, to get by on only two meals a day. There have been reports of food riots in various parts of the country since 1991.[61] In mid-1994 there were claims that a cholera epidemic was spreading.

Can the regime survive this growing crisis? There have been examples - notably in Latin America - of states undergoing a period of economic decline without the government falling as a consequence. But the rate of decline in the

---

57. Kim Jong Il showed few signs of reformist inclinations prior to coming to power, but this does not mean that he did not harbor them privately.
58. "Pyongyang continues to rely on *Juche* economic policy," *Vantage point*, vol. XVII, no. 8, August 1994, p. 2.
59. "South Korea: Seoul says N. Korean economic slump continues," Reuters, November 18, 1994.
60. Yong-Sup Han, "China's leverages over North Korea," *Korea and world affairs*.
61. "North Korea beset by minus economic growth during first half of 1993," *Vantage point*, vol. XVI, no. 8, September 1993, p. 19.

North has averaged around 5 per cent a year for the past four years. If this continues to the year 2000, the North's economy will have declined by over 55 per cent compared to 1990. It is difficult to believe that any regime can survive this sort of precipitous decline over the long term.[62]

Pyongyang clearly hopes that the benefits which will flow from the October Agreement - including access to free oil and the prospect of increased foreign trade and investment, and access to international financial institutions, will reverse its disastrous economic decline. Yet it is by no means clear that this will happen. The fact that *political* restrictions on economic interchanges may ease does not mean that the international community will necessarily rush to trade and invest in the North.

For most countries, North Korea is simply not a very attractive trading and investment partner under current circumstances. It tried an open-door investment strategy in the 1970s and failed. It did, however, succeed in running up - and reneging on - huge foreign debts. In 1994, Pyongyang is apparently still refusing to discuss repayment of its debts, despite the fact that it is soliciting new investment. The debt issue will likely remain a major reason for international reluctance to invest in North Korea.

In the mid-1980s, well before the nuclear issue had become a barrier to economic interaction with the outside world, the regime passed a joint-venture law and sought to encourage foreign investment. But by 1990, relatively few joint-venture businesses had been established and most of the foreign partners were from the Chongryun community in Japan, whose investments were as much politically as economically motivated.

In 1993, the North enacted a new series of laws, again designed to attract foreign investment, but this time the focus was on so-called free economic zones rather than joint ventures. Pyongyang's preference is for foreign investment to flow to export industries which will generate desperately needed foreign currency.

---

62. There are several counter-arguments to the "collapsist" thesis. First, the regime will blame the nation's problems on the "imperialists" and their "lackeys" and the people may well believe this because their only source of information is the state. Second, with a $800 - $1,000 per capita income the North's economy can halve and people will still be better of than Filipinos or Vietnamese - economic decline is not a threat to survival. Third, the repressive apparatus of the state will deal swiftly, efficiently and ruthlessly with any dissent. However, much the same arguments could have been used to argue that repressive regimes in the former Soviet Union and Eastern Europe would not collapse. They did.

But it is not clear that the DPRK will be an attractive export platform for most foreign investors. The regime's future political stability is questionable, its population is unused to international production and management practices, its currency is not convertible, its bureaucracy is pervasive and inefficient, and its economic and communications' infrastructures are primitive. Unlike other Asian states, it cannot compensate for such disadvantages by offering very low wages. Per capita GNP is estimated to be between $800 and $1,000 a year - much higher than the Philippines, or Vietnam, or the lower-wage parts of China, all of which have been far more welcoming to foreign investors.

South Korea may nevertheless wish to encourage investment in the North despite these disadvantages, in part because it sees such investment as lessening the costs of reunification and improving what will eventually be part of its own economy. Individual South Korean corporations have a defensive interest in investment in the North; they cannot risk being left out of a major part of their future domestic market. On November 7, 1994, ROK President Kim Yong Sam announced that his government would lift its two-year-old ban on business contacts with the North and said that Seoul would back any application by Pyongyang to join APEC.[63] South Korea's preferred scenario sees Chinese-style economic reforms introduced throughout North Korea, leading to a revival of the economy and the evolution of a more pluralistic political system. Ideally, the latter will facilitate the process of reunification while a revived DPRK economy will ensure an economic "soft landing" when reunification is actually implemented.

But notwithstanding South Korea's particular interests in trading with, and investing in, the North, Kim Yong Sam's government may find building better economic relations with its neighbor politically difficult, if not impossible, if there is no satisfactory progress in the North-South dialog, and if the North maintains its campaign of vilification against the South.

It is difficult to be optimistic about the prospects for North-South dialog given that the history of past talks has been one of unrelieved failure. Within weeks of the October Agreement being signed, the North was suggesting that it would not resume its inter-Korean dialog until the South apologized for its failure to show proper respect when Kim Il Sung's death was announced. Subsequently, Pyongyang added more preconditions. The South would have to apologize for past

---

63. "South Korea: S. Korea lifts ban on business with North," Reuters, November 7, 1994.

behavior on the nuclear issue and abolish its national security law. On November 22 a North Korean radio broadcast stated that "absolutely no dialogue can be made with the Kim Yong Sam regime."[64] And the signing of the October Agreement has in no sense slowed the inflammatory anti-South rhetoric emanating from Pyongyang. The DPRK media continues to use language like "puppets," "criminal clique" and "bastards" to describe the government in Seoul. Kim Yong Sam's conservative critics already believe the October Agreement to be a sellout, and will make life very difficult for the government if there is no progress in the North-South Korean dialog.

In addition to probable external reluctance to invest in the DPRK, there are the regime's own concerns about the political risks of economic liberalization. Only with market reforms throughout its economy can the North hope to reverse the decline in its economy. But market liberalization creates obvious political risks for the regime - notably those which arise from the job insecurity and rising prices for previously subsidized goods which are the inevitable concomitants of reform. At present the regime can blame its economic problems on external factors. Such a strategy would be impossible if the problems in question (such as inflation and unemployment) were the obvious and unambiguous consequence of government policy.

Liberalization has longer-term risks as well. Market reform devolves economic power away from the state, strengthens civil society and, in so doing, threatens the long-term stability of the regime. Hardliners in the North are acutely aware of the corrosive impact of China's surging market-driven and decentralized economic development on the authority of the central government.[65] An essay by Kim Jong Il in *Rodong Shinmun* on November 4, describing as "traitors" those who embraced the "illusion" of capitalism, has been seen as a serious critique of China's economic reform package.[66] Concern about the possibly destabilizing impact of Chinese-style reform has led the North to seek to keep foreign invest-

---

64. "North Korea: Pyongyang reportedly rejects inter-Korean governmental talks," Reuters, November 24, 1994.

65. To note this is not to deny that much of the market sector is controlled by members of the Chinese Communist Party; it is to assert that the logic of liberal-market capitalism is, by definition, antithetical to centralized control over the economy by the state. The fact that elements of the market system are owned/controlled by party functionaries does not lessen this contradiction, it simply complicates it.

66. "Kim Jong Il believes in final victory of socialism," *Korea Times*, November 11, 1994, refers to this essay.

ment projects relatively isolated from the rest of the economy in special free economic zones like those at Nampo and Najin-Sonbong; the Tumen River scheme is perhaps the most ambitious of these efforts. But investment restricted largely to these zones and focused on exports will not be enough to revive the domestic economy.

Economic recovery will also be constrained by the continuing energy crisis. The 500,000 tonnes of heavy oil that the North can expect to receive each year as a result of the October Agreement will not be nearly enough to cancel the regime's oil deficit. Even with the extra oil, the North will still have little more than half the amount it had in 1990 - the year the economic decline started. There is also no guarantee that the Chinese, who will shortly have to start importing oil themselves, will continue to provide oil on a barter basis. The regime had hoped to reduce its reliance on oil by boosting coal production. This strategy appears to have failed. According to South Korea's National Unification Board, coal production in 1993 was 27.7 per cent lower than in 1987. Total power output is around 40 per cent lower than demand.[67]

The October agreement, in other words, is unlikely to lead to developments which will reverse the decline of the DPRK economy.

Conclusion

The Agreement struck between the United States and North Korea in October 1994 is a good one, even though it provides no solid guarantee that the North will reveal the true history of its past nuclear activities. The agreement is important primarily because it prevents what would otherwise have been a major expansion in the North's nuclear weapons' program.

Critics have attacked the Agreement because it does not require the North to submit to inspections for as much as five years, and because the existing nuclear facilities will not have to be destroyed for nearly ten years. But although a

---

67. "North Korea: Seoul daily describes energy crisis in North Korea," Reuters, November 11, 1994.

worrying precedent for the global non-proliferation regime, these delays have a positive side. Time is not on the North's side.[68]

The regime's long-term predicament was well described by Aidan Foster-Carter some three years ago:

> ... the North Korean system is in terminal crisis; there is as yet little sign of a will to seek a cure; and even if the medicine of reform were to be swallowed in doses large enough to be efficacious, the side effects would render the patient fatally vulnerable to yet other maladies. (This last is very well understood in Pyongyang, which of course explains the reluctance to reform.)[69]

Given the uncertainties that surround the October Agreement, given the possibilities that a clandestine nuclear program of some sort may exist, only the demise of the DPRK regime can guarantee the demise of the DPRK's nuclear program. The controversial inspection issue will not need to be addressed before 1999, by which time the North's economy may well have been in decline for almost a decade. No regime can withstand this sort of decline indefinitely. The DPRK's eventual, but inevitable, demise, in addition to ending more than 50 years of unrelieved Stalinist repression, will be a major plus for the global non-proliferation regime.[70]

---

68. Pyongyang may believe that the four- to five-year breathing space it has now bought will enable it to decrease still further its reliance on oil and permit its agriculture to recover after successive poor harvests, caused in part by bad weather. By this time the oil prospecting, which has been underway for some time in North Korean waters, may also have borne fruit.

69. Aidan Foster-Carter, "Prospects and pathways for Korean reunification," in: Andrew Mack (ed.), *Asian flashpoint* (Sydney: Allen and Unwin, 1993), p. 174.

70. There is some concern that South Korea may seek to keep whatever nuclear program it inherits from the North.

Appendix I

Chronology regarding safeguards in DPRK, International Atomic Energy Agency, Vienna

1. A comprehensive safeguards' agreement with the DPRK entered into force on April 10, 1992, permitting verification that all nuclear material and all nuclear facilities in the DPRK were used exclusively for peaceful purposes and assessment of whether the initial declaration of material and facilities (received on May 4, 1992) is complete and correct. The DPRK declared holdings of plutonium of less than 1 kilogram.
2. During 1992 the Agency's analysis of samples from the reprocessing plant indicated inconsistencies that led the IAEA to conclude more plutonium exists: whether grams or kilograms is unknown.
3. In late 1993/early 1994 the Agency requested access to, and samples from, two non-declared sites which were apparently related to nuclear waste. This was declined and the DPRK declared the sites to be non-nuclear and military.
4. The matter was referred to the Security Council in spring 1993. The Council endorsed the Agency's position, urged the DPRK to cooperate, urged the Director General to seek consultations with the DPRK and urged member states to seek to promote a solution.
5. On March 12, 1993 the DPRK announced its intention to withdraw from the NPT.
6. During 1993 the United States especially had many contacts with the DPRK aimed at finding some settlement which would take account of security concerns of the DPRK and seek full nuclear transparency on the part of the DPRK.
7. The DPRK declared on June 11, 1993 that it "suspended the effectuation of its withdrawal" from the NPT.
8. On February 15, 1994, after lengthy talks with the IAEA, a detailed understanding was reached with the IAEA about conducting inspections that the Agency requested - with the exception of the two non-declared, apparently waste-related sites.
9. An inspection was performed in March 1994, but was blocked on very important points in the reprocessing plant.
10. The Agency reported the matter to the Security Council which endorsed the Agency's request.
11. After further talks between the DPRK and other states, the DPRK accepted Agency inspection of the points earlier blocked. These inspections have been performed and analysis of the results will be available in due course.
12. At about the same time, the DPRK informed the Agency that it intended to refuel the 5 MW (electrical) Experimental Nuclear Power Reactor, loaded in 1986 and operated since 1987. The Agency immediately informed the DPRK that - as it had told DPRK authorities already in February 1993 - it wished during such refueling to select a number of fuel rods, segregate them from the others, secure them so that they would

not be replaced by others and examine them. This was requested because an examination of the rods might show how long they had been in the reactor. This presupposes availability of a representative sample of rods and knowledge of exactly where they had been located. If it were found that some or all the rods in the reactor had been there for a shorter time than eight years, there could exist non-declared nuclear material, spent fuel, or perhaps plutonium and waste.

13. The DPRK first ignored the IAEA's request to select a sample of rods and stated that the Agency could verify that the discharged fuel would not be diverted. Later it answered that such selection and segregation was incompatible with the DPRK's "unique status."

14. When the discharge of fuel continued without agreement and the Secretariat saw the possibility of this particular path to verify the DPRK's nuclear inventory closing, it reported the situation to the Security Council and the Board of Governors.

15. As communications between the Agency and the DPRK indicated that the DPRK was ready to consult about the issue of inspections, the Agency sent officials for talks to the DPRK. They explained again the urgency of the measures requested by the Agency and again met complete rejection of the measures because of the DPRK's "unique status."

16. At this stage, when already well over half of the fuel in the reactor had been discharged, the DPRK described a method which it claimed would enable the Agency in the future - after they had reached a package agreement with the United States and abandoned its "unique status," prevented a valid future examination which could have confirmed or negated its claim that the fuel which has now been discharged was the first fuel in the reactor and that no earlier fuel had been taken out for possible reprocessing and plutonium separation. The Agency is not saying this has been the case, but it cannot exclude it.

Appendix II

Agreed Framework between the United States of America and the Democratic People's Republic of Korea, Geneva, October 21, 1994

Delegations of the Governments of the United States of America (US) and the Democratic People's Republic of Korea (DPRK) held talks in Geneva from September 23 to October 17, 1994, to negotiate an overall resolution of the nuclear issue on the Korean peninsula.

Both sides reaffirmed the importance of attaining the objectives contained in the August 12, 1994 Agreed Statement between the US and the DPRK and upholding the principles of the June 11, 1993 Joint Statement of the US and the DPRK to achieve peace and security on a nuclear-free Korean peninsula. The US and the DPRK decided to take the following actions for the resolution of the nuclear issue:

I. Both sides will cooperate to replace the DPRK's graphite-moderated reactors and related facilities with light-water reactor (LWR) power plants.

1) In accordance with the October 20, 1994 letter of assurance from the US President, the US will undertake to make arrangements for the provision to the DPRK of a LWR project with a total generating capacity of approximately 2,000 MW (electrical) by a target date of 2003. The US will organize under its leadership an international consortium to finance and supply the LWR project to be provided to the DPRK. The US, representing the international consortium, will serve as the principal point of contact with the DPRK for the LWR project.
   — The US, representing the consortium, will make best efforts to secure the conclusion of a supply contract with the DPRK within six months of the date of this Document for the provision of the LWR project. Contract talks will begin as soon as possible after the date of this Document.
   — As necessary, the US and the DPRK will conclude a bilateral agreement for cooperation in the field of peaceful uses of nuclear energy.

2) In accordance with the October 20, 1994 letter of assurance from the US President, the US, representing the consortium, will make arrangements to offset the energy foregone due to the freeze of the DPRK's graphite-moderated reactors and related facilities, pending completion of the first LWR unit.
   — Alternative energy will be provided in the form of heavy oil for heating and electricity production.
   — Deliveries of heavy oil will begin within three months of the date of this Document and will reach a rate of 500,000 tonnes annually, in accordance with an agreed schedule of deliveries.

3) Upon receipt of US assurances for the provision of LWRs and for arrangements for interim energy alternatives, the DPRK will freeze its graphite-moderated reactors and related facilities and will eventually dismantle these reactors and related facilities.
   — The freeze on the DPRK's graphite-moderated reactors and related facilities will be fully implemented within one month of the date of this Document. During this one-month period, and throughout the freeze, the International Atomic Energy Agency (IAEA) will be allowed to monitor this freeze, and the DPRK will provide full cooperation with the IAEA for this purpose.
   — Dismantlement of the DPRK's graphite-moderated reactors and related facilities will be completed when the LWR project is completed.
   — The US and the DPRK will cooperate in finding a method to store safely the spent fuel from the 5 MW (electrical) experimental reactor during the construction of the LWR project, and to dispose of the fuel in a safe manner that does not involve reprocessing in the DPRK.

4) As soon as possible after the date of this document, US and DPRK experts will hold two sets of expert talks.
   — At one set of talks, experts will discuss issues related to alternative energy and the replacement of the graphite-moderated reactor program with the LWR project.
   — At the other set of talks, experts will discuss specific arrangements for spent fuel storage and ultimate disposition.

II. The two sides will move towards full normalization of political and economic relations.

1) Within three months of the date of this Document, both sides will reduce barriers to trade and investment, including restrictions on telecommunications' services and financial transactions.
2) Each side will open a liaison office in the other's capital following resolution of consular and other technical issues through expert-level discussions.
3) As progress is made on issues of concern to each side, the US and DPRK will upgrade bilateral relations to the Ambassadorial level.

III. Both sides will work together for peace and security on a nuclear-free Korean peninsula.

1) The US will provide formal assurances to the DPRK, against the threat or use of nuclear weapons by the US.
2) The DPRK will consistently take steps to implement the North-South Joint Declaration on the Denuclearization of the Korean peninsula.

3) The DPRK will engage in North-South Korean dialog, as this Agreed Framework will help create an atmosphere that promotes such dialog.

IV. Both sides will work together to strengthen the international nuclear non-proliferation regime.

1) The DPRK will remain a party to the Treaty on the Non-Proliferation of Nuclear Weapons (NPT) and will allow implementation of its safeguards' agreement under the Treaty.
2) Upon conclusion of the supply contract for the provision of the LWR project, *ad hoc* and routine inspections will resume under the DPRK's safeguards' agreement with the IAEA with respect to the facilities not subject to the freeze. Pending conclusion of the supply contract, inspections required by the IAEA for the continuity of safeguards will continue at the facilities not subject to the freeze.
3) When a significant portion of the LWR project is completed, but before delivery of key nuclear components, the DPRK will come into full compliance with its safeguards' agreement with the IAEA (INFCIRC/403), including taking all steps that may be deemed necessary by the IAEA, following consultations with the Agency with regard to verifying the accuracy and completeness of the DPRK's initial report on all nuclear material in the DPRK.

Kang Sok Ju, Head of the Delegation for the Democratic People's Republic of Korea, First Vice-Minister of Foreign Affairs of the Democratic People's Republic of Korea

Robert L. Gallucci, Head of the Delegation of the United States of America, Ambassador at Large of the United States of America

Table 1 North Korea's nuclear facilities

Facility and Location	Capacity	Start up date and Supplier
1st Reactor (Yongbyon)	IR8MW thermal	1965, USSR
2nd Reactor (Yongbyon)	30MW thermal	1987, DPRK
3rd Reactor (Yongbyon)	200MW thermal	1995, DPRK
4th Reactor (Taechoon)	700MW thermal	1996, DPRK
"Hot cells" (Yongbyon)		1965, USSR
Reprocessing Plant (Yongbyon)	200 tonnes p.a.	Near Completion, DPRK
Nuclear Waste Disposal Facility (Yongbyon)		DPRK
Fuel Fabrication Plant (Yongbyon)	200-300 tonnes p.a.	1985-1986, DPRK
Uranium Concentration		1982 (Pakchon)
Plants (Pyongsan and Pakchon)		1990 (Pyongsan)
Uranium Mill (Kusong)	?	?
Uranium Mines (Hungnam, Pyongsan, Ungki, Sunchon)	Reserves 26 million tonnes (of which some 4 million tonnes are said to be recoverable)	

Sources: Taewoo Kim, "South Korea's nuclear dilemmas," *Korea and world affairs*, vol. XVI, no. 2, summer 1992, p. 255; and *Defense white paper*, Ministry of Defense, Republic of Korea, p. 67.

3 After the Cold War: Prospects for Nuclear Arms Control in South Asia[1]

Virginia I. Foran

Introduction

Many proliferation analysts believe that the Cold War may have helped to keep the lid on nuclear proliferation, by spreading an implicit superpower nuclear umbrella over states that otherwise might have tried to develop the bomb. If this is true, then the end of the Cold War should have brought a rapid increase in the number of countries trying to build the bomb. In contrast to predictions, however, the end of the Cold War has not yet produced a change in proliferation strategies of India and Pakistan.

In the following paragraphs, I will present an overview of nuclear proliferation in South Asia prior to the end of the Cold War as seen by the traditional non-proliferation community; I will then discuss in detail the current status of each state's nuclear programs and their respective nuclear policies. Next, I will attempt to evaluate aspects of the post-Cold War environment influencing each state's current position on nuclear arms control. In conclusion, some policy recommendations are presented.

1. Support for the writing of this article from the W. Alton Jones Foundation and the Institute for the Study of World Politics is gratefully acknowledged. I also appreciate the research assistantship of Evan Medeiros and Brian Weinberger, the methodological contributions of Devin T. Hagerty and Michael J. Cain, and helpful comments by Peter Lavoy, Bill Potter, Mitchell Reiss, and Sandy Spector.

M. van Leeuwen (ed.), The Future of the International Nuclear Non-Proliferation Regime, 57-123.
© 1995 *Kluwer Academic Publishers. Printed in the Netherlands.*

South Asia during the Cold War

During 1986-1987, the Carnegie Endowment for International Peace convened a task force to discuss the security concerns of India and Pakistan. Observations noted were: both states possessed the capability to manufacture nuclear weapons within a few weeks but neither state had deployed any to date; and serious ongoing hostilities existed between the two states that could potentially erupt into war. In addition, citing regional and superpower threats to their security that necessitated maintaining a nuclear weapons' option, both states claimed that as long as the United States and the Soviet Union maintained their own nuclear arsenals, they had the right to follow suit.[2] Yet the task force concluded that a "full-fledged arms race on the Subcontinent is still avoidable."[3] At first glance, not much has changed since that 1988 assessment.

India's motivation for a nuclear weapons' option stems from the 1962 surprise invasion by China, and from Pakistan's 1972 decision to develop nuclear weapons. During the Cold War years, India's nuclear policy was based on two steadfast claims; that its 1974 test was a "peaceful nuclear explosion," and that it would never deploy nuclear weapons.[4] Aspects of this policy are consistent with Prime Minister Nehru's view that nuclear weapons would not increase India's security, but that nuclear technology could contribute to India's overall economic and technological development.[5] True Indian security, he stated, required all

---

2. *Nuclear weapons and South Asian security, report of the Carnegie Task Force on Non-Proliferation and South Asian Security*, (Washington, DC: Carnegie Endowment for International Peace, 1988), pp. 7-19.

3. *Nuclear weapons and South Asian security*, p. 5. The report also articulated policy recommendations. See *Nuclear weapons and South Asian security*, pp. 77-117. Similar analysis and conclusions have been reached by Stephen Philip Cohen, "Nuclear neighbors," in: Cohen (ed.), *Nuclear proliferation in South Asia*, pp. 1-20.

4. India's decision not to build openly a nuclear weapons' deterrent against China after the Chinese test at Lop Nor in 1964, suggests that the Indian test was intended as a symbolic response to China's nuclear capabilities. Regarding the timing of the 1974 test, many believe that India was responding indirectly to US intervention in the 1971 Indo-Pakistani War, when Washington deployed the aircraft carrier Enterprise to the Bay of Bengal. Others believe the Indian Prime Minister, Indira Gandhi, may have ordered the test in order to bolster her own political support.

5. Rikhi Jaipal, "The Indian nuclear situation," *International security*, vol. 1, no. 4 (spring 1987), pp. 45-6; and Brahma Chellany, *Nuclear proliferation: the US-Indian conflict*, (New Delhi: Orient Longman, 1993), pp. 1-4.

nations to renounce nuclear weapons entirely.[6] India would become committed to maintaining a nuclear weapons' option to deter a second military invasion from China, border incursions from a nuclear-capable Pakistan, and would refuse to accede to the NPT due to its discriminatory nature. Throughout the Cold War period, there were individuals and political parties that advocated India becoming a fully declared nuclear-weapon state, but the executive leadership always chose to remain technically true to Nehru's original policy.

Pakistan's nuclear program seems to be directly tied to India's nuclear capability. Secretly launched in 1972 after being defeated by India in the 1971 war over East Pakistan (now Bangladesh), Pakistan's nuclear program began in earnest in 1974 after India's test of an atomic device. Since then, although Pakistan is believed to have obtained specific bomb design information from China, and clandestinely obtained the majority of its nuclear infrastructure from Western Europe and North America, it has neither conducted a nuclear test, nor declared itself a nuclear-weapon state. Twice during the Cold War, however, the head of the Pakistani nuclear program, Dr Abdul Qadeer Khan, claimed that Pakistan had the ability to manufacture nuclear weapons.[7] Each time, these claims were later denied. Throughout the period, Pakistani leaders have offered their accession to the NPT if India would also do so.[8]

For both states, while details of their respective nuclear programs and infrastructure have leaked out over the years, information and evidence of a clear military strategy for their recessed nuclear capabilities has remained ambiguous.

OPAQUE PROLIFERATION AND EXISTENTIAL DETERRENCE

What has emerged from both states is a nuclear policy dominated by the employment of "existential" nuclear deterrence strategy. This type of deterrence charac-

---

6. A. Appadorai and M.S. Rajan, *India's foreign policy and relations* (New Delhi: South Asia Publishers Private Ltd, 1985), p. 229, and G.G. Mirchandani, *India's nuclear dilemma* (New Delhi: Popular Book Services, 1968), p. 159.
7. Kuldip Nayar, "India forcing us to go nuclear: A.Q. Khan," *Muslim* (Islamabad), March 1, 1987. Then in 1989, the Chief of the Army Staff, Mirza Aslam Beg, stated that "both the nuclear option and the missiles act as a deterrent, and these in turn contribute to the total fighting ability of the army, which acts as a deterrent to the enemy." See Mushahid Hussain, "Pakistan 'responding' to change," *Jane's defence weekly*, October 14, 1989, p. 779.
8. Leonard S. Spector with Jacqueline R. Smith, *Nuclear ambitions*, (Boulder, CO: Westview Press, 1990), pp. 63-117.

terizes a strategy that relies on communicating to one's enemies a "certain irreducible risk that an armed conflict might escalate into a nuclear war."[9] States with undeclared nuclear weapon capabilities rely almost exclusively upon existential deterrence because none of their enemies' capability is verifiable. As a result, each state cannot rule out the possibility that their adversaries can defeat them militarily.[10] The term "opaque proliferation" is used to describe the type of nuclear proliferation that occurs when an existential deterrence strategy is adopted.[11]

Opaque proliferation mixes a "public posture of restraint with the covert development of nuclear weapons, or at least the option to build them quickly."[12] This description matches the cases of India and Pakistan. As Devin Hagerty notes, it is understandable why a potential proliferant would try to hide the early stages of nuclear weapons' research and development. Most proliferants develop nuclear weapons in response to security threats, and would not want to warn their adversary of what potentially lay ahead. One has to question, however, why a state would choose not to advertise its nuclear weapons' capability and thereby obtain the full deterrent value of the weapons. It has been argued that there are both international and domestic costs associated with overt weaponization that current proliferating states have to bear. These costs may affect a state's decision to test, to declare its capability, and eventually to deploy the weapons in a deterrent fashion, forcing a state to proliferate at some level below a fully declared state. *The decision to develop nuclear weapons, therefore, should no longer be thought of as a binary choice (develop or not develop), but rather as a continuous one,*

---

9. Marc Tractenberg, "The influence of nuclear weapons in the Cuban Missile Crisis," *International security* 10, no. 1 (summer 1985), p. 139. McGeorge Bundy, "Existential deterrence and its consequences," in: Douglas MacLean (ed.), *The security gamble: deterrence dilemmas in the nuclear age* (Ottawa, J.J.: Rowman and Allanheld, 1984), pp. 3-13.

10. See Devin T. Hagerty, "Opaque proliferation, existential deterrence, and nuclear stability," chapter two of draft dissertation, "The power of suggestion: opaque proliferation, existential deterrence, and the South Asian nuclear arms competition," University of Pennsylvania, May 1994. This section relies heavily on Hagerty's original analysis.

11. "Opaque proliferation" was first described by Benjamin Frankel in "Notes on the nuclear underground," *The national interest*, no. 9 (fall 1987), and further developed by Avner Cohen and Benjamin Frankel, "Opaque nuclear proliferation: methodological and policy implications," *Journal of strategic studies* 13, no. 3, September 1990.

12. Devin T. Hagerty, "The power of suggestion," p. 257.

along a continuum from a completely covert capability to a fully declared capability. Each state's choice of its specific level of proliferation will depend on the international and domestic costs incurred and the security benefits it revives.[13]

With respect to the costs on the international level, overt weaponization incurs international opprobrium, at least from members of the NPT regime. In recent years, the number of states supporting the regime has increased, and some, like the United States, have enacted domestic legislation penalizing would-be proliferators by making it more difficult to openly seek the technology and resources needed for nuclear weapons' capability. Indeed, Ben Frankel claims that overt weaponization has been de-legitimized by the NPT.[14] Frankel also argues that the Cold War bipolar international system reduced the need for states to overtly weaponize, since some deterrence was provided to all states by the competing superpowers.[15]

For states with limited resources, burgeoning populations, and popularly elected governments like India, overt weaponization at any stage may have been too costly. Similarly, India and Pakistan may have thought that overt weaponization might trigger a premature arms race with their enemies or invite a preemptive military strikes on development sites, radically increasing the overall costs of the program. Also, both India and Pakistan had to take the evolving international non-proliferation regime into account during their decision-making period, although the way they experienced it was very different. The non-proliferation norm was gaining strength during the 1960s and, in fact, Gandhi is believed to have contributed to it with his lessons on non-violence. Shlomo Aronson describes India as a case of "self-imposed opacity," originating from Gandhi's lessons, and resulting in a "moral legacy" that makes overt nuclear proliferation less likely.[16]

Pakistan's leaders did not view weapons and arming as negatively as Ghandi and his followers, possibly making the threshold between covert and overt proliferation in Pakistan more tenuous. In fact, unlike India, Pakistan's government has been dominated by military leaders, and even when there has been

---

13. See footnote 10.
14. Benjamin Frankel, "Notes on the nuclear underground," p. 125.
15. See Benjamin Frankel, "The brooding shadow: systemic incentives and nuclear weapons proliferation," *Security studies* 2, nos 3/4, (spring/summer 1993), pp. 37-78.
16. Shlomo Aronson, *The politics and strategy of nuclear weapons in the Middle East: opacity, theory, and reality, 1960-1991* (Albany, NY: SUNY Press, 1992), pp. 290ff.

civilian leadership, the military has played a significant role in decision-making on the nuclear program. This military culture lends itself rather well to overt weaponization.[17] In addition, Pakistan has a smaller nuclear infrastructure to target than India, reducing the potential costs of weaponization further if the military was worried about pre-emptive strikes. Pakistan's military dictatorship may have been in a better position than India's popularly elected leaders to withstand the domestic economic costs of its nuclear program simply because it did not have to respond directly to public opinion. Despite these reduced domestic constraints to overt proliferation, Pakistan still chose an opaque path. This may be because of the vulnerability of the Pakistani nuclear program. From its inception, Pakistan's program was dependent on external resources, and as a result was extremely vulnerable to international pressure from the NPT regime, particularly export controls. In addition, Pakistan had to balance its program with the military and financial relationship it had with the United States and US non-proliferation demands.[18]

To summarize, while both India and Pakistan had clear motives to develop nuclear weapons during the Cold War period, they also experienced international and domestic constraints to their nuclear programs which influenced their decision to choose an opaque proliferation strategy.

Current Nuclear Status of India and Pakistan

INDIA

The 1974 atmospheric test of an atomic device, the unsafeguarded nuclear reactors and plutonium reprocessing facilities, ongoing research efforts in uranium enrichment technology, and persistent testing of nuclear capable missiles, have contributed to 20 years of skepticism regarding the truth of New Delhi's

---

17. Devin T. Hagerty, "Opaque proliferation, existential deterrence, and nuclear stability," pp. 12-13.
18. For details on Pakistan's clandestine efforts see David Albright and Mark Hibbs, "Pakistan's bomb: out of the closet," *Bulletin of the atomic scientists*, July/August 1992, pp. 38-43; *India and Pakistan: pressures for nuclear proliferation*, INR Report 778-AR, Assessments and Research, Bureau of Intelligence and Research, US Department of State, Washington, DC, February 10, 1984.

official position, that its nuclear program is entirely peaceful. The Indian government has contributed even further to this skepticism by making various ambiguous remarks over the years implying that India could assemble a bomb in a relatively short period of time.[19] Despite this circumstantial evidence of India's *de facto* nuclear weapons' capability, it is *still* widely believed that New Delhi has not deployed any nuclear weapons to its military forces. As a result, non-proliferation specialists must be content with making estimates of New Delhi's nuclear weapons' *potential*, based on the amount of unsafeguarded fissile material and principally weapon-grade plutonium that may be available for nuclear weapons' use. Conservative estimates conclude that New Delhi will have enough fissile material by 1995 for as many as 80 bombs.[20]

Nuclear Infrastructure and IAEA Safeguards. The basic question is how, precisely, might India use its nuclear infrastructure, which is also employed for peaceful nuclear research and for the production of electricity, to produce fissile material - principally plutonium - for nuclear arms. To determine this perfectly, it is necessary to know the size and operating history of all research and power reactors brought on-line to date and the extent to which the plutonium-bearing spent fuel has been separated at India's reprocessing plants. This information, however, is largely unavailable because India has not disclosed many details of the operating history of its nuclear infrastructure and has not accepted international monitoring by the International Atomic Energy Agency (IAEA). A reasonable estimate can nevertheless be made using generic information about the design of

19. M.R. Balkrishnan (ed.), "Collected scientific papers of Dr. P.K. Iyengar: volume 5 selected papers and speeches on nuclear power and science in India," (Bombay: Bhabha Atomic Research Center, 1991), p. 247, cited in David Albright and Mark Hibbs, "India's silent bomb," *Bulletin of the atomic scientists*, September 1992. p. 27. Also "India retracts statement on nuclear capability," Reuters, February 8, 1992, (0851); "Country prepared to meet Pakistani nuclear 'threat,'" *All India Radio Network*, (1530), February 8, 1992 (FBIS-NES-92-028, February 11, 1992, pp. 43-4).

20. See David Albright, Frans Berkhout, and William Walker, *World inventories of plutonium and highly enriched uranium* (Stockholm: SIPRI, 1992), pp. 160-61. Their estimate includes the high-quality plutonium produced at each of India's research reactors (CIRUS and Dhruva) and the small amount of high-quality plutonium produced at the start-up of India's unsafeguarded power reactors (MAPP I/II and NAPP I/II).

facilities and making some explicit technical assumptions about India's nuclear production capacities.[21]

David Albright has emphasized some well-founded assumptions in his estimate of India's nuclear weapons' potential. First: Indian scientists are not likely to use low-grade plutonium, like that produced in power reactors, for nuclear bombs. While all grades of plutonium can be used in a nuclear device, states that have the ability to produce high-grade plutonium tend to prefer it for weapons' design over reactor-grade plutonium, as it is less likely to fission spontaneously and is therefore more reliable. Second: Indian research reactors are producing weapon-grade plutonium, while the power reactors produce reactor-grade plutonium.[22] Given this, only a small number of facilities are regarded as part of India's stockpile of unsafeguarded plutonium and corresponding nuclear weapons' potential.

Contributing Facilities. India's oldest facility is the 33-year old Canadian-supplied CIRUS research reactor located at the Bhabha Atomic Research Center (BARC). CIRUS is not subject to IAEA safeguards but is governed by Indian-Canadian agreements relating to the acceptable use of plutonium produced there. Canada does not, however, conduct any inspections to verify these agreements. India's plutonium infrastructure also includes the Dhruva research reactor, also at BARC, which has operated since 1986, although its power was significantly upgraded in 1988. Dhruva is not subject to any safeguards or restrictions on the production of plutonium or reprocessing. Albright estimated the total amount of weapon-grade plutonium that CIRUS and Dhruva have produced over their life span by calculating how much thermal energy the reactors can produce in one day and multiplying that by a capacity factor, that is, an estimate of how well the reactors have

---

21. A complete listing of all known nuclear-related facilities and their respective status with the IAEA can be found in Appendix A.

22. The quality of plutonium is gauged by the number of fissile isotopes (PU_{239} and PU_{241}) it contains. The even numbered isotopes (PU_{240} and PU_{242}) are more likely to fission spontaneously and are thus considered less stable for weapon purposes. Ideally, weapon designers prefer plutonium that has the highest number of odd-numbered isotopes as possible. Lower burn-up rates do not allow sufficient time for the non-fissile plutonium isotopes to build up in the spent fuel. Hence, the low burn-up rates of the research reactors produce a higher grade of plutonium than the higher burn-up rates of power reactors. See Albright, *et al.*, pp. 14-17.

operated over the years.[23] According to these calculations, as of 1994, the Dhruva and CIRUS research reactors alone had produced enough unsafeguarded weapon-grade plutonium for between 49 and 80 bombs (assuming that all spent fuel produced from CIRUS and Dhruva up to 1992 has been reprocessed).[24]

India is currently operating eight power reactors and nine others are in various stages of construction or repair. Although India's nuclear power plants are not believed to be producing weapon-grade plutonium at this time, only two sites are under safeguards of any kind. As a result, a worst-case estimate of India's nuclear weapons' potential cannot rule out the possibility that at some time in the future, power reactors could produce weapon-grade plutonium, or that the existing stockpile of unsafeguarded reactor-grade plutonium could be diverted for weapons use.[25]

Currently safeguarded facilities include the two US-supplied reactors at Tarapur, and the Rajasthan I and II nuclear power plants. In October 1993, the 30-year-old agreement between the US and India to supply fuel to the two reactors at Tarapur expired, reopening the subject of safeguards for India as a whole.[26] During the year prior to expiry, India took the position that it would no longer be required to keep the Tarapur units and their spent fuel under IAEA inspection after the agreement had lapsed. Indian officials also stated that India would consider itself free to reprocess spent fuel from the Tarapur reactors, a right restricted by the original agreement. The controversy ended when a bilateral

---

23. The capacity factor takes into account the relative operating performance of the facilities. For example, the Dhruva research reactor was closed for almost a year in 1987 due to operating problems, but has operated without further difficulty for the past four years, up to its rated capacity of 100 megawatts. The smaller 40-megawatt CIRUS reactor was slowed by fuel fabrication problems in mid-1990, which caused it to be run at half power for six months.

24. Appendix B shows all assumptions and calculations made in obtaining the estimates.

25. All the power reactors, except at Tarapur, are CANDU reactors which can be refueled continuously. CANDU reactors have the capability to produce various grades of plutonium depending on how fast or slow the uranium fuel is fed through the reactor. The "online" refueling capacity permits plant operators to select a fueling cycle that maximizes the economically efficient production of electricity by using relatively long burn-up periods or one that maximizes the production of weapon-grade plutonium by moving the uranium fuel through these reactors more rapidly than normal. It should be noted, however, that although changing the fueling cycle is possible, it is more easily said than done, as it can create serious technical difficulties with the operation of the facility.

26. Leonard S. Spector, *Nuclear proliferation today*, (New York: Vintage Books, 1984), pp. 31-7, 46-8.

safeguards' agreement between India and the IAEA, which was voluntarily drafted by India, was finalized and approved by the IAEA Board of Governors in February 1994. The agreement established permanent safeguards in exchange for international assistance in keeping the Tarapur plants operational.[27] India possesses enough fuel to keep the plants running through 1995 and has not yet asked for any additional fuel or assistance.

The Rajasthan reactors are under permanent IAEA inspection, but neither Canada, which supplied the plants, nor the Soviet Union, which supplies the heavy water, retained the right to approve the reprocessing of spent fuel. India has, in fact, separated plutonium originating from the Rajasthan Power Station (RAPS), which remains under IAEA monitoring.

Reprocessing Facilities. India has readily acknowledged that it is extracting plutonium produced in its unsafeguarded reactors and has announced a program to separate several tonnes of the material by next century - potentially sufficient for hundreds of nuclear weapons - ostensibly to serve as fuel for advanced breeder reactors. It is not known how much of the spent fuel has already been reprocessed. India has two large-scale reprocessing plants currently operating - the PREFRE plant at Tarapur and one at BARC. A third plant is under construction at Kalpakkam. All of these are unsafeguarded, but when fuel from one of the safeguarded plants is reprocessed, IAEA inspections are applied.

The reprocessing plant at BARC is designed to process only metallic fuel, such as used in the CIRUS and Dhruva reactors. It is large enough to handle all the spent fuel produced by these reactors.[28] As a result, there are no technical capacity constraints on reprocessing all the weapon-grade plutonium produced by Indian research reactors - the main suspected source of India's nuclear weapons' potential.

The PREFRE plant has been operating since 1977 and can reprocess spent fuel from any of India's nuclear power plants. When spent fuel from RAPP I and II is being reprocessed at PREFRE, IAEA safeguards are applied and extend to any separated plutonium. When fuel is reprocessed from a reactor that is not subject to IAEA inspections, however, no safeguards apply. Given that BARC can

---

27. "Agreement with IAEA on Tarapur safeguards," *The Hindu*, February 24, 1994, p. 1 (JPRS-TND-94-011, May 16, 1994, p. 21).

28. The BARC plant can reprocess up to 30 tonnes of spent fuel per year, totalling 570 tonnes. The best estimate of CIRUS and Dhruva's output only totals approximately 120 tonnes.

only be used to reprocess CIRUS and Dhruva fuel, all remaining unsafeguarded fuel would have to be reprocessed at the PREFRE plant. The extent to which the PREFRE plant has been used to separate unsafeguarded plutonium is not publicly known. In any case, India's reprocessing capability is constrained by the 100 tonnes per year operating capacity of PREFRE.

A worst-case estimate of India's nuclear weapons' potential would assume that part of PREFRE's capacity would be used to reprocess the weapon-grade plutonium that is produced by the start-up of the unsafeguarded power reactors.[29]

Other Facilities. In addition to the above facilities, India is currently operating a 15-megawatt fast breeder test reactor (FBTR) at Kalpakkam. This reactor has been operating since 1993 and may eventually contribute to India's nuclear weapons' potential. In addition, although India's nuclear program has concentrated on plutonium production, the uranium enrichment route to producing fissile material has not been neglected. In 1985, a former Director of the Department of Atomic Energy, Raja Ramanna, announced that a centrifuge cascade at BARC had operated successfully. At the end of 1992, the facility consisted of 100 centrifuges.[30] Construction of a second facility near Mysore in Karnataka state started in 1987, although production of enriched uranium apparently did not begin until mid-1990 because of construction delays.[31] In 1991 India failed to list the Mysore plant on an inventory of facilities that it agreed to exchange with Islamabad, and Pakistan objected. New, unchallenged lists were exchanged in August 1992, allowing an agreement on not attacking nuclear facilities. In January 1994, Indian

---

29. The Albright *et al.* estimate takes this into account.
30. From a list of facilities now being exchanged between India and Pakistan as a result of confidence-building measures adopted after the 1990 Kashmir crisis. It is regarded as a secret document, but was believed to have been obtained by *News of Rawalpindi*. See David Albright *et al.*, *World inventory*, p. 162, fn. 27.
31. BARC comprises a 100-machine cascade; the Karnataka facility is believed to have several hundred operating centrifuges producing three separative work units per machine per year. The rationale for the enrichment program remains unclear, although the uranium could be used in a variety of projects, including the fueling of nuclear submarine reactors, the development of a thermonuclear capability, or the supply of fuel for nuclear reactors such as those located at Tarapur. India also has a laser uranium enrichment program. "Second Indian enrichment facility using centrifuges is operational," *Nucleonics week*, March 26, 1992.

and Pakistani Foreign Secretaries exchanged lists again: both lists were identical to the ones delivered in 1992.[32]

India is believed to be undertaking projects relevant to the production of thermonuclear bombs, and it has been widely speculated that if Pakistan tested an atomic bomb, India might respond with the test of a thermonuclear device to demonstrate its continuing lead in the field.[33]

Potential Nuclear Delivery Vehicles. India has developed two nuclear-capable, surface-to-surface ballistic missiles - the Prithvi and the Agni, with ranges of 150 and 1,500 miles respectively. Both missiles have been tested several times. The Indian government maintains that both systems are for use with conventional warheads, but no state has ever deployed a ballistic missile as complex and expensive as the Agni to carry conventional ordnance. The Agni's range is enough to be used against Pakistan, but a much longer-range missile would be needed to reach many of China's major cities and important military installations.

In April 1994, some experts speculated that funding for the Agni missile program would not be renewed, especially since the original program of three tests had been completed in February of that year. The speculation coincided with efforts by the US government to persuade India to cap its missile program, making even the slightest delay in funding for the program appear as if New Delhi was yielding to Washington's pressure.[34] During spring and summer 1994, however, New Delhi more than made up for that delay by carrying out tests of the short-range (9 km) Trishul, putting its pilotless Lakshya missile (300 km) into

---

32. *Report to Congress: update on progress toward regional non-proliferation in South Asia*, as required by the Foreign Assistance Act of 1961, amended, section 620F(c), April 1994, pp. 6-7.

33. Testimony of William Webster, Director of Central Intelligence, Hearings on Missile and Nuclear Proliferation, Committee on Governmental Affairs, US Senate, May 18, 1989; *Department of Atomic Energy, annual report 1988-1989* (Bombay: Government of India, 1989), p. 3; Albright and Hibbs, "India's Silent Bomb," *The bulletin of atomic scientists*, September 1992, p. 30.

34. At the time of writing, it is not believed that the Agni program will receive new funding. See "Paper reports Agni missile program 'temporarily capped,'" *The Hindustan Times*, April 20, 1994 (FBIS-NES-94-076, April 20, 1994, p. 57). Capping the Agni program may not necessarily mean that India is through with research and development of nuclear-capable missiles. If India is primarily concerned with countering Chinese nuclear weapons, a much longer-range missile capability would be needed.

production, and threatening to deploy the Prithvi along Pakistan's border, illustrating India's clear intentions of not yielding to international pressure.[35]

Future development plans may include a missile with intercontinental range. In 1992, the US government sanctioned the Indian Space Research Organization (ISRO) after discovering that Russia intended to sell three cryogenic rocket engines, along with the relevant technology, to India for their Geostationary Satellite Launch Vehicle program (a cryogenic rocket burns liquid oxygen and gaseous hydrogen and can be used to boost satellites into geostationary orbit). Washington argues that the technology could also be used for intercontinental ballistic missile development and that technology transfer would violate the Missile Technology Control Regime (MTCR), although at the time, neither Russia nor India belonged to the MTCR and disputed the U.S. claim. The sanctions were lifted in July 1994, after Russia and India agreed to the transfer of seven of the engines without the technology. The ISRO later stated that it did not need the technology as it expected to launch its own indigenously manufactured cryogenic engine within four years.[36] Other missile-related technology in which India has invested includes cruise missile and pilotless target aircraft. Capabilities in this field are currently, however, still believed to be limited.[37]

India also possesses several advanced fighter-bombers capable of delivering nuclear weapons against Pakistan, including the British and French-supplied Jaguars, French Mirage-2000, and Russian-supplied MIG-23, MIG-27, and MIG-29s. In early 1993, India was believed to be negotiating with Russia to purchase a MIG-31 strategic interceptor, but apparently changed its mind and finalized a deal to purchase an additional 30 MIG-29s in April 1994, this in response to the US government's offer to release 38 F-16s to Pakistan, in exchange for Islamabad's

---

35. See "India's Trishul missile test fired," UPI (New Delhi) (1518), August 1, 1994. The US government states that although there are Prithvi missiles near the Pakistani border, they have not been officially "deployed," and are there for testing reasons only. There have been no official Indian Governments statements clarifying the official status of the Prithvi as of this writing.

36. See "India to make rockets that worry US, Russia," Reuters, (0714), New Delhi, July 27, 1994; "US ends sanctions, Indian space official says," Reuters, (0914), Bangalore, July 16, 1994; "Development of indigenous cryogenic engine discussed," *The pioneer*, April 25, 1994, p. 1 (JPRS-TND-94-011, May 16, 1994, p. 22).

37. See Brahma Chellany, "India develops cruise missile technology," *UPI*, September 23, 1992; W. Seth Carus, *Cruise missile proliferation in the 1990s* (Washington, DC: Praeger Publishers/Washington Paper, 1992), p. 41.

promise to cap its nuclear program - an offer Pakistan has refused. India could use these aircraft to reach targets within China's borders, but longer-range aircraft would be needed to reach principal cities.[38]

All these elements - large amounts of weapon-grade fissile material, various sophisticated delivery systems, paired with India's refusal to renounce nuclear weapons and allow full inspection of its nuclear facilities - indicate India's consistent strategy of not ruling out a nuclear response to security threats, despite its official nuclear policy.

PAKISTAN

Likewise, Pakistan's official policy is that its nuclear program is for peaceful purposes only. Over the years, however, Pakistani leaders have made statements directly referring to Pakistan's nuclear deterrent capability.

As recently as August 1994, Benazir Bhutto's government categorically denied that Pakistan possesses a nuclear bomb, in response to statements made by the former Prime Minister, Nawaz Sharif.[39] Officially, Pakistan's current policy regarding the status of its nuclear program is that, in the course of its development of a peaceful nuclear program, Pakistan has acquired the capability to develop nuclear weapons, but it has made a specific decision not to produce them.[40] This denial seems somewhat contradictory in light of the Berlin police report in August 1994, stating that evidence of planned or successful shipments of plutonium to Pakistan was found during intensive international searches conducted to stop smuggling of radioactive materials from the former Soviet Union. The Pakistani government, however, claims the police report is false.[41]

---

38. The typical combat radius for the aircraft is 500 to 600 miles (800 to 1,160 kilometers).
39. Sharif was quoted by the Pakistan Press International as stating, "I confirm Pakistan possesses the atomic bomb," and that if India attacked Pakistan, it could trigger a "nuclear holocaust as both countries possess atomic bomb." See Narayanan Madhavan, "India's Rao under pressure on Pakistan bomb claim," Reuters, August 24, 1994, (0702); Alistair Lyon, "Pakistani ex-Premier stands By nuclear revelation," Reuters, August 25, 1994 (0347); Alistair Lyon, "Pakistani leaders deny nuclear bomb claim," Reuters, August 24, 1994 (0716).
40. Alistair Lyon, "Pakistani leaders deny nuclear bomb claim," Reuters, August 24, 1994 (0716).
41. See "Pakistan denies involvement in nuclear smuggling," Reuters, August 18, 1994, (1035); "India says Pakistan behind nuclear smuggling," Reuters, August 19, 1994, (0746).

As in the Indian case, an evaluation of Pakistan's capabilities has to be partially based on educated assessments.

Nuclear Infrastructure and IAEA Safeguards.[42] Pakistani Prime Minister Zulfikar Ali Bhutto, father of current Prime Minister Benazir Bhutto, initiated Pakistan's efforts to develop nuclear weapons in 1972, shortly after Pakistan's 1971 loss of East Pakistan during a war with India by broadening Pakistan's nuclear energy program (begun in 1955 with the assistance of Canada and the United States) to include the goal of obtaining fissile material for nuclear weapons.[43] Due to Pakistan's limited indigenous technological capability, Bhutto also began a program of clandestine procurement of components for a nuclear bomb.[44] Both aspects of the Pakistani nuclear program were accelerated after India's test of a nuclear explosive device in May 1974.[45]

Since Pakistan is not a signatory of the Nuclear Non-Proliferation Treaty, the only safeguards imposed on its nuclear facilities are those upon which supplier countries have insisted. As a result, only two currently operating nuclear facilities in Pakistan are under IAEA safeguards. These include Pakistan's first research reactor (Pakistan Research Reactor - PARR-1), which Islamabad obtained from the United States in 1965, and Pakistan's first nuclear power reactor (KANUPP), which was obtained from Canada in 1972. A 1991 effort to purchase a power reactor from France had to be cancelled because of France's decision to require full-scope safeguards on all major nuclear exports. More recently, Pakistan has negotiated to purchase a 300-megawatt nuclear power plant from China (Chas-

---

42. This section relies heavily on written assessments by Leonard S. Spector, Senior Associate, Carnegie Endowment for International Peace.
43. Details on Pakistan's nuclear infrastructure in Appendix C.
44. With the inception of US President Dwight D. Eisenhower's Atoms for Peace program, Pakistan organized its Atomic Energy Agency in 1955 and began to train personnel in the United States. In 1971, Prime Minister Bhutto announced his plan to develop nuclear weapons at a secret meeting of Pakistani scientists in Multan. See Steve Weissman and Herbert Krosney, *The Islamic bomb* (New York: Times Books, 1981), pp. 43-6; and Ashok Kapur, *Pakistan's nuclear development* (London: Croom Helm, 1987), chs 3 and 4.
45. The US State Department analysis regarding the impact of India's 1974 "peaceful nuclear explosion" on Pakistan's nuclear program in: "The Pakistani nuclear program," June 23, 1983, US Department of State document SECRET/NOFORN/ORCON, National Security Archives, hereafter referred to as "The Pakistani nuclear program." See also Steve Weissman and Herbert Krosney, *The Islamic bomb*, p. 75.

ma), and while the Chasma plant will be under IAEA safeguards, China is not insisting that Pakistan obtain full-scope safeguards, a condition that is becoming very common among major nuclear suppliers.[46] Islamabad will still encounter difficulties completing the facility as the plant uses some French and German equipment and technology and both states have insisted that Pakistan negotiate a full-scope safeguards' agreement before they complete their contractual obligations.[47]

A few indigenously built facilities fill out Pakistan's nuclear infrastructure. However, most, if not all, of them have benefited from technology and equipment obtained from outside sources. These facilities include a uranium enrichment facility (Kahuta), a small uranium enrichment research and development plant (Golra), a pilot-scale reprocessing plant (New Labs), a small plutonium separation facility (at the Pakistani Institute of Nuclear Science and Technology, PINS-TECH), and an incomplete plutonium production reactor (Khusab).

Bhutto's original nuclear weapons' program anticipated using plutonium as its primary source of fissile material, and just prior to the 1974 Indian test, Bhutto began negotiating with the French government to purchase a reprocessing plant. After considerable pressure from the United States, however, France suspended delivery of many of the components, and finally cancelled the entire contract.[48] Shortly before his execution, Bhutto revealed how critical the reprocessing plant was to the Pakistani nuclear program, when he declared that "all we needed was the reprocessing plant," and Pakistan would be "on the threshold of a full nuclear capability."[49] With the plutonium route to nuclear weapons blocked for the time

46. In 1992, the Nuclear Suppliers Group revised its voluntary guidelines to require all non-nuclear-weapon states to negotiate a full-scope safeguards agreement before "significant, new exports may be transferred" from supplier states. Although the requirement did not actually take effect until January 1, 1993, France announced its intentions to retroactively enforce the provision on it's sales to Pakistan. China is not a member of the NSG and does not abide by these voluntary guidelines. See Tadeusz Strulak, "The Nuclear Suppliers Group," *The nonproliferation review*, vol. 1, no. 1 (fall 1993), p. 5.

47. See Mark Hibbs, "No chance for Sino-Pakistani reactor deal, Western vendors say," *Nucleonics week*, February 6, 1992, p. 2; "Pakistan feeling NSG pressure on supply for Chinese PWR export," *Nuclear fuel*, July 20, 1992, p. 13.

48. The contract was originally signed only six months after India's 1974 nuclear test; see Leonard S. Spector, *Nuclear proliferation today* (New York: Vintage Books, 1984), pp. 74-81.

49. Zulfikar Ali Bhutto, *If I am assassinated ...* (New Delhi: Vikas, 1979), p. 138.

being, Pakistan turned its attention to the uranium enrichment method, where other efforts had been made since 1975.

During the late 1970s and especially during the 1980s, Pakistan sought to build up its uranium enrichment capability by clandestinely seeking equipment and technology from many European nations and the United States. Pakistan obtained an entire uranium conversion plant with the help of a German business-man who was later convicted for bypassing West German export control laws.[50] In addition, it is believed that most of the centrifuges operating at the Kahuta uranium enrichment facility are based on either German or Dutch design.[51] Less successful were Pakistan's attempts to purchase high-speed electronic switches, known as krytrons, and reflector materials from the United States.[52] Overall, six Pakistani nuclear projects have depended on raw material or design information clandestinely obtained from outside sources.[53]

Pakistan's efforts to procure parts of its nuclear infrastructure continue even today. At times, outside suppliers have been persuaded by the United States and other members of the non-proliferation regime not to sell nuclear-related equip-ment and technology to Islamabad. The effect of this interference has only been to delay, not prevent, Pakistan's progress.

Estimate of Nuclear Weapons' Potential. An estimate of Pakistan's nuclear weapons' capability conducted in 1992 states that Pakistan had enough fissile

---

50. A uranium conversion plant is needed to convert raw uranium into uranium hexafluoride, the type of chemical uranium used in centrifuges. See Albright and Hibbs, "Pakistan's bomb: out of the closet," *Bulletin of the atomic scientists*, July/August 1992, p. 39; Leonard S. Spector with Jacqueline R. Smith, *Nuclear ambitions* (Boulder, CO: Westview Press, 1990), p. 34.
51. Albright and Hibbs, "Out of the closet," pp. 40-41.
52. For a full discussion of these and other clandestine Pakistani efforts see, Leonard S. Spector, *The undeclared bomb* (Cambridge, MA: Ballinger Publishing Company, 1988), pp. 136-9; Leonard S. Spector, *Going nuclear* (Cambridge, MA: Ballinger Publishing Company, 1987), pp. 105, 114-16; Leonard S. Spector, *The new nuclear nations*, pp. 22-40.
53. Leonard S. Spector lists these projects as the Kahuta enrichment plant, the uranium hexafluo-ride plant at Dera Ghazi Khan, the expansion of Pakistan's uranium enrichment capability, a plant to produce tritium, a tritium purification plant, and other material and equipment needed to manufacture nuclear weapons. See Spector and Smith, *Nuclear ambitions*, p. 35.

material for 6-7 nuclear devices.[54] Another estimate, also based on the amount of fissile material produced in Pakistan, roughly doubles the first, reporting that Pakistan could have as many as 10-13 bombs.[55] Like India, however, Pakistan is not believed to have completed the production of any of its potential weapons, choosing to stop just short of putting the necessary components together.[56]

Although calculations may vary, an estimate of the amount of fissile material and other necessary components available, either through indigenous production or clandestine procurement, is central to any evaluation of Pakistan's nuclear program. There are only a few facilities that are suspected of contributing to Pakistan's nuclear weapons' potential.

Contributing Facilities. Because Pakistan has chosen the uranium enrichment path of nuclear weapons' development, the key facilities are the uranium enrichment plants. There are two such facilities: a gas centrifuge plant at Kahuta and a small uranium research and development plant at Golra, both located near Islamabad.

The Kahuta gas centrifuge plant was built in the late 1970s and early 1980s and began operating in 1984. It is believed that China assisted Pakistan with

---

54. Based on the amount of weapon-grade uranium Pakistan is believed to have obtained from China in the early 1980s, and the amount produced by the Kahuta plant between 1986 and late 1991, when production is believed to have stopped. If Pakistan has relied on a bomb design obtained from China, each nuclear weapon would use approximately 15 kilograms of weapon-grade uranium and weigh 180 kg. Regarding the transfer of uranium by China, see "Pakistan's atomic bomb," *Foreign report*, January 12, 1989, p. 1. Regarding the output of the Kahuta plant, see "Memorandum for Dr Kissinger; subject: official visit of Pakistan Prime Minister Mohammed Khan Junejo: background and talking points," July 18, 1986, in: Virginia I. Foran (ed.), *The making of US foreign policy: US nuclear non-proliferation policy, 1945-1990* (London: Chadwyck-Healey, 1992), hereafter referred to as "Memorandum for Dr Kissinger." For the estimate of seven weapons, see "Testimony of Robert Gates," Committee on Governmental Affairs, US Senate, January 15, 1992; "Pakistan has seven nuclear weapons," Reuters, December 1, 1992.
55. David Albright and Mark Hibbs, "Out of the closet," p. 38.
56. Representatives of the US Central Intelligence Agency have testified before Congress that it has "no reason to believe that either India or Pakistan maintains assembled or deployed nuclear bombs," but that "both countries have all of the parts or can make the parts on very short notice." See "Testimony of Robert Gates," before Committee on Governmental Affairs, US Senate, January 15, 1992; *Report to Congress: update on progress toward regional non-proliferation in South Asia*, as required by the Foreign Assistance Act of 1961, amended, section 620F(c), April 1994.

building the centrifuges and supplying uranium hexafluoride, the unenriched uranium material used in the centrifuges.[57] According to US government sources, the plant was designed to produce enough weapon-grade uranium for "several" devices per year, although this estimate can never be verified as Pakistan is not obligated to place the facility under safeguards. Uranium mining and processing facilities that provide the fuel for Kahuta are not under safeguards either, allowing Pakistan complete secrecy over its uranium enrichment process.[58]

During an official visit to Washington DC in June 1989, Prime Minister Benazir Bhutto announced that Pakistan had stopped producing weapon-grade uranium. During the spring 1990 Kashmir crisis, however, Pakistan is believed to have resumed production until mid-1991. Taking this brief pause in uranium production into account, the Kahuta facility could have produced enough uranium for "several" devices per year for roughly four years (1986-1989 and 1990-1991). Based on the amount and design of the centrifuges believed to be operating, the Kahuta plant alone could have produced enough weapon-grade uranium for between three and five nuclear weapons per year. This would place Pakistan's current nuclear weapons' potential somewhere between twelve and twenty nuclear bombs if there has been no further production of highly enriched uranium.[59]

---

57. Dr A.Q. Khan, a Pakistani metallurgist believed to have stolen gas centrifuge designs from Urenco, announced in 1984 that Kahuta was producing low enriched uranium. By 1986, however, US intelligence sources strongly believed that Kahuta was producing highly enriched weapon-grade uranium. See Albright and Hibbs, "Out of the closet," p. 39. For information on the Chinese assistance, see "The Pakistani nuclear program;" for 1986 enrichment levels see, Bob Woodward, "Pakistan reported near atom weapons production," *Washington Post*, November 4, 1986.

58. See "Memorandum for Dr Kissinger," and "Pakistani nuclear program."

59. Estimates range from 1,000 operating centrifuges out of 14,000 installed, up to 3,000 operating centrifuges. Most of the operating centrifuges are believed to be based on German Urenco designs known as G-1 and G-2, with a few earlier-generation centrifuges of German and Dutch design. Albright and Hibbs believe that most of Pakistan's centrifuges are of the G-2 design which has an estimated capacity of 5-6 separative work units per year (SWU), with a few G-2 and smaller-capacity centrifuges capable of 2-3 SWU rounding out the operating machines. Assuming a mix of centrifuges and taking an average of the operating capacity producing between 3-5 SWU per year, Kahuta could produce between 9,000-15,000 SWU per year. This is enough for 45-75 kilograms of weapon-grade uranium per year, which using a Chinese bomb design of 15 kilograms, is enough for 3-5 nuclear weapons per year.

The Golra plant was constructed during the early 1980s. Reports indicate that the facility is mostly dedicated for research and development of uranium enrichment technology, and is therefore probably not contributing very much to Pakistan's nuclear weapons' potential.[60] According to Western intelligence sources, however, the facility has been used to test advanced-design centrifuges that were eventually installed at Kahuta.[61] It was also the subject of some controversy between India and Pakistan in 1992 when Islamabad failed to include it on the list of facilities exchanged with New Delhi.

Reprocessing Facilities. Pakistan has continued to undertake plutonium reprocessing activities despite being thwarted at the beginning. A pilot-scale reprocessing plant called New Labs was built adjacent to the Pakistani Institute of Nuclear Science and Technology near Rawalpindi. Based on blueprints provided by France, the plant is believed to have been completed in 1991. It is not known, however, whether it is operational at this time, as Pakistan may still not have enough unsafeguarded fuel for reprocessing to warrant its operation.[62] It is believed, however, that New Labs could expand its reprocessing capability if Pakistan was eventually able to increase its plutonium production. PINSTECH is also the site of a plutonium separation lab, built in the basement of the institute. However, even if both these plants were up and running, only the Karachi Nuclear Power Plant (KANUPP), subject to IAEA safeguards, is currently capable of producing spent fuel for reprocessing. In order to produce plutonium

---

60. This estimate matches an October report stating that Pakistan is believed to have stockpiled more than 200 kilograms of weapon-grade HEU. See Mark Hibbs, "Bhutto may finish plutonium reactor without agreement on fissile stocks," *Nucleonics week*, October 6, 1994, pp. 10-11; Simon Henderson, "Pakistan builds second plant to enrich uranium," *Financial Times*, December 11, 1987; Neil R. Lewis, "Reports of Pakistan uranium plant weighted," *New York Times*, January 10, 1988; "Pakistan denies new enrichment plant," *Nuclear engineering international*, February 1988, p. 7; "Second Indian enrichment facility using centrifuges is operational," *Nucleonics week*, March 26, 1992; "India and Pakistan fail to include new SWU plants on exchanged lists," *Nuclear fuel*, March 30, 1992.
61. Albright and Hibbs, "Out of the closet," p. 42.
62. Albright and Hibbs, "Out of the closet," p. 42.

for nuclear weapons, Pakistan would have to violate the trilateral safeguards' agreement negotiated with Canada and the IAEA.[63]

During testimony provided by the former head of Neue Technologien GmbH, on trial for illegally selling a uranium conversion plant to Pakistan, it was revealed that a new plutonium production reactor has been under construction near the Indus River at Khusab since approximately 1989, and that Pakistani agents had solicited the German firm to supply equipment for it. It is believed to be a 70-MW (thermal) plant, moderated by heavy water. China is also believed to have supplied some of the equipment for the plant. As of late 1994, the facility was not under IAEA safeguards.[64] If completed, the reactor would provide Pakistan with a supply of unsafeguarded plutonium. The plant is on the list of facilities the United States is trying to ensure are "never finished" because they would affect any future global treaty on fissile material cut-off. Pakistan has threatened to complete the reactor, now believed to be approximately 50 per cent finished, unless India agrees to freeze its fissile material stockpiles at a level equivalent to Pakistan.[65] During the summer of 1994, at the Conference on Disarmament where multilateral discussions for a global fissile material cut-off were being held, Pakistan proposed that a simple ban on future production of fissile materials was not enough, but that existing stockpiles should be declared and then put under safeguards. With the exception of India, all non-aligned nations accepted this proposal. Most Western nations, however, disapproved, and

---

63. It is not believed that Pakistan has violated the agreement, although there is some concern that between 1980 and 1982, Pakistan may have loaded undeclared fuel into KANUPP, removed it and subsequently reprocessed it at New Labs. In any case, the amount reprocessed would be too small for a nuclear device. In 1982, IAEA safeguards were improved to reduce the possibility of violations of this type occurring without detection. See Leonard S. Spector, *Nuclear proliferation today*, pp. 93-4; "Pakistani nuclear program."

64. There is no specific information regarding the type of equipment China has provided to Pakistan. However, Article III.2 of the NPT prohibits transfers of equipment designed for a nuclear reactor to a non-nuclear-weapon state without IAEA safeguards. See Leonard S. Spector and Mark McDonough, *Global spread of nuclear weapons 1995*, forthcoming (Washington, DC: Carnegie Endowment for International Peace, 1995).

65. Mark Hibbs, "Bhutto may finish plutonium reactor without agreement on fissile stocks," pp. 10-11.

in late 1994 were pushing instead for a simple cut-off, leaving existing stockpiles free from safeguards.[66]

Power Plants and Research Reactors. The US-supplied PARR-1 reactor is also at the PINSTECH site. In 1992, PARR-1 was modified to operate on 19.9 per cent enriched uranium rather than 93 per cent enriched uranium previously provided by the United States.[67] PARR-1 production capacity was doubled at this time (from 5 to 10 megawatts), but the reactor is under IAEA safeguards and it is still too small to produce significant amounts of plutonium.

In 1992, Pakistan agreed to purchase a 300-megawatt nuclear power plant from China. China has proceeded with the sale despite its 1992 accession to the NPT and its corresponding obligation not to supply nuclear material or technology to states which are not under full-scope safeguards by the IAEA.[68] The sale is significant as no other country has been willing to sell a plant to Pakistan since former Prime Minister Zulfikar Ali Bhutto's efforts to purchase the French reprocessing facility in 1976.[69] More recently, it has been reported that 60 Pakistani operators of the Chashma Nuclear Power Plant are being trained in basic safety and maintenance procedures at a Chinese school.[70]

Weaponization. Pakistan is believed to have received weapon-design information from China, including the weapon design tested at Lop Nor in 1966. That design

---

66. Interview with Thomas Zamora-Collina, Institute for Science and International Security, December 1994; Mark Hibbs, "Bhutto may finish plutonium reactor without agreement on fissile stocks," pp. 10-11.
67. Shahid-ur-Rehman Khan and Rauf Siddiqi, "Pakistan marks 25 nuclear years with upgraded research reactor," *Nucleonics week*, May 28, 1992, p. 11.
68. "Pakistan gets confirmation on Chinese reactor ... but loses French PWR," *Nuclear engineering international* (March 1992), p. 7; Mark Hibbs, "Pakistan feeling NSG pressure on supply for Chinese PWR export," *Nuclear fuel*, July 20, 1992, p. 13; "Work begins on Chinese supplied nuclear plant," *Frontier post*, July 21, 1992 (FBIS-NES, July 31, 1992, p. 55).
69. "Pakistan-China defense cooperation: an enduring relationship," *International defense review*, 1 (1993), p. 110.
70. "PRC to train 60 Chashma nuclear plant operators," *Islamabad radio Pakistan network*, April 26, 1994 (FBIS-NES-94-080, April 26, 1994, p. 59).

is believed to require a solid sphere of approximately 15 kilograms of weapon-grade uranium with a hollow core surrounded by high explosives and a tamper.[71] There is some evidence that Pakistan may have pursued technology relevant to thermo-nuclear weapons as well. There are reports that PARR-1 was illegally used to irradiate lithium targets, a key process in the production of tritium, which is used to boost the yield of nuclear bombs to thermo-nuclear levels. The technology and material were supplied by German firms.[72]

Potential Nuclear Delivery Vehicles. Pakistan is believed to be pursuing two nuclear-capable missile systems, neither of which have yet been deployed. The Hatf-I and Hatf-II missiles are short-range ballistic missiles capable of reaching targets within 85 kilometers and 300 kilometers respectively. Their design is believed to based on the French Dauphin and Eridan sounding rockets, and are modified with the help of France and China for missile use.[73]

Pakistan is also seeking to acquire the Chinese M-11 missile system, which is capable of carrying nuclear warheads to targets 300 kilometers away. As early as 1991, the United States believed that Pakistan had acquired M-11 *test* missiles and launchers from China.[74] After unsuccessfully trying to persuade China to halt the transfer, the United States imposed sanctions (Category 2) on China and the Pakistani Space and Upper Atmosphere Research Commission in accordance with MTCR prescriptions. In early 1992, after China had agreed to abide by the

---

71. Albright and Hibbs, "Out of the closet," p. 43.
72. Reportedly, two (then) West German firms provided Pakistan with small amounts of tritium gas, a tritium purification and storage plant, and other material needed. See Mark Hibbs, "Illegal export charges may spur tighter German export controls," *Nucleonics week*, January 5, 1989; Mark Hibbs, "German firms exported tritium purification plant to Pakistan," *Nuclear fuel*, February 6, 1989; John J. Fialka and Thomas F. O'Boyle, "West German firms admit supplying nuclear-weapons material to Pakistan," *Wall Street Journal*, April 21, 1989; Testimony of Reinhard Heubner, Federal Prosecuting Attorney, Hanau District, before the Second Parliamentary Investigating Committee of the German Bundestag, Bonn, April 15, 1989, p. 60.
73. John Harvey and Uzi Rubin, "Assessing ballistic missile proliferation and its control," (Stanford, CA: Stanford University Center for International Security and Arms Control, 1992), p. 75.
74. John J. Fialka, "Pakistan seeks Chinese missile, US believes," *Wall Street Journal*, April 5, 1991; R. Jeffrey Smith, "Chinese missile launchers sighted in Pakistan," *Washington Post*, April 6, 1991; "Official hopes for delivery of Chinese missiles," *Hong Kong AFP*, June 13, 1991 (FBIS-NES, June 13, 1991, p. 28).

MTCR standards on exports, the United States lifted the sanctions.[75] By late 1992, however, China was reported to be delivering operational missiles to Pakistan again.[76] China maintains that the missiles are shorter-range systems than those prohibited by the MTCR.[77] Unable to verify China's claims, in August 1993 the Clinton administration placed two-year trade and economic sanctions against the Chinese Ministries of Defense and Aerospace Industries and eight Chinese companies. Similar sanctions were placed against Pakistan,[78] although by September 1994 there was still no independent confirmation that Chinese M-11 missiles have been deployed in Pakistan. In October 1994, however, China signed a statement with the United States formally agreeing not to export missiles capable of the range and payload specifically *or inherently* prohibited by the MTCR.[79] In return, the US sanctions against China would be lifted. The anticipated arrival of Chinese missile technicians in Islamabad, in addition to reports that Islamabad paid an installment of $15 million in 1988 for a number of M-11 missiles, launchers, and a team of Chinese trainers, leads one to wonder if, despite China's formal agreement with the United States, it is simply a matter of time before deployment of the missiles is confirmed.

---

75. Bill Gertz and Warren Strobel, "US set to drop sanctions if China obeys missile pact," *The Washington Times*, January 30, 1992.
76. According to US officials, there was strong evidence that M-11s were shipped in November 1992, although spy satellites were unable to confirm this at the time. See Bill Gertz, "Pakistan-China deal for missiles exposed," *The Washington Times*, September 7, 1994, p. A1.
77. The MTCR prohibits the sale of missiles or parts of missiles that can deliver a 500 kilogram payload a distance of at least 300 kilometers. See Barry Schweid, "US-China," *Associated press*, October 5, 1994, (0150); R. Jeffrey Smith, "China said to sell arms to Pakistan," *Washington Post*, December 12, 1992.
78. The sanctions were imposed under "Category 2" of the MTCR. Stronger "Category 1" sanctions will be imposed if China has transferred a "complete missile system" to Pakistan. See Bill Gertz, "China may suffer for missile dealings," *The Washington Times*, September 8, 1994, p. A4; Jon B. Wolfstahl, "US imposes sanctions over China's missile transfers," *Arms control today* (September 1993), p. 27.
79. By gaining Chinese acquiescence on "inherent capability," the United States believes it has resolved the difference of opinion on whether the M-11 missile system, which the Chinese government asserts has a range of 290 km, falls under the MTCR guidelines. See "Joint United States-People's Republic of China statement on missile proliferation / Joint United States-People's Republic of China statement on stopping production of fissile materials for nuclear weapons," US Department of State, Office of the Spokesman, October 4, 1994.

Pakistan currently possesses as number of French Mirage jets and has also acquired sophisticated nuclear-capable fighter-bomber aircraft such as the F-16. In agreeing to sell the plane to Pakistan, the United States insisted that Pakistan not use them to deliver nuclear weapons, and periodically monitors the F-16s to verify that they have not been modified.[80] Sales of F-16 planes and spare parts were slowed and eventually halted as a result of President Bush's 1990 failure to certify that Pakistan does not possess a nuclear explosive device, triggering implementation of the Pressler Amendment.[81] Although the Clinton Administration offered Pakistan a one-time waiver of the Pressler Amendment in March and April 1994, releasing 38 additional F-16s already paid for by the Pakistani government in exchange for a "verifiable cap" on Pakistan's nuclear program, as of fall 1994, Islamabad has publicly rejected the American offer and has demanded that the funds for the planes be returned to the Pakistani government.[82]

Potential Impact of Post-Cold War Environment

Evaluating the prospects for nuclear arms control in South Asia requires assessing the impact of the post-Cold War environment on India's and Pakistan's current proliferation motives and constraints. While some post-Cold War predictions of proliferation identify important factors in making this assessment, they each imply one or two factors will significantly alter the proliferation situation in the world. Benjamin Frankel argues that the end of bipolarity is likely to encourage states to

---

80. "Opening statement of Senator Richard Lugar," *Hearings on the implementation of the Pressler Amendment*, Committee on Foreign Relations, US Senate, July 30, 1992.
81. The 1985 Pressler Amendment to the 1961 Foreign Assistance Act bans all US military aid to Pakistan unless the President of the United States can certify that Pakistan does not "possess a nuclear explosive device." See Foreign Assistance Act of 1961, section 620E(e).
82. In May 1994, Pakistani Foreign Minister, Sardar Assef, announced that Islamabad would agree to allow "non-intrusive inspections of its nuclear facilities by the United States to help improve bilateral relations." However, the US Congress did not appear to support the one-time waiver, and Pakistani enthusiasm has waned. Meanwhile, Assef's statements caused an uproar and demands that the government resign. See John Thor-Dahlburg, "In Pakistan, US envoy upbeat on arms limits," *Los Angeles Times*, April 10, 1994, p. A6; Anwar Iqbal, "Pakistan to allow nuclear inspection," *UPI*, Islamabad, May 18, 1994; Raja Asghar, "Pakistan wants money back if no US fighters," Reuters, Islamabad, August 10, 1994, (0620).

proliferate,[83] while Devin Hagerty has argued that it will lead to a better coordinated non-proliferation regime and less proliferation. In addition, Hagerty argues that the economic liberalization programs being pursued by India and Pakistan will force greater dependency on international financial institutions which are largely controlled by supporters of non-proliferation, causing an indirect constraint on their nuclear programs.[84] In a different context, Peter Feaver argues that the risk of proliferation in South Asia will continue as long as the prospects for inter-state conflict over Kashmir remain high.[85] These discussions, however, do not agree on what the deciding factors that will affect proliferation in the post-Cold War world are, nor on what kinds of proliferation will ultimately result. Perhaps it is a too difficult task to evaluate how proliferation has changed since the end of the Cold War, when, as Leonard Spector has so aptly put, we are not sure what has been holding the dike so far.

Given that building a causal model of proliferation after the Cold War is probably premature, I would like to suggest a framework for describing and analyzing some of the events and factors believed to effect the prospects for nuclear arms control in South Asia. Hopefully this framework will contribute to building the much-needed consensus to conduct proliferation analysis in the post-Cold War world.

---

83. Benjamin Frankel, "An anxious decade: nuclear proliferation in the 1990s," *Journal of strategic studies* 13, no. 3, September 1990, p. 2; Benjamin Frankel, "The brooding shadow: systemic incentives and nuclear weapons proliferation," pp. 37-78.
84. Devin T. Hagerty, "Opaque proliferation, existential deterrence, and nuclear stability," pp. 14-15.
85. Feaver examines what happens when states with opaque nuclear programs decide to weaponize rapidly during a crisis situation, such as the ongoing conflict between India and Pakistan over Kashmir. He points to the general danger of weaponization during crisis periods. Feaver argues, moreover, that in opaque states, where there is little or no development of any military strategy incorporating nuclear weapons, the military and the political leadership is likely to behave erratically, perhaps even irrationally. It becomes crucial, therefore, to include some assessment of potential crisis situations in the region. Peter D. Feaver, "Proliferation optimism and theories of nuclear operations," *Security studies* 2, no. 3/4, (spring/summer 1993), pp. 176-7.

A FRAMEWORK FOR ANALYSIS

A full description and explanation of the effect of post-Cold War events on South Asian nuclear arms control would first have to posit what domestic and international factors are more likely to influence nuclear arms control than others and why. Second, given those events, how are decision-makers likely to influence the direction of policy? Third, what interactive effects are likely to occur between the decision-makers that will influence the ultimate outcome? Once these are established, a causal model of proliferation can be achieved. I will focus on sketching the first two steps. However, I am not suggesting that each of the factors thought to influence proliferation in the South Asian region is a result of the end of the Cold War, but more simply, *that the factor has occurred since that period and could have an impact on the state's deterrence strategy and ultimately its proliferation posture.*

I will use a simple heuristic device to organize the two levels at which the effects could occur: I will evaluate the events in light of their effect on moving India and Pakistan away from their current opaque nuclear status and existential deterrence strategy towards either fully declaring (that is, less opaque) or fully renouncing their nuclear capability (that is, more opaque). As the Cold War was an international phenomena only indirectly effecting South Asia, most of the identified factors which could affect the region stem from the international level as opposed to the domestic level. Nevertheless, general political and economic changes stemming from the end of the Cold War have occurred at the domestic level.

POST-COLD WAR INTERNATIONAL FACTORS AFFECTING INDIA AND PAKISTAN

The prediction that the non-proliferation regime would be seriously challenged in the post-Cold War era by states who could no longer rely on extended deterrence previously supplied by the competing superpowers, and who compensated for the loss of security with their own nuclear weapons programs, assumes that security threats to these states remain at Cold War levels and that there is little or no countervailing pressure from the non-proliferation regime. During the Cold War, both India and Pakistan believed that the extended deterrence their respective superpower patrons were prepared to offer would be so unreliable that they opted for a mixed strategy, balancing increases in conventional military capabilities with opaque nuclear programs. Even with a mixed strategy, the end of bipolarity and corresponding superpower patronage wreaked havoc on both states' conventional military capabilities. Both have attempted to make up the difference, but their financial resources limit their efforts. Compensating for their loss of security, however, some threats to the region have lessened, and for those that have not, the end of the Cold War has enabled the international non-proliferation regime to increase pressure on states. As a result, the proliferation consequences of the end of the Cold War are not likely to be as dire as previously predicted.

India. Concluded in August 1971, the Indo-Soviet Treaty had formalized the economic and military relationship already emerging between the two participants. In particular, the former Soviet Union extended generous terms of trade and credit to India for the purchase of military equipment, spare parts, and technology rights, and, most importantly, included a loose defense pact. The defense pact was noted in Article IX of the Treaty and required each state to come to the aid of the other in the event of attack by a third state.

With the dissolution of the Soviet Union at the end of 1991, a new requirement for hard currency transactions rather than the more flexible rupee-rouble barter arrangement of the past had to be negotiated, and the valuable supply line of defense equipment was in question.[86] Moscow had accepted rupees or barter goods as payment in the past, but the fifteen independent republics refused to agree to the old methods of payment. India was unable to make the hard currency payments the suppliers demanded and soon found itself in a conventional military spare-parts crisis. India also lost a valuable ally, as Moscow quickly indicated that it wanted to renegotiate the Friendship Treaty, but without Article IX. In January 1993, the leaders of India and Russia met to sign a new 20-year Friendship Treaty, which significantly stops short of re-extending a military umbrella to India. The loss of Moscow's support was highlighted by its unprecedented endorsement of a Pakistani nuclear-weapon-free zone proposal during a November 1991 vote in the UN General Assembly - the first time that Moscow had voted against India in the UN. Similarly, the fate of two 1,000-megawatt reactors to be built by the Soviet Union at Koodankulam was no longer assured, as Russia refused to confirm its role in the reactor project. New Delhi has reportedly

---

86. One expert estimates that Soviet hardware constituted between 60 and 70 per cent of all of India's weaponry. See J. Mohan Malik, "India copes with the Kremlin's Fall," *Orbis*, winter 1993, pp. 69-87. Also "India's Westward gaze," *Jane's defence weekly*, January 9, 1993, pp. 18-19.

decided to substitute two smaller, indigenously constructed reactors at the same site instead.[87]

The international tempest triggered in 1992 by the proposed sale of cryogenic rocket boosters by Russia to India indicates that future transactions with possible nuclear applications will be subject to a higher level of international scrutiny. During the Cold War, the Soviet Union might have ignored international complaints regarding the transfer of cryogenic technology. Since the end of the Cold War, however, Russia has been on the defensive to show that it is concerned about nuclear proliferation, especially because of leaks originating from Russia or one of the former Soviet republics. Officially sanctioning the transfer of questionable technology would not have contributed positively to Russia's non-proliferation credentials.[88]

India has not made radical efforts to acquire new military suppliers,[89] but has preferred to continue to negotiate with Russia (most likely because of its existing military equipment). To compensate for the reduced levels of military imports since the dissolution of the Soviet Union, however, there is also some indication that India is attempting to produce more conventional military equipment itself.[90] To resolve the dilemma of access to new military equipment, India has sought to increase familiarity and access to Western military technology and hardware through co-production efforts and joint military exercises.[91] In April 1994, Prime Minister Narasimha Rao authorized a 20 per cent increase in defense spending over the 1992/93 budget, which totalled $6.75 billion (still only 3 per cent of its gross national budget). Only very small increases had been made in

---

87. Brahma Chellaney, "Yeltsin pledges not to sell military technology to Pakistan," *UPI*, January 29, 1993, (06:22).

88. William Potter has noted that Russia's change of heart on transferring the cryogenic rocket technology to India may have more to do with the financial incentives the United States provided to Russia along with the prospect of joint US-Russian space ventures. Still, would such joint ventures have been possible during the Cold War? Furthermore, would a questionable technology transfer have even caught the attention of Cold War diplomats?

89. See P. Stoban, "Developments in military power: 1988-93," *Asian strategic review 1992-93* (New Delhi: The Institute for Defense Studies and Analyses, 1993), p. 97.

90. See Jasjit Singh, "Trends in defense expenditures," *Asian strategic review 1992-93* (New Delhi: The Institute for Defense Studies and Analyses, 1993), pp. 50-51.

91. "India's Westward gaze," *Jane's defence weekly*, January 9, 1993, pp. 18-19.

previous years, and were not even enough to keep up with the rate of inflation.[92] In addition, since the end of the Cold War, India's defense spending as a proportion of the entire Indian budget has also decreased, from a high of 17.09 per cent in 1987 to 14.69 per cent in 1992, the last available date. Although some might point to the 20 per cent increase as exorbitant and a clear response to the end of the Cold War, other factors suggest that India's reaction has been rather muted.

Pakistan. Pakistan's military relationship with the United States was also a factor of the Cold War. Pakistan's relationship with the United States actually began with the 1954 Mutual Defense Assistance Act, which first authorized US military sales to Pakistan. With the 1958 Baghdad Pact, Pakistan sought to establish a close military alliance with the United States in order to balance its conventional inferiority *vis-à-vis* India. The United States, for its part, sought reliable allies on the Asian borders of the Soviet Union, as well as influence *vis-à-vis* China and the Middle East. Pakistan was eager to meet those needs.

The United States grew concerned, however, when it became known that Pakistan was clandestinely trying to purchase technology and components for a uranium enrichment facility. In 1976, the US Congress responded by passing the Symington Amendment to the Foreign Assistance Act of 1961, which prohibits US economic assistance to states that import uranium enrichment technology without corresponding IAEA safeguards. Under this law, aid to Pakistan was cut off in mid-1979 - but not for long. When the Soviets invaded Afghanistan in December 1979, the United States sought ways of contributing to the defeat of the Soviet-backed government in Kabul. The Reagan administration argued to the US Congress that both Cold War and non-proliferation objectives could be obtained if the Symington Amendment was waived and economic and military assistance to Pakistan released. Pakistan would then be able to aid anti-communist guerrillas in Afghanistan, and at the same time improve its conventional weapons' capability *vis-à-vis* India, making its nuclear weapons efforts unnecessary. The waiver was obtained, and by 1981 Pakistan had a $3.2 billion aid package that included 40 F-16 fighter bombers, as well as other conventional arms that could be used in the

---

92. Jasjit Singh, "trends in defense expenditure," p. 41, gives recent defense spending figures as a percentage of GDP. See also Selig S. Harrison and Geoffrey Kemp, *India & America: after the Cold War*, Report of the Carnegie Endowment Study Group on US-Indian Relations in a Changing International Environment (Washington, DC: Carnegie Endowment for International Peace, 1993), pp. 21-2.

Indo-Pakistan theater. However, in approving this assistance, the US Congress enacted the Pressler Amendment, named for its sponsor, South Dakota Senator Larry Pressler, which requires the President to certify that Pakistan does not possess a nuclear explosive device. In a clear illustration of the primacy of Cold War politics over non-proliferation goals, Presidents Reagan and Bush made these certifications until 1990, only a few months after the Soviets withdrew from Afghanistan, despite increasing evidence that Pakistan was becoming nuclear capable. The US government asserted that Pakistan had crossed the threshold in early 1990 when Islamabad manufactured cores for several nuclear weapons,[93] although in 1991, Pakistani government officials stated that further production of weapon-grade nuclear materials and weapon components had been frozen.[94]

Given the radical loss of financial and military assistance since the United States' 1990 decision, one should expect that Pakistan's defense spending as a percentage of the government's total budget would have to increase to make up the difference. Indeed, in contrast to the previous trend of a gradual reduction in the defense portion of Pakistan's government spending, there has been a significant increase in spending since the US decision.[95] This rise has enabled Pakistan to build up its conventional military capital stocks. Whether this increase indicates that Pakistan feels less restraint on its nuclear program is not clear. Indeed, there is important evidence to the contrary.

Since 1991, the Pakistani government has sought to re-establish US assistance by trying to gain acceptance as an undeclared nuclear-weapon state. Pakistani Foreign Minister Sharhayar Khan, probing the United States' attitude, stated *in Washington* in February 1992 that Pakistan possessed all the elements for a nuclear device, and that the program had been frozen.[96] At that time, however, the United States' criteria for re-establishing aid were that the program had to be rolled back to its 1989 status, and, specifically, that all existing nuclear-weapon cores had to be destroyed.[97] Pakistan soon discovered that it would indeed have

---

93. See "Pak-US relations in the 1990s," *Nation*, August 16, 1991.
94. See "Khan notes freeze on program," *Karachi AMN*, February 9, 1992, (JPRS-TND, April 3, 1992, p. 6).
95. Jasjit Singh, "Trends in defense expenditures," p. 59.
96. "Nuclear game-plan," *Patriot* (New Delhi), March 27, 1993, p. 4, (JPRS-TND-93-017, Pakistan's nuclear admission puts pressure on India, June 7, 1993, p. 13).
97. Mushahid Hussain, "Nuclear issue: ball is now in Pakistan's court," *Nation*, November 29, 1990.

to freeze at the 1989 level if it wanted to re-establish aid, for the United States was not willing to accept Pakistan's undeclared nuclear-capable status.

Recent efforts by the US government to seek a one-time waiver of the Pressler Amendment and allow delivery of some of the F-16s, already paid for by Pakistan prior to the 1990 cut-off, in return for a verifiable cap on Pakistan's nuclear program, may indicate a slight change in non-proliferation attitude towards the region. It is still unclear what the requirements of a "verifiable cap" are, but at first glance they may be less restrictive than earlier efforts to "roll-back" the program. A US change in non-proliferation attitude may not matter in the long run, however, as domestic elements in Pakistan are increasing the pressure on the Bhutto government to reject all international influence - unless there is a corresponding "verifiable cap" on India's program.[98] India has refused this suggestion, citing its ongoing security concerns with China, but has made a counterproposal to discuss caps on *all* nuclear-capable states.[99]

China. China's role in events in South Asia during the Cold War is too frequently left out of proliferation discussions. Although not a primary Cold War actor, China's attitude towards the region has also been changing since the end of US-Soviet rivalry, and this change has made a significant difference. During the Cold War, China supported the Pakistani government, while its relations with India were antagonistic. In addition to its surprise invasion of northern India in October 1962, Beijing sent a military warning to India during the 1965 war over Kashmir, which contributed to India's acceptance of the UN Security Council's cease-fire terms. Then, during the 1971 war over East Pakistan, Beijing sent valuable arms to an under-supplied Pakistani army. Since the dissolution of the Soviet Union, however, China has participated in a series of discussions with India in an attempt to reconcile relations. Most importantly, China and India have signed an agreement easing their 32-year-old border dispute. Although the actual border still cannot be drawn, India and China have agreed not to disagree about it any longer.

Relations between India and China are still far from perfect. China is still not receptive to India's long-time security concerns over Chinese military superiority, and Beijing is still suspected of assisting Pakistan's nuclear program despite its 1992 accession to the NPT. It is not believed likely that China would support

---

98. "Pakistan will not roll back nuclear potential: Bhutto," April 16, 1994.
99. Hamish McDonald and Ahmed Rashid, "Half a deal," *Far Eastern economic review,* April 21, 1994, pp. 22-3.

Pakistan in the event of a military crisis, as it did in 1971, but it cannot be ruled out. For improvements in nuclear arms control to occur, China would have to be more willing to participate in discussions involving constraints on its nuclear program and improve its non-proliferation behavior, particularly in the export control area.

US and Russian behavior towards India and Pakistan has changed since the end of the Cold War. Without competing foreign policy goals, the United States and Russia's individual behavior and multilateral cooperation on non-proliferation matters became stronger than before; and although China's record on non-proliferation is troublesome, Beijing has taken steps to reduce tensions with one of its Asian rivals. The general prediction that the end of bipolarity alone would contribute to more overt weaponization does not appear accurate in South Asia. Perhaps there are other post-Cold War international factors influencing this outcome.

The Urgency of Regional Conflicts. If the aftermath of Iraq's 1990 attack on Kuwait, and the intensive multilateral attention North Korea received during 1993 and 1994, are any indication of current international cooperation on non-proliferation, the governments of India and Pakistan may be less likely to chance becoming the target of such new non-proliferation zeal. New Delhi and Islamabad cannot doubt that an overt nuclear program will attract intense international scrutiny, pressure, and even sanctions. In fact, as countries like South Africa, Brazil and Argentina renounce their nuclear programs, and prospects for arms control in the Middle East improve, all eyes are turning on South Asia. This does not mean that the international non-proliferation regime will be successful in its efforts to pull India and Pakistan back from the nuclear brink, but it may sober each states' actions and perhaps even inter-state relations (rhetoric not withstanding). In addition, without the prospect of international backing, Pakistan's worst-case scenario, of the Indian army splitting Pakistan down the middle, is not likely to occur, and India may not have to worry about the Pakistani-backed insurgency in Kashmir erupting into a full-fledged military maneuver by the Pakistan army.[100] If a crisis were to occur, it is more likely that the major powers would make it absolutely clear, as they did during the 1990 Kashmir crisis, that they would not

---

100. See Devin T. Hagerty, "Pakistan-India relations: Kashmir and the nuclear question," in: Charles H. Kennedy and Rasul B. Rais (eds), *Pakistan: 1994* (Boulder, CO: Westview Press, 1994).

intercede on the behalf of either state. Given that there has been so much concern that the ongoing Kashmir conflict would trigger a nuclear war between India and Pakistan, it is also likely that the major powers would choose to force a solution that neither state would like (as they did in 1965).[101]

Confidence-Building during and after the Cold War. One should also ask whether the potential for conflict in South Asia is as high as some believe. Many proliferation scenarios rest on the early interpretations of the 1990 Kashmir crisis. Since 1990, however, there have been several reports that the Kashmir crisis was not nearly as serious as previously believed.[102] These reports provide a more accurate account of the events of the crisis, and seem to justify a revision of the earlier proliferation predictions. The non-proliferation regime and international efforts are also having an impact on the potential for crisis. In fact, during the last three years, Non-Governmental Organizations outside South Asia, along with agencies of the US government, have sponsored several face-to-face negotiations of sophisticated confidence-building measures (CBMs) designed to avoid crisis in Kashmir and elsewhere on the Subcontinent, to foster better relations between India and Pakistan, and to build up prospects for regional and multilateral arms control agreements. Although rhetorical statements continue to be made by both states, there has been significant progress in introducing these CBMs into the region.[103]

---

101. See Leonard S. Spector, "India-Pakistan war: it could be nuclear," *New York Times*, June 7, 1990, p. A23; and James Woolsey, *US security policy vis-à-vis rogue regimes*. Also Seymour Hersh, "On the nuclear edge," *New Yorker*, March 29, 1993, pp. 56-69; and William E. Burrows and Robert Windrem, *Critical mass: the dangerous race for superweapons in a fragmenting world* (New York: Simon and Schuster, 1994), pp. 61-85.

102. Michael Krepon and Mishi Faruqee, *Conflict prevention and confidence-building measures in South Asia: the 1990 crisis*, Occasional Paper 17 (Washington, DC: The Henry L. Stimson Center, April 1994); and Aziz Hanifa, "Ex-envoys deny '90 showdown," *India abroad*, February 25, 1994.

103. See Brahma Chellany, "The challenge of nuclear arms control in South Asia," *Survival* 35, no. 3 (fall 1993), pp. 121-36; Moonis Ahmar, "War avoidance between India and Pakistan: a model of conflict resolution and confidence-building in the post-Cold War era," *Strategic studies* (winter 1993), pp. 3-26; *Report to Congress: update on progress toward regional non-proliferation in South Asia*, as required by the Foreign Assistance Act of 1961, amended section 620F(c), April 1994.

During the Cold War, there was only one confidence-building agreement concluded in the region: the Shimla Accord, intended to normalize Indo-Pakistani relations in the wake of the war over East Pakistan in 1971. This accord pledged to settle disputes peacefully. It was successful in restoring diplomatic relations, returning captured territories, releasing prisoners of war, and restoring communications and travel links between the two states, but it did not actually resolve any of the existing disagreements between the two states. Recently, Pakistan has argued that the Shimla Accord provides the basis for accepting the United Nations' resolutions urging that a plebiscite be held to determine Kashmir's status. India disagrees, saying that the accord simply means that no third-party negotiations are possible in resolving disputes between the two states. India knows that any plebiscite in Kashmir where 80 per cent of the population is Muslim will come out in Pakistan's favor.

In sharp contrast, the post-Cold War era is significant for the number of agreements that have been initiated and concluded between the two states. The following is a listing of these agreements and CBMs:

1. Agreement to Notify of Military Exercises - In the wake of the 1987 Brass Tacks military exercise which almost resulted in war, in August 1992 India and Pakistan exchanged instruments of ratification on an agreement providing for advance notice of military exercises, maneuvers, and troop movements.
2. Agreement on Non-Attack of Nuclear Installations - First negotiated in 1988, this agreement provides for India and Pakistan to exchange detailed information on their nuclear weapons and research facilities on an annual basis, and promises that both states will not attack the sites listed. The Agreement came into force in 1992 after the two states exchanged lists for the first time. The lists were exchanged again in 1994.
3. Military Hotline Agreement - A communications "hotline" was established after the May 1990 Kashmir crisis between the respective military leaderships (Director General Military Operations), to share timely information regarding military exercises, maneuvers, and air-space violations.
4. Air-Space Violations Agreement - In April 1991, India and Pakistan signed an accord allowing each other to fly-over rights. In August 1992, another agreement allowed for fly-overs and landing by military planes.

5. Chemical Weapons Convention - In late 1992, both states agreed to ban the production, stockpiling and use of chemical weapons. No verification measures were included. India and Pakistan acceded to the CWC in 1993.[104]

There have also been a number of agreements concluded between India and China.[105] Since the 1991 visit of Premier Li Peng to New Delhi, China and India have agreed to implement the following CBMs: a ceiling on troop deployments along the Himalayas; clarification of the line of control; mutual agreement not to use force to change the border; prior notification of troop maneuvers; a "hot line" communication link; periodic meetings of border-force commanders; and measures to deter air-space violations. Since these were proposed, India and China have also reduced the number of troops on the Siachen Glacier, have instituted the "hot line," and have made progress on establishing cease-fire lines.

Finally, there are a number of multilateral CBM proposals. The Five Power Conference, formally proposed by Pakistan (but encouraged by the United States), would gather China, Russia, the United States, India and Pakistan together to discuss a South Asian non-proliferation system. India, however, has opposed the conference on the grounds that Chinese nuclear weapons and weapons' deployments would not be discussed, so the United States has proposed to hold separate but parallel talks with India and Pakistan in Washington. This time, the Pakistanis rejected the offer on the basis that separate talks would undermine the Five-Power proposal. Although it is unlikely that a Five Power Conference will occur in the near future, by the end of 1994, both states continued to discuss aspects of non-proliferation with the United States, indicating some willingness to cooperate.

The United States has urged Pakistan and India to participate in negotiating a global verifiable ban on all fissile material production, a regional nuclear test ban, and acceptance of IAEA safeguards on specific nuclear installations. Also, the United States has begun a dialogue with China to seek support for American non-proliferation objectives in South Asia.

Besides enthusiastically supporting the Chemical Weapons Convention, India has pledged to support a Comprehensive Test Ban Treaty, and a No-First-Use

---

104. Once the CWC enters into force, acceptance of international verification is obligatory.

105. To date, all CBMs and arms control proposals discussed between India and China have been in the conventional area. China has refused to enter into official discussions with India on nuclear matters.

Agreement among all nuclear-capable states.[106] In January 1994, India proposed negotiations with Pakistan on six different CBMs, including: ensuring peace along a Line of Control in Kashmir; withdrawal from the Siachen Glacier; settlement of boundaries along Sir Creek and a maritime boundary in Indian Ocean; resolving differences on the Tulbal Navigation Project (Wallar Barrage) in Kashmir; extending the Agreement on Prohibition of Attack on Nuclear Facilities and Installations to population and economic centers; and a no-first-use of nuclear "capability" agreement. Pakistan was abrupt in its rejection of this last proposal, saying that since Pakistan was not a nuclear power, a no-first-use agreement was not possible. As far as the proposals on Kashmir were concerned, Pakistani Foreign Secretary Shaharyar Khan said "None ... goes into the depth of the issue."[107]

In January 1994, Pakistan proposed that India and Pakistan discuss arrangements for holding a plebiscite in Kashmir, and ways for reducing tension. India rejected the plebiscite, but agreed to examine the second issue further.

While the dramatic increase in CBM-related activities are not necessarily *caused* by the end of the Cold War, one cannot ignore the fact that so many measures have been negotiated since. The Kashmir conflict, unfortunately, has proven almost impossible to resolve. Given that the roots of the crisis are in the 1947 partition of colonial India, and that domestic factors in both countries contribute to the conflict, a full solution seems far off.

SOME CONCLUSIONS REGARDING INTERNATIONAL FACTORS AFTER THE COLD WAR

For both India and Pakistan, the pressures to increase their security because of a real loss of superpower patronage at the end of the Cold War, may be balanced by an increase in international cooperation on non-proliferation. The international non-proliferation regime is able to impose real costs on the development of nuclear programs and is now also trying to contribute to resolving the issues that

---

106. India has co-sponsored United Nations' resolutions (with the United States and others), urging the conclusion of a multilateral convention on a fissile material production cut-off, and the negotiation of a Comprehensive Test Ban Treaty. See *Report to Congress: update on progress toward regional non-proliferation in South Asia*, as required of the Foreign Assistance Act of 1961, amended, section 620F(c), April 1994.

107. *Report to Congress*, p. 7.

motivate proliferation in the first place. It is these factors, along with some domestic factors discussed below, that to date have contributed to preventing radical departures from either India's or Pakistan's opaque nuclear weapons' postures.

POST-COLD WAR DOMESTIC FACTORS AFFECTING INDIA AND PAKISTAN

Domestic factors, such as the Gandhian legacy of nuclear disarmament and Nehru's promise not to develop nuclear weapons, contributed to India's decision to maintain an opaque nuclear posture. Similarly, low levels of indigenous technical capability required Pakistan to depend on foreign suppliers for the majority of its technological resources, increasing the nuclear program's vulnerability to outside pressure, and essentially raising its overall cost. These constraints, in addition to concerns of pre-emptive attacks on nuclear facilities, and a potential arms race with opponents, persuaded both states - in the face of vocal domestic constituencies that advocated becoming fully declared nuclear-weapon states - to keep their nuclear programs opaque.

How have these domestic factors changed since the end of the Cold War? How may they affect India's and Pakistan's nuclear postures? And, in particular, how has the breakdown of the Cold War patron-client relationships impacted on the domestic costs and benefits of each state's proliferation strategy?

Since the end of the Cold War, both India and Pakistan have experienced dramatic changes to their economic, social and political fabric. Again, however, further analysis would be required to assess whether this was more than a coincidental factor. Confounding the analysis, however, is that both states began to open up their economies in the late 1980s, making it difficult to isolate any independent domestic economic effects from the end of the Cold War. Given this confusion, I will rely on what Pakistanis and Indians themselves have argued about their own respective domestic situations and then postulate any potential connection between the end of the Cold War and prospects for nuclear arms control.

INDIA: 1991-1994

By the Cold War's end, India's economy, stagnant from years of low growth, and the political system, weakened by continual corruption and recent minority governments, were both in crisis. Exacerbating these difficulties was India's need to find a new trading partner and political ally to replace the dissolving Soviet Union. These factors led to dramatic changes in the economic structure and political fabric of India, which in turn led to a reshuffling of the incentives and constraining factors of India's opaque proliferation posture. Despite this reshuffling, India's nuclear program remains opaque. For the foreseeable future, although India's nuclear capability continues up the proliferation ladder, New Delhi is neither inclined to conduct any nuclear tests nor declare itself a nuclear-weapon state. Both economic and political factors appear significant in explaining this.

Economic Factors. By the time the Soviet Union was dissolved at the end of 1991 and it became apparent that long-standing liberal trading practices between India and the republics of the former Soviet Union would need to be renegotiated, the economic situation in India was already grim. The growth rate of the GDP had dropped to 5 per cent from the 10.4 per cent level reached in 1988-89, and inflation was on the rise. India was facing a serious foreign exchange reserve crisis, and was forced to request a bail-out from the IMF. The IMF granted the request but imposed strict financial conditions, including devaluing the Indian rupee. The only way to compensate for the devaluation and the loss of the Soviet market was to find new export markets - a difficult task in the midst of a world-wide recession.[108] In this respect, the end of the Cold War could not have happened at a worse time for India.

Finance Minister Manmohan Singh, an economist appointed for his financial acumen and political objectivity by Prime Minister Rao, had the unsavory task of attempting to remedy the economic situation without losing the political support needed for Rao to remain head of the government. Singh boldly chose to introduce a radically different economic policy whose objective was to transform India's socialist-based economy into a "market-friendly" one.

This change in economic policy meant the loss of socialism as a political ideology. The dissolution of the Soviet Union served to exacerbate this loss, providing clear evidence for some that capitalism had somehow "won" the economic Cold War.[109] Soon, implementation of IMF economic performance

---

108. K. Shanker Bajpai, "India in 1991: new beginnings," *Asian survey* 32:2 (February 1992), p. 212.
109. K. Shanker Bajpai, former ambassador to the United States, has noted the broad impact of this change. See his "India in 1991," p. 210.

criteria, such as balancing the government budget, liberalizing licensing agreements, and easing regulations on foreign collaborators, became the shibboleth for succumbing to international pressure on all kinds of unrelated issues such as Kashmiri self-determination, human rights, intellectual property rights, not to mention US proposals for nuclear arms control in the region. The fiscal conditions imposed by the IMF were seen by Indians as interference in India's economy by Western states that neither understood the complexities of the Indian economic system nor respected the enormous fiscal and social responsibilities of the Indian government. Critics of the bail-out suggested that financial assistance might come at the price of India's autonomy. At best, the loans, although necessary for India's survival, became embarrassing for a nation that had prided itself on self-reliance.[110] These views were also influenced to some degree by India's self image as an emerging global power with the potential of becoming a militarily powerful state.[111] As a result, Indian policy-makers could not avoid being suspicious of the motives of their new collaborators, particularly the United States. This distrust was not a new aspect of US-Indian relations, but a remnant from Cold War years.

During the Cold War, India's non-alignment policy was designed to allow New Delhi to side with either the Soviet Union or the United States and other Western powers when it was in Indian interests. In actual practice, however, Indian political sympathies more often lay with the former Soviet Union than with Western powers.[112] With the end of the Cold War, even in theory, a non-alignment policy made little sense. Some Indian leaders sensed an opportunity to redefine India's position as the leader of the non-aligned states into the leader of the Third World. However, the stagnant economy and lack of cohesive political leadership prevented Delhi from rising to the occasion. Still, even if New Delhi was not in the best position to dictate its views, it was determined not to be shunted aside in the post-Cold War international environment.

---

110. See Bernard Weinraub, "Economic crisis forcing once self-reliant India to seek aid," *New York Times*, June 29, 1991.
111. Stephen Philip Cohen makes this argument in "India as a Great Power: perceptions and prospects," in: Philip Oldenburg (ed.), *India briefing 1991* (Boulder, CO: Westview Press, 1991), p. 46.
112. Steve Cohen has noted that India's relations with the United States and other Western powers are viewed as an extension of the colonial experience, whereas relations with the Soviet Union were viewed as equals. See Cohen, "India as a Great Power: perceptions and prospects," p. 58.

Take away non-alignment and the de-facto political alliance with the Soviet Union, however, India's views of the future were unclear. It would be politically unpalatable to turn to the United States, particularly when India and the United States had been on opposite sides of the table for nearly 30 years. In addition, there was a growing sentiment that the United States would try to manipulate India into a position of dependency and perpetual poverty. The opening of India's economy meant competition with such American icons as Pepsi and IBM. During the Cold War, the terms of trade with the Soviet Union usually included a technology transfer as well, enabling Indian companies to manufacture their own version of sophisticated imports within a few years. The terms of trade with the United States were never as generous and have remained unchanged, although the amount of trade has increased in recent years. Consequently, it becomes clearer why the honeymoon in US-Indian relations after the Cold War was so brief.

Many of India's foreign policy elite believed that without the Cold War competition, friendship would finally flourish between the two democratic giants. American hopes were also high, especially regarding the liberalization of the Indian economy, and the US sought to support it by enthusiastically backing India's financial requests to the World Bank and IMF, and even seeking to balance its own policies in the region. However, the enthusiasm waned on both sides after a number of miscues and misstatements, revealing that the dominant issue in US policy towards India was still India's nuclear program.

Political clumsiness in US policy was interpreted by the Indian Government as old-fashioned heavy-handedness trying to take advantage of India's weak political and economic position to force it to alter its traditional approach to nuclear non-proliferation. India, perceiving itself surrounded by powerful Western capitalists in a changing international political environment, had few options but to become further entrenched as an opaque nuclear state - at least for now. Some of the progress made in bilateral and multilateral non-proliferation negotiating forums was spoiled by this re-trenchment.

At first, for example, the United States' 1990 decision to implement the Pressler Amendment on Pakistan was a positive indication to India that Washington was no longer fooled by Pakistan's reassurances that it did not possess a nuclear weapons' capability. This dramatic change in policy, along with American support for India's economic liberalization plans, meant that by the time President Clinton took office in 1993, optimism in US-Indian relations had reached its highest level. Most Indians quickly latched on to Clinton's ideological references to President John F. Kennedy, whose affinity with immigrant Indians had been idealized over the years, as another indication that relations would be warmer and more balanced than during the Cold War.[113] Specifically, the Indian Foreign Ministry assumed that the United States would finally agree to lower American barriers to technology transfer, increase foreign aid, and, most importantly, drop all political pressure on India's nuclear program.

Expectations in the US were similarly high, but for very different reasons. Recognizing that India could no longer rely militarily or economically on the Soviet Union, many US policy-makers assumed that India had no choice but to turn to the United States. As a result, the United States was indeed willing to discuss improvements in trade relations, but it did not believe that all pressure on the nuclear program had to be dropped. Officially, the United States would stop insisting that India sign the NPT, but would continue to look for ways to cap and then roll-back the nuclear program. The assumption was that India would have to bargain its nuclear program away for trade benefits and financial assistance. But as soon as the Indians realized US goals, traditional hard-line approaches to the United States and on nuclear policy re-emerged.

President Clinton's decision to reassign the highly experienced US Ambassador, Thomas Pickering, from New Delhi to Moscow sent a disappointing signal to India that Russia was still more important than South Asia. Making the situation worse, no suitable US Ambassador to India could be found for over a year. US attempts to seek possible areas of compromise in the Kashmir crisis promptly backfired when Assistant Secretary of State for South Asia, Robin Raphel, questioned the Instrument of Accession of Jammu and Kashmir to India, a document the Indian government regarded as fully recognized by previous US administrations.[114] US Deputy Secretary of State Strobe Talbott's trip to South Asia, to test the waters for a US plan to lift the Pressler Amendment in order to sell additional (nuclear capable) F-16s to Pakistan, was the last straw.

The United States proposed that the F-16s would be exchanged for a "verifiable cap" on the Pakistani nuclear program. The implication was that a similar quid pro quo was also available to India, and India had only to negotiate what it wanted. Talbott also presented a personal invitation to Indian Prime Minister Rao from President Clinton to come to the United States to "review the global and

---

113.   See J.N. Dixit, "Indo-US relations in perspective," *The Hindu*, April 6, 1994; Sandy Gordon, "Capping South Asia's nuclear weapons programs: a window of opportunity?," *Asian survey* 34, no. 7, July 1994, p. 664.

114.   J.N. Dixit, "Indo-US relations in perspective."

bilateral issues with the goal of advancing US-Indian relations and promoting understanding and friendship between our two peoples."

The range of issues became all too clear during secret talks held in London prior to the Indian Prime Minister's visit to Washington scheduled for May 1994. It appeared that the discussions were exclusively focused on the kinds of security guarantees India would want from the permanent members of the UN Security Council and other large powers in exchange for capping its nuclear program. This proposal would never be accepted back in New Delhi for two fundamental reasons. First, security guarantees offered in an environment where there was less than complete trust and respect between partners were impossible. Second, the offer of security guarantees still failed to address India's traditional concerns over China's nuclear program and demands for a universal non-proliferation regime.[115]

US policy triggered the worst possible response among Indians because it was devised without taking into account India's economic vulnerability and growing suspicion of Western, particularly US, objectives in the region. The policy itself also appeared to many Indians to be an indication of continued American deference to Pakistan and strategic moves against Indian security interests. American efforts to provide F-16s to Pakistan again indicated to many Indians that US efforts to gain influence in India had failed, so Washington was merely striking up its alliance with Pakistan again. Finally, the US approach focused too much of its high-level attention on pressuring India to cap its nuclear program, but not enough on India's concerns with global proliferation. This had the affect of slighting the Indian perspective. As a result, the Indian government was criticized for even discussing the issue with US officials. Some suggested that Talbott should have been sent home without seeing the Prime Minister,[116] as political opposition leaders rallied around the nuclear program as a source of prestige.

---

115. Sandy Gordon, "Capping South Asia's nuclear weapons program," p. 664; Raju Santhanam, "Rao in a bind over 'downgraded' US trip," *The statesman*, April 30, 1994, pp. 1, 9; Manoj Joshi, "PM caught in a dilemma over London talks," *Times of India*, April 29, 1994; "Furore in Rajya Sabha over PM's US visit," *The statesman*, April 28, 1994.

116. As it was, the meeting with Rao was delayed for over 24 hours. See John Thor Dahlburg, "Pakistan, India rebuff US proposal to reduce danger of nuclear war," *Los Angeles Times*, April 8, 1994.

Political Factors. Even if the US approach to India had not been predominantly focused on the nuclear issue, it is not clear whether India would have been ready for a new relationship with the United States. The minority-led government was not robustly supported, and was still suffering from a period of internal upheaval that dated back to the last years of the Soviet Union. Any change in the *status quo* would have triggered attacks from the political opposition and destabilized the fragile political bargain that allowed Prime Minister Rao to stay in power.

The followers and descendants of Gandhi and Nehru had dominated the Indian political landscape during the Cold War, but this had changed with the assassination of Rajiv Gandhi during the spring 1991 elections. Acting President of the Congress (I) Party became Narasimha Rao, who had opted out of the election for health reasons, but was known for his loyalty to the Congress Party and service to three Prime Ministers. He was only expected to remain until new elections could be scheduled.[117]

The Congress (I) Party's principal competitor in the elections was the Hindu nationalist party, the Bharatiya Janata Party (BJP). Many voters believed that the BJP and other Hindu parties should be given a chance to accomplish what the Congress Party had been promising for years but had failed to provide.[118] With the Congress (I) Party's political support on the wane, the size of the BJP grew in recent years and had been widely noticed in India and abroad for campaigning for a declared nuclear weapons' capability and a fundamentalist Hindu government.[119]

The 1991 elections, therefore, provided choices at both ends of the political spectrum. On one, was Congress (I), standing for experienced traditional leadership; on the other, the untested, more radical BJP. The election results were mixed. The Congress Party (I) regained control of the government, but was unable to win a majority. It was forced for the first time to lead a minority government.[120] Rao persuaded party stalwarts to unanimously entrust him to

---

117.   S. Venkateshwaran, "Rao tipped to head Congress temporarily," *News India*, May 31, 1991, pp. 1, 40.

118.   Steve Coll, "Indian voter alienation undercuts prospects for producing a mandate," *Washington Post*, June 12, 1991.

119.   See "BJP President urges Delhi 'to go nuclear,'" *Indian express*, February 9, 1992, p. 1 (JPRS-TND-92-008, March 26, 1992, p. 27).

120.   See Mark Fineman, "Congress Party seeks a Prime Minister," *Los Angeles Times*, June 20, 1991, pp. A8-9, and "Getting down to business," *Asia week*, July 5, 1991, pp. 33-5.

guide the Congress (I) Party into a new age of politics without the Gandhi and Nehru families. Many critics believed that because "Rao represent[ed] the old, traditional Congress Party culture," there would be few innovative policies.[121] Others believed that during this time of international and domestic upheaval, an older, experienced leader was needed to calm the nation down.[122] All, however, believed that change would be forced upon the Congress Party and the Indian government soon.

Arguably the more important result of the 1991 election was that the BJP increased its strength in parliament to 119 seats. It also won control of the state of Uttar Pradesh, a Congress Party stronghold, and became India's dominant opposition party. Election winnings among other parties were so widely dispersed that even with the support of Congress Party allies, the Rao government would need partial support of the BJP in order to survive. This would then force the Congress Party to modify its condemnation of Hindu nationalism and other aspects of the BJP platform.[123] As a result, a new political bargain for India was struck, making the 1991 election the strongest challenge ever to the secular principles of government championed by Nehru and Gandhi, and to Gandhi's anti-nuclearism and Nehru's pledge not to develop nuclear weapons.

The BJP and the Viswa Hindu Parishad stimulated religious and ethnic tensions, which climaxed in the notorious Ayodhya crisis.[124] This crisis lead to a major confrontation between the national Rao government and the BJP leadership. Many other parties, because of a lack of coherence, failed to support the

---

121. Steve Coll, "Gandhi supporter chosen to be India's next Premier," *Washington Post*, June 21, 1991.
122. Bernard Weinraub, "Congress Party loyalist with a calming hand," *New York Times*, June 22, 1991.
123. Manju Parikh, "The debacle at Ayodhya: why militant Hinduism met with a weak response," *Asian survey* 33, no. 7, July 1993, pp. 676-80.
124. After an earlier, thwarted attempt in 1990, in 1992 radical Hindus succeeded in tearing down the more than four centuries-old Babri mosque in the city of Ayodhya. The mosque, they claimed, had been built on the site of an ancient Hindu temple. This lead to a major confrontation between the national government and the leaders of the BJP-led state government. See Manju Parikh, "The debacle at Ayodhya: why militant Hinduism met with a weak response," *Asian survey* 33, no. 7, July 1993, pp. 673-84. Also Walter Andersen, "Lowering the level of tension," *India briefing 1992* (Boulder, CO: Westview Press for the Asia Society, 1992), pp. 23, 27-8.

government on this issue, forcing the Rao government to moderate its positions in the face of a powerful BJP.[125]

The influence of the BJP was also strongly felt just prior to Prime Minister Rao's visit to the United States in May 1994 to discuss US non-proliferation proposals, when BJP leader Manohar Joshi demanded that Rao publicly declare India's commitment to its nuclear option before departing for the United States.[126] Given this intense attention, it would have been almost impossible for Rao to respond positively to the American proposals and survive politically.

Despite the complaints about Rao's leadership, the government has so far survived. Some believe that this is not because of Congress (I) Party strength, but because of the "inability of any group, either within a party or a party as a whole, to provide a wider appeal."[127] In the midst of so much change, the electorate longs for stability.

What is clear is that the price for Indian domestic political stability may be to fray the edges of the secular traditions in Indian government. Perhaps more out of habit than forethought two positions are emerging: suspicion of Western motives in Indian economic affairs, and a tenacious hold on India's nuclear option. Political support for a declared nuclear capability seems to have grown, but is constrained among other things by the poor economic health of the country. Even if the economic situation improves, it will still be a very long time before a pro-nuclear BJP gains control of the Indian government.

Barring any radical increases in external military threats from China or Pakistan (which are not expected), with India's economic picture still dim, it is unlikely that the BJP's pro-nuclear position will encourage dramatic increases in India's nuclearization. However, without opposition support for nuclear arms control in the region, any Indian government will be unable to partake in any arms control initiative that does not have global non-discriminatory implications.

---

125.   Manju Parikh, "The debacle at Ayodyha," p. 676, citing "The BJP's calculations," *Indian express* (Hyderabad), December 23, 1992, p. 8; I. Gopalakrishnan, "Session polarized by Ayodhya," *India abroad* (New York), January 1, 1991, p. 24.

126.   "Clarify stand on n-arms: BJP," *The Times of India*, April 29, 1994.

127.   K. Shankar Bajpai, "India in 1991," p. 212.

PAKISTAN: 1991-1994

Three factors have significantly dominated Pakistan's domestic landscape since the end of the Cold War. The first is Pakistan's efforts to maintain peaceful transfers of political power from one party to another. The second was the October 1, 1990 decision by the United States to suspend economic and military aid under the Pressler Amendment to the 1961 Foreign Assistance Act, because of Pakistan crossing the nuclear weapons' threshold by manufacturing weapon cores. The third is the economic liberalization policies begun under Prime Minister Nawaz Sharif.

Political Factors. The election of Benazir Bhutto as Prime Minister in December 1988 began Pakistan's transition from partial military dictatorship to democracy. The Bhutto government, however, inherited substantial political baggage from the military dictatorship that would eventually contribute to her political demise in 1990. Along with President Ghulam Ishaq Khan, and Chief of the Army Staff Mirza Alsam Beg, Bhutto inherited the Eighth Amendment to the Constitution, which allowed an unelected President the extraordinary power to terminate any Prime Minister's term and call new elections. President Khan used this power to dismiss Bhutto on August 7, 1990 on the grounds of rampant corruption and the inability to govern. It is widely believed, however, that Beg and Khan were simply remaining loyal to the now dead Zia who had overthrown Zulfikar Ali Bhutto, Benazir's father, in 1977.[128] It has also been suggested that the Pakistani army criticized Benazir Bhutto's accommodating approach to negotiations in Kashmir and Afghanistan, and her inability to persuade the US government to cease pressuring Pakistan on its nuclear program. Moreover, the United States did not appear willing to fully back Pakistan during the 1990 Kashmir crisis.[129]

In October 1990, Prime Minister Mian Nawaz Sharif was elected to take Bhutto's place. He also inherited Zia's Eighth Amendment, President Khan and

---

128. The army is also believed to have been behind an earlier effort to depose Bhutto. See Salamat Ali, "Military targets," *Far Eastern economic review*, September 3, 1992, p. 16. For the 1990 deposition, see "Army was behind Benazir's Ouster," *News India*, July 31, 1992.

129. Michael Krepon and Mishi Faruqee, eds, *Conflict prevention and confidence-building measures in South Asia: the 1990 crisis*, pp. 7-8.

General Beg, but his political support was much broader based than Benazir Bhutto's had ever been.

In the 1990 elections, Sharif's Islamic Democratic Alliance captured more than a two-thirds' majority in the National Assembly and ruled all four provinces. The deposed Benazir Bhutto and her People's Democratic Alliance party immediately charged that the election had been stolen, but only after the government began to investigate Bhutto for corruption and misuse of power, did she put aside efforts to work within the political system and encourage demonstrations in the streets.[130]

The Sharif government thus faced fierce opposition from the very beginning. In addition, Sharif's election coincided with the US decision to withhold economic aid, forcing an immediate shortage of funds. To compound problems, local terrorism persisted in the Sind, and economic confidence in the government and the country's financial institutions were further shaken by the Bank of Credit and Commerce International scandal. To hold his coalition government together, Sharif was forced to expand his cabinet to a record 48 ministers and various advisers. The cynical general population half expected the military to take advantage of Sharif's political vulnerability and take control of the government.[131] The saving grace came with the retirement of Zia's old hand, army chief General Beg. The new military leadership, directed by General Asif Nawaz Janjua, immediately made it clear that it was not going to ally itself with any political faction, laying any thought of military intervention in the budding democracy to rest, at least for a short time.[132]

When General Nawaz died of a heart attack in January 1993, President Ghulam Ashaq Khan, knowing that he had to face elections later that year and wanting a strong political advocate in the regime's leadership, decided to appoint

---

130. Khan suggests that with the elections of 1988 and 1990, there is the emergence of a two-party system in Pakistan (the PDP and IJI), with other minor parties claiming only local influence. The difference in the popular vote between the two parties was actually very small - 0.53 per cent. However, the IJI won 106 seats, while the PDP won only 44. Their domestic and foreign policy programs also converged. See Khan, "Pakistan in 1991," pp. 198-9.
131. Khan, "Pakistan in 1991," pp. 198-9.
132. *Dawn* (Karachi), August 18, 1991, cited by Khan, "Pakistan in 1991," p. 200.

his own man. Prime Minister Sharif immediately contested the President's action and eventually announced that he wanted to repeal the Eighth Amendment.[133]

Benazir Bhutto suddenly found herself being politically courted by both the President, who had earlier dismissed her, and the Prime Minister, whose government she had relentlessly criticized. Meanwhile, President Khan invoked the Eighth Amendment, dismissed Sharif's government for corruption and harassment of opponents, and installed an interim government under caretaker Prime Minister Mir Balkh Sher Mazari. Bhutto's Pakistan's People's Party (PPP) became Mazari's principal supporter. This time, however, the Pakistan Supreme Court stepped in and, in response to Sharif's petition against the dissolution of the National Assembly, found the presidential order "illegal" and "unconstitutional." The Court's action was in direct contrast to past behavior when it historically sided with the "military-bureaucratic establishment at critical junctures in the nation."[134] Zia's legacy of a political-military bureaucracy was finally being replaced by new political institutions.

The political maneuvering by the reinstated Nawaz Sharif and President Khan continued with no resolution, until in the summer of 1993 both were persuaded to simultaneously resign. Just as Sharif symbolized new political forces in the country after Bhutto's dismissal in 1990, those forces now "demanded a more popularly based government that would be free to answer the needs of a disparate as well as desperate nation."[135] The dual resignation provided a political "second chance" for Benazir Bhutto who was re-elected as Prime Minister in October 1993, albeit with an even shakier coalition than in 1988.[136]

Given this political climate, how has the end of the Cold War affected the domestic political agenda and, in turn, the prospects for nuclear arms control?

---

133. The crisis escalated even further when General Nawaz's widow alleged that her husband had been poisoned in a plot involving some politicians close to the Prime Minister. See Tahim Amin, "Pakistan in 1993: some dramatic changes," *Asian survey*, vol. 34, no. 2, February 1994, pp. 191-2.

134. Tahim Amin, "Pakistan in 1993: some dramatic changes," pp. 192-3.

135. Lawrence Ziring, "The second stage in Pakistani politics: the 1993 elections," *Asian survey*, vol. 33, no. 12, December 1993, p. 1179.

136. For details on Bhutto's governments, see *The Economist*, December 3, 1988, p. 25; also Samina Yasmeen, "Democracy in Pakistan: the third dismissal," *Asian survey* 34, no. 6, June 1994, p. 573, and Tahir Amin, "Pakistan in 1993: some dramatic changes," pp. 195-6.

During Bhutto's first term, her lack of outward support for the nuclear program may have contributed to her unpopularity with her co-leaders, General Beg and President Khan.[137] By contrast, Prime Minister Sharif made it clear during his initial months in power that the nuclear program would not be compromised despite US non-proliferation efforts.[138] During his term, however, Sharif appeared to contradict those early statements and supported various aspects of nuclear arms control for Pakistan. In 1991 alone, Sharif not only proposed the Five-Power Talks, but managed to refreeze the nuclear program soon after General Beg's retirement in August of that year.[139]

In the summer of 1994, out-of-office Sharif made several statements confirming Pakistan's possession of an atomic bomb, explaining that he was doing so to prevent Bhutto from quietly trying to get rid of the nuclear program.[140] In April 1994, Bhutto had been under direct US pressure to agree to a verifiable cap of the nuclear program in exchange for a one-time release of 38 F-16s prohibited from export under the Pressler Amendment. Even before Secretary Talbott could land

---

137. Harvard-educated Benazir Bhutto was generally thought to be sympathetic to US non-proliferation views, but she was also her father's daughter. It is believed that Pakistan stopped production of weapon-grade uranium just prior to Bhutto's election in 1988, but that the program was accelerated during the 1990 Kashmir crisis. Benazir Bhutto claims that she did not authorize the acceleration, a claim that has been disputed by General Beg. See "General on Bhutto's commitments to nuclear program," *Frontier post*, January 7, 1993 (FBIS-NES, January 8, 1993, p. 51).

138. See "Sharif says nuclear program 'prime objective,'" *Islamabad domestic service*, December 7, 1990 (FBIS-NES, December 7, 1990, p. 58); "Pakistan will 'never bow,'" *Washington Post*, December 8, 1990; Stephen Coll, "US seeking deal on Pakistani aid," *Washington Post*, December 1, 1990.

139. A Pakistani businessman working in Singapore was named as Prime Minister following the resignations of President Khan and Prime Minister Nawaz Sharif. During his short-lived tenure, Prime Minister Moeen Qureshi became the first Prime Minister to publicly announce that Pakistan's nuclear program had been "capped" (sc. by his predecessor). This announcement was never withdrawn or contradicted by the Pakistani government. See Tahir Amin, "Pakistan in 1993: some dramatic changes," pp. 194-5.

140. Alistair Lyon, "Pakistani ex-Premier stands by nuclear revelation," Reuters, August 25, 1994, (0347). The statement is particularly interesting since Sharif uses the words "nuclear bomb" rather than "nuclear capability," and raises the issue of whether Pakistan had crossed the threshold from an undeclared nuclear-weapon state to a declared nuclear-weapon state, although the declaration is coming from a *former* Prime Minister. See C. Uday Bhaskar, "South Asian n-agenda needs to be redefined," *The statesman*, August 31, 1994, p. 1.

in Islamabad, Prime Minister Bhutto made it clear that the quid pro quo was unacceptable, stating to the media that "Pakistan has paid for the planes, and the United States should either deliver the planes or return the money."[141] The American proposal, as noted, aimed to create conditions in South Asia conducive to a dismantling of nuclear weapons in both India and Pakistan. While the current formula was unsatisfactory, Bhutto did express "support for the objectives underlying the proposal," and agreed to work on "developing an approach acceptable to both the US and Pakistan."[142] Nawaz Sharif received a briefing from American diplomats on the visit and was presumably capitalizing on Bhutto's decision to even negotiate with the United States. It is difficult to see his criticism of Bhutto in the summer of 1994 as anything but trying to maximize on public sentiment for political purposes.[143]

In essence, Benazir Bhutto and Nawaz Sharif pursued identical political strategies. When they are out of power, they criticize the other for undermining Pakistan's national security and the national pride placed in Pakistan's nuclear program; but when they are in power, they opt to balance the pro-nuclear position of the Pakistani military, and continue to seek a compromise with their traditional US allies. While balancing a pro-nuclear faction is not the most ideal non-prolifer-

---

141. Indeed, Pakistan had already paid over $680 million for the planes. See "Pakistan, India rebuff US proposal to reduce danger of nuclear war," *Los Angeles Times*, April 8, 1994; John F. Burns, "India unmoved in arms talks with the US," *New York Times*, April 9, 1994. Meanwhile, during Talbott's visit, Pakistani Army Chief of Staff, General Abdul Waheed, was in Washington, DC, making it absolutely clear that the army would not back a cap to the nuclear program in exchange for "a few pieces of hardware." See "The F-16 challenge: Benazir comes under domestic pressure over the American conditions attached to the sale," *India today*, April 30, 1994, p. 56.

142. The "approach" focuses on precisely defining what the criteria are for verifying the cap on the nuclear program. After all, the Pakistani government has stated that the program has already been (unilaterally) capped. What kind of verification does the United States need? See "Well done Ms Bhutto and Gen. Waheed!," *The Friday Times*, April 14-20, 1994, p. 1; "The F-16 challenge: Benazir comes under domestic pressure over the American conditions attached to the sale," *India Today*, April 30, 1994, pp. 56-9; Tahir Amin, "Pakistan in 1993," p. 198.

143. A June 1991 Gallup poll taken in Pakistan gave astounding support to the Pakistan nuclear program - 71 per cent of those asked "favored rejection of American aid rather than giving up the nuclear program, and 87 per cent were in favor of Pakistan making nuclear weapons." See Khan, "Pakistan in 1991," p. 205, citing *News* (Islamabad), July 2 and 7, 1991.

ation outcome, it is better than what could result if either Bhutto or Sharif maintained the same position inside the government as they advocated from the outside. The end of the Cold War, however, may be forcing both political leaders to change their strategy.

It is clear from public opinion polls and the response to Sharif's August 1994 statements, that no Pakistani Prime Minister would be able politically to survive a complete dismantlement of the nuclear program (certainly not without a corresponding dismantlement of the Indian program, for which the prospects are not promising). The US non-proliferation pressure on Pakistan, increased after the end of war in Afghanistan and the end of the Cold War, has served to increase the symbolism that the nuclear program holds, and has pushed Pakistan towards redefining its foreign policy away from its unreliable superpower ally. If the political leadership is perceived to be giving in on this issue, within this fragile democracy, both the loyal and disloyal opposition are waiting for the opportunity to seize power. This political fragility is compounded by two significant economic factors of Pakistan's post-Cold War years.

Economic Factors. In December 1990, Prime Minister Sharif initiated economic reforms designed to accelerate the pace of Pakistan's economic growth through deregulation and privatization. The plan was enthusiastically welcomed when first announced, but when it was implemented, the government was severely criticized, mainly because the plan lacked transparency and implementation had been too hasty.[144]

By the time of the US decision to suspend aid, Pakistan's external debt was $18 billion. The government faced internal budgetary shortages amounting to 5.2 per cent of its gross domestic product, and a balance of payments deficit of $2.1 billion. In addition, the unemployment rate was climbing, reaching 13.45 per cent during 1990-91, while inflation had reached 12.29 per cent. In May 1991, the Finance Minister announced that debt servicing and defense expenditures for 1991-92 would require 53 per cent and 47 per cent respectively of all revenue. In other words, there were *no funds* for social services, not to mention development programs.[145]

---

144.   Khan, "Pakistan in 1991," pp. 201-2.
145.   Khan, "Pakistan in 1991," pp. 200-201, citing Finance Minister Sartaj Aziz's speech, published in *Dawn*, May 31, 1991.

As if the liberalization policies were not enough, the suspension of US aid, along with the impact of the Gulf War, causing increases in oil and petroleum prices and sending Pakistani workers in Kuwait and Iraq home, contributed to a serious strain on Pakistan's balance of payments and domestic budget. The only positive news was a healthy growth rate for the Pakistani economy, resulting in all IMF and World Bank conditions being met and a subsequent relaxation of foreign exchange regulations.[146] This could not alter the basic result, however, as the political leadership faced an extremely vulnerable economy and an extremely unhappy electorate whose expectations about their social conditions had previously been rising.

All three of the above factors contributed to a confusion among Pakistan's leaders. The suspension of US aid was a clear signal that economic or political relations with the United States might not ever be the same. The leadership knew that changes in foreign policy might be necessary, but due to the terrible economic conditions, it was not clear what changes would be supported on the domestic level.

Immediately after the suspension of US aid to Pakistan in 1990, there was a very strong feeling that the United States was "tilting" towards India. The implementation of the Pressler Amendment, US National Security Adviser Robert Gates's visit during the 1990 Kashmir crisis (during which he is reported to have told the Pakistani leadership not to count on US support in the event of war), US support of India's requests from the International Monetary Fund and World Bank, and growing joint US-Indian military cooperation, including military exercises, joint service in the UN-sponsored Somalia mission, and refueling of US jets during the second Gulf War, all contributed to this perception.[147] At the same time, Russia's attitude to Pakistan seemed to improve, as highlighted by Vice-President Alexander Rutskoi's announcement in December 1992 that Russia and Pakistan would sign a Friendship Treaty similar to the Treaty between India and the former Soviet Union. In addition, Russia backed away from its traditional support of India's position on Kashmir as "an integral part of India" and instead

---

146.   Khan, "Pakistan in 1991," pp. 200-201.

147.   See Shekhar Gupta and W.P.S. Sindhu, "Cautious maneuvers," *India today*, June 30, 1992, pp. 34-5; William Scally, "Rao says US-India ties entering 'bold new era,'" Reuters (1328), May 18, 1992; and "Cosying up to Washington," *Asia week*, February 14, 1992, pp. 23-4.

recognized Pakistan's view of Kashmir's disputed status. There was, indeed, ample reason for Pakistan to be confused about its foreign policy.[148]

Pakistan was also uncertain about its relations with traditional Arab friends in the wake of the second Gulf War; it did not want to worsen its relations with the United States, although Americans were largely viewed as anti-Islamic; its relations with India were not improving; and in the wake of the Afghan War, rival *mujahideen* factions were fighting for control of Afghanistan.[149] In the meantime, the dissolution of the Soviet Union had set loose a flurry of independent Central Asian states, reminding Pakistan of its glorious role in the Moghul Empire and, at the same time, raising the fear that ethnic minorities within its own borders would seek independence as well.[150]

In post-Cold War fashion, instead of seeking one direction, Pakistan has sought to balance its relations with old friends, the United States and China, and, sparked by economic imperatives, with new relations, with the new Central Asian states. In November 1992, the founding members of the Economic Cooperation Organization (ECO) - Pakistan, Iran and Turkey - welcomed seven additional members: Afghanistan, Azerbaijan, Uzbekistan, Turkmenistan, Tajikistan, Kazakhstan, and Kyrghystan. Immediate plans were made for infrastructural and economic cooperation.[151] This multi-directional foreign policy has provided Pakistan with some room to counterbalance the non-proliferation demands of the United States. If ECO is successful, Pakistan might be able to satisfy some of the economic demands of its electorate and reduce its dependence on the west and its non-proliferation goals, potentially loosening the constraints on Pakistan's nuclear program. As of this writing, initial enthusiasm for ECO has waned somewhat, but could emerge again in the near future.

OBSERVATIONS REGARDING POST-COLD WAR DOMESTIC FACTORS

Since the end of the Cold War, both India and Pakistan appear to have experienced rather dramatic increases in the amount of political support for their

148.   See "Marriage is out, so play the field," *Asia week*, February 14, 1992, p. 24.
149.   See Rais A. Khan, "Pakistan in 1991," pp. 203-6; Rais A. Khan, "Pakistan in 1992," pp. 135-40; and Tahir Amin, "Pakistan in 1993," pp. 197-9.
150.   See Rais A. Khan, "Pakistan in 1992," pp. 135-7.
151.   See Rais A. Khan, "Pakistan in 1992," p. 137.

respective nuclear programs. In both cases, this support has been stimulated by the political opposition, and, interestingly, it has been stimulated in similar ways.

Major political forces in India and Pakistan have identified each state's nuclear program as a primary source of national pride and regional, if not international, prestige. Political leaders are capitalizing on the desire and need to redefine both states' positions in the international system after the dissolution of the Soviet Union, and as such are reluctant to give up any measure of power the states perceive they have - at least until the policy makers are sure it will not contribute to their objectives. The BJP and the Muslim League are simply capitalizing on this confusion.

Both factors suggest that the nuclear issue has become such a domestic lightening rod in India and Pakistan, that it may become insulated from changes in the external variables that motivated the state to seek nuclear capability in the first place. Even if Prime Ministers Rao and Bhutto wanted to move away from their opaque proliferation strategies, they would not be able to do so. Holding all other domestic and international factors constant, this variable is pushing India and Pakistan closer to a declared nuclear strategy. However, if the pro-nuclear parties gained political power, they would still have to overcome the economic constraints faced (at least if they were to govern by democratic means) to affect a radical change up the proliferation ladder in either state. Barring lasting economic deprivation, for the foreseeable future it appears that nuclear arms control in South Asia will depend on whether the nuclear issue can be de-politicized enough to allow it to be considered in a serious fashion.

Middle-of-the-Road Conclusions and Policy Recommendations

The nuclear capability of both India and Pakistan has increased since the end of the Cold War, but there has not been a radical departure from either state's proliferation strategy. Instead, India and Pakistan appear to be continuing to edge up the proliferation ladder while denying that they possess a bomb. This does not imply, however, that the end of the Cold War has gone unnoticed. It simply means that the changes to each state's proliferation incentives and constraints that have occurred since the end of the Cold War have led to the same outcome, even if that outcome has come about in a different fashion than before.

The most important factors originally influencing India's decision to develop a nuclear weapons' capability were China's invasion in 1962, Pakistan's military relationship with the United States and China, and Islamabad's decision in 1972 to develop its own nuclear capability. Pakistan in its turn has been primarily motivated by India's progress on its nuclear program.

By late 1994, India's relations with China had improved, and ostensibly the overall Chinese military threat to India was reduced. Beijing, however, has given no indication that it is willing to discuss nuclear arms control on an equal basis with India, or anyone else for that matter. On the other hand, the loss of the Soviet Union and the United States as India and Pakistan's respective superpower patrons has contributed to both states feeling vulnerable and confused. This has dramatically reinforced public opinion in support of the nuclear program, as a symbol of national prestige and source of security in the midst of this change. Meanwhile, India's relations with Pakistan are not improving, leaving that incentive unaltered. Pakistan's original motive for developing nuclear weapons has not improved either, and in fact some argue that India's imminent deployment of the Prithvi will make things much worse. While the variance in each incentive is difficult to measure, the changes appear as fluctuations, not as radical dramatic departures from policy. This leads to the conclusion that international incentives for proliferation in South Asia have remained at about the same level as during the Cold War years.

Constraints to proliferation on the international level, on the other hand, may be increasing if one considers that Cold War politics limited the amount of pressure that was placed upon India and Pakistan. Recently, by contrast, the United States has made efforts to balance its non-proliferation objectives in both states, non-governmental organizations have focused on negotiating solutions to conflict issues in the region, and the non-proliferation regime has concentrated its attention on South Asia as one of the few remaining regions of proliferation concern. In addition, progress on the international negotiation of non-proliferation measures, such as the Comprehensive Test Ban Treaty and the fissile material cut-off, will address some of the complaints from both states (in particular India) regarding global, non-discriminatory non-proliferation.

Meanwhile, on the domestic level the economic constraints to both states' nuclear programs have been exacerbated by the loss of superpower financial and trade relationships, and the decision by both states to open up their economies.

The Indian government remains ambiguous about how and whether the new Prithvi missile will be deployed. In addition, other missile systems have not received the political or financial support consistent with a less opaque nuclear program. India may be gauging Pakistan's (and perhaps the international community's) response to its actions. Pakistani leaders are realizing more and more that they need to appear to be responsive to the economic and social needs of the electorate if they are to stay in power. As a result, the economic conditions may continue to act as a constraint to radical movements up the proliferation ladder, as they did during the Cold War. This domestic political dynamic is also operating in India.

On the other hand, because the political opposition in each country has seized upon the nuclear issue as a symbol of national pride and a necessity for the state's secure future, keeping the electorate happy could do the most damage to prospects for nuclear arms control in the region and may produce ironic conclusions as far as proliferation analysis is concerned.

Post-Cold War predictions of nuclear proliferation spiraling out of control were based on an assumption that *international factors*, such as the Cold War alliance system, were largely responsible for keeping proliferation in check. In the absence of these factors, proliferation would hence be left unchecked. However, the analysis here leads to a different conclusion. In the case of South Asia, it may be the *domestic-level factors*, in particular the political support of nuclear weapons, that could potentially contribute to radical change in the proliferation strategies of both states. Non-proliferation policy efforts, therefore, may want to focus on domestic-level factors if progress is to be made on nuclear arms control in the region, especially on de-linking the nuclear issue from India's and Pakistan's national prestige.

RECOMMENDATIONS FOR NON-PROLIFERATION

With respect to South Asia, there are two approaches to de-politicizing the nuclear issue on the domestic level, and thereby reducing the nuclear incentives, that could have some effect. The first, pragmatic strategy requires the ruling party or coalition to appear to adopt the opposition party's view of the nuclear issue as its own. In other words, when possible, do not allow the opposition to occupy the moral high ground when it comes to the state's nuclear program. Indian Prime Minister Rao seems to have adopted this strategy at some level by paying lip service to his critics on the nuclear issue, especially regarding the defense budget and missile testing programs. This strategy can be weakened when critics do not accept the declaration of policy as actual policy and make repeated demands for evidence of progress on nuclear weapons' development. However, if the issue can be de-politicized enough, so that maintaining the *status quo* on the nuclear program becomes acceptable, then in the event of the opposition gaining political power, there will be no increased incentive to speed up the program.

The second, more straightforward strategy focuses on de-legitimizing the nuclear programs as sources of national pride and prestige. While this strategy is very difficult and complex, the United States and Russia were recently successful in implementing this approach to help persuade Ukraine to transfer the nuclear weapons on its soil to Russia for dismantlement. The United States and others should broaden the range of issues discussed with New Delhi and Islamabad. Too much focus on the nuclear issue in bilateral or multilateral forums, particularly at high levels, reinforces the impression that the only reason to have any discussion whatsoever is to resolve the proliferation problem. In addition, dwelling on the nuclear issue alone provides an incentive for India and Pakistan, if ever they want to move down the proliferation ladder, to use their nuclear program as a bargaining chip to gain huge financial and perhaps even political concessions in return for becoming non-nuclear states.

Bilateral discussions could include issues such as the kinds of economic and development goals held by India and Pakistan for the next century and what can be done to facilitate achieving these goals. In the long run, the price of this approach may actually be lower than what was negotiated in the case of Ukraine, · as it encourages mutually beneficial trust rather than a payment extracted for actions taken.

This approach will also contribute to a natural decline in the salience of the nuclear issue as a symbol of national prestige that will occur over time as India and Pakistan adjust their foreign policies to post-Cold War conditions and gain confidence with respect to their relative roles in the international system.

Because of Nehru's adagium, the prestige of the Indian nuclear program has been tied with technological progress rather than with military security. Perhaps, efforts can be made to reinforce any existing remnants of Nehru's view by encouraging public discussion of the effects of nuclear weapons, involving the support of appropriate Indian and Pakistani researchers.

A hard-line approach would be to increase the economic pressure on India and Pakistan, particularly as both states increasingly have to respond to democratic demands for costly development and social programs. But even if the current economic situations of India and Pakistan indicate that losing or delaying part of the international loans both states receive would force the government to reconsider the allocation of its funds, such an approach might merely increase the state's resolve to maintain the program. In any case, it could encourage the political opposition to advocate an even more aggressive position on nuclear weapons. Overall, this approach should be seen as a policy of last resort.

Related efforts could include continuing technology sanctions on India and Pakistan and broadening the IAEA's inspections currently conducted there. In general, however, sanctions can evoke combative reactions. This approach, therefore, is probably less effective, and less desirable than the incentive approach.

In conclusion, to detect the possibility of changes in India or Pakistan's proliferation strategies, one must begin by evaluating changes in the domestic and international factors that led both states to choose an opaque proliferation path. Only then can realistic non-proliferation policies be developed.

Appendix A India

Name/Location of Facility	Type/Status	IAEA Safeguards
Power Reactors		
Tarapur I	Light water, LEU, 150 MWe/ Operating	Yes
Tarapur II	Light water, LEU, 150 MWe/ Operating	Yes
Tarapur III	Heavy water, nat. U, 500 MWe/ Site preparation	No
Tarapur IV	Heavy water, nat. U, 500 MWe/ Site preparation	No
Rajasthan I Kota	Heavy water, nat. U, 207 MWe/ Operating	Yes
Rajasthan II	Heavy water, nat. U, 207 MWe/ Operating	Yes
Madras I Kalpakkam	Heavy water, nat. U, 220 MWe/ Operating	No
Madras II	Heavy water, nat. U, 220 MWe/ Operating	No
Narora I	Heavy water, nat. U, 220 MWe/ Temporarily shut down	No
Narora II	Heavy water, nat. U, 220 MWe/ Operating	No
Kakrapar I	Heavy water, nat. U, 220 MWe/ Operating	No
Kakrapar II	Heavy water, nat. U, 220 MWe/ Commissioned	No
Kaiga I Karnataka	Heavy water, nat. U, 220 MWe/ Under construction	No
Kaiga II	Heavy water, nat. U, 220 MWe/ Under construction	No
Rajasthan III Rota	Heavy water, nat. U, 220 MWe/ Under construction	No

Name/Location of Facility	Type/Status	IAEA Safeguards
Rajasthan IV	Heavy water, nat. U, 220 MWe/ Under construction	No
Koodankulam I	Light water, LEU, 500 MWe/ Site preparation	No
Koodankulam II	Light water, LEU, 500 MWe/ Site preparation	No
Research Reactors		
Apsara Trombay	Light water, medium-enriched uranium, 1MWt/Operating	No
Cirus Trombay	Heavy water, nat. U, 40 MWt/ Operating	No
Zerlina Trombay	Heavy water, variable fuel, 400 Wt/Decommissioned	No
Purnima II Trombay	Uranium-233, .005 KWt/ Dismantled	No
Purnima III Trombay	Uranium-233, 30 KWt/Operating	No
Kamini Kalpakkam	Uranium-233, 30 KWt/Operating	No
Dhruva Trombay	Heavy water, nat. U, 100 MWt/ Operating	No
Fast Breeder Test Reactor (FBTR), Kalpakkam	Plutonium & nat. U, 15 MWe/ Operating	No
Uranium Enrichment		
Trombay	Pilot-scale ultracentrifuge plant/Operating	No
Rattehalli	Pilot-scale ultracentrifuge plant/Operating	No
Reprocessing (Plutonium Extraction)		
Trombay	Medium-scale/Operating	No

Name/Location of Facility	Type/Status	IAEA Safeguards
Tarapur	Large-scale/Operating	Only when safeguarded fuel is present[152]
Kalpakkam	Laboratory-scale/Operating	No
Kalpakkam	Large-scale/Under construction	No
Kalpakkam	Fast breeder fuel reprocessing plant/Under construction	No
Uranium Processing		
Jaduguda	Mining and milling/Operating	N/A
Hyderabad	Uranium purification (UO_2)/ Operating	No
Hyderabad	Fuel fabrication/Operating	Partial
Trombay	Uranium conversion (UF_6)/ Operating	No
Trombay	Fuel fabrication/Operating	No
Tarapur	Mixed uranium-plutonium oxide (MOX) fuel fabrication/Operating	Only when safeguarded fuel is present
Heavy Water[153]		
Nangal	Operating	No
Baroda	Intermittent operation	No
Tuticorin	Operating	No
Talcher	Operating	No

152. The IAEA is planning to establish a permanent presence at this facility beginning in June 1994. This is to implement India's recent agreement to place fuel from the Tarapur I and II reactors, soon to be reprocessed at this plant, under IAEA safeguards in perpetuity. India plans to reprocess the spent fuel to produce plutonium for mixed-oxide fuel (MOX) to be sued for refueling the Tarapur reactors. Indian officials have given indications that India may also apply IAEA safeguards at the Kalpakkam reprocessing facility.

153. Output of these facilities has been far below their design capabilities, necessitating clandestine imports of heavy water. See Leonard S. Spector with Jacqueline R. Smith, *Nuclear Ambitions*. (Boulder, CO: Westview Press, 1990), pp. 73-75.

Name/Location of Facility	Type/Status	IAEA Safeguards
Kota	Operating	No
Thal-Vaishet	Operating	No
Manuguru	Operating	No
Hazira	Operating	No

HEU   = Highly Enriched Uranium
LEU   = Low-Enriched Uranium
nat. U = Natural Uranium
MWe   = Millions of watts of electrical output
MWt   = Millions of watts of thermal output
KWt   = Thousands of watts of thermal output

Sources: Leonard S. Spector with Jacqueline R. Smith, *Nuclear Ambitions*. (Boulder, CO: Westview Press, 1990); "World Survey: Waiting for a New Dawn," *Nuclear Engineering International*, June 1991, p. 22; "Hope for Foreign Reactors Ends in Both India and Pakistan," *Nucleonics Week*, January 23, 1992, p. 3; Shahid-ur-Rehman Khan, "India and Pakistan Exchange Lists of Nuclear Facilities," *Nucleonics Week*, January 9, 1992, p. 10; Mark Hibbs, "Second Indian Enrichment Facility Using Centrifuges is Operational," *Nucleonics Week*, March 26, 1992, pp. 9-10; Mark Hibbs, "India and Pakistan Fail to Include New SWU Plants on Exchanged Lists," *Nuclear Fuel*, March 30, 1992, p. 6; "Kakrapur Startup," *Nuclear Engineering International*, November 1992, p. 12; "AEC Denies Reports on Making Atomic Bombs," *Patriot*, October 23, 1992, reprinted in *JPRS-TND-92-046*, December 11, 1992, p. 11; Interview with Indian official, February 1993; "World Nuclear Industry Handbook," *Nuclear Industry International*, 1993; Neel Patri, "Indian Budget Gives No Increase in Nuclear Plant Building Money," *Nucleonics Week*, March 11, 1993; Neel Patri, "India Scaling Down Kundankulam As Russian Reactor Plan Fades," *Nucleonics Week*, April 15, 1993, p. 13; Neel Patri, "Thorium-Burning Kakrapar-1 Declared Commercial by NPC," *Nucleonics Week*, May 13, 1993, p. 4; "India: FBTR Raising Power," *Nucleonics Week*, December 16, 1993, p. 15; Mark Hibbs, "India May Apply IAEA Safeguards on Future Plutonium Separation," *Nuclear Fuel*, February 14, 1994, p. 9; Mark Hibbs, "Safeguards Deal on TAPS BWRs Left Consent Issue Unresolved," *Nucleonics Week*, March 10, 1994, p. 7; Neel Patri, "Narora-1 Turbine Fire Spoils Indian Nuclear Production, Profits," *Nucleonics Week*, April 7, 1994, p. 3; Neel Patri, "Indian Lawmakers Criticize Cost, Delays in Nuclear Power Program," *Nucleonics Week*, April 28, 1994, p. 2; Neel Patri, "India Might Take Another Look at Plans to Expand Heavy Water Plant," *Nuclear Fuel*, May 9, 1994, p. 14.

Appendix B Probable contribution of CIRUS and Dhruva reactors to India's nuclear weapons potential-1994

Reactor	MW(t) /day	Capacity %[154]	Years of operation	Kg PU per year	Total kg Pu produced	Total kg Pu available for weapons[155]	Potential no. of weapons (8 kg-5 kg/-bomb)
CIRUS	40	65	33 (1960-93)	9.490	313.170	303.68	37-60
Dhruva	25	65	2 (1986-88)	5.931	11.862	11.862	1-2
Dhruva after up-grade	100	65	5 (1989-93)	23.725	118.625	94.9	11-18

Assumptions:
1. Total energy output/year or Total MWth/day = (X MWth/day)(365 days)(% reactor capacity)
2. Weapons grade Pu/year = (1 gram PU)/(1 MWth/day)
3. Assumes that both reactors produce only weapons grade plutonium requiring an approximate "burn-up" rate of 1000 MW per day / tonne of uranium fuel.
4. Assumes that all spent fuel produced through 1992 has been reprocessed. Estimate of number of weapons based on this assumption. See calculations below.

Calculations:
CIRUS   40(365)(.65) = 9490 MWth/day or 9.490 kg PU/year
            9.490 (33 years) = 313.170 kg PU total production
            9.490 (32 years) = 303.68 kg PU available for weapons

DHRUVA25   (365)(.65) = 5931.25 MWth/day or 5.931 kg PU/year
            5.931(2 years) = 11.862 kg PU total production - all available for weapons

            100 (365)(.65)) = 23725 MWth/day or 23.725 kg PU/year
            23.725(5 years) = 118.625 kg PU total production
            23.725(4 years) = 94.9 kg PU available for weapons

Total PU: 313.170 + 11.862 + 118.625 = 443.657 kg PU total production
Total available for weapons: 303.68 + 11.862 + 94.9 = 410.442 kg PU = 49 -> 80 weapons

---

154. The "capacity" is the percentage at which the reactor is assumed to be operating.
155. It is estimated that 95-99 per cent of the total plutonium produced will be available for weapons use after reprocessing. To keep it simple, I have assumed that 100 per cent is available and that all spent fuel up to 1992 from these two reactors has been reprocessed.

Appendix C Pakistan: Nuclear Infrastructure

Name/Location of Facility	Type/Status	IAEA Safeguards
Power Reactors		
KANUPP Karachi	Heavy-water, nat. U, 125 MWe/ Operating	Yes
Chasma	Light-water, LEU, 300 MWe/ Under construction	Planned
Research Reactors		
Pakistan Atomic Research Reactor (PARR) Rawalpindi	Light-water, originally HEU, modified to use LEU fuel, 10 MWt/Operating	Yes
PARR 2 Rawalpindi	Pool-type, light-water, enriched uranium(?), 27 KWt/Operating	Yes
Research/Plutonium Production Reactor, Khusab	HEU, 50 MWt/Under construction	No
Uranium Enrichment		
Kahuta	Large-scale ultracentrifuge facility/Operating	No
Sihala	Experimental-scale ultracentrifuge facility/Operating	No
Golra	Ultracentrifuge plant reportedly to be used as testing facility/ Under construction? Operating?	No
Reprocessing (Plutonium Extraction)		
Chashma	Terminated by France (1978); construction may be nearly complete using indigenous resources	No
New Labs Rawalpindi	Cold tests conducted; not known to be operating	No
PINSTECH Rawalpindi	Experimental-scale plant	No

Name/Location of Facility	Type/Status	IAEA Safeguards
Uranium Processing		
Dera Ghazi Khan	Uranium mining and milling/ Operating	N/A
Lahore	Milling/Operating	N/A
Dera Ghazi Khan	Uranium conversion (UF_6)/Operating	No
Chashma/Kundian	Fuel fabrication/Operating	No
Heavy Water		
Multan	Operating	No
Karachi	Operating	No
Tritium Purification		
150 km south of Rawalpindi	Tested in 1987	No

HEU   = Highly Enriched Uranium
LEU   = Low-Enriched Uranium
nat. U   = Natural Uranium
MWe   = Millions of watts of electrical output
MWt   = Millions of watts of thermal output
KWt   = Thousands of watts of thermal output

Sources: Leonard S. Spector with Jacqueline R. Smith, *Nuclear Ambitions* (Boulder, CO: Westview Press, 1990); U.S. Department of State, "The Pakistani Nuclear Program," June 23, 1983, SECRET/NO-FORN/ORCON; released under the Freedom of Information Act to the National Security Archive, Washington, DC, January 17, 1991, pp. 1-5; U.S Department of State, "Memorandum for Dr. Kissinger; Subject: Official Visit of Pakistan Prime Minister Mohammad Khan Junejo: Background and Talking Points," July 18, 1986, SECRET/SENSITIVE, released under the Freedom of Information Act to the National Security Archive; Hedrick Smith, "A Bomb Ticks in Pakistan," *New York Times Magazine*, March 6, 1988, p. 38; "Pakistan's Atomic Bomb," *Foreign Report*, January 12, 1989, p. 1; "U.S.-Supplied Nuclear Research Reactor Modified," *Agence France Presse*, March 17, 1991, in *FBIS-NES*; R. Jeffrey Smith, "Pakistan Can Build One Nuclear Device, Foreign Official Says," *Washington Post*, February 7, 1992; Gene Kramer, "U.S.-Pakistan," *Associated Press*, February 10, 1992; Rauf Siddiqi, Ann MacLachlan, "No 'Direct Progress' in Talks, But Pakistan, U.S. Continue Effort," *Nucleonics Week*, February 20, 1992, p. 15; "France and Pakistan in Accord on Compensation," *Nuclear Engineering International*, March 1992, p. 7; Mark Hibbs, "Second Indian Enrichment Facility Using Centrifuges is Operational," *Nucleonics Week*, March 26, 1992, p. 10; "Khan Notes Freeze on Program," Karachi, *AMN*, February 9, 1992, in *JPRS-TND*, April 3, 1992, p. 6; "Work on Plant Begins," *The Frontier Post*, July 31, 1992, in *JPRS-TND-92-027*, August 5, 1992, p. 12; interview with senior

U.S. official, fall 1992; David Albright and Mark Hibbs, "Pakistan's Bomb: Out of the Closet," *The Bulletin of the Atomic Scientists*, July/August 1992, p. 38; Shahid-ur-Rehman, "Chinese Official Says Chasma Design is Near Completion," *Nucleonics Week*, December 17, 1992, pp. 8-9; Mark Hibbs, "India and Pakistan Fail to Include New SWU Plants on Exchanged Lists," *Nuclear Fuel*, March 30, 1992; Ali Sarwar Naqvi, "Don't Blame Pakistan," *Washington Post*, July 16, 1992; "Pakistan Has Seven Nuclear Weapons," Reuters, December 1, 1992 (reporting on an NBC News report stating that Pakistan possessed "at least seven" nuclear devices); Shahid-ur-Rehman Khan, "Construction Officially Underway by CNNC for Pakistan's Chashnupp," *Nucleonics Week*, August 5, 1993, p. 5; William C. Potter and Harlan W. Jencks, *The International Missile Bazaar* (Boulder, CO: Westview Press, 1994), pp. 81, 84; U.S. State Department, "Report to Congress: Update on Progress Toward Regional Nonproliferation in South Asia," April 1994; Alistair Lyon, "Pakistani Leaders Deny Nuclear Bomb Claim," Reuters, August 24, 1994; Steve Pagani, "IAEA Says Unable to Verify Pakistan Atom Bomb Report," Reuters, August 24, 1994; Alistair Lyon, "Pakistani Ex-Premier Stands By Nuclear Revelation," Reuters, August 25, 1994; "U.S. Warns China, Pakistan Against Missile Sale," *Reuters*, September 7, 1994; R. Jeffrey Smith and Thomas W. Lippman, "Pakistan M-11 Funding Is Reported," *Washington Post*, September 8, 1994; Sid Balman, Jr., "China-U.S.: China Rebuts U.S. Missile Claim," *United Press International*, October 3, 1994; Interviews with U.S. officials, fall 1994; Elaine Sciolino, "U.S. and Chinese Reach Agreement on Missile Export," *New York Times*, October 5, 1994; Daniel Williams, "U.S. Deal With China Allows High-Tech Sales in Exchange for Pledge," *Washington Post*, October 5, 1994; Mark Hibbs, "Bhutto May Finish Plutonium Reactor Without Agreement on Fissile Stocks," *Nucleonics Week*, October 6, 1994, p. 10.

4 Nuclear Proliferation in the Middle East

Marianne van Leeuwen

Introduction

Since time immemorial, the Middle East has been ridden with armed conflicts, and during this century, arms races have been raging in the region with special intensity. This can partially be explained by the area's recently discovered source of affluence: oil. Oil-producing countries, and regional powers subsidized by them, have spent fortunes on buying and in some cases producing advanced conventional weapons, but increasingly also on obtaining the capability to produce non-conventional systems. On several occasions during recent decades, the Middle East has witnessed the use of non-conventional - chemical - weapons in battle and against civilians.

Nuclear proliferation in the Middle East, as far as incentives are concerned, has developed into a network pattern, linking one (would-be) perpetrator to another by motivation, and in various ways involving officially acknowledged nuclear-weapon states through extra-regional ramifications. Within this complex pattern, two major regional conflicts have become linked, even though their causes are not related: the conflict between Israel and its Arab neighbors, and that between Iraq and Iran.

The various arms races have been fueling each other and cannot really be treated entirely separately. Nevertheless, on the following pages the focus is on nuclear proliferation, and reference to the "other" arms races will be made from that perspective. The motivations for a number of regional powers to try and obtain a nuclear weapons capability are analyzed. The progress of their efforts is briefly evaluated, and some options to stem nuclear proliferation are indicated. As Israel has played a pivotal role in the proliferation problem in the Middle East, attention is first directed at its policies and the options for changing them.

M. van Leeuwen (ed.), The Future of the International Nuclear Non-Proliferation Regime, 125-153.
© 1995 *Kluwer Academic Publishers. Printed in the Netherlands.*

Israel

MOTIVATIONS

To date, the state of Israel is the only country in the Middle East which has actually built nuclear weapons. It has obtained its nuclear option for security reasons: Arab states *en masse* rejected Israel's existence in 1948 and some continue to do so today. The security motivations were intensified by Israel's traumatic historical background. During the 1950s, Israel cooperated closely with France on security issues. At the time of the June War of 1967, however, the French position on arms' deliveries deeply disappointed the Israelis. After then, the United States became Israel's most powerful friend. Their security relationship became very close but was problematic at times, and, moreover, it was never formalized in a treaty.[1] Israel has never acceded to the Nuclear Non-Proliferation Treaty.

The prevailing view on Israel has long been that of a small, weak and peaceful country surrounded by implacable Arab enemies. In fact, ever since the beginning of its history as a contemporary independent state, Israel's military weakness has been exaggerated. In 1948, 1956, 1967, 1969-1970, 1973 and 1982-1985, Israel has proven its superiority in battle. Still, Israeli planners based their nation's defense on worst-case scenarios, the worst imaginable scenario being that all Israel's Arab enemies would unite and create an effective military coalition which would succeed in annihilating the Jewish state, while external powers sat by and watched or even supported the Arab coalition.

Two pillars of Israel's military philosophy have consequently been that the country should be as independent from others as possible in its defense, and that it should maintain a qualitative edge over its regional enemies. Through its indigenous conventional arms industry (counted world-wide among the best of its kind), and through procurement of state-of-the-art weaponry, especially, since 1967, from the United States, Israel has made certain that its conventional weapons are superior to those of its enemies. Apart from that, it has developed non-conven-

---

1. I have written about this in somewhat more detail in Marianne van Leeuwen, *Changing hearts? The Bush administration, American public opinion, and the Arab-Israeli conflict* (The Hague: Netherlands Institute of International Relations "Clingendael," 1991), pp. 17-19.

tional weapons,[2] and in that category, the most striking advance has been made in the nuclear section.

CAPABILITIES

The story of the birth of Israel's nuclear capabilities has been told in detail elsewhere.[3] The headlines are as follows. After the Suez crisis of 1956, there blossomed in secret a mutually profitable cooperation in nuclear-arms production between Israel and France. The French helped Israel to a research reactor with excellent plutonium production qualities, and to the designs for a reprocessing plant. These became the central installations at the nuclear complex constructed near the desert town of Dimona. Allegedly, the French also provided Israeli scientists with nuclear test results. From Norway, the Israelis bought heavy water, needed for moderating their Dimona reactor. Besides that, they themselves developed heavy water production technology. Uranium stocks (natural and highly enriched) were obtained from various foreign sources, sometimes in "adventurous" fashion, while modest but significant quantities could be mined at home.

When President de Gaulle, set on improving French-Arab relations, forbade French cooperation on the construction of the reprocessing plant in 1960, Israel had made enough progress to finish the installation anyhow. By 1970 it was producing and separating plutonium in significant quantities. By the time of the

---

2. It has been assumed that Israel has chemical weapons, while it is sometimes claimed that it has at least a production capacity for biological weapons as well. Efraim Karsh, Martin S. Navias and Philip Sabin (eds), *Non-conventional-weapons' proliferation in the Middle East: tackling the spread of nuclear, chemical, and biological capabilities* (Oxford: Clarendon Press, 1993), pp. 2-3. Israel has ratified the 1925 Geneva Protocol prohibiting the use of "asphyxiating, poisonous, or other gases, and of bacteriological methods of warfare," and it has signed the Chemical Weapons Convention of 1993; but it has not signed the Biological Weapons Convention of 1972.

3. E.g. Steve Weissman and Herbert Krosney, *The Islamic bomb: the nuclear threat to Israel and the Middle East* (New York: Times Books, 1981), pp. 105-28. Pierre Péan, *Les deux bombes* (Paris: Fayard, 1982); Frank Barnaby, *The invisible bomb: the nuclear arms race in the Middle East* (London: Tauris, 1989); Seymour M. Hersh, *The Samson option: Israel's nuclear arsenal and American foreign policy* (New York: Random House, 1991); Leonard S. Spector and Jacqueline R. Smith, *Nuclear ambitions: the spread of nuclear weapons 1989-1990* (Boulder, San Francisco, Oxford: Westview Press, 1990), pp. 149-74.

1973 October War, Israel was a nuclear-weapon state. During the 1970s, research was initiated on uranium enrichment including centrifuge and laser technology.

In 1986, the Israeli nuclear technician Mordechai Vanunu, who had worked for many years in the Dimona complex, provided spectacular details on Israel's option to the *Sunday Times*.[4] He was then abducted, tried and convicted in Israel on charges of high treason. His statements have not been rebutted. According to Vanunu, Israel was producing lithium deuteride and tritium in addition to plutonium. These materials can be used as the explosive core of thermonuclear weapons and as boosters in advanced fission weapons. Based on this information, specialists have calculated that by 1990, Israel may have been in the possession of some 100 to 200 nuclear fission explosives, and, according to some, possibly even some fusion devices as well.[5] Israel has bought and built various delivery vehicles capable of carrying nuclear explosives that could reach targets all over the Arab world and some on the territory of the former Soviet Union.[6] Its nuclear arsenal may since have grown by about 40 explosive devices per year.[7]

AND USE

As Israeli authorities have never publicly acknowledged the country's nuclear capability, analyses of that capability's use are necessarily speculative. With that proviso in mind, the following can be said. The nuclear option has fitted perfectly in the overall strategy of providing security independence and regional military superiority. It counterbalances Arab superiority in manpower and conventional weapons, as well as the chemical and biological capabilities that some Arab states have started to develop.

For a long time, specialists have concluded that Israel would use nuclear (fission) warheads as a weapon of last resort, and then in a counter-city rather than a counter-force role. Israel, they assumed, would try to invoke immediate help from outside (read: the United States), by hitting, for instance, Damascus or Baghdad with nuclear weapons.

---

4. His information is analyzed in Frank Barnaby, *The invisible bomb*.
5. Most specialists deny, however, that fusion weapons can be built without testing.
6. Israel has produced various types of ballistic missiles; one, the Jericho 2, with a range of 1,450 km.
7. For a survey of assessments, see Spector and Smith, *Nuclear ambitions*, pp. 159-64.

More recently some specialists, basing their conclusions on the Vanunu revelations concerning the large numbers and the advanced type of nuclear explosives produced since the early 1980s, have claimed that counter-force use would now be part of the Israeli strategy as well.[8]

SCENARIOS

Israel might make tactical use of its nuclear weapons, for instance, if in a war situation Jordan allowed Iraqi troops passage through its territory on their way to attack Israel. The Israeli army would try to carry its defensive actions to the western part of Jordan. Facing the threat of large-scale ground attacks on Israel's heartland, it might decide to use nuclear weapons to stop the enemy's advance before it reached Israel. As, however, Iraq's military power has been severely crippled and Jordan made peace with Israel in October 1994, this scenario is at present theoretical. It seemed less far-fetched, however, during the Kuwait crisis. During that episode, too, it was widely believed that Israel might retaliate with nuclear weapons against any chemical attacks by Iraq.

Plausible scenarios for the immediate future, in which Israel's security would be threatened in such a way as to provoke Israel to use nuclear weapons either counter-force or counter-city, are hard to imagine. It is less difficult, however, to envisage developments motivating Israel to cling to its nuclear option.

In principle, a Syrian offensive against Israel could be extremely dangerous, for instance, if chemical weapons were used widely. The present Syrian leadership, however, has always been characterized by caution and pragmatism, and that attitude has been strengthened by the melting of the Cold War. The last Soviet leadership discouraged the Syrians from trying to achieve "strategic parity" with Israel, and Moscow's relationship with Israel's patron, the United States, has improved rapidly, as has its relationship with Israel itself. Since the demise of the Soviet Union, Syria has been entirely without superpower patronage. Its involvement in the "peace process" - which has been growing less reluctant - indicates that Damascus prefers to obtain concessions from Israel without fighting. A change in the Syrian leadership, however, might create hazardous uncertainties. Domestic unrest might erupt. A conflagration involving Israel could then develop. Apart from that, any enlargement of Syria's arsenal of ballistic missiles, chemical

---

8. Barnaby, *The invisible bomb*, pp. 54-55.

or even biological weapons would be viewed with great concern in Jerusalem. Even though such eventualities might not cause Israel to use its nuclear weapons, they would certainly hamper denuclearization.

As long as a moderate Egyptian leadership stays in power, the Egyptian - Israeli peace will not be broken. However, a fundamentalist take-over in Egypt - whether violent or not - would probably lead to a rapid worsening in Egyptian-Israeli relations and could lead to the suspension of peace. Even without a resumption of warfare, this would be considered as extremely adverse in Jerusalem. In addition, Israel would have to reckon with the possibility that a radical Islamic Egyptian government would contract alliances with other anti-Israeli regimes. Egypt has participated in a program to develop ballistic missiles and must be considered capable of arming such missiles with chemical warheads.[9] That knowledge makes a political reversal in Egypt even more ominous to Jerusalem. Again, such developments would at least block denuclearization by Israel.

Similar speculations can be made about Jordan. As long as King Hussein reigns, peace with Israel will continue. The royal succession has been provided for: in case of the king's death, his brother Hassan is to take over. If the succession were to proceed without a hitch, Jordanian policy towards Israel would not become more hostile. But the succession might be challenged and this might lead to a radical take-over or intervention in Jordanian politics by Syria and possibly Iraq. Such eventualities would be interpreted as grave security risks by Israel and would motivate it to stick to its nuclear option.

It is very hard to imagine security risks originating in Lebanon severe enough to cause Israel to maintain its option or even use its nuclear weapons. Such dangers could only arise in combination with dramatic reversals of policy in Syria.

Somewhat further down the road, Iran, Libya and even Iraq may achieve nuclear-weapons' options. Libya and Iran dispose of chemical-weapons' capabilities right now, while they are trying to improve the range of their delivery systems. All three have stayed aloof from the "peace process." If they were to achieve a nuclear option, Israel would interpret this as a deadly threat. It would, again, rule out voluntary denuclearization by Jerusalem and under certain

---

9. Until the summer of 1989, Egypt cooperated with Argentina and Iraq in the so-called Condor 2 project, focused on the development of a ballistic missile with a range of over 1,000 km. Egypt possesses a large number of Scud missiles of the 280 km range which may be equipped with chemical warheads.

circumstances might lead to conventional preemptive strikes by Israel or even to nuclear exchanges. Iran, especially, is seen by Israel as an extremely dangerous potential enemy.

AND REALITIES

While destabilizing chains of events may take place in the future, it must be noted that ever since Egypt made peace with Israel in 1979, a revival of the strong Arab military coalition against the Jewish state has been considered impossible even by Israel's fiercest enemies, and, if anything, seems less realistic after the start of bilateral and multilateral peace negotiations. So far, these negotiations have been more successful than many initially dared to hope. Israel's immediate security problems derive from difficulties with the implementation of Palestinian autonomy in the Gaza Strip and Jericho. Violence may become more widespread if the economic situation in the (former) occupied territories should further deteriorate. Armed confrontations between Jewish settlers and Palestinians may increase in intensity. The Palestinian authorities may prove unable or unwilling to control armed attacks against Israeli targets by members of radical groups like Hamas or Islamic Jihad. The PLO may even be ousted from its leadership position by these radical groups.[10] Nuclear weapons, however, would not help Israel solve security problems caused or aggravated by such developments.

On balance, scenarios in which an Israeli government would consider using nuclear weapons are very speculative, but it is not difficult to perceive reasons for Israel to maintain its undeclared nuclear capability as a deterrent against (non-conventional) attacks by present or future regional foes.

INTERNATIONAL LEVERAGE

There are other ways in which to use a nuclear option, however, and these Israel has already practiced. According to some, there have been several instances in which the Israeli leadership ordered nuclear weapons to be made ready.[11] It is

---

10. The present Israeli government, for that matter, may be succeeded by a right-wing government bent on torpedoing the "peace process."

11. Nadav Safran, *Israel: the embattled ally* (Cambridge, MA: Cambridge University Press, 1978), pp. 483 and 488-490. Also see Shlomo Aronson with Oded Brosh, *The politics and strategy of nuclear weapons in the Middle East: opacity, theory and reality, 1960-1991. An*

said to have happened during the October War of 1973, when the Israeli army was about to break down under the pressure of the combined Syrian-Egyptian attacks. By readying the missiles, Golda Meir's cabinet is said to have emitted an SOS that was picked up, as was intended, by the United States, prompting it to speed up an airlift of conventional weapons.

It allegedly happened again early in 1991, when Israel was hit by Iraqi Scud missiles during the Gulf War, even though it had stayed out of the military coalition against Iraq. Unshielding nuclear-tipped missiles has allegedly been a means for the Shamir government to obtain US ABM Patriot missiles and even - a first in American-Israeli relations - the stationing of American military personnel trained in handling the Patriots. Israel may possibly want to maintain its option for such "diplomatic" purposes until a full-fledged Middle East peace is established, even though the likelihood of another Arab-Israeli war has receded dramatically.

Apart from that, Israel can use its nuclear option as a major bargaining item in arms control negotiations with its Arab negotiating partners.

REVERSING THE PROCESS

Israel's military prowess has caused deep concern among its Arab neighbors. The Egyptians, the Syrians, the Jordanians and most of all the Lebanese have suffered great losses in confrontations with Israel. They and other Arab states have resented its overwhelming power, even if a number of them have resigned themselves to its existence as in 1979 when Egypt concluded a formal peace agreement with it. Arguably, Israel's nuclear option has been a major incentive for non-conventional-weapons proliferation in the Middle East. More specifically, Libya's and Iraq's attempts at obtaining chemical and nuclear capabilities, and Syria's chemical-weapons' program can partially be traced back to Israel's option,

---

Israeli perspective (Albany: State University of New York Press, 1992), pp. 143-9. Aronson doubts the story that Minister of Defense Dayan ordered, or considered ordering, the *use* of nuclear missiles during the October War. For a contrasting version see Stephen Geen, *Living by the sword: America and Israel in the Middle East* (Brattleboro: Amana Books, 1988), pp. 90-92 and 98-99. See also Yezhid Sayigh, "Middle Eastern stability," in: Karsh, Navias and Sabin (eds), *Non-conventional-weapons' proliferation*, pp. 189-190; and Yezhid Sayigh, "Reversing the Middle East nuclear arms race," *Middle East report*, vol. 22, no. 4, July-August 1992, p. 17.

while that option may also have provided an extra incentive for allegedly revived Iranian nuclear-weapon plans.

From this point of view, denuclearization by Israel would mean an important step towards deproliferation in the Middle East. Led by Egypt, Arab states have indeed insisted on the demolition of Israel's nuclear weapons as a first step in the negotiating process, a major condition for a comprehensive peace and, of course, for creating a regional nuclear-weapon-free zone. This line of argument, however, ignores the fact that Iran, Iraq and even Libya have strong incentives for their nuclear ambitions that are unrelated to Israel, while none of these countries have indicated any serious willingness to make peace with Israel even if it would disarm itself completely.[12]

As no Israeli government has ever admitted the country's nuclear capabilities, the present political leadership can hardly take a public position on nuclear *dis*armament in the context of the peace negotiations. Israeli experts close to the government, however, have spoken out. Countering the Arab argument, they have stated that their country can only consider nuclear disarmament at the very end of the "peace process," and that regional disarmament agreements should include *all* forms of non-conventional weapons as well as various conventional systems. By the same token, the establishment of a nuclear-weapon-free zone (NWFZ) in the Middle East would only be feasible at the very end of the peace process.[13]

For two decades now, Israeli governments have advocated a regional NWFZ, but as a result of direct negotiations between the regional powers, that is, not as a

---

12. In the summer of 1994, the press reported that Iraq had been approaching Israel about the possibilities for reaching a peace accord, in order to gain international acceptability and the lifting of sanctions. To judge the sincerity of such tenders, if they were indeed made, it should be remembered that the Iraqi leadership made pacific sounds during the first Gulf War, saying that it would not thwart the Palestinians if they could conclude an acceptable peace with Israel. Only a few years later, however, Iraq threatened to destroy Israel with chemical weapons and attacked it with Scuds.

13. See, for example, Shalheveth Freier, "Non-proliferation and issues of regional and global security," *Disarmament*, vol. 16, no. 3, 1993, pp. 66-91. Also Gerald M. Steinberg, "Middle East arms control and regional security," *Survival*, vol. 36, no. 1, spring 1994, pp. 126-31. Yezhid Sayigh, a Palestinian scholar and coordinator of the Palestinian negotiating team to the multilateral arms control talks, has argued in support of the arms control timing schedule proposed by Israeli authors. See his article "Reversing the Middle East nuclear race," *Middle East report*, vol. 22, no. 4, July-August 1992, p. 18.

measure imposed by the United Nations where Israel feels itself at an overwhelming diplomatic disadvantage.[14] In addition, Israeli spokespeople have indicated a strong preference for a regional safeguards' system,[15] based on intrusive mutual inspections among the parties involved rather than a "standard" safeguards' system under the International Atomic Energy Agency.[16] Egypt, by contrast, has over the years promoted the idea of a NWFZ under United Nations auspices and safeguarded by the IAEA, and has found general support from Arab states for its position. Arab proposals have stressed the need for immediate Israeli ratification of the NPT as a non-nuclear-weapon state (which would automatically mean Israeli acceptance of full-scope safeguards). Israel, however, would only feel free to comply if it became convinced that *all* its former regional enemies (including Libya, Iran, and Iraq) had truly buried their hatchets.

Israel, then, will not agree soon to do away with all of its nuclear weapons. Yet it may consider taking some first unilateral steps. It would have to convince its Arab partners in the peace negotiations that these steps are worthy of some form of reciprocity, and would need intermediaries in the effort as long as it continues to refuse to acknowledge its nuclear-weapons capabilities. In this respect (as well as in others), the bilateral talks between Egypt and Israel on nuclear issues that were initiated in the fall of 1994 may offer opportunities.

Specifically, Israel might agree to "cap" its production of explosive material and freeze its arsenal. Already in May 1991, American President Bush called for a verifiable ban on the production and acquisition of weapons-grade nuclear material as part of his comprehensive proposal for arms control in the Middle East. In 1992, the US administration entered into bilateral talks with Israel on the subject.[17] In September 1993, the Clinton administration, pursuing the Bush initiative, proposed a world-wide policy of capping plutonium production as a pillar of its nuclear non-proliferation policy. In the case of Israel, the plan makes sense. For one thing, if the Vanunu assessments are correct, the Israeli arsenal is

---

14. Barnaby, *The invisible bomb*, pp. 158-9.
15. Similar to that of OPANAL under the Treaty of Tlatelolco.
16. See Freier, "Non-proliferation and issues of regional and global security."
17. C. Hardenberg (ed.), *The arms control reporter: a chronicle of treaties, negotiations, proposals, weaponry & policy 1993* (Cambridge, MA: The Institute for Defense and Disarmament Studies, 1993), 453.B.148.

amply equipped as it is.[18] For another, the life-span of the Dimona reactor, Israel's main plutonium and only tritium producer, is beginning to near its end. Within the next decade, the Israeli government will anyway have to decide whether to end the production of plutonium and tritium or build a new reactor. Even if construction could be achieved without external help, it would be noticed and have an adverse effect on the peace negotiations. The plutonium already produced in the Dimona reactor will retain its weapon-quality for a long time. Tritium, however, decays relatively quickly.[19] Without a reactor or an alternative neutron source to produce new supplies of tritium, the booster weapons or fusion option would die a "natural death." This would represent a significant first *dis*armament step.

Implementation of a decision to cap the production of nuclear explosive materials would require nimble diplomatic footwork and managerial and technical support, particularly from the United States. Israel would probably refuse intrusive, international verification of its nuclear complex at Dimona until the conclusion of a comprehensive peace. Yet the Arab partners would, quite reasonably, demand trustworthy verification of some sort. A crucial question, then, would be whether reliable methods for non-intrusive verification are available or could be developed shortly. All would depend on guarantees by non-intrusive means that the Dimona reactor was shut down and that material already irradiated was not being reprocessed. In addition, assurances would be needed that no alternative means were used to produce tritium, while the enrichment research program would either have to be transferred to civilian purposes and placed under international control, or ended. It may be possible to detect from the outside whether the reactor and reprocessing plant are in use if Israel were to allow perimeter tests (the taking of ground and air samples fairly close to the nuclear complex).[20] The IAEA has recently made progress in developing and testing such technologies, and from a technical point of view at least, it would be logical

---

18. This, however, is precisely why Arab negotiators may not accept a capping proposal as a serious suggestion.
19. Its half-life is about 12 years.
20. For technical details on environmental monitoring, see R.J.S. Harry's contribution to this publication.

to have the IAEA perform the surveys.[21] However, verifying from the outside the cessation of enrichment research experiments would be virtually impossible. In this respect, very much would depend on Arab confidence in Israeli assurances. At a later stage, and maybe in a phased procedure, Israel would have to subject its plutonium stocks to regular inspections.

Skeptics may well stress the formidable difficulties involved and belittle the importance of capping as a confidence-building measure. Yet as long as there is no comprehensive peace in the Middle East, no Israeli government will be pressurized into accepting policies that in its view impair its defensive capabilities, and capping may be the only feasible result in the near future.

Iran

MOTIVATIONS

Iran's nuclear proliferation efforts are shrouded in ambivalence. Iran ratified the NPT as a non-nuclear-weapon state in 1970, although according to the prevailing American position based largely on statements by intelligence officers, secret nuclear-weapons' research was initiated by the late Iranian Shah in the margin of his vast civilian nuclear program, and was focused on three tracks: weapon design, reprocessing technology, and enrichment technology.[22] The Shah reportedly stated in 1975 that if other regional powers one day became nuclear, Iran could not lag behind.[23] In 1974, India performed a "peaceful" nuclear explosion. One year later, Iraq was laying concrete foundations for its nuclear program. Both developments could be viewed as detrimental to the Shah's regional power and as incentives for an Iranian nuclear-weapons' program.

---

21. If Israel felt uncomfortable about the IAEA inspections, it could be allowed to send along an observer of its own. The IAEA has already been considering ways to facilitate and improve safeguards in the Middle East. See IAEA Board of Governors General Conference GOV/2682-GC(XXXVII), September 6, 1993, *Application of IAEA safeguards in the Middle East: report by the Director General to the Board of Governors and to the General Conference*, and the annexed letters from Egypt, Iraq, Israel, Lebanon, Libya and Syria.
22. Spector and Smith, *Nuclear ambitions*, p. 206; Akbar Etemad, "Iran," in Harald Müller (ed.), *A European non-proliferation policy: prospects and problems* (Oxford: Clarendon Press, 1987), p. 207.
23. Hardenberg, *The arms control reporter 1993*, 453.E.7.

During the Shah's reign Iran's relations with Israel, although unofficial, were warm and mutually profitable. Therefore, the Iranian program, if it existed at the time, was presumably not initiated primarily as a reaction to Israel's option. Possible motivations could have been the Shah's desire to underpin his ambitions for regional leadership, a wish to strengthen his hand against his aggressive competitor for regional power - Iraq - and a wish to deter Soviet expansionism.

A former head of the Iranian Atomic Energy Commission, Akbar Etemad, has, however, emphatically denied that there was a weapons' program under the Shah.[24] He recalls discussing the issue with the Shah. According to him, the Shah did not believe in the effectiveness of a nuclear deterrent against the former Soviet Union but relied on conventional strength (with which he was generously provided by the United States) both against Moscow and Baghdad. The Shah, Etemad claims, also felt that a weapons' option would damage Tehran's security relations with the West.

On the other hand, by the end of the 1970s the Iranian monarch became worried about the tendency in industrialized countries, especially the United States, to restrict the export of sensitive products and technology for civilian purposes. Although he denied planning the construction of a reprocessing plant and contented himself with financial rather than intellectual partnership in the Eurodif enrichment venture, reprocessing and enrichment studies may have been performed on a research level while he was in power.[25]

It is relevant to note the uncertainties surrounding the beginnings of Iran's option, because the activities of the new regime, which came into power in 1979, are considered by the American sources referred to earlier to have been built on foundations laid by the Shah. If there were no foundations, and if, particularly, there was no weapons' technology research program, that makes it even more difficult to assess any recent progress.

As far as motivations for a putative Iranian nuclear-weapons' program are concerned, some shifts and changes have arguably taken place in the post-imperial period, while other arguments have been reinforced.

---

24. Etemad, "Iran," pp. 212-14.
25. Etemad, "Iran," pp. 206 and 212-14.

Statements made by leading Iranian spokespeople have fed fears that Iran is working on a nuclear-weapons' program. They certainly show a willingness to ignore the commitments that Iran accepted when it ratified the NPT.[26]

The new rulers have claimed a leadership role in the Islamic world. They might wish to strengthen this position by the possession of nuclear weapons. In addition, they may feel that the world of Islam needs a nuclear capability in reply to the capabilities of other "ideological worlds."

They have expressed the belief that Israel should be annihilated, and the Israeli nuclear-weapons' capability probably adds grist to their mill. From a pragmatic perspective, however, Tehran has little to fear from Jerusalem as long as it does not actually threaten Israel's security. Iran's practical efforts against Israel so far have been concentrated on sponsoring terrorist activities against Israeli targets, mainly in Lebanon. Such actions, however brutal, do not present a vital threat to the Israeli state. In addition, for quite some time under the new regime Iran continued to obtain spare parts for its armaments from Israel, in spite of all its virulent verbosity. Israel might be anathema, but at the same time it was a very useful silent ally in Iran's war with Iraq. This suggests that Iran's leaders are perfectly capable of exchanging their ideological zeal for pragmatism when it comes to finding effective solutions to pressing security situations.

Iran, of course, has confronted a deadly threat from Iraq. Iraq probably initiated a nuclear-weapons' program during the 1970s and has certainly invested heavily into such an endeavor during the last decade. Security-inspired arguments for the Iranian regime to produce nuclear (and chemical) weapons could be Iraq's bombing of Iranian nuclear construction sites and even more so Iraq's activities in non-conventional weapons' procurement, these in combination with the inflaming of deep-seated conflicts, interlaced with religious fervor. During the Iran-Iraq war of the 1980s, Iraq was the first to make extensive use of chemical weapons against Iranian soldiers, but Iran replied in kind. In so doing, both countries violated their solemn commitments under the Geneva Protocol, and arguably lowered the threshold for employing non-conventional weapons.

In the early years of the Khomeini leadership, fear of Soviet expansionism may have been an additional security argument. Tehran had to take a grim view of the Soviet invasion of Afghanistan in December 1979. Ideologically speaking,

---

26. Leonard Spector, "Nuclear proliferation," in Karsh, Navias and Sabin (eds), *Non-convention-al-weapons proliferation*, pp. 142-3 and 145.

Tehran and Moscow if anything were even further apart than they had been when the Shah was still in power. However, since the dramatic political changes in the Soviet Union which have culminated in its dissolution, these arguments have arguably lost persuasiveness.

CAPABILITIES

As part of the Shah's civilian nuclear program, numerous Iranians received training abroad and at home. Iran's new fundamentalist leaders, however, initially stopped most of the program and many of those involved left the country. Western suppliers, mainly from West Germany, drastically reduced their services. For one thing, continued cooperation became hazardous during the Iran-Iraq war when the reactor construction sites proved to be within Iraq's striking distance. Moreover, the West German government distrusted the new regime and discouraged the resumption of activities by German industry after the Iran-Iraq war had ended.

The research program, however, was reportedly able to continue without major interference. Many of the research staff stayed and continued working. Additional training was reportedly provided by the People's Republic of China.[27] Research was even expanded when a new center was opened in Isfahan in 1984. Moreover, after a few years the Iranian leaders reversed their policy on the nuclear power program, tried to persuade Iranian nuclear physicists and technicians to come back from exile and searched for alternatives to take the place of West German suppliers. In the spring of 1994 it was reported that Russia was willing to perform the task.[28] In addition, prospecting for uranium sites has been successful. It is estimated that Iran's proven reserves can sustain a major nuclear power program for considerable time and would certainly be sufficient to provide source material for the production of explosive devices.[29] Tehran also reportedly bought substantial quantities of uranium concentrate from South Africa in 1988 and 1989.

There are no public signs of the construction of reprocessing or uranium-enrichment installations; there have been no reports in open sources about pilot installations of that kind with the exception of one small calutron provided by

27. Spector, "Nuclear proliferation," p. 144.
28. *Jomhuri-Yeeslami*, April 13, 1994, p. 4.
29. Etemad, "Iran," p. 206.

China[30] and finally, in December 1993, a special visit by the IAEA's deputy Director-General of safeguards (who, we may assume, had been briefed extremely well), did not bring to light any suspicious activities. Only in one respect is there substantial evidence: Iran is acquiring aircraft and medium-range ballistic missiles capable of delivering nuclear warheads.[31]

Judging by publicized data, the strongest evidence for any nuclear-weapons' plans on the part of the radical Islamic regime in Tehran seems circumstantial: the way in which Iran conducts its relations with the outside world, and more particularly its involvement in international terrorism, its proven chemical-weapons' production and use, and its interest in ballistic missiles. Until more concrete data are publicized on Iran's nuclear efforts, it remains largely a matter of (dis)taste to decide how serious a proof these factors represent. If Iran has a program, it will probably take a decade at least before it can reach the nuclear threshold. That leaves time for preventive action.

PREVENTIVE ACTION

Iran would need substantial outside help in realizing a nuclear-weapons' option. A general international embargo on the sale of relevant (nuclear and dual use) materials and knowledge to Iran would force Tehran to postpone any weapons' plans for a considerable time, long enough, perhaps, to see the advent of a leadership more willing to abide by its commitments under international treaties. Western industrialized countries are at present going even further, and refusing to help Iran even with the non-controversial parts of a civilian nuclear program. A case can be made that this stringent policy violates the right of Iran under the NPT to develop its civilian nuclear program, and may even provide it with a motive to secede formally from the Nuclear Non-Proliferation Treaty. There are, moreover, suppliers who - out of principle or for commercial reasons - do not wish to follow

---

30. Spector mentions this in "Nuclear proliferation," pp. 144-5. Electromagnetic enrichment of uranium, for which calutrons were developed in the United States during the Second World War, is an outdated technology but it works. Iraq made substantial progress with its calutron program before the installation was discovered by the indications of an Iraqi defector, and dismantled. It takes much more than just one calutron to obtain weapons-grade uranium, however.

31. *The military balance 1993-1994* (London: Brassey's for the International Institute for Strategic Studies, 1993), p. 223.

the Western policy of denying supplies. Russia, for example, has reportedly agreed to help out with the construction of reactors for the planned power station at Busher that was originally assigned to a West German company. The reactors are reportedly not of a particularly proliferation-prone design and will fall under IAEA safeguards. Potentially more dangerous support, however, might come from China and North Korea, which have aided Iran in the build-up of its non-conventional arsenals and are both capable of providing sensitive nuclear knowledge or hardware. There is as yet not much evidence that they are doing so, although China is reported to have provided Iran with a small calutron (see footnote 30). It has, finally, repeatedly been alleged that Iran was hiring nuclear experts in the former Soviet Union and that it had succeeded in buying nuclear-weapons' components or even complete weapons there. Additionally, it has been claimed that is was cooperating with Pakistan in the nuclear-weapons' field. None of these allegations have so far been publicly substantiated.[32]

Possibilities to address Iran's putative motivations for nuclear proliferation vary. Little can be done about the argument that Iran needs a reply to Israel's nuclear capability; that capability will not disappear in the near future, while Tehran would probably refuse to consider a less unlikely development, Israel capping the production of nuclear explosives, as a significant step towards future denuclearization. In fact, and to reverse the argument, Iran's regional intentions and overall military capabilities are arguably one major reason for Israel to maintain a nuclear option. As to Iran's security concerns about its western neighbor Iraq, those concerns must have abated considerably since the end of the second Gulf War. For the foreseeable future, international efforts to prevent Iraq from resuming its weapons' programs will continue. Iran could hardly wish for more.

The Iranian regime has earned itself a bad reputation in large parts of the world. It is investing in a nuclear program with quite respectable civilian purposes, that yet may have a weapon component. Its actions deserve being watched carefully and adequate precautions are called for. The short-term danger, however, seems to be overstated by some American sources, and some of the remedies that are being applied may actually worsen the situation.

---

32. *The military balance 1993-1994*, p. 233.

Iraq

MOTIVATIONS

In 1969, Iraq was one of the first countries to ratify the Nuclear Non-proliferation Treaty as a non-nuclear-weapon state. Like Israel, Iraq never admitted it wanted nuclear weapons, and it did not provide many public clues as to its motivations. So it must be assumed that the Iraqi regime was driven by its ambitions for regional Arab leadership, its traditional rivalry with Iran, and the conviction that Israel's nuclear option deserved an "Arab" reply in kind, especially after June 1981 when the Israeli air force destroyed Iraq's largest research reactor when it was about to go critical.

The second Gulf War and its aftermath have dealt a severe blow to Iraq's ambitions. Yet the measures ordered by the United Nations Security Council to verify that Iraq will not revitalize its non-conventional-weapons' program bear witness to the continuing international distrust of Iraq's intentions. The distrust is well founded. Nothing fundamental has changed in Iraq's political management. The old leaders are still in power. They are angered and frustrated by the humiliation visited upon them by the international community and they may be counted upon to try and regain their old regional clout by every trick in the book. They have allegedly already taken steps to reopen covert supply lines to support a reanimated weapons plan. The country's nuclear knowledge is still intact. Some defections aside, the weapons team is still there.

Ironically, however, even most opponents of Saddam Hussein's rule would not like to see Iraq irretrievably weakened, as that might cause increased instability in the Gulf region and in particular strengthen Iranian influence to a dangerous level. Especially if Iran were to develop a nuclear weapons' capability, that would be a grim prospect for the Gulf region and far beyond. Evidence of an Iranian nuclear-weapons' program would obviously be a major incentive for the rulers in Baghdad to revert to their non-conventional-weapons' production efforts.

CAPABILITIES

Presuming two phases in Iraq's nuclear-weapons' program so far, the first before Israel's bombardment of the Tammuz-1 (Osirak) reactor in June 1981, and the second between then and 1991, it can be concluded that Iraq started by focusing on plutonium production and later switched its research and development efforts to various methods of uranium enrichment. In addition, it has made a great effort to obtain, through purchasing or production, the means to deliver non-conventional bombs or warheads, especially ballistic missiles. During the 1980s it collaborated with Argentina and Egypt on the development of a medium-range missile, the Condor 2.[33]

During the first phase, Iraq overtly received substantial external support. The French provided two research reactors fueled with highly enriched uranium. The larger one, in particular, had excellent plutonium-breeding qualities if the core was cloaked in natural or depleted uranium. Iraq bought large quantities of both uraniums from Italy, Portugal, Niger and Brazil. The French also agreed to work with Iraq on fast breeder technology. The Italians provided Iraq with basic reprocessing technology. The IAEA was kept informed and inspections were scheduled for as soon as relevant material was involved. The Israelis, however, removed the linchpin from this putative scheme to produce plutonium by destroying the Tammuz-1 in a spectacular air raid.

During the second phase, Iraq concentrated on acquiring the capability to enrich uranium. Spending enormous amounts of money and spreading its buying operations among a large number of countries, it tried to hide its tracks from the public eye, the IAEA or even its suppliers. This operation started in 1982. Iraq's approach has been to get hold of as much sensitive technology and material as possible, meanwhile seeming to cooperate fully with inspections by the International Atomic Energy Agency. Most Western countries sympathized with Iraq in its war against Iran. It was not fashionable to draw attention to the unattractive characteristics of the regime in Baghdad. Only by 1989 did suspicions about Iraq's nuclear activities rise again in public. When Iraq invaded and annexed Kuwait, the US administration presumably reacted with such decisiveness not only because international law had been violated and oil supply-lines might be threatened, but also because the situation provided an opportunity to put a stop to Iraq's efforts at nuclear-weapons' production before it was too late. Just how far the Iraqis had advanced toward their nuclear option only became clear after the war was over.

When Baghdad had admitted defeat in the spring of 1991, the United Nations Security Council decided that Iraq's non-conventional weapons and their produc-

---

33. Spector and Smith, *Nuclear ambitions*, pp. 193 and 196-197.

tion sites should be destroyed.[34] In addition, the Council ordered an ongoing system of verification and control to prevent Iraq from reverting to its undesirable efforts.[35] This included checking future sales or supplies (including dual-use items) by third parties to Iraq. Although the leaders in Baghdad tried to sabotage the work of the United Nations Special Commission (UNSCOM) and IAEA teams, the inspectors managed to provide a host of data on ways, means and progress of the Iraqi programs, and to have essential parts of these destroyed. The most striking elements with regard to the nuclear program are briefly enumerated here.[36]

Iraq was working on various uranium enrichment techniques: gas centrifuge, chemical separation, and most notably electromagnetic isotope separation. International experts had considered the latter method so outdated as to be no longer relevant. As it turned out, Iraq had made most progress with precisely this unexpected technique. In addition, evidence was found of a well-advanced program to acquire and test the non-nuclear parts of nuclear explosives. Finally, plans came to light for the production of lithium-6, suitable both in fission weapons (as a booster) and as explosive material in fusion weapons.

Educated estimates now affirm that Iraq was within two years of producing highly enriched uranium in substantial quantities when it invaded Kuwait.[37] Obviously, the lead time for realizing a nuclear option has become much longer now, but the country nevertheless has a substantial advantage over beginners in the field. It has at its disposal critical knowledge and designs, and may still use the services of certain suppliers with whom it has worked before. However, large-scale production of nuclear explosive devices and their delivery vehicles seems impossible for as long as the verification effort lasts. Obtaining the components for a small "primitive" option would remain very difficult, but might just be feasible.

---

34. Security Council Resolution 687, adopted April 3, 1991.
35. Security Council Resolution 715, adopted October 11, 1991; accepted by Iraq November 26, 1993.
36. Details on the findings in IAEA General Conference GC(XXXV)/978, September 16, 1991, *Iraq's non-compliance with its safeguards obligations* plus attachments. Also David Albright and Mark Hibbs, "Iraq's quest for the nuclear grail: what can we learn?," *Arms control today*, July-August 1992, pp. 5-8.
37. Spector, "Nuclear proliferation," pp. 136-41; Tim Trevan, "Ongoing monitoring and verification in Iraq," *Arms control today*, May 1994, pp. 11-15.

PREVENTING RECIDIVISM

The urge of Iraq's beleaguered leaders to produce non-conventional weapons is probably stronger now than it has ever been. Considering Baghdad's proclivity to deceitfulness, it may not be presumed that UNSCOM and IAEA inspectors have covered the terrain fully and destroyed all relevant material and installations.[38] From this perspective, continuation of close verification and control measures is necessary for at least as long as the present leadership remains in power.

Before 1991 Iraq had managed to build an unsafeguarded nuclear program parallel to its officially declared activities. Most of the related efforts had gone unnoticed by either the IAEA or foreign intelligence services, including those of the United States. Iraq had also violated its safeguards agreement with the IAEA by reprocessing, but not reporting, a small quantity of irradiated material from a safeguarded research reactor. In short, the safeguards system of the International Atomic Energy Agency was shown to be in need of strengthening.

The IAEA has reacted to the challenge. It has reconfirmed its right to perform inspections at short notice, of undeclared as well as declared facilities. More generally it is more assertive in the interpretation and implementation of its safeguarding tasks. It has been evaluating the possibilities for close cooperation with intelligence services in order to be informed on time of covert goings-on, and it is preparing the upgrading and further modernization of its safeguards techniques.

Under the aegis of the Nuclear Suppliers Group many suppliers, shocked by the information about Iraq's covert program, decided in 1992 to impose the condition of full-scope safeguards on all their nuclear exports, and added a large number of dual-use items to their previous trigger list.

Such measures should slow down any future Iraqi attempts at proliferation (and those of other countries with nuclear ambitions) but they cannot provide foolproof guarantees, certainly not as long as the present regime remains in power and there is money to be made through irresponsible sales. A change in the political leadership of the country would be a first condition for restoring international confidence in Iraq's good intentions. Continuation of the present UN sanctions might help to produce such political change, although, of course, they

---

38. For an alarming evaluation, see *Iraq rebuilds its military industries: a staff report*, prepared by Kenneth R. Timmerman for the House Foreign Affairs Subcommittee on International Security, International Organizations and Human Rights, June 29, 1993.

could never be formally aimed at such a result. Besides that, a domestic rebellion may produce serious regional instability with all concomitant dangers.

Libya

MOTIVATIONS

Although Libya ratified the Nuclear Non-Proliferation Treaty, during the 1970s its leaders went on a well-documented nuclear-weapons' chase. Over the years, Libya's leader Qaddafi has gone on record with conflicting statements concerning his nuclear intentions, stressing that "the Arab nation" has a right to build the bomb, but also repeating that Libya is neither capable nor willing to produce nuclear weapons on its own.[39]

Libya's motivations for trying to obtain nuclear weapons have been strongly colored by ideology, but also arguably have a security angle. Ideologically, the regime led by Colonel Qaddafi has prided itself to be the most uncompromising and principled opponent of Israel's existence. In order to substantiate this claim, it has felt that it had to acquire the same spectacular lethal military power as its demonized enemies, Israel, the United States and more generally Western industrialized countries that are supportive of Israel. Qaddafi presented this ambition as a drive for an "Arab" or more widely an "Islamic" nuclear bomb against the "Jewish" or "capitalist" bomb. In reality, however, Libya has participated only marginally in the struggle against Israel, while its claim to Arab leadership - or Islamic leadership for that matter - has been challenged if not ridiculed by most other regional rulers.

Unlike a number of other Arab states, Libya has not been an actual target for the Israeli defense forces. In that respect, Libya's option lacks a serious security argument. By its extremely hostile attitude towards Israel, by its involvement in terrorist activities against Israeli citizens and friends of Israel, including American citizens, Libya, however, antagonized the United States so strongly that the US attacked Libyan targets several times during the 1980s. Here, one might argue, is a belated, added security motivation for Libya's nuclear longings: to keep the United States from pushing too hard without having to give in to Washington's

---

39. See Hardenberg, *The arms control reporter 1993*, 453.E.5. for some samples.

demands. The reverse argument, however, is at least as plausible: that the United States will not hesitate to use military force against Libya's regime again, should Libya one day succeed in approaching the nuclear threshold. Not many Arab neighbors would deeply mind. Even if some Arab rulers are sympathetic in principle to the idea that there should be an Arab, or an Islamic, answer to Israel's nuclear capability, they would not entrust this fatal responsibility to Qaddafi.

CAPABILITIES

Libya's ambitions have reached much further than its technical abilities. The country lacks indigenous expertise and sensitive installations. It boasts a single research reactor which was built by the former Soviet Union, and this installation is under IAEA safeguards, has been operated largely by Russian personnel, and is generally considered innocuous.

Libya, however, is rich and can offer substantial amounts of money for foreign expertise or even for ready-built nuclear weapons should these become available on the international black market. It has followed that approach in the past, when it tried to buy weapons in China or financed the Pakistani nuclear program, allegedly hoping in vain for some rewards in kind. During recent years there have been worries and speculations about Libya trying to obtain fissile material from East European traffickers or attempting to hire nuclear specialists from the former Soviet Union. So far, however, no evidence to substantiate such speculations has emerged publicly.

The country does have a substantial arsenal of mainly short-range ballistic missiles[40] and has been trying to develop its own missiles, with the help of German firms.[41]

PREVENTIVE ACTION

Even though Qaddafi has not publicly expressed his desire for nuclear weapons for some time, there are factors suggesting that a stringent non-proliferation policy is still recommended. The patterns in his conventional weapons' acquisitions, and the efforts he has put into obtaining a chemical weapons' production

---

40. *The military balance 1993-1994* mentions 40 FROG-7 and 80 Scud-B.
41. Spector and Smith, *Nuclear ambitions*, pp. 180-81.

capability[42] are only the most striking indications that the country's leader is ambitious and ruthless. Attempts to address Libya's proliferation motivations must be deemed futile as long as the present regime stays in power. There is little chance that Colonel Qaddafi will cease to believe that Israel should be destroyed or that capitalism should be defeated.

Because of Libya's technical deficiency in the nuclear field, a policy of denial is still an effective way to keep the country from becoming nuclear. This policy can count on the (silent) support of many of Libya's Arab neighbors.

Algeria and Syria?

MOTIVATIONS, AND WHAT SHOULD BE DONE ABOUT THEM

Only recently, Algeria and Syria have been mentioned as potentially interested in a nuclear-weapons' option, mainly by American sources,[43] but the accusations are based on very shallow public evidence indeed. There are no statements on record by the political leaders of either country which point to a desire to acquire the capability to produce nuclear weapons. In the case of Algeria, it is impossible to think of arguments - however Machiavellian - that make sense. In Syria's case, it has been suggested that Syria might be looking for an option to compensate for the loss of the Soviet Union as superpower patron.[44] The Syrian Defense Minister claimed in the mid-1980s that the Soviet Union would provide it with nuclear weapons if it were to come under Israeli nuclear attack. It is hard to believe, however, that Moscow ever made such a promise, and it cannot be accepted as proof that, with the demise of the alleged Soviet nuclear support, Syria would want the wherewithal to fend for itself. Another argument might theoretically be that Syria, which is seriously involved in the Middle East "peace process" from which it intends to gain the maximum profit possible, could use the hint of a future nuclear option as a bargaining chip in its negotiations with Israel. But there

---

42. Libya reportedly used chemical weapons during its intervention in the civil war in Chad. See Julian Perry Robinson, "Chemical-weapons proliferation," in Karsh, Navias and Sabin (eds), *Non-conventional weapons' proliferation*, p. 76.
43. Spector, "Nuclear proliferation," pp. 145-51.
44. Spector, "Nuclear proliferation," in Karsh, Navias and Sabin (eds), *Non-conventional-weapons' proliferation*, p. 147.

is no public evidence that the Syrian leaders have been indulging in either consideration.

CAPABILITIES

The basis for the mini wave of speculations about an Algerian or Syrian nuclear option has been that both countries have of late shown an interest in setting up modest nuclear programs.

Algeria did so without making its activities public and moreover with the help of China, which has provided the country with a large reactor (as well as many weapons systems). China is suspected of generally being less than responsible in its nuclear and arms exports.[45] Meanwhile, however, Algeria has placed this controversial installation under IAEA safeguards. It has moreover announced that it will ratify the NPT, by which it will commit itself to full-scope safeguards. The Algerian authorities have pressing domestic emergencies to cope with, so the delay in ratification can be explained by this rather than any ulterior motives.

Syria, which ratified the NPT in 1969 as a non-nuclear-weapon state and concluded a safeguards agreement with the IAEA in 1992, has shown some interest in buying a miniature neutron source reactor and enriched uranium from China. It was also considering building a modest nuclear power station, but these considerations have not led to concrete plans so far.[46] Syria does have a substantial arsenal of ballistic missiles and aircraft capable of delivering nuclear explosives.[47]

PREVENTIVE ACTION

In view of the above, no special preventive action seems required. If Israel decides to cap its production of plutonium and tritium in the context of the multilateral negotiations on regional arms control, that ought to present a disincentive to Syria - if it really fosters nuclear weapons' plans in the first place.

---

45. Spector, "Nuclear proliferation," pp. 147-50.
46. Spector, "Nuclear proliferation," p. 146.
47. *The military balance 1993-1994*, pp. 130-31.

Conclusions

In the Middle East, proliferation of non-conventional weapons capabilities is a symptom of deeply disturbed security relations, aggravated by real or affected ideological fervor. Merely a handful of countries, however, is actively involved. Only one, Israel, has passed the nuclear threshold. The others: Iran, Iraq and Libya, are years if not decades away from realizing options unless they manage to find a shortcut by buying complete systems from the former Soviet Union.

Still, the situation is difficult to defuse, because of the thoroughness of the conflicts that have stimulated proliferation, and because the incentives for proliferation cannot be reduced to one origin. The Arab-Israeli conflict has been an important factor, but certainly not the only one. The driving force behind Iraqi and Iranian proliferation is mutual distrust and animosity.

It would be conducive to progress in Arab-Israeli negotiations and, eventually, to the prospects for denuclearization of the Middle East, if Israel made clear its willingness to reduce its nuclear capability as much as possible. As a first step, it should cease the production of plutonium and tritium. Depending on positive and concrete Arab reactions, it should then in a phased process hand over its plutonium stocks to regular inspections.

The Arab countries currently involved in the "peace process" should follow the Egyptian and Jordanian examples and refrain from making the conclusion of a peace treaty with Israel dependent on complete destruction of its nuclear arsenal. They should cooperate with plans for more general regional arms reductions and refrain from new attempts at non-conventional weapons' proliferation. They should try to use whatever influence they have with Libya, Iraq and Iran to persuade them to recognize Israel. Israel cannot be expected to fully abandon its nuclear option until those countries have made peace with it.

Separate from this, in order to tackle the second major cause for proliferation in the Middle East, sustained international efforts will be needed to help create and support endurable peaceful relations between Iran and Iraq.

Basically there are two technical instruments to slow down proliferation in Iran, Iraq and in Libya, as they are largely dependent on external help if they want to produce nuclear weapons: controls on nuclear exports and sales of dual-use technology, and denial of certain exports. Denial policies especially, however, may become controversial. They can be interpreted as conflicting fundamentally with Article IV of the NPT, which states that "all the Parties to the Treaty undertake to facilitate, and have the right to participate in, the fullest possible exchange of equipment, materials and scientific and technological information, for the peaceful uses of nuclear energy." Iraq, Iran and Libya (as well as Syria) have all ratified the Treaty as non-nuclear-weapon states. Iraq and Libya have undoubtedly violated their obligations, so it was therefore justifiable to subject them to international policies of denial. In the cases of Iran and Syria, however, such a policy cannot be defended so easily as long as no hard evidence of efforts towards nuclear proliferation is presented, and as long as calls for an embargo by certain Western countries are not based on clearly formulated, justifiable public criteria. Arguably, nuclear supplier states have a right to decide for themselves not to sell to certain would-be customers. On the other hand, if they are parties to the NPT, as is the case with all the members of the Nuclear Suppliers Group, they are also bound by Article IV of the Treaty. In sum, although a policy of denial may work for the time being, it may also have the effect of harming the credibility of the NPT.

Safeguards are a much more neutral means. The International Atomic Energy Agency must be enabled to continue to improve its safeguards techniques, and to utilize its right to perform special inspections if necessary. In this context it must be allowed to act upon serious intelligence information from its member states. The strict limits placed on Iraq's civilian nuclear activities must be observed, and the verification and monitoring system now in place must be continued until the political situation in Iraq changes fundamentally. The nuclear programs of Iran and Libya must be carefully monitored as well, and their leaders must be held to their NPT obligation of cooperating with full-scope safeguards. Arguably, sales to Iran and Libya of sensitive nuclear or dual-use technology should continue to be discouraged, because their leaders have already shown that they will use non-conventional weapons in violation of their countries' solemn commitments. Fully impeding the development of civilian nuclear programs in discredited non-nuclear-weapon states that are party to the NPT, however, quite apart from the feasibility of such a policy, might be counterproductive, as it might present those countries with an excuse to leave the Treaty.

The Non-Proliferation Treaty and the international norm it embodies have been severely tried in the Middle East. Iraq and Libya have violated their commitments, Iran is under suspicion of doing the same, and Israel has persistently refused to ratify at all. Painful questions have been raised about the Treaty's effectiveness, and the willingness and ability of the international community to enforce its implementation. Israel's refusal to ratify has caused Arab spokespeople to question their own countries' adherence, and to question the desirability of the

Treaty's indefinite extension. Arguably, it has strongly hampered efforts to establish a nuclear-weapon-free zone in the Middle East and may hamper the implementation of advanced plans to create such a zone on the African continent.[48]

On the other hand, the need for a strong non-proliferation norm is felt even more intensely in the Middle East, precisely because the possibility of nuclear war is less remote, less unthinkable here than in most other parts of the world. Regional political leaders are aware of this, as witnessed by the various proposals for nuclear-weapon-free zones. Although the realization of such zones may still be far off, there are opportunities for incremental steps towards this final goal that are supported by regional states, at least in theory. These need not be steps in the dark. There is a useful precedent in the form of the Tlatelolco system in Latin America; there is also the example of denuclearization by South Africa. Both precedents were caused by fundamental changes in the politics of the countries concerned, but they were facilitated to a large extent because they could be embedded in an international non-proliferation system. The participating countries could establish safeguards in cooperation with the IAEA, and have their intentions constitutionalized through ratification of the NPT.

Hopefully, the Middle East will be able to follow a similar route in the next century.

---

48. For a discussion of this problem see David A.V. Fischer, "Africa as a nuclear-weapon-free zone," *Disarmament*, vol. XIV, no. 3, 1991, pp. 115-16: and Nathan Shamuyarira, "Africa as a nuclear-weapon-free zone (continued)," *Disarmament*, vol. XV, no. 1, 1992, pp. 122-3.

Table 1 Nuclear Cycles in the Middle East

Country	Algeria	Israel	Iran	Iraq	Libya	Syria	Saudi-Arabia
member IAEA	yes	yes	yes	yes	yes	yes	yes
member NPT	no	no	yes	yes	yes	yes	yes
power reactors in operation	no	no	no	no	no	no	no
research reactors	Nur (1MW)s As Salam (15MW)s	IRR 1 (5 MW)s IRR 2 (40? 70? 150? MW)!	TRR (5MW)s HWZPRs MNSRs	Tammuz 1 (destroyed) Tammuz 2 (800KW)s# IRT-2000 (5MW)s#	Tajoura (10M-W)s	no	no
uranium resources	(phosphate rock mining)	yes (phosphate rock mining)	yes	no	no	no	no
uranium treatment	no	yes! (purification, conversion)(?)	no	yes!# (purification, conversion)	no	no	no
heavy water production	no	yes! (?)	no	no	no	no	no
fuel fabrication	no	yes! (?)	no	#	no	no	no
reprocessing	no	yes! (?)	yes (pilot)	#	no	no	no
enrichment	no	R&D and pilot! (?)	R&D	#	no	no	no
production tritium, lithium deuteride	no	yes! (?)	no	no	no	no	no

Legend: s = under IAEA safeguards; ! = unsafeguarded; (?) = unconfirmed; # = de-activated or dismantled by UNSCOM/IAEA

Sources: International Atomic Energy Agency, GC (XXXV)/978, 16 September 1991 "Iraq's compliance with its safeguards obligations;" International Atomic Energy Agency, *IAEA yearbook 1993*, Vienna, 1993; International Atomic Energy Agency, *The annual report for 1993*; *The arms control reporter*, vol. 12, 1993 and vol. 13, 1994, section 453, Institute for defense and disarmament studies (Cambridge MA 1993, 1994); Frank Barnaby, *The invisible bomb. The nuclear arms race in the Middle East*, I.B. Tauris, London 1989; Leonard S. Spector with Jacqueline R. Smith, *Nuclear ambitions. The spread of nuclear weapons 1989-1990* (Boulder, San Franscisco, Oxford: Westview Press, 1990).

5 The Nuclear Proliferation Challenge from the Soviet Successor States: Myths and Realities

William C. Potter

Few non-proliferation issues have attracted more international attention than the collapse of the Soviet Union and the inheritance of its nuclear assets by the Soviet successor states. Myriad articles on "loose nukes," "Ukrainian launch codes," "brain drain" and "nuclear mafia" are among the popular manifestations of this concern in the mass media. The Soviet Threat Reduction Act of 1991 (or the Nunn-Lugar Cooperative Threat Reduction Program as it is commonly known) is illustrative of the seriousness with which the US government also viewed the proliferation dangers from the former Soviet Union.

More often than not, both popular and official expressions of concern over the nuclear risks emanating from the post-Soviet states have not been matched by sound understanding of the sources of the proliferation problems or the obstacles in the way of their solution. Indeed, a great deal of misinformation has been published and numerous misconceptions propagated, which impede efforts to mitigate the proliferation risks. This chapter identifies a number of these "myths" and seeks to provide corrective information.

Myth No. 1: The Post-Soviet States have been Slow to Denuclearize and to Assume their NPT Obligations. In fact, the pace of denuclearization in the former Soviet Union has been remarkably fast since the collapse of the Soviet state. All of the thousands of tactical nuclear warheads that were dispersed over fourteen of the fifteen former Soviet republics were redeployed on Russian territory by mid-1992.[1]

---

1. Turkmenistan appears to have been the only Soviet republic without nuclear weapons on its territory.

M. van Leeuwen (ed.), The Future of the International Nuclear Non-Proliferation Regime, 155-166.
© 1995 *Kluwer Academic Publishers. Printed in the Netherlands.*

The dismantling and removal of the strategic nuclear weapons on the territories of Belarus, Kazakhstan and Ukraine has also been proceeding at a rapid pace.[2] By the end of September 1994, 45 of the 81 SS-25s that had been stationed in Belarus had been transferred to Russia;[3] all strategic bombers and associated cruise missiles formerly deployed in Kazakhstan had been moved to Russia, as had 44 of the 104 SS-18s;[4] nearly half of the 130 SS-19s deployed in Ukraine had been dismantled[5] and 37 of the 46 SS-24s had been deactivated (that is, their warheads have been removed).[6]

The process of engaging the post-Soviet states in the international non-proliferation regime has also proceeded rapidly. By the end of October 1994, twelve of the fourteen non-Russian successor states had joined the Nuclear Non-Proliferation Treaty as non-nuclear-weapon states.[7] The two most recent adherents were Turkmenistan (September 29, 1994) and Moldova (October 11, 1994). Today, only Tadjikistan and Ukraine remain outside of the NPT regime. Although these new members of the NPT have the potential to play a major constructive role at the 1995 NPT Extension Conference, it would be a mistake for either the United States or Russia to assume that all or most of the new adherents will automatically follow the Russian or US lead to support indefinite extensions of the Treaty.[8]

---

2. See *Nuclear successor states of the Soviet Union: nuclear-weapon and sensitive export status report*, (Carnegie Endowment for International Peace and the Monterey Institute of International Studies, draft, November 1994); and "Nuclear weapons deactivizations continue in FSU," *Arms control today*, November 1994, p. 27.
3. The redeployment is expected to be completed by mid-1996.
4. The SS-18 warheads presently remain in storage in Kazakhstan. See "Nuclear weapons deactivizations continue in FSU," p. 27. According to Russian press reports, all nuclear warheads in Kazakhstan will be removed to Russia by mid-1995, and all missile silos will be dismantled by mid-1997. See *Radio free Europe/Radio liberty report*, May 4, 1994.
5. "Remarks prepared for delivery by Secretary of Defense William J. Perry to the Henry L. Stimson Center, September 20, 1994."
6. Under the terms of the January 14, 1994 Trilateral Statement, all SS-24s must be deactivated by mid-November 1994.
7. Editor's note: subsequent to the submission of this chapter, Ukraine acceded to the NPT in December 1994.
8. The United States and Russia have both been slow to assist the new NIS adherents prepare for the 1995 Conference.

If the good news is that almost all of the successor states are now party to the NPT, the significant bad news is that Ukraine remains outside of the fold.[9] The prospects for near-term accession, while uncertain, are nevertheless better than they have been since 1991.

The balance between proliferation incentives and disincentives in Ukraine has never been strongly in favor of nuclear weapons retention. The principal incentives or pressures to "go nuclear" have been pursuit of a deterrent capability *vis-à-vis* Russia and, to a lesser extent, the quest for greater international autonomy and prestige. Domestic political factors, bureaucratic politics, and a desire to trade a nuclear posture for economic side payments have also influenced Ukraine's nuclear stance at different points in time since the collapse of the Soviet Union. The most significant underlying constraints have been economic and political in nature, especially fear of political and economic reprisals by other states, and isolation from the international community.[10]

The relative influence of these factors, as well as other potential proliferation determinants such as public opinion, has varied over time and has often been associated with a number of situational variables. These factors include leadership change and domestic and regional crises, most notably Crimea's move to assert independence and the confrontation with Russia over the Black Sea Fleet.

The Trilateral Statement of January 14, 1994 is often cited as a milestone in Ukraine's circuitous path towards NPT accession.[11] In it, President Kravchuk reiterated his commitment that Ukraine would accede to the NPT as a non-nuclear-weapon state in the "shortest possible time." In return, Ukraine was promised compensation for the removal of nuclear warheads on its territory as well as additional economic assistance. In addition, Presidents Clinton and Yeltsin pledged that once the START 1 Treaty entered into force and Ukraine became a non-nuclear-weapon state that is party to the NPT, the United States and Russia would reaffirm their obligations to refrain from the threat or use of force against the territorial integrity or political independence of Ukraine.

---

9. Editor's note: see note 7.
10. See Victor Zaborsky, *Nuclear disarmament and non-proliferation: the evolution of the Ukrainian case*, (Cambridge, MA: Center for Science & International Affairs, Harvard University, June 1994).
11. A dissenting view is provided by Steven Miller, "Ukraine, the Trilateral Agreement, and the future of denuclearization," IISS *Strategic comments*, February 23, 1994.

The Trilateral Statement may have been helpful in addressing the security concerns of some Ukrainian parliamentarians. The Rada's decision on February 3, 1994 to accept the Statement and to reverse its prior opposition to key non-proliferation provisions of the Lisbon Protocol to the START 1 Treaty, however, probably had more to do with the growing awareness that the main threat to Ukraine's territorial integrity loomed from within rather than outside the country. This threat was in the form of Crimea's attempt to assert its independence from Ukraine, a danger not likely to be mitigated by nuclear weapons. Indeed, accession to the NPT may have been perceived as having the positive effect *vis-à-vis* Crimea of triggering Russia's reaffirmation of Ukraine's territorial integrity.

The one new development that may complicate the Rada's decision on NPT accession is the October 21, 1994 "Agreed Framework" between the United States and the Democratic People's Republic of Korea (DPRK). This framework is likely to be perceived in Ukraine as a high states' sellout to North Korea's nuclear weapons' program and may persuade some Ukrainian parliamentarians to hold out for a larger package of Western assistance, perhaps including new nuclear reactors to replace those at Chernobyl.

Myth No. 2: All Sensitive Nuclear Facilities and Weapons-Grade Materials in the Former Soviet Union are Based in Russia. This myth, which confuses dedicated nuclear weapons' production facilities with other sources of weapons-grade material, is in part responsible for the careless accusations made during the summer of 1994 that the nuclear material seized at Tengen, Landshut, and Munich in Germany must have come from a Russian nuclear facility.

In fact, although the bulk of the Soviet Union's nuclear assets are concentrated in Russia, not inconsequential nuclear fuel-cycle facilities, as well as stocks of highly enriched uranium (HEU) and dual-use nuclear materials and technologies, are found in other successor states.

These nuclear assets include uranium mining and milling centers in Estonia, Kazakhstan, Kyrgyzstan, Tadjikistan, Ukraine, and Uzbekistan; nuclear research and training centers in Armenia, Belarus, Georgia, Kazakhstan, Ukraine, and Uzbekistan; and research reactors at many of these centers, some of which are fueled with highly enriched uranium.[12]

---

12. For more detailed information on the nuclear assets of the non-Russian successor states, see William Potter (with Eve Cohen and Edward Kayukov), *Nuclear profiles of the Soviet successor states* (Monterey, CA: Monterey Institute of International Studies, 1993).

There is evidence, for example, that 33-35 kg of weapons-grade uranium is stored at the Institute of Power Engineering Problems at Sosny, near Minsk. At least 22 kg of uranium enriched to 90 per cent is also present at the Baikal-1 and IGR reactor complexes at the Semipalatinsk test site in Kazakhstan. Well over three times that amount appears to be stored in bulk form at the Khar'kiv Technical Institute in Ukraine, although Ukraine has reported only a small portion of that amount to the IAEA. There are also fourteen nuclear power reactors in commercial operation in Ukraine, two in Lithuania, and one in Kazakhstan. The reactor in Kazakhstan at Aktau (formerly Shevchenko) is a liquid-metal fast breeder used for both desalination and electricity generation purposes. It is capable of producing over 100 kilograms of plutonium a year, and was also involved in experiments in the early 1990s in which fuel assemblies derived from weapons material were loaded into the reactor. This was feasible because the reactor was designed to use mixed-oxide (MOX) fuel.[13]

Kazakhstan is also the site for the Ulba Metallurgy Plant, the major facility in the former Soviet Union for fabricating nuclear fuel assemblies. This plant at Ust-Kamenogorsk in eastern Kazakhstan produces nearly all of the fuel pellets used in post-Soviet-manufactured reactors and may in the past have fabricated highly-enriched uranium fuel for Soviet naval propulsion reactors. Approximately 600 kilograms of HEU was stored at the plant until fall 1994 when it secretly was transferred to the United States. In addition, the plant is the largest producer in the former Soviet Union of beryllium, a metal used in civilian nuclear power reactors and also in the manufacture of nuclear weapons. Other major production sites for dual-use nuclear-related items such as hafnium and zirconium are found in Ukraine.

Perhaps the best kept secret is the existence of a gas centrifuge factory located in Bishkek, Kyrgyzstan. This factory, formerly run by the Soviet military, is now, at least in part, a joint-stock company closely linked to the uranium processing center at Kara-Balta.[14]

Although the nuclear assets of the non-Russian republics (with the possible exceptions of Kazakhstan and Ukraine) are unlikely to support an indigenous nuclear weapons' program, they do pose significant risks in terms of diversion

---

13. The MOX fuel seized at Munich on August 10, 1994 is reportedly similar to that used previously at Aktau (personal communication to William Potter by Kazakhstan nuclear engineer, August 1994).

14. CIS Nuclear Database, Monterey Institute of International Studies.

and unregulated nuclear exports. Those dangers are heightened by the primitive state of export controls in the former Soviet Union outside Russia, the underdeveloped state of material accounting and physical protection in most of the successor states, and the failure to enlist any of the non-Russian successor states as members of the Nuclear Suppliers Group (NSG).[15] The risk of division is also aggravated by the absence of international safeguards at most nuclear facilities in the newly independent states.[16]

Myth No. 3: Russia has Lax Export Control Guidelines and a Long History of Export Control Abuse. Contrary to popular perceptions, the Soviet Union generally followed a very stringent nuclear export policy. This policy was instituted in 1958 after the Soviet leadership realized that its "peaceful" nuclear aid to China was being utilized for military purposes, and continued until the late 1980s. It was part of a broader non-proliferation policy that included extensive consultation and cooperation with the United States. This cooperation persisted even during the most troubled periods of the superpowers' relations in the 1970s and 1980s.

The problem with respect to export controls in Gorbachev's Soviet Union and today's Russia is not that there is an absence of good export control regulations or well-trained experts. Russia inherited almost all of the Soviet Union's nuclear export control structure and personnel. As a consequence, it was much better positioned than the other former republics to regulate nuclear exports. Beginning in late 1991, Russia also adopted a number of important new presidential decrees, presidential directives, and governmental regulations designed to adapt the export control process to the post-Soviet environment. Most important of these was Presidential Decree No. 388, issued on April 11, 1992, which provides the legal basis for the new export control structure in Russia. Other important decrees and regulations established control lists regulating the export of nuclear-related dual-use material, equipment, and technology; stipulated Russian adherence to the policy of "full-scope" safeguards as a condition of export; and endorsed Russian

---

15. The failure to include non-Russian NIS representatives in the NSG is a consequence of both disinterest on the part of some relevant successor states and the lack of unanimity on the issue of new NIS members by the current NSG parties. Regrettably, the NSG in 1994 adopted a new policy to allow non-members to participate only once as an observer. As a consequence, Ukraine is no longer able to attend, despite its desire to do so.
16. Although IAEA safeguards agreements have been concluded with many of the successor states, the agreements have entered into force only for Latvia and Lithuania.

observance of the Nuclear Suppliers Group Guidelines.[17] It should be noted that the legal basis for the Russian export control system derives from executive decrees and not from national legislation.[18]

Although Russia has taken important positive steps to regulate nuclear exports, these actions have been undermined by a number of other developments. They include: (1) the change in the relative influence of organizational actors in the export control policy-making process (especially the decline in the influence of the Ministry of Foreign Affairs and the rise of the Ministry of Foreign Economic Relations and the Ministry of Atomic Energy); (2) the greater consideration in export decisions now given to the acquisition of hard currency; (3) the demise of the nuclear export monopoly formerly enjoyed by Techsnabexport and the corresponding proliferation of private nuclear entrepreneurs with access to nuclear material, equipment, and technology; (4) the virtual absence of custom controls between Russia and the other post-Soviet states; and (5) the underdeveloped state of export controls and the lack of trained export control personnel in the non-Russian successor states.

As a consequence of the porous borders between Russia and the other newly independent states, it is extraordinarily short-sighted of Western governments not to provide more export control assistance to the non-Russian successor states, including those without nuclear weapons on their territory. At the present time, there are no meaningful export controls in place in the Baltic states which serve as major transit points for rare earth metals and other dual-use goods. A country such as Kyrgyzstan that seriously wants to stem the flow of illicit exports, cannot

---

17. A detailed discussion of Russian export control developments is provided in Y. Simachev and A. Kokopev, "Export controls in Russia," paper presented at the workshop on Export Controls in the NIS: Legislative and Administrative Challenges and Opportunities, Minsk, October 3-4, 1994. See also William Potter, "Nuclear exports from the former Soviet Union: what's new, what's true," *Arms control today*, January/February 1993, pp. 3-10; and Elina Kirichenko, "Nuclear non-proliferation export controls of Russia," CIS non-proliferation project working paper, Monterey Institute of International Studies, November 1993.

18. An exception to this general phenomenon is the law adopted on April 29, 1993 that established criminal penalties for the unlawful export of raw materials, materials, equipment, knowhow, and services useful for creating arms and military equipment. See *Nuclear successor states of the Soviet Union*, p. 34.

even find a donor for $35,000 worth of radiation detection equipment to support its principal border crossing with Uzbekistan.[19]

Myth No. 4: MINATOM and the Ministry of Defense have Custody over All Weapons-Grade Nuclear Material in Russia. One of the most widespread myths with serious non-proliferation policy implications is that the Ministry of Atomic Energy (MINATOM) and the Ministry of Defense are the sole custodians of nuclear weapons-grade material in the Russian Federation. This faulty assumption appears to have led the US government to concentrate its assistance efforts in material control and accounting and physical protection with MINATOM and the Ministry of Defense. This focus has been to the exclusion of two other key actors that control large stocks of HEU for Russia's naval propulsion reactors: the Ministry of Shipbuilding and the Committee for the Defense Industry. One might argue, in fact, that the most dangerous and immediate problem involving the potential for nuclear diversion in the former Soviet Union involves the enormous stockpile of HEU controlled by these two bodies.

This fresh fuel, much of it enriched to between 70 and 90 per cent, supports the operation of over 200 nuclear-powered ships in the Russian Navy's Northern and Pacific Fleets, as well as seven civilian nuclear ice-breakers. Fuel elements containing HEU from this stockpile were stolen in late 1993, but were reportedly recovered in Russia in July 1994. The stockpile may also have been the source of the tiny quantity (800 milligrams) of HEU seized at Landshut, Germany, in mid-June 1994.

Fresh nuclear fuel stockpiles for naval reactors are located near Severomorsk, Severodvinsk, and Vladivostok.[20] New fuel for naval reactors is reportedly under the control of the Ministry of Shipbuilding, while strategic stocks of fuel are under the control of the Committee for the Defense Industry. The stocks of reactor fuel appear to be located together, although they are under the control of two different bodies.[21]

This duality of control, the existence of dual material accounting systems, and the reluctance of either body to date to cooperate with the Russian nuclear regulatory body, Gosatomnadzor, creates conditions that could be exploited by

---

19. Proceedings of the NPT Extension Conference workshop, Almaty, Kazakhstan, October 10-12, 1994.
20. *Nuclear successor states of the Soviet Union*, draft, November 1994, p. 19.
21. Author's interviews with safeguards specialists from the Kurchatov Institute, June 1994.

individuals or organized groups seeking access to the HEU. Although separate material accounting systems exist on paper at the nuclear fuel stockpiles, no physical inspections or checks of the nuclear material inventories have been conducted in the past decade - if ever. Material accounting, to the extend that it was employed, tended not to be facility-specific and was mainly used for central planning and financial purposes.[22] Material control relied on a system of personal responsibility in which a designated person was entrusted with the nuclear material until it was passed on to another designated individual.[23]

A team of safeguards' experts at the Kurchatov Institute is now attempting to persuade Russian authorities to introduce a modern system of material control and accounting at the propulsion reactor fuel-storage facilities. At the present time, however, Gosatomnadzor, which technically has authority for assuring physical protection and material accounting, can at best provide an item count of sealed fuel containers. Access is reportedly limited because of bureaucratic resistance to what is perceived as undue intrusion by another organization and because of concern by the Ministry of Shipbuilding and the State Committee for the Defense Industry that Gosatomnadzor will discover that serious safeguards problems persist.

Myth No. 5: The Cases of Nuclear Seizures in Germany in Spring and Summer 1994 were the First Cases of Weapons-Grade Diversion in the Former Soviet Union. It is important to distinguish between confirmed cases of diversion of weapons-grade material from nuclear facilities in the former Soviet Union and the transport of such material to other states. There remain relatively few cases of confirmed - as opposed to reported - diversions of weapons-grade material. There are, however, at least several cases of diversion which predate the seizures in Germany in 1994. The most serious involve the disappearance of an undisclosed quantity of HEU from the "Luch" nuclear research facility at Podolsk near Moscow and the theft (and subsequent recovery) of three fuel elements containing HEU from a naval base in Murmansk.

The former diversion is confirmed by MINATOM documents. This case, along with concern about lax security at nuclear research centers and interim

---

22. See Oleg Bukharin, "Soft landing for bomb uranium," *Bulletin of the atomic scientists*, September 1993, p. 46.
23. See Vladimir Sukhoruchkin, quoted by Edith Lederer, "Russian nuclear safeguards," Associated Press, April 28, 1994.

storage facilities for plutonium from dismantled weapons, led MINATOM in 1993 to adopt an internal directive on strengthening safeguards, especially of HEU and plutonium.[24] Financial difficulties and inter-agency bureaucratic battles, however, appear to have delayed implementation of the directive.[25]

Although most alleged thefts of nuclear bomb material in fact involved low-enriched uranium of no direct use in a nuclear weapons' program, one cannot dismiss the possibility that large quantities of weapons-grade fissile material have been diverted. This possibility stems from the existence of lax physical protection and shoddy material control and accounting practices at many, if not most, civilian nuclear facilities in the former Soviet Union. In early 1994, for example, Gosatomnadzor ordered the closure for six months of Moscow's Research Institute for Non-Organic Substances because of lax arrangements for protecting plutonium at the site.[26]

In another example of material control underdevelopment, senior officials at the Institute of Power Engineering Problems in Belarus acknowledged that because of sloppy accounting practices in the past, they did not know the precise amount of HEU at their own facility.[27] Given the small amount of material in question at the Belarus facility (between 33 and 35 kilograms of HEU enriched to 90 per cent), one can imagine the uncertainty at nuclear facilities in Russia that possess HEU and plutonium stocks thousands of times larger. Under such conditions, it is probably impossible at the present time to distinguish between "material unaccounted for" (MUF) and material that has been stolen.

Myth No. 6: There were Four Serious Cases in which Weapons-Grade Material from the Former Soviet Union was Seized in Germany in 1994. This myth is a recent but widespread one, that has been repeated regularly by the Western media. The four cases routinely mentioned are:

(1) Six grams of Pu-239 seized in Tengen on May 10, 1994;

---

24. See Oleg Bukharin, "Technical aspects of proliferation and non-proliferation," paper presented at the Conference on Multilateral Security: Eurasia and the West, Barnett Hill, England, July 11-15, 1994.

25. *Ibid.*

26. Testimony of Leonard S. Spector before the House Foreign Affairs Committee, Subcommittee on International Security, International Organizations, and Human Rights, June 27, 1994.

27. Author's interviews in Minsk, June 1994.

(2) Seizure at Landshut, Bavaria, on June 6, 1994 of 800 milligrams of U-235 enriched to 87.7 per cent;

(3) Seizure by Bavarian state police on August 10, 1994 of over 300 grams of mixed-oxide fuel that was on board a Lufthansa flight from Moscow to Munich; and

(4) Purchase by a Hamburg journalist pretending to be an undercover policeman of what was reported to be a tiny sample of Pu-239 at a Bremen train station on August 16, 1994.

Only the Tengen and Munich cases are of major proliferation significance. The first case, which involved the inadvertent seizure of a small quantity of extraordinarily pure plutonium (99.78 per cent), is important because it alone of the recent German cases was not a sting operation. It may also have involved a real prospective buyer.[28]

The Lufthansa case is significant because of the relatively large quantity of material that was seized and indications that its procurers were in a position to deliver much more.[29] The so-called Bremen case, although usually lumped together with the other three, in fact involved a speck of plutonium from a smoke detector and was no different than many earlier inconsequential cases.[30]

Neither the Tengen and Munich contraband, nor that at Landshut, appears to have been the product of dedicated nuclear weapons' production - despite initial German statements to the contrary. Collectively, however, the three cases demonstrate that a variety of weapons-grade material is available for illicit sale from multiple sources in the former Soviet Union.

---

28. For a detailed analysis of the Tengen case see Mark Hibbs, "Russian data suggests Pu was enriched by Arzamas - 16 Calutrons," *Nuclear fuel*, August 15, 1994, pp. 9-10; and Hibbs, "Plutonium, politics, and panic," *Bulletin of the atomic scientists*, November/December 1994, pp. 24-31. See also William Potter, "Nuclear security in the post-Soviet states," *The non-proliferation review*, spring/summer 1994, pp. 61-5.

29. See Hibbs, "Plutonium, politics, and panic."

30. The Bremen case is also sometimes discussed in the context of a fifth "Flensburg case" involving an earlier seizure of a minuscule sample of plutonium from a Soviet manufactured smoke detector. See Mark Hibbs, "IAEA meeting on smuggling problem avoids sensitive data sharing issue," *Nuclear fuel*, November 7, 1994, p. 13.

Conclusion

Numerous myths and misconceptions notwithstanding, significant nuclear proliferation threats from the Soviet successor states do exist. Most of these dangers have underlying economic and political causes that will not disappear soon and are not amenable to outside intervention. As a consequence, Western efforts, at best, are likely to make a difference at the margins. The West can and should, however, try to make that difference.

There is no shortage of good recommendations for Western assistance, some of which have actually been adopted as governmental policy. They include efforts to foster the growth of indigenous non-proliferation expertise, to encourage more routine and extensive sharing of Western-Russian intelligence regarding illicit nuclear exports and organized crime activities, and to expedite the delivery of financial and technical assistance in the area of export control, physical protection, and material control and accounting. What has too often been lacking in Western policy has been prompt implementation. These delays in the delivery of promised assistance have given rise to tremendous cynicism in the post-Soviet states and have also undermined support for assistance programs in the US Congress. Blame for the halting pace of policy implementation can be found in both donor and recipient countries, and includes extensive inter-agency wrangling and bureaucratic politics. The speed and impact of non-proliferation assistance, however, has also been impeded by a poor understanding of the nuclear infra- structure and the domestic sources of nuclear policy-making in the former Soviet Union (especially in the non-Russian states) and by the reluctance of Western governmental agencies to work more closely with non-governmental organizations in the pursuit of mutual non-proliferation objectives.

Western efforts to encourage nuclear proliferation restraint in the Soviet successor states are also undermined by the prevalent view there that Washington, Bonn, Paris, and London often do not practice what they preach. As a conse- quence, the ability of the Western powers to gain allies in the former Soviet Union for the 1995 NPT Extension Conference, as well as for other non-proliferation initiatives, may well depend on the perceptions in the post-Soviet states' capitals of the consistency with which the West applies its non-proliferation standards and the extent to which the Western nuclear-weapon states (and Russia) are prepared to forego nuclear testing, restrain their arms exports, and reduce their own nuclear arsenals. This challenge is difficult, but not unreasonable, for the West to meet.

6 IAEA Safeguards and Non-Proliferation

R. Jörn S. Harry

Introduction

Great concern existed about the risks of horizontal proliferation after the Second World War, and this concern was reflected in the Nuclear Non-Proliferation Treaty of 1968.[1] Full-scope safeguards were called for in the Treaty, to be implemented by the International Atomic Energy Agency in Vienna, which had already been founded in 1957.[2] This new safeguards' task put more emphasis on the general safeguards' task of the IAEA, which was only one of its functions in connection with its "regular" technical mission of stimulating the safe application of nuclear energy for civilian purposes all over the world. IAEA safeguards are based on the cooperative attitude of the inspected states.

At the time the NPT was formulated, it was widely feared that some developed states would become nuclear. The application of safeguards allayed those fears for many years. Nowadays some of the developing states have acquired enough nuclear technology to be considered serious nuclear-weapon threshold states. They appear, however, still to be dependent on some technologically advanced special products from highly advanced states. The international non-proliferation regime has been supplemented with new measures like the Nuclear Suppliers Guidelines, containing export restrictions and controls. IAEA safeguards, too, have had to adapt to the drastic political and technical changes in the world.

About twenty-five years ago, the upsurge in hijacking of airplanes and other acts of terror, together with two cases of theft of natural uranium, stimulated

---

1. "Treaty on the non-proliferation of nuclear weapons," reproduced in IAEA document INFCIRC/140.
2. IAEA, *IAEA statute*, as amended up to December 28, 1989, IAEA, Vienna, 1990.

M. van Leeuwen (ed.), The Future of the International Nuclear Non-Proliferation Regime, 167-203.
© 1995 *Kluwer Academic Publishers. Printed in the Netherlands.*

attention for physical protection as a means to contain sub-national proliferation. The IAEA played its role in a timely fashion, although it has a limited mandate in this area.

Recent years have witnessed drastic reductions in nuclear-weapon arsenals, from which large stockpiles of nuclear-weapon material are emerging. That material will have to be kept under control for a long period, triggering proposals for international control and safeguards' arrangements, for which, it will be argued here, the International Plutonium Storage, as negotiated about fifteen years ago, offers an acceptable model.

In sum, horizontal proliferation, sub-national proliferation, and vertical proliferation are three aspects of the nuclear weapons' problem that the IAEA can help to address. The process of strengthening the effectiveness of IAEA safeguards has been getting more attention since the 1990 NPT review conference. The revelations after the second Gulf War stimulated this process strongly. Major questions now are: what role will the member states of the IAEA allow it to play in this context, and what improvements in IAEA safeguards are needed and acceptable?

Safeguards and the NPT

According to the NPT, non-nuclear-weapon states have to accept IAEA safeguards on all source and special fissionable material in all peaceful nuclear activities of the state. The preamble of the NPT poses that parties are: "to further the application ... of the principle of safeguarding effectively the flow of source and special fissionable materials by use of instruments and other techniques at certain strategic points." These two principles were the basis for the modern full-scope safeguards' system of NPT safeguards, that was formulated by negotiations in the IAEA Safeguards Committee during 1970 and 1971, and published in IAEA document INFCIRC/153 in 1972.

Until the end of the 1960s, the IAEA safeguards' system had developed organically, and was in principle only covering a limited number of submitted nuclear activities, plants or amounts of nuclear or non-nuclear material.[3] By

---

3.   IAEA, "The Agency's safeguards," INFCIRC/26, March 30, 1961; and INFCIRC/26/Add.1, April 9, 1964; IAEA, "The Agency's safeguards system (1965, as provisionally extended in 1966 and 1968)," September 16, 1968, INFCIRC/66/Rev. 2.

focusing now on all nuclear material[4] in all nuclear activities, no explicit proof of the "peaceful" use of installations, equipment, or non-nuclear material was required, and an element of arbitrary judgment could be avoided. Material accountancy, recording in the facility, and reporting to the IAEA, followed by regular inspection of the correctness of the reporting, form the backbone of the IAEA safeguards' system. Additional measures of containment and surveillance support the conclusions on non-diversion of the nuclear material, based on independent IAEA verification of the flow and physical inventory compared with the book values of the state declarations. The Book Physical Inventory Difference (BPID), or as it is usually known, the Material Unaccounted For (MUF), is the main yardstick of the objective and rational system, as formalized in the safeguards' document INFCIRC/153.[5]

By concentrating on the nuclear material, the new system removed some traditional concerns about industrial espionage. From the point of view of nuclear weapons' proliferation, it was deemed sufficient, because the fabrication of a nuclear weapon is impossible without weapons-grade nuclear material, which was not freely available at all. It was further argued that all other parts of a nuclear explosive device could be obtained on the open market or produced without major technical problems.[6]

Article II of the NPT commits non-nuclear-weapon states not to manufacture or acquire nuclear weapons. IAEA safeguards mainly verify the declared nuclear material and installations, and compliance with other aspects of the NPT was not included in the scope of IAEA safeguards. Nevertheless, safeguards could not exclude the existence of proscribed activities like the unreported production of nuclear-weapon-usable material or the construction of a workshop for the assem-

---

4. Throughout this chapter, "nuclear material" means any source or any special fissionable material as defined in Article XX of the NPT statute. The term source material shall not be interpreted as applying to ore or ore residue.
5. "The structure and content of agreements between the Agency and states required in connection with the Treaty on the Non-Proliferation of Nuclear Weapons," INFCIRC/153 (Corr.), IAEA, Vienna, June 1972.
6. This might be true for a uranium-based weapon, but a plutonium-based weapon needs a much more sophisticated implosion design for the conventional explosives part. Openly published reports on the IAEA on-site inspections in Iraq under the UN Security Council Resolution 687 (1991) proved that export restrictions on advanced technology have seriously hindered the rate of progress of the Iraqi weaponization program- in this respect.

bly of a nuclear explosive device, otherwise there was no need to apply safe-guards.

More than twenty years of safeguards' application have proven the success of that limited approach. There is so much international interdependence involved in the nuclear power generation of today, and such large commercial interests are at stake, that no state has ever misused a real nuclear power plant for the production of its first nuclear weapon. Military programs, by contrast, have stimulated development of nuclear technology for peaceful purposes. Nuclear proliferation will be reversed, in a manner of speaking, when nuclear material gained from the dismantlement of nuclear weapons will be used in a civilian program, implying that it will be subject to safeguards and finally be fissioned in nuclear power plants or research reactors.

Experience over many years has showed that inspectors have on occasion noticed suspect activities that suggested a violation of the NPT. Some cases were resolved quietly, others remained a problem for a longer time. Such cases were reported to the IAEA Board of Governors and in the Annual Report to the General Conference of the IAEA. Present problems with special inspections in North Korea demonstrate how strongly the application of IAEA safeguards depends on the cooperation of the inspected state. In any case the present situation leads to a clear political signal.

INTERPRETATION OF VERIFICATION

The use of the word verification in the safeguards' document INFCIRC/153 suggests an overly restricted misinterpretation.[7] This was particularly caused by Articles 28 and 29.[8] These articles are mentioned in Part II of INFCIRC/153,

---

7. From *Bulletin of peace proposals 1977*, vol. 8, no. 1, p. 9; F. Barnaby, at that time Director of SIPRI: "A Party to the NPT could legally manufacture the components of any number of nuclear weapons, and the non-nuclear parts of the weapons could be assembled. Only when the fissile material was placed into one of the devices would the Treaty be broken."

8. 28. The Agreement should provide that the objective of safeguards is the timely detection of diversion of significant quantities of nuclear material from peaceful nuclear activities to the manufacture of nuclear weapons or of other nuclear explosive devices or for purposes unknown, and deterrence of such diversion by the risk of early detection.

29. To this end the Agreement should provide for the use of material accountancy as a safeguards measure of fundamental importance, with containment and surveillance as important complementary measures.

which contains the technical specifications of procedures for the application of safeguards. Hence it does not give a comprehensive definition of obligations in connection with the NPT, it merely defines the technical rules of the IAEA verification of the declared nuclear activities. This should not be reversed to interpret that part of the verification as verification of all NPT obligations of the state.

A wider interpretation of the NPT obligations is defended in a thorough study by George Bunn and Roland M. Timerbaev, two principal negotiators of the text of the NPT.[9] The study argues that the safeguarding tasks given to the IAEA under the NPT include ensuring that a state does not take those distinctive steps in the development process, generally known as "weaponization," that lead up to the actual assembly of a nuclear explosive device or weapon. Possibilities for a wider interpretation of INFCIRC/153 will be dealt with later on in this paper.

In a 1991 report on disarmament to the United Nations, the meaning of verification has been directly related to the accepted Treaty obligations.[10] Verification is described as a process which establishes whether state parties are complying with their obligations under an agreement. The process of verification consists of multiple steps which include monitoring; collection of information relevant to obligations under arms limitation and disarmament agreements; analysis of the information; and reaching a judgment as to whether the specific terms of an agreement are being met.

A wider acceptance of this understanding of verification will give more body to the safeguards' activities of the IAEA. Such an interpretation demands the IAEA also to come into action when a state prepares or develops nuclear activities which do not fit into the declared program of normal civil activities. Or to state it more cooperatively: the IAEA should help to remove all credible suspicions of nuclear weapon ambitions by adequate inspections.

---

9. G. Bunn, R.M. Timerbaev, "Nuclear verification under the NPT: what should it cover, how far may it go?," PPNN Study Five (Southampton, UK: Mountbatten Centre for International Studies, University of Southampton for Program for Promoting Nuclear Non-Proliferation, April 1994).

10. Department for Disarmament Affairs, Report of the Secretary-General, "Study on the role of the United Nations in the field of verification," Disarmament Study Series 20, A/45/372 (New York: United Nations, 1991).

Recent Developments in IAEA Safeguards' Implementation

At the IAEA General Conference in September 1991, the Netherlands made a statement on behalf of the European Community and its member states with a set of proposals that could be implemented relatively quickly. The measures included:

— an early submission of design information on new nuclear plants;
— the effective use by the IAEA of special inspections, including the use in relation to undeclared nuclear facilities;
— setting up by the IAEA of a universal register of exports and imports of sensitive nuclear equipment and verification of the safeguarded use of that equipment;
— an obligation to declare all nuclear materials, including uranium ore concentrate produced in the territory of the state;
— a notification to the IAEA Board of Governors for any application for exemption of safeguards, before it is accepted.

The first two proposals were rapidly accepted by the IAEA Board of Governors. However, agreement on the third issue was reached only after longer discussions and modifications. The result is the voluntary implementation of the reporting scheme agreed upon in February 1993. This demonstrates, not only in wording but also in practice, that such an agreement is always based on consensus and sometimes many compromises. Truly universal adherence has not yet been reached. Implementation of safeguards becomes increasingly complicated by such voluntary options when they are not universally followed. Further proposals include taking into consideration the openness and transparency of the inspected state, reflected for instance in the rights of access for inspectors and the use of additional information sources. The IAEA is evaluating a number of measures and recommendations for improving the cost-effectiveness of its safeguards' system. This evaluation is performed through a two-year development program known as Program 93+2.[11] The program evaluates six specific areas:

---

11. R. Hooper, "IAEA development program for a strengthened and more cost-effective safeguards' system," *International nuclear safeguards 1994, vision for the future* (proceedings of a symposium, Vienna, March 14-18, 1994, vol. 1 (Vienna: IAEA, 1994), pp. 255-69.

— cost analysis of present safeguards' implementation;
— assessment of potential cost-saving measures;
— environmental monitoring techniques for safeguards' application;
— increased cooperation with State Systems of Accounting and Control;
— improved analysis of information on a state's nuclear activities;
— and enhanced safeguards' training.

Technical safeguards' aspects of this program are included later in this chapter. The New Partnership Approach with EURATOM, by which the IAEA is going to make more effective use of the results of this supra-national safeguards' system of the European Union, has also to be mentioned as a recent improvement in IAEA safeguards' efficiency.

The IAEA's Secretariat, which is employed as an international civil service, is highly qualified and generally speaking has performed well.[12] Its safeguards' personnel, in particular, has maintained a high technical professional level, in accordance with the rule from the Statute that prescribes that in recruitment "efficiency, technical competence, and integrity" are to be paramount, with geographical considerations secondary. It will be hard put, however, to cope with a substantial increase in responsibilities and tasks if it is not expanded and if the organization's financial means are not bolstered. Particular attention should be given to the complications created by the fact that staff are usually employed on short-term contracts. This means that, as a rule, a relatively large fraction of the personnel is not yet experienced enough to perform the more complicated tasks, for which not enough experienced personnel is available. This is, for instance, reflected in long-outstanding facility attachments that regulate the specificities of the safeguards' implementation per nuclear facility.

Safeguards in Balance with International Cooperation

After 1945, the dual-use potential of nuclear energy was clearly recognized, and international policies were developed to promote its use for civilian purposes but at the same time strongly discourage and preferably prevent its use for military

---

12. Ellis Morris (ed.), *International verification organizations*, Center for International and Strategic Studies (Toronto: York University, 1991).

ends. Shortly after the Second World War, the United Nations discussed the establishment of a central authority which should administer all uses of nuclear energy. That initiative, known as the Baruch Plan, failed. In the first eleven years of man-controlled fission, technological information was kept secret and severe constraints were imposed on the international trade of nuclear material and equipment. Nevertheless, the Netherlands and Norway successfully developed their nuclear technology and started a reactor on July 30, 1951 in Kjeller, Norway, at an open scientific centre. There were similar developments world-wide, proving that secrecy of information is no suitable instrument to ensure non-proliferation of nuclear technology. On the contrary, it led to an increase in independent nuclear activities, which represented a proliferation risk as illustrated by the development of "peaceful nuclear explosions" (PNEs) which were considered acceptable - even the NPT has an article that deals with them. PNEs were included in the Tlatelolco Treaty, and India tested a "peaceful nuclear explosive device" in 1974.

President Eisenhower's famous "Atoms for Peace" speech of December 8, 1953 marked a turning point. Bilateral and international peaceful nuclear cooperation started under strict non-proliferation conditions. At first, safeguards were implemented by the United States, but they were soon delegated to the international organizations EURATOM and the IAEA.

The IAEA was founded in 1957 on the authority of the United Nations as an autonomous intergovernmental organization. Its task is to further the use of atomic energy for peaceful purposes and to ensure at the same time that atomic energy would not be misused for military purposes. Hence, from the beginning, it had a safeguarding task, embedded in the wider scope of peaceful applications of nuclear energy.[13] Safeguards developed as a specialist vocation, strongly supported by technical developments in measurement and monitoring techniques. The wide application of full-scope safeguards according to the NPT stimulated the technical development of safeguards based on systematic analysis and its formalization in INFCIRC/153. The IAEA to date is the only verification organization that is functioning on a world-wide scale.

---

13. For further details, see *Facts about the IAEA*, (Vienna: IAEA, 1991).

Safeguards' Acceptance

The safeguards' activities of the IAEA (and, within the European Union, by the supra-national organization EURATOM) are aimed at internationally acceptable assurances. The scope of these assurances is necessarily limited to the peaceful, or declared, use of the inspected nuclear activities. The effectiveness of safeguards, moreover, depends on the cooperation of individual states. Existing budgets, availability of manpower with special skills, and limitations of the authority to verify circumscribe the application of technical safeguards further.

Acceptance of safeguards in the nuclear field may be strengthened by verification systems that were recently created in other areas. Thus, the strength of the EURATOM safeguards' system is enhanced by political and economical ties enforced through the Maastricht treaty. The 1992 Chemical Weapons Convention (CWC) contains new approaches to inspections. The same goes for the Treaty on Conventional Armed Forces in Europe and the Treaty on Open Skies. These Treaties offer opportunities for new approaches to the verification of nuclear non-proliferation.[14] It is possible that when these new approaches become internationally acceptable, states that have not yet ratified any, or all, of the existing Treaties will be persuaded. But such developments depend at least partially on the development of verification techniques.

For the application of IAEA safeguards in states that acceded to the NPT, a special safeguards' agreement has still to be concluded between the IAEA and the "client" state or group of states. When safeguards are challenged, or suspicion of Treaty violation cannot be removed, the IAEA can request access for a special inspection. However, if the state refuses, the IAEA cannot directly enforce access to suspect installations or install sanctions. For important decisions in this context, the IAEA is, first of all, dependent on the political support of its Board of Governors and its General Conference. In these bodies not only safeguards' proponents, but also members, including non-NPT members, who view safeguards differently, participate in the decision-making process.[15] In the final

---

14. An example is the result of the Conference on Security and Cooperation in Europe, (that is, the Charter of Paris for a New Europe), Conference on Security and Cooperation in Europe, signed at Paris on November 21, 1990.
15. All member states are commonly tied together by the broad mandate of the IAEA that includes the stimulation of all peaceful uses of atomic energy. Hence the IAEA safeguards have always been based on a wide consensus between differently oriented member states. A

stage, however, the IAEA reports on violations to the United Nations Security Council, which, by its Charter, has the means to compel a non-nuclear-weapon state to accept IAEA safeguards' inspections or, if necessary, to invoke appropriate sanctions.

Horizontal Non-Proliferation and Safeguards

PEACEFUL NUCLEAR ACTIVITIES AND SAFEGUARDS IN THE CONTEXT OF INTERNATIONAL COOPERATION

Total energy consumption in the world will grow rapidly because of the continuous growth of world population. At the same time, the largest share of the substantial economic growth will take place in developing states, especially in South-East Asia. These developments will also stimulate energy demands.[16] At the 1992 World Energy Conference, no clear statements were made regarding the share of nuclear power in the total energy production of the states. All energy resources, however, including nuclear energy, must be developed in view of the "minimal regret" strategy in relation to the CO_2 problem and its far-reaching consequences. The developed states are best equipped to support a sustainable growth by the controlled use of nuclear energy. But the right to an equal share of the development cannot simply be denied to developing states. This again raises the dual-use dilemma of nuclear energy.

The International Fuel Cycle Evaluation, a world-wide technical study, concluded in 1979 that there is no technical way of solving the proliferation problem. Some nuclear fuel-cycles are more, others less attractive for a state with weapon aspirations. But starting a nuclear-weapons' production program is essentially a political decision by governments.[17] And if sufficient resources are

---

one-sided development has thus been avoided, which has contributed to the general acceptability of safeguards.
16. J.R. Frisch, K. Brendow and R. Saunders (eds), *World energy horizons 2000-2020*, Proceedings of the 14th Congress of the World Energy Conference, Montreal 1989 (Paris: Éditions Technip, 1989); World Energy Council, *World Energy Council 15th Congress, Madrid, 1992*, (London: WEC, 1992).
17. INFCE Technical Coordinating Committee, *International nuclear fuel-cycle evaluation*, summary volume, (Vienna: IAEA, March 1980).

available locally, nuclear weaponization cannot easily be stopped from the outside. IAEA safeguards, however, have to detect such developments if the peaceful nuclear fuel-cycle is misused.

Spectacular improvements in safeguarding the commercial nuclear fuel-cycle have been achieved, particularly in safeguarding plants using the sensitive technologies of enrichment, reprocessing and plutonium containing mixed-oxide fuel fabrication.[18] These improvements were stimulated by commercial interest in these plants and by the international interdependence of both the technology and the commercial operations. In particular the multinational cooperation of organizations like Eurodif and Urenco are actually realizations of the idea of regional fuel-cycle centers.[19]

During the past two decades, controls and restrictions on sensitive exports have been added to safeguards as technical means to prevent proliferation, particularly by the adoption of the Zangger list,[20] and the recently reviewed Nuclear Suppliers Guidelines.[21] According to these Guidelines, exports of nuclear material and other specific material, equipment, or technology to non-nuclear-weapon states are to be subject to full-scope safeguards and the application of minimum levels of physical protection in the receiving state.[22] This is

18. For enrichment, consensus was reached in F. Brown, "Hexapartite safeguards project overview," *ESARDA* Bulletin 5, 1983, pp. 6-7. For reprocessing, a similar status has been reported in IAEA, *Report of the LASCAR forum: large-scale reprocessing plant safeguards. Approved at the fifth LASCAR plenary meeting, Shimoda and Tokyo, Japan, May 1992* (IAEA: Vienna, 1992). A technical account of safeguarding modern reprocessing is given in S. Kaiser and R. Howsley *et al.*, "THORP: the route to a safeguardable plant," 15th Annual Symposium on Safeguards and Nuclear Material Management, Augustinianum, Rome, Italy, May 11-13, 1993, *ESARDA* 26, EUR 15214 EN, CEC DG XIII, Luxembourg (1993), and related papers pp. 101-19.
19. "Regional fuel-cycle centers, 1977 report of the IAEA study project," 2 vols, (Vienna: IAEA, 1977).
20. IAEA, "Communications received from member states regarding the export of nuclear material and of certain categories of equipment and other material," INFCIRC/209, (Vienna: IAEA, 1974), and its corrections, modifications, additions.
21. IAEA, "Communications received from certain member states regarding guidelines for the export of nuclear material, equipment or technology," INFCIRC/254/Rev.1/Part 1 Nuclear Transfers, and /Rev.1/Part 2 Nuclear-related Dual-use Transfers (Vienna: IAEA, 1992).
22. Paradoxically, in the application of the safeguards, the IAEA uses higher limits for the amounts of nuclear material (e.g. exemption limit is 10 tonnes of natural uranium, and the Nuclear Suppliers Guidelines trigger safeguards on natural uranium above the limit of

politically sufficient to ensure that the supply of nuclear material and of other specific material, equipment or technology is protected against the risks of horizontal proliferation and against possible terrorist attacks by sub-national groups.

It is to be hoped that, apart from commercial interests, political concern in the nuclear fuel-cycle will also continue to support financially the good record on security and safeguards of the nuclear fuel-cycle. A prolongued lowering in the commercial demand for civilian nuclear services and materials like plutonium may otherwise discourage privatized industry to maintain, in the long run, the necessary high standards of control.

INTERNATIONAL CREDIBILITY OF SAFEGUARDS BASED ON OPENNESS

The IAEA regularly publishes its safeguards' inspection results.[23] Evaluations of declarations and verification results are documented, and the inspectorate has published its criteria.[24] The IAEA also publishes the list of inspected facilities in its Annual Reports. Its safeguards' effectiveness assessment (a priori) and

---

500 kg).

23. IAEA, "Safeguards," *Annual Report for 1993*, GC(XXXVIII)/2, (Vienna: IAEA, 1994); and similarly for the European Union, *The safeguards operations report 1989-1990 of the European Commission to the Council and the European Parliament: European Safeguards Directorate*, "Report on the Operation of EURATOM Safeguards (presented by the Commission)," SEC{92}80 def., (Brussels: Commission of the European Communities, January 24, 1992).

24. J.A. Larrimore, "IAEA safeguards criteria," *Journal of nuclear materials management*, May 1993, pp. 19-23. W. Gmelin, *et al.*, "Contributing to goals and concepts for safeguards implementation," 13th Annual Symposium on Safeguards and Nuclear Material Management, Avignon, France, May 14-16, 1991, *ESARDA* 24, EUR 13686 EN, CEC DG XIII, (Luxembourg, 1991), pp. 31-4. W. Gmelin, "Safeguards in the European Community," 11th Annual Symposium on Safeguards and Nuclear Material Management, Luxembourg, May 30-June 1, 1989, *ESARDA* 22, EUR 12193 EN, CEC DG XIII, (Luxembourg, 1991), pp. 17-21. W. Gmelin, B. Math, W. Stanners, E. van der Stricht, B. Love and G.V. Landresse, "Implementation questions relating to inspection goals and safeguards effectiveness," 7th Annual Symposium on Safeguards and Nuclear Material Management, Liège, May 21-23, 1985, *ESARDA* 19, CEC JRC Ispra (Va.) (1985), pp. 17-27; W. Gmelin, B. Math, B.W. Sharp, W. Stanners, G.V. Landresse and B. Love, "Invited paper, notes on inspection goals" 6th Annual Symposium on Safeguards and Nuclear Material Management, Liège, May 21-23, 1985, *ESARDA* 17, CEC JRC Ispra (1984), pp. 19-24.

evaluation (a posteriori) are performed by the organization's own staff with input and support from the General Conference, the Board of Governors, the Standing Advisory Group on Safeguards Implementation, member state Support Programs, and Consultants and Advisory Groups.[25] Member states participating in these groups get a detailed insight into the technical aspects of the safeguards' implementation.

States can also judge the professional performance of the IAEA inspectors in the state, by exercising their right to accompany them. The exchange of information among the different groups helps member states to define their support work according to the needs, and also to provide information on developments to the IAEA informally. It is important that both the IAEA and the member states provide the required monetary resources for this exchange of information. Also, the normal exchange of scientific information through publications, symposia and the personal contacts at international meetings must not be neglected. All of these activities are required to keep the scientific experience regarding safeguards up to date. There is a continuous need for optimization by new techniques, which can help to achieve formalized, objective and, if possible, quantified results.[26]

Safeguards are designed to build confidence in the peaceful use of nuclear energy. The confidence results from a process in which the sometimes opposing, or at least mistrusting, parties get acquainted and gradually learn to trust one another. Thus the sharing of the benefits of nuclear power between states, helped by the IAEA as intermediary, has contributed to the struggle against horizontal proliferation. In this process the IAEA safeguards played the leading part. Unfortunately, the continually re-emerging distrust in the protection of confidential information by the IAEA, and states' unjustified fears of being exposed openly in the annual safeguards' reports threatens transparency and the stability of the system.

---

25. V. Bragin and L.D.Y. Ong, "Report of the Advisory Group Meeting on Safeguards Assessment and Evaluation Methods, May 17-21, 1993," IAEA internal document IOM SGCP-599 460-M7.AG-824 from DIR-SGCP to the Director General, June 30, 1993.

26. F.J. Walford, "Characterization of C/S Devices and Systems (A review of progress)," AEAFS-150(H)/SRDP-R 195, (Harwell, AEA Technology, 1993).

Sub-National Non-Proliferation and Physical Protection

AN INTERNATIONAL NORM FOR PHYSICAL PROTECTION

In the United States, safeguards normally include physical protection. In the European tradition this is seen as a separate subject. The protection of nuclear material and nuclear installations against unauthorized actions is the prerogative of sovereign states. Therefore, a distinction has been made between physical protection as an element of "national safeguards," and the "international safeguards" of the IAEA.

The IAEA has regularly convened meetings on physical protection with experts from member states who drew up the IAEA guidelines for the physical protection of nuclear material. The IAEA first published these guidelines in June 1972. Later that year, a terrorist attack on Israeli participants in the Olympic Games in Munich triggered international public awareness of the dangers of terrorism.

The IAEA guidelines have been reviewed and adapted according to the experience gained and the increasing needs for improved physical protection.[27] The guidelines set the international norm for physical protection in bilateral arrangements between states and in national regulations. A proposal to include radioactive sources in the physical protection guidelines was rejected. For radioactive sources, the existing regulations on handling dangerous goods were deemed more appropriate, in view of the generic difference between the comprehensive set of rules and regulations controlling the handling of nuclear material, and the necessity to formulate comparable rules for all aspects of the control of these (in toxicity respects much more) dangerous goods.

INTERNATIONAL COOPERATION ON PHYSICAL PROTECTION

Recent years, however, have witnessed several cases of irresponsible trafficking in quite strong radioactive sources, creating radiation hazards for innocent bystanders. In some states the general public is insufficiently protected against such dangers. Investigation of the origin of the radioactive material and measures

---

27. IAEA, *The physical protection of nuclear material*, INFCIRC/225/Rev.3, (Vienna: IAEA, 1993).

to avoid recurrence should have been undertaken, but at the time of writing little is publicly known about these cases, the necessary follow-up and preventive counter-measures. The incidents can be seen as harbingers of more criminal business involving relevant amounts of weapons-grade material.

After 1972, the importance of a Convention on the Physical Protection of Nuclear Material, to establish cooperation for international transport of nuclear material, was pointed out repeatedly.[28] Between October 1977 and October 1979, government representatives discussed and proposed the final text of the Convention. The Convention addresses international cooperation in physical protection for civil nuclear installations. Specifically, it deals with physical protection issues related to international transport of nuclear material and legal issues involving attacks on civil nuclear activities. The Convention constitutes the highest level of international regulations for physical protection that could be agreed upon at that time. It has never been possible to extend at least its cooperation aspects to nuclear material for military applications. That such an extension would be sensible, however, was illustrated some two years ago, when small quantities of plutonium, incorporated in detectors for chemical warfare, were discovered in a hotel lobby. This was probably the first time that an attempt to sell plutonium of military origin on the black market was discovered. The catch of quantities of more than 1 gram of plutonium in Germany during the summer of 1994 also proved the deficiencies of physical protection measures in some states. These cases, moreover, show that the NPT safeguards' premise, that nuclear weapons-grade material is not available, is going to erode.

How soon will it be possible to adapt the non-proliferation strategy to this new fact of life, and what has to be done in that area? This strongly depends upon a thorough investigation of the discovered cases and a proper assessment of the possibility that more have occurred.

IMPROVEMENT OF INTERNATIONAL CREDIBILITY IN EFFECTIVE PHYSICAL PROTECTION

There is still no possibility for independent international verification of the level required for physical protection. Sovereign states make their own assessment of

---

28. "Convention on the Physical Protection of Nuclear Material," legal series, no. 12, IAEA, Vienna, 1982.

the probable threat and scrutinize the adequacy of their physical protection measures. This is the basis for the international assurance of adequate physical protection measures by these states. Bilateral and multilateral cooperation on this sensitive subject exists, but in normal circumstances it is not referred to openly. The findings of high-quality nuclear material in 1994 undermine international confidence in the system solely based on national physical protection.

This unsatisfactory state of affairs should be changed. Progress in international cooperation concerning the safety of civil nuclear installations may serve as an example. In the past, states considered regulations for nuclear safety as being the responsibility of governments. After the Chernobyl accident, however, attitudes have changed: many states have invited IAEA safety teams to visit and advise them on the safety of their nuclear power plants. At the IAEA 1994 General Conference on Tuesday September 20, the Convention on Nuclear Safety was opened by the Director General for signature. By signing the convention, states oblige themselves to meet agreed international standards of nuclear safety and to report on the safety performance achieved.

The issue of physical protection is urgent. Unauthorized removal or misuse of nuclear material is of significance in the context of proliferation by states, and may even become a threat in civil war. It becomes conceivable that the civilized world will have to face more complex proliferation risks, involving activities of sub-national groups which may have international consequences. Their objective is most probably limited to a credible nuclear threat. Various forms of harmful collaboration aimed at nuclear proliferation may occur, between sub-national groups, and even between states or a state and a sub-national group. This means that the subjects of the three sections - physical protection, horizontal proliferation and vertical proliferation - can no longer be treated completely separately.

Vertical Non-Proliferation and Safeguards

NUCLEAR DISARMAMENT

The former Soviet leader Gorbachev and US President Reagan agreed that a nuclear war cannot be won and must never be fought. They started a nuclear disarmament process which requires careful control of both nuclear and non-nuclear components. In the first proposals for controlling the stockpiles of fissile material from these nuclear weapons, a 10 per cent uncertainty has been accepted as reasonable. Since the United States and Russia still possess large numbers of nuclear weapons, the agreement on this high value of relative uncertainty may be considered justified as it helps avoid too large and probably unnecessary safe-guards' expenses. The arrangement, however, introduces another discriminatory element in the relationship between the nuclear haves and the nuclear have-nots, as the latter have to accept lower uncertainty values. This becomes even more important when both have to prove they do not produce nuclear weapons.

As part of its non-proliferation policy, the Clinton administration plans to make the excess highly-enriched uranium (HEU) and plutonium from US weap-ons subject to the US-IAEA Voluntary Safeguards' Agreement.[29] A disadvantage of this agreement is the existence of the right to withdraw nuclear material from the safeguarded inventory. In his policy statement to the United Nations General Assembly of 1993, however, President Clinton indicated that the material should be removed permanently from military use. This would put the American policy in line with the draft of the International Plutonium Storage (IPS) system, which provides for permanent safeguards even after material has been withdrawn from IPS custody. The US has proposed to allow IAEA inspectors to view the weapon components stored at the Department of Energy's Pantex facility near Amarillo, Texas, but under the condition that methods are developed by which the IAEA can credibly verify the material while sensitive weapons' design information is still protected.

In addition, the Americans have also advocated a multilateral convention prohibiting the production of HEU or the separation of plutonium for nuclear weapons (cut-off). The United States will seek broad multilateral support for its approaches, but will be prepared to act unilaterally when necessary.

The dismantlement of nuclear weapons will take many decades. High-quality fissile material will become available for reutilization in civilian nuclear activities, and, arguably, destruction by fission for commercial purposes is the only respon-sible way to deal with the material. Perhaps President Clinton's remark at the UN General Assembly that the released plutonium should not be stockpiled for a long

---

29. M. Hibbs and A. Maclachlan, "US will put IAEA safeguards on 'excess' fissile material," *Nucleonics week*, vol. 34, September 16, 1993, (New York: McGraw-Hill Publication, 1993), pp. 1 and 10-11.

term, may be seen in this context.[30] As a result of nuclear disarmament, large stockpiles of weapons-grade material will be created that have to be protected and safeguarded for a long time.

HIGHLY ENRICHED URANIUM FROM DISMANTLEMENT

The United States has agreed with Russia to buy low-enriched uranium produced by the Russians from 500 tonnes of HEU out of the former Soviet nuclear-weapon program. Initially, annual conversion will consume 10 tonnes of HEU; after five years, this is to be increased to 30 tonnes of HEU each year. The present US nuclear weapon complex will contain at least 250 tonnes of HEU. In total the United States produced 994 tonnes of HEU between 1940 and 1992.[31] Commercial use of all this HEU from dismantled weapons will distort market conditions if conversion and utilization are speeded up. The 500 tonnes of Russian HEU, for instance, correspond with three times the annual world demand for low-enriched uranium. Moreover, the Russian/US deal for HEU pitches the price of the resultant low-enriched uranium at just below market prices.

Part of the American HEU is consumed by the naval propulsion reactors and research reactors in the United States and abroad. The US administration, however, propagates the reduction of the level of enrichment in fuel for research reactors, as part of its non-proliferation policy. This particular policy is counter-productive for two reasons. For one thing, a small number of not yet internationally safeguarded US research reactors and well-safeguarded research reactors outside the United States needs highly enriched fuel for advanced research and for

---

30. For estimates of the world inventory of plutonium and highly enriched uranium, see D. Albright, F. Berkhout and W. Walker, *World inventory of plutonium and highly enriched uranium, 1992,* (Oxford: Oxford University Press for SIPRI, 1993).

31. *Nuclear fuel,* vol. 19, no. 14, July 4, 1994. This figure includes all enrichments above 20%, but it is a more accurate starting point than other estimates in the public domain. Other estimates of HEU are related to weapon-grade uranium. Consumption in naval propulsion, weapons' tests and research reactors in and outside the United States can probably account for about 150 tonnes. But there remains an appreciable stockpile, in the order of 600 tonnes of HEU, of different enrichments outside nuclear weapons. It will be in various forms including irradiated reactor fuel, material not meeting specifications, scraps, discards, and wastes. This is indicative for the complexity of the safeguards verification tasks ahead.

the production of radioactive sources for medical applications.[32] Moreover, as insiders have pointed out, the 20 per cent limit is quite arbitrary. In this lower-enriched fuel more plutonium is formed in small but worrisome amounts. This last point will cause unnecessary extra problems with transport, handling, and recycling or disposal regulations for the irradiated nuclear material.

PLUTONIUM FROM DISMANTLEMENT

Fissioning of the plutonium (and the same applies to HEU) will at least result in 24,000 kWh of heat per gram of material fissioned. This physical fact should render the material commercially attractive, if the societal development around the nuclear fuel-cycle allows its use. Plutonium destruction in existing reactors or specially designed fast reactors will anyhow change the separated plutonium into spent fuel with a fresh amount of fission products. As long as it can be seen as a valuable energy source, the nuclear material will be kept in the commercial fuel cycle and under adequate safeguards and physical protection. If, on the contrary, plutonium is considered as waste, there is no economic incentive to invest in its further protection and safeguards. The logic consequence of the positive attitude of Russia and the negative attitude of the United States of the further use of plutonium makes it impossible to conclude an agreement on Russia's weapon plutonium in the same way as has been done for the HEU. In any scenario, however, the interim storage of this nuclear material from the weapon program will be necessary for a long time.[33]

Recycling and disposal indeed present new problems in the context of large-scale nuclear disarmament. A recent study of proposals to dispose of the expected large quantities of weapons-grade plutonium recommends fixing it together with highly radioactive waste in glass[34] for final geological disposal. This proposal neglects some facts of life. Radioactive fission products are decaying relatively

---

32. The use of highly enriched uranium is imperative for obtaining the highest possible neutron flux density, for example: a more intense irradiation allows the production of a larger amount of short-living radio-isotopes.

33. W. Panofsky, *The management and Disposition of Excess Weapons Plutonium* (US National Academy of Sciences, Committee on International Security and Arms Control, January 1994).

34. Anatoli Diakov, Harold Feiveson, Helen Hunt, Edwin Lyman, Marvin Miller and Frank von Hippel, "Disposition of separated plutonium," *Science & global security*, vol. 3, no. 3-4, March 1993.

rapidly compared to plutonium. The radiation shield by which the fission products protect the plutonium decreases accordingly, which means that the plutonium becomes increasingly accessible again over the years.

The problem of final disposal of radioactive waste has not yet been solved at all. Today's plans are all aimed at retrievable storage. One outstanding objection against final disposal is the long half-life of alpha-emitting nuclides like plutonium. But in the case of retrievable storage, the stored plutonium also becomes increasingly problematic from a proliferation point of view. Its total quantity will not be easily verifiable anymore, as it is mixed together with decaying fission products. If no commercial use is found for this dangerous material, it will probably not get the necessary safeguard attention.

PLUTONIUM AND SUSTAINABILITY

From a perspective of long-term storage feasibilities, then, the US policy to try to convince other states to stop commercial reprocessing is counter-productive. Free development of the peaceful fuel cycle under strict non-proliferation conditions should be maintained, for reasons of principle *and* non-proliferation practice. US scientists have taught others how to reprocess, and strong efforts have been made to perform reprocessing activities in a safe and demonstrably peaceful way, fitting into a reliable MOX fuel-cycle for light-water reactors and more fast-breeder reactors in the future. Recycling plutonium and low-enriched uranium after reprocessing represents a prudent use of the world's natural resources based on an environmental objective to minimize the production of waste. Recycling is preferred in all other areas of industrial enterprise for reasons of environmental conservation. By continuing the reprocessing option, it will be possible to produce for each fissioned atom roughly another fissionable atom out of the abundantly available fertile materials ^{238}U or ^{232}Th. It was with that sustainability perspective in mind that all efforts to develop the civil nuclear-power cycle have been made. Without that perspective the total amount of fissionable uranium in the world that could reasonably be explored would not have justified the large efforts invested.

From a non-proliferation point of view, reprocessing and enrichment are best organized in an international setting. International commercial and technical interdependence and the creation of multinationals like Eurodif and Urenco in the nuclear fuel-cycle have stabilized the proliferation risks of the large-scale application of the sensitive technologies, reprocessing and enrichment.

APPROACHING TOTAL NUCLEAR DISARMAMENT

If and when total disarmament is approached, the uncertainty value accepted for safeguards will have to be carefully revised. Inspections of the civil fuel-cycle of nuclear-weapon states must be performed in order to deter, or detect with timeliness, secret fabrication of nuclear-weapons' material. These inspections can be organized along the procedures of the Chemical Weapons Convention, or full-scope safeguards can be invoked. Since "denuclearized" states will continue to have an appreciable weapons technology, it may be necessary to revise the IAEA safeguards' criteria regarding timeliness and significant quantities. This may still be a remote problem, but that should not keep us from considering ways and means to address it.[35]

And the IAEA again has relevant experience to offer, as it has already been active in helping to install a safeguards' system in states that have voluntarily abandoned their weapons' programs. The application of full-scope safeguards in denuclearizing states serves a clear purpose. Moreover, it will take away one galling form of discrimination in the NPT, which has been used against the Treaty by its antagonists. Gradually building up the system, and adjusting it to the situation within the IAEA international consensus structure, will not, however, be an easy task.

Finally, it must be stressed that adequate measures are still needed in order to be sure that nuclear weapons or their components do not disappear and end up in the hands of unauthorized users. In the civil fuel-cycle, advanced safeguards and physical protection equipment are available. Similar techniques and measures should be applied for all military nuclear material, not only in the five official nuclear-weapon states, but everywhere where more than minute quantities of civil or military weapon-usable nuclear material are present.

---

35. David Fischer, *Stopping the spread of nuclear weapons, the past and the prospects* (London: Routledge, 1992), p. 3. "There is of course no way of disinventing the bomb and it is unlikely that the world will ever re-enter a pre-atomic Garden of Eden. It is not incontrovertibly obvious that we should try to do so; it was no earthly paradise. What is essential is not that distant goals should eventually be reached but that the movement towards them should continue. The last steps on this road will be the most problematic and controversial but there is no need to anticipate difficulties that may lie in the remote future.

To stop the spread of nuclear weapons while nuclear technology expands, it is also essential that nuclear energy outside the nuclear-weapon nations (and increasingly in them) be used for civilian purposes only and that its civilian use be clear for all to see."

Improving IAEA Safeguards with Respect to Uranium-Ore Concentrate

Following the second Gulf War, the disclosure of a large electromagnetic uranium enrichment program in Iraq made clear that the misuse of natural uranium can also lie at the basis of a weaponization endeavor. Safeguards' inspectors and the IAEA could have been well aware of the acquisition and production of natural uranium in Iraq, but it seems that the point had been neglected for many years. The interpretation of the safeguards' rules for that part of the fuel cycle needs to be revised.[36]

INFCIRC/153 Article 34 states that natural uranium has to be placed under full-scope safeguards when the material has reached a composition and purity suitable for fuel fabrication or for being isotopically enriched, and leaves the plant or the process stage in which it has been produced. The article also mentions that reporting on imports and exports of natural uranium is not required if the material is exported or imported for specifically non-nuclear purposes. The word specifically, however, implies that something has to be specified. It had generally been accepted that under the NPT a state is not obliged to report the indigenous production of natural uranium, including its non-nuclear use. The text of Article 34 only suggests that there is nuclear material "subject to safeguards" which lingers before the "starting point" when "the nuclear material shall become subject to the other safeguards' procedures specified in the Agreement." If no obligation is attached to the material it can be used freely for any unknown purpose.

Technically it is, one must assume, possible to use nuclear material in an illicit nuclear-weapon program before it reaches the conditions of the generally accepted "starting point of safeguards." The Smyth Report, which covers developments between 1940 and 1945,[37] hints at the ambiguity introduced by the definition of "starting point." The first reactor by E. Fermi was made critical by using a large amount of cold-pressed uranium oxide powder. This material

---

36. As I have argued elsewhere in a detailed study on the starting point of safeguards. See R.J.S. Harry, "The starting point of IAEA safeguards, aspects of safeguards on ore concentrates," 15th Symposium on safeguards and nuclear material management, Augustinianum, Rome, Italy, May 11-13, 1993.

37. H. DeWolf Smyth, *Atomic energy for military purposes, the official report on the development of the atomic bomb under the auspices of the United States Government, 1940-1945*, (Princeton, NJ: Princeton University Press, 1948).

probably did not meet the high technical specifications of today's fuel fabrication. New types of reactor fuel, and new processes for enriching uranium, will probably use other compounds of uranium, or they can tolerate unusual levels of impurities. These are all characteristics that are difficult to verify by inspectors.

During recent decades various new techniques for isotope separation have been investigated and more or less successfully applied (to name a few: gas-centrifuge, nozzle, stationary wall centrifuge, plasma centrifuge, laser, chemical separation, chemical reaction by isotope selective laser activation). The non-nuclear use of uranium metal has also been developed, for example as radiation shielding, or as counter-weight, and in particular for military purposes as armoring and as armor-penetrating ammunition.

The enrichment route to a nuclear weapon is made more attractive by this evolution. Under the present IAEA practice, unsafeguarded natural uranium can be introduced in an unknown and covert enrichment process without being noticed. Obviously, this implies a major proliferation risk, particularly if highly enriched material can be converted to the metal pieces of a nuclear weapon in a military plant that is normally used to making ammunition that contains uranium. Sometimes reality surpasses fantasy. Several nuclear-threshold states have investigated and some succeeded in their nuclear-weapon ambition by using of uranium enrichment. It might therefore be prudent if the IAEA gives a positive interpretation to the concept "subject to safeguards" that also applies before "the nuclear material shall become subject to the other safeguards' procedures specified in the Agreement."

Arguably, then, a full reporting obligation should be introduced on all natural uranium ore concentrate produced or imported, and a right of the IAEA to inspect this. This does not imply the full application of safeguards as defined in INFCIRC/153 for the more important categories of nuclear material. The system could be quite effective if it follows the same practice as EURATOM does for these materials.

In the EURATOM safeguards' system the producers of uranium ore concentrates have to keep account of their production and despatches, and to report annually.[38] For the IAEA situation an estimation of the involved manpower

---

38. From Commission regulation (EURATOM) No 3227/76 of October 19, 1976, published in the *Official journal of the European Communities* of December 31, 1976, no. L 363.
   Article 29. Any person or undertaking extracting ores on the territory of a Member State shall keep accounting records thereof. These records must indicate, in particular, the tonnage

expected can be derived from the EURATOM experience which has been published regularly.[39] It has been roughly estimated on the basis of EURATOM experience, that for all installations in the world the annual IAEA workload for safeguarding uranium ore concentrate shall on average amount to less than 80 man-days of inspection. The inspection right does not imply the need for a full annual coverage by inspections, but allows for a random sampling approach.

If the IAEA adopts the interpretation that states must submit all nuclear material to safeguards, including reports on all natural uranium ore concentrate that has left the mining and milling stage, and if, consequently, the IAEA has the right to verify the correctness of these reports, the Agency is in a better shape to detect this earliest stage of a weapon acquisition route. Mining and ore concentration generate large quantities of radioactive wastes. These operations might therefore give additional opportunity for detection, for example by aerial survey or by environmental sampling, if the subjected state allows the use of these detection methods. If universal adherence can be reached by a voluntarily accepted obligation to report on all exports and imports of natural uranium and all indigenous production irrespective of use, there remains little chance that undeclared attempts to acquire natural uranium would remain unnoticed.

The type of reduced safeguards' verification described here could also be applied to all nuclear material with low strategic value which is present in large amounts in the fuel cycle, such as natural or unirradiated low-enriched uranium reactor fuel. Under this system, no very detailed extra reporting and inspection burdens on large-size mining and milling activities are necessary. The efficiency of this verification can be improved by using additional free gathering of information, as is applied, for instance, by checking the OPEC member states' oil production levels.

---

and average uranium and thorium content of the ore extracted and of the stock at the mine, and proof of shipment, stating the date, consignee, and quantity. Such records shall be kept for at least five years.

Article 30. No later than the end of January each year, producers of ores shall inform the Commission, in accordance with the form set out in Annex VII, of the amount of material dispatched from each mine during the previous year.

Article 31. Any person or undertaking exporting ores to non-Member States shall inform the Commission thereof, in accordance with the form set out in Annex VII, on the actual date of dispatch.

39. *Safeguards operations report 1989-1990 of the European Commission to the Council and the European Parliament*; SEC(92) 80 def.

Improving IAEA Safeguards with Respect to Detection of Undeclared Nuclear Activities

SPECIAL INSPECTIONS

One of the arguments in the preceding paragraphs was that the IAEA safeguards pursuant to the NPT should cover all nuclear material in all nuclear activities in the non-nuclear-weapon states. Consequently, the declarations of the states have to be complete and the IAEA has the right and obligation to verify this completeness. If suspicion remains, the provision of INFCIRC/153 on special inspections can be applied to discover "undeclared" activities or facilities. These inspections are prescribed if the IAEA concludes that information received is not adequate to allow it to fulfill its responsibilities. The IAEA had until recently never invoked this part of the safeguards' rules. Now, however, its Board has underscored this right, in the understanding that the "special inspection" option will be used only in very rare occasions.

Implementation of special inspections depends very much on the cooperation of the inspected state, as the recent case of North Korea painfully shows. In some other cases where suspicions were raised, the states themselves invited "visits" by IAEA officials to remove suspicion. However desirable, such "visits" can never replace a proper special inspection.

ENVIRONMENTAL MONITORING

After the second Gulf War the United Nations Security Council adopted Resolution 687, giving unprecedented rights to IAEA personnel working in the framework of the United Nations Special Commission (UNSCOM) to deny Iraq any capability that could be used to develop nuclear weapons. Subsequently,[40] the IAEA was asked to develop a plan for future ongoing monitoring and verification of Iraq's compliance with its obligations. This plan includes the application of environmental monitoring techniques to sediments and waterways. The IAEA convened a consultants' group meeting on environmental monitoring in 1993. One of its conclusions was that "the use of a structured environmental sampling program as part of routine safeguards' inspection activities has the potential to

---

40. In UNSC Resolution 715 (1991).

provide a cost-effective and valuable source of information ...."[41] The detection of signs of enrichment or reprocessing is unlikely to provide unambiguous identification of such an undeclared activity. It would, however, focus IAEA attention on particular sites or countries and trigger further investigations. The report also acknowledges that the success of a long-range monitoring program would be improved if supplementary information (for example, supplied by member states) is taken into account.

The expectation that a cost-effective technique can be developed to decide with more confidence that safeguards coverage in a state is complete, may drastically change the general approach to safeguards. It is, for instance, unlikely that a state without a reprocessing capability will try to produce nuclear weapons by diverting irradiated fuel. Safeguards can be adapted to the character of a state's capabilities.[42]

For environmental sampling techniques it is necessary to know what to look for, to sample with careful precautions, and to apply sophisticated analytical techniques. The evaluation should beware of false alarms that could easily discredit outcomes. The environmental sampling techniques have to deal with quite a spectrum of innocent background radiation. The presence of declared nuclear activities in particular will generate higher backgrounds which render long-range detection impossible, even by measurements of nuclear material. Inspectors have to be allowed more intrusive access rights at facilities if the system is to work demonstrably. In the earlier mentioned IAEA safeguards' development, Program 93+2, tests are performed which aim particularly at short-range applications.

Basically, two different routes are available to start an autonomous nuclear-weapon program: the enrichment route and the reactor route. Both have to be checked.

---

41. *Consultants group meeting on environmental monitoring and special analysis methods for safeguards, final report*, (Vienna: IAEA, March 30-April 2, 1993).

42. In a conference paper to the INMM, I have discussed the possibilities for the detection of undeclared nuclear activities, both from the technical side and from an unconventional interpretation of INFCIRC/153. See R.J.S. Harry, "IAEA safeguards and the detection of undeclared nuclear activities," *Nuclear materials management*, vol. XXII, INMM 34th Annual Meeting Proceedings, Scottsdale, Arizona, July 18-21, 1993, pp. 109-14.

THE UNDECLARED ENRICHMENT ROUTE

The enrichment route to a nuclear weapon is short, but very demanding technically. The enrichment plant is currently the only potential "undeclared" stage before weapons' production in a program, in which nuclear material is handled that can be covered under an arrangement of temporary non-application of safeguards for military use, according to Article 14 of INFCIRC/153, or a limited amount of nuclear material that is exempted according to Article 37. Conversion of highly-enriched uranium into metal pieces can be concealed in a military plant where depleted or natural uranium is customarily used for non-nuclear use.

For the production of the first explosive device of simple design, a minimum of 25 kg of ^{235}U contained in highly-enriched uranium is assumed to be required. For safeguards this amount is called the significant quantity. This corresponds with about 5 tonnes of natural uranium as source material, which can easily be stored in a single large transport container. An enrichment capacity of about 5 tonnes separative work is needed.

It is assumed that infra-red satellite observation has a detection limit of a local energy emission of a few megawatts. The energy needed for the aerodynamic and the diffusion enrichment process are nearly equal. Production by these processes of a significant amount of ^{235}U in one year would entail about 12 GWh, or a steady power of 1.4 MW during the whole year. For centrifuge enrichment much less energy is needed: 0.3 GWh, or 35 kW continuously during one year. The last power level, the equivalent of a running car engine, will not attract particular attention.

In the form of uranium hexafluoride (UF_6) the nuclear material involved produces in total about 0.5 x10^6 neutrons per second. It has been assessed[43] that against the natural background at sea level, neutron detection of the UF_6 tails, and product is possible at distances of up to about 100 meters. The conditions for this are that no shielding is applied, and efficient neutron detectors are used. Concealment can be achieved by using small batches of UF_6 and the application of shielding. Comparable results were reported about an experiment to detect nuclear

---

43. J.K. Aaldijk, R.J.S. Harry, J.L. Wieman, J.T. Markin and J.E. Stewart, "Neutron area monitoring in the cascade hall of a centrifuge enrichment plant," Proceedings of the sixth annual symposium on safeguards and nuclear material management, May 14-18, 1984, Venice, Italy, CEC, JRC, Ispra (Va.), *ESARDA* 17, pp. 103-9.

weapons.[44] A neutron background from declared nuclear activities nearby will render the detection possibilities very low when direct inspection access, near to the UF_6-containing equipment, is denied.

If access is obtained to bulk amounts of UF_6, a gamma-spectrum measurement can give an assessment of the degree of enrichment by the enrichment-meter approach, while neutron measurements can give a rough estimate of the amount of UF_6 involved.

For detection by environmental sampling, relatively few possibilities exist. Uranium as such is normally present in the environment. The chemical conversion processes can be hidden in legitimately non-safeguarded activities that apply similar chemical reactants. The annual emission of UF_6 of a 1,000 tonne SW/a centrifuge plant is estimated to be less than 25 grams of uranium. There is an environmental background of natural uranium that further reduces the insignificant chance for detection of deviating isotopic composition. Only if some small representative samples could be obtained, is high-performance mass spectrometry capable of detecting small deviations in isotopic composition.[45] Such deviations have been used to trace differences in the origin of the material, caused by differences in natural isotopic fractionation, nuclear reactions of the uranium isotopes or contamination by non-natural uranium.[46]

The enrichment route to nuclear weapons may be short, but it is also technically complex. The sensitive details of diffusion or centrifuge enrichment technology have never been published. States that have wanted to apply uranium enrichment have had great difficulties in obtaining the equipment and materials to fabricate and operate an unsafeguarded facility. Nuclear suppliers' information might be helpful for the detection of attempts to gather the necessary technology beyond the needs of the declared program. The potentials for this use of additional information are also a subject of the IAEA safeguards' development, Program 93+2.

---

44. S.T. Belyaev, V.I. Lebedev, B.A. Obinyakov, M.V. Zemlyakov, V.A. Ryazantsev and V.M. Armashov, "The use of helicopter-borne neutron detectors to detect nuclear warheads in the USSR-US Black Sea experiment."

45. In the order of 10^{-5} in the $^{234}U/^{238}U$ ratio, and an occurrence of 1.10^{-6} in the $^{236}U/^{238}U$ ratio.

46. K. Mayer, W. De Bolle, A. Alonso and P. de Bièvre, "Accurate determination of isotope abundances in natural uranium of different origins," personal communication.

THE UNDECLARED REACTOR, OR PLUTONIUM ROUTE

The reactor route to a nuclear weapon has always been considered to be technologically more attractive. It can be based on openly published information, and less specialized techniques are necessary. For the fabrication of a significant quantity of 8 kg of ^{239}Pu by neutron irradiation of uranium, about 35 grams of neutrons are required, neglecting losses. At least 8 kg of uranium has to be fissioned for that neutron production. The irradiation has to be followed by a chemical separation step before the significant amount for weapon production becomes available. Because plutonium with a low content of higher nuclides is desired, several times more chemical-separation effort is needed than is usual for reprocessing commercially used reactor fuel.

A fully covert project that intends to produce one significant amount per year needs a natural uranium reactor of at least 25 MW$_{th}$ and a reprocessing capacity in the order of at least 10 tonnes of heavy metal per year. For the reactor, nuclear-grade graphite (several hundreds of tonnes) and/or heavy water (significant amount 20 tonnes D$_2$O$_{eq}$) is necessary, otherwise the reactor needs enriched uranium.

Because of the complexity of this route, there are many more chances for detection. Exchanges of materials, equipment, and experienced personnel between undeclared and declared activities enhance the possibility for safeguards' detection. Only small experimental activities in this area can be hidden successfully in the declared fuel cycle. During the last years, two cases of such hidden experimental small quantities of plutonium production and separation have been reported.

The reactor power level enables detection by infra-red satellite observation. Neutron detection of such an operating reactor is also possible, at a distance of about 100 meters, provided that no legitimate neutron sources are nearby, and no extra neutron shielding has been applied.

The undeclared reprocessing plant is particularly sensitive for environmental monitoring because of various discharges. A declared reprocessing plant operating nearby (within a few kilometers distance), however, renders detection by environmental sampling impossible. There are, moreover, several expensive technical possibilities to conceal the reprocessing activity.

The neutron emission from weapons-grade plutonium enables detection at distances of about 10 meters if the material is unshielded. The large size of the processing equipment, and the emission probabilities of fission products and the chemicals applied in the Pu-route, make this route detection-prone. This applies in particular when inspectors get access, or can at least come close. The background of declared reprocessing activities nearby may disturb detection capability, requiring more intrusive access rules for inspections at declared facilities.

EXOTIC AND FUTURISTIC UNDECLARED ROUTES

Little consideration has been given up until now to the implications of the thorium cycle. This route is less attractive because uranium or plutonium are needed to start a thorium-containing reactor. For the fabrication of a significant quantity of 8 kg ^{233}U by neutron irradiation of thorium, at least 35 grams of neutrons are required. Starting with thorium irradiation, an attractive proliferation route may be the chemical separation of ^{233}Pa, which, with a half-life of 27 days, decays to pure ^{233}U. But relatively more reprocessing effort may be needed than for the more well-known separation of plutonium. The highly radioactive decay chain of ^{232}U-daughter nuclides makes the commercial use of this fuel cycle less appealing.[47] As far as is known, the existing nuclear-weapon states have never used ^{233}U for a nuclear explosive device, although in the United States 1.4 tonnes ^{233}U have been produced in the past.[48]

Strong neutron sources, other than nuclear reactors, are not safeguarded. Scientific research and programs for nuclear transmutation to "burn" actinide waste has rekindled interest in these neutron sources. In the distant future fusion reactors, too, will form a strong neutron source. These sources can be used to irradiate fertile material (thorium or uranium) or actinide waste to create fissile nuclides, which are not covered by the definition of special fissionable material in the IAEA Statute (for example, ^{237}Np and some isotopes of Cm and Cf).[49] These isotopes have attractive fission properties, but because of their radioactive decay are less easy to handle and to convert into a nuclear explosive device. Nevertheless, if available, these isotopes could probably be used to "upgrade" conventional nuclear material. These isotopes are mentioned recurringly in speculations on

47. J.D. Thorn, C.D. John and R.F. Burstall, "Thorium fuel cycles," in W. Marshall (ed.), *Nuclear Power Technology*, vol. 2: Fuel Cycle (Oxford: Clarendon Press, 1983).

48. IAEA: *International nuclear fuel-cycle evaluation: advanced fuel-cycle and reactor concepts*, STI/PUB/534 (Vienna: IAEA, March 1980).

49. G. Kindleben, *Kritikalitätssicherheit*, KTG-Seminar Bd. 3, (Cologne: Verlag TÜV Rheinland, 1986).

advanced nuclear-weapon designs.[50] A non-nuclear-weapon state that has ratified the NPT is less liable to be suspected at an early stage of pursuing a weapons capability. If it succeeds in developing exotic (futuristic or outdated) weapons production technologies, it may succeed in hiding its program until the very last minute, even if it is subjected to advanced safeguards, and then use its newly acquired option to support a deterrent or compellent foreign policy.

Improvement of IAEA Safeguards by Openness and Transparency of the State

Before the February 1992 meeting of the IAEA Board of Governors, Director General Hans Blix said: "Perhaps the broad objective of safeguards may be said to be the creation of a regime of openness and transparency and thereby to create confidence."[51]

Allowing greater inspection freedom on a voluntary basis can contribute to more confidence in the state's adherence to the NPT obligations, with respect to the suspicion of undeclared facilities or activities. Increased confidence might enable a reduction in the area of routine inspections, because some diversion scenarios, such as undeclared reprocessing, become highly incredible.

It has been proposed to give states the opportunity to go far beyond their current obligations to demonstrate that they are not proliferators.[52] New characteristics of openness and virtually unrestricted access for inspectors would be added to build confidence in the conclusions drawn by the IAEA. For that purpose the IAEA should be allowed to use nearly the same tools that the state has at its disposal to demonstrate that there are no clandestine facilities. Of course, it is impossible to give absolute proof of the absence of undeclared facilities, but with

---

50. F. Barnaby, "Red mercury, is there a pure fusion bomb for sale?," *International defense review* 6/1994. This publication also speculates about the option of a fusion weapon that can start without a full fission core.

51. IAEA, "IAEA inspections and Iraq's nuclear capabilities," IAEA/PI/A35E 92-01473 (Vienna: IAEA, April 1992).

52. J.G. McManus and D.B. Sinden, "A new safeguards approach," Proceedings of the 15th Symposium on safeguards and nuclear material management, May 10-13, 1993, Rome, Italy, CEC, JRC, Ispra (Va.), *ESARDA* 26. Also published in *Nuclear materials management*, vol. XXII, INMM 34th Annual Meeting Proceedings, Scottsdale, Arizona, July 18-21, 1993, pp. 19-25.

this openness the IAEA could reasonably conclude so with great confidence. Some limitations on these access rights may remain in the areas of industrial commercial sensitivity, national security and private property. The Convention on Chemical Weapons has provisions of so-called "managed access." A similar provision could allow IAEA inspectors to apply short-range radiation monitoring and environmental monitoring techniques to solve problems in this area.

Unannounced inspections have a higher probability of the detection of undeclared facilities and activities. The Safeguards Agreement currently ties unannounced inspections to the routine inspections at facilities, and in extreme circumstances IAEA inspectors, like citizens or national nuclear inspectors, have the right to move freely in the state, and their free information gathering is not restricted. Publication of a list of "locations outside facilities," that is, of places where relatively small amounts of nuclear material subject to safeguards are present, would add to the transparency already provided by the IAEA' s Annual Report of a list of facilities. Public scrutiny could also support safeguards' implementation.

An assessment performed by the IAEA in the Program 93 + 2 will indicate the effectiveness of this new approach to reach better transparency, and also the costs and safeguards' benefits involved. The traditional counter-argument must be expected: "absence of evidence of undeclared activities is no valid evidence of the absence of undeclared activities." The different monitoring techniques mentioned before, however, can be applied under a scheme of free access for inspectors.[53]

Lessons from the Iraqi Case

Even if full NPT-safeguards are in place, a well-separated and secret military program has little chance of being detected by the interpretation of routine safe-guards that prevailed before the second Gulf War. Iraq's weaponization program illustrates this point sufficiently. The lack of general openness in the Iraqi state and the lack of freedom of information-gathering in Iraq helped to keep a lot of information on the weaponization program secret. What became known before the second Gulf War was of a speculative nature. Before the war, the "excellent"

---

53. As proposed by McManus and Sinden in "A new safeguards approach."

Iraqi cooperation with the IAEA inspectors on their few routine inspections served to keep the inspectors from free additional information-gathering.

A dedicated state with sufficient resources will, in the end, be successful in developing a nuclear weapons' program, even if it is based only on indigenous development. However, it is doubtful that such a program can be kept completely secret. Obtaining materials and equipment externally on a free market has been made more difficult by the continuing improvements in export controls, which now also include dual-use items. Measures to detect secret nuclear weapons' programs have also improved, for example by the developments in environmental monitoring and the systematic information collection on relevant exports and imports, and its analysis.[54] Only if a state can obtain the essential materials for its nuclear weapons' program unsafeguarded from another state, does detection of that program become a completely different job.

The UN Special Commission (UNSCOM) inspections after the second Gulf War are performed on a completely different legal basis than the ordinary safeguards' inspections. But even this important legal support by the United Nations Security Council did not prevent the UNSCOM teams experiencing some disturbing delays in the inspection and access to some crucial information. As also illustrated by North Korea, the denial of prompt IAEA access for special inspections makes it impossible to remove suspicions. Although admittedly some UNSCOM discoveries were based on sheer good luck, the scrutiny of the nuclear material bookkeeping was important in bringing the truth to light.

IAEA safeguards, as in the EURATOM system and formulated in the IAEA Statute,[55] should include the right of unhampered access by inspectors to all places, persons and information, as necessary. The inspectors should also be familiar with the local safeguards' concepts, and with local culture and language.[56] In the present optimization of safeguards, preference is often given to automated equipment. That is all right, as long as it removes some dull routine work from inspectors and frees them for the exercise of their proper job and high skills. In many situations, however, the replacement of intelligent human observa-

---

54. One of the subjects under study in the Program 93+2.
55. Article XII.6.
56. R. Schenkel and W. Kloeckner, "The role of non-quantifiable aspects in nuclear safeguards," *Nuclear materials management*, vol. XXII, INMM 34th Annual Meeting Proceedings, Scottsdale, Arizona, July 18-21, 1993, pp. 303-8.

tion by automated equipment is a loss of important additional inspection possibilities.

The number of inspections allowed according to INFCIRC/153 strongly depends on the total amount of nuclear material present in the facility in question. There is a stepwise increase in the maximum inspection frequency from one inspection per year to fifty or more if the amount of nuclear material increases above 5 effective kilograms.[57] Based on such a formula the state could keep the amount of IAEA inspections drastically lower than required for good safeguards, by distributing the nuclear material over a few small facilities. In fact the inspection frequency was surprisingly low in Iraq, and in other states that have a few declared nuclear activities. In its revised criteria for the planning of inspection activities, the IAEA is now taking into account the sum of all effective kilograms of nuclear material present in a state, in order to erase this loophole.

Nuclear material accountancy, supported by on-the-spot inspections, remain the backbone of all safeguards' systems. Most discoveries in the case of Iraq were made on the spot by inspectors who knew very well what to look for, and who were allowed to pose the right questions to the Iraqis. A scrupulous and persistently repeated analysis of the data and continuing interrogations by the UNSCOM teams were needed in order to get the complete information on all nuclear material, including all source material, in Iraq.

The UNSCOM-IAEA inspections in Iraq illustrate how much inspection work is involved in an open-ended search throughout a state. One year of nuclear inspections involved the equivalent of one-fifth of the world-wide total annual IAEA inspection effort. The inspection teams made use of many specialists for dedicated inspections. The introduction of similar new elements in IAEA inspections will also have financial consequences, which the member states must be willing to bear.[58]

---

57. "Effective kilogram" means a special unit used in safeguarding nuclear material. The quantities expressed in "effective kilograms" allow to compare different kinds of nuclear material. For plutonium and pure ^{235}U it is its weight in kilograms; for uranium it is dependent on the enrichment in such a way that it accounts for the difficulties to enrich or its value for use in a nuclear reactor.

58. Eric Chauvistré, "The implications of IAEA inspections under Security Council Resolution 687," Research Papers no. 11, United Nations Institute for Disarmament Research, Geneva, (New York: United Nations, 1992).

Three Classical Lacunae of IAEA Safeguards

Traditionally, three potential loopholes have been identified in NPT safeguards.[59]

Firstly, inspectors cannot seek out undeclared clandestine facilities, and may overlook them. The discoveries in Iraq showed this. A whole electromagnetic enrichment program, including a special hydroelectric-power dam, had been overlooked by the intelligence community.

Remedies are the reconfirmation of the IAEA right for "special inspections," the voluntary supply of relevant information to the IAEA, the improvement under discussion at the "starting point" of safeguards, the early submission of design information, and the voluntarily engagement to enter into a universal reporting scheme for nuclear material and specified equipment and non-nuclear material. Most of these measures have been agreed quite rapidly since the discoveries in Iraq. They are also aimed at giving the IAEA the possibility to discover a programmatic mismatch in the nuclear activities of the state.

Secondly, the inspectorate cannot follow nuclear material placed in non-proscribed military use, like the nuclear reactor in a submarine. This is still a theoretical problem, but it has to be solved in the near future, when the cut-off of production of nuclear-weapon material by the nuclear-weapon states will necessitate the extension of safeguards. Reactor fuel can be provided[60] with a safeguards' seal that can remain safely on the nuclear fuel elements at all times, even

---

59. L. Scheinman, "Political aspects of NPT safeguards," in R.B. Leachman and P. Althoff (eds), *Preventing nuclear theft: guidelines for industry and government*, Symposium of implementing nuclear safeguards, October 25-27, 1971, Kansas State University (New York: Praeger, 1972).

60. A full load of nuclear fuel elements for the material test reactor, the EU's HFR in Petten, the Netherlands, had once been sealed with ultra-sonic seals from the fabrication plant onwards. The seals allowed verification of the integrity and identity of the nuclear fuel elements. However, the experiment has never been completed properly at the reprocessing end of the life of the nuclear fuel. Another successful application experiment of seals in the reactor core was conducted at the VAK reactor in Germany; see Chr. Brückner, H. Heger, L. Pachl, R. Dennys, J.M. McKenzie, L.A. Suber and J.F. Patterson, "Test of an LWR fuel assembly sealing system in a demonstration experiment at the Kahl experimental nuclear power station," Proceedings of the sixth annual symposium on safeguards and nuclear material management, Cini Foundation, Venice, Italy, May 14-18, 1984, *ESARDA* 17, (Commission of the European Communities, Joint Research Centre Ispra, 1984).

when it is placed in the core of a reactor. So this remaining theoretical problem can be solved.

Thirdly, safeguards cannot meet the problem of denunciation by a state once it has attained a level of sophistication and a stockpile of fissile material enabling it to rapidly convert such material to the manufacture of nuclear weapons. Whatever may be the case, safeguards at least fulfill their function of bringing such a move into international daylight, together with a reasonably correct estimate of the nuclear capabilities of that particular state.

Conclusions

IAEA safeguards have supported the development of international nuclear cooperation. Strong international economic ties around nuclear activities and multinational nuclear industries have grown that have helped to reduce proliferation risks.

Over the years, the focus of non-proliferations concerns has shifted from technologically highly developed states to developing states and sub-national groups. Collusion between states and such groups cannot be ruled out.

It essentially takes a political decision by a state to start a nuclear weapons' program. If the IAEA only applies safeguards to the declared nuclear activities of the state, a secret weaponization program has a chance to go undetected, as in Iraq.

The main function of the IAEA safeguards is to give timely international warning that diversions are occurring from the declared nuclear activities. Increased emphasis on the verification of NPT obligations has led to improvements in the system. Several measures to enhance the detection capabilities of IAEA safeguards, beyond the declared nuclear activities, have been agreed upon. The implementation of other measures is still under discussion, development, or investigation.

Every state that is subject to safeguards has to conclude its own safeguards' agreement, and some improvements can only be accepted on a voluntary basis. Universal adherence to the new elements of safeguards' implementation, however, is still very desirable in order to avoid the creation of a patchwork regime, in which every state can accept its own particular mix of measures.

The support of IAEA member states for strengthening safeguards, both technically and with relevant information from national technical means, is essential. The value of human observation and experience as an element of inspections is of the utmost importance. Increased use of technical measures can ease the inspectors' tasks, so they can better concentrate on relevant issues, but instruments should not replace human observation.

Recent developments in the trafficking of radioactive sources and nuclear material underscore the need for stronger international cooperation on physical protection, including measures covering military installations.

The IPS scheme should be made applicable for the creation of international confidence in the safe, safeguarded and secure storage of the unavoidable stock-piles of nuclear-weapon material that will emerge from dismantlement, as well as the excess amounts of separated plutonium from civil reprocessing.

Strong national policies on non-proliferation should avoid taking recourse to a policy of denial, as was followed during the first decade of the development of the controlled nuclear chain reaction. The "Atoms for Peace" approach of building relations on the basis of supply, and demanding strong guarantees, has been most successful since. The development of more proliferation-resistant nuclear technology has to fit into this development of commercially attractive, safe and reliable nuclear energy for a sustainable future.

7   Proliferation, Threat, and Learning: The International and Domestic Structures of Export

William K. Domke

Introduction: International and Domestic Structures

The pattern of successive national policies and international arrangements aimed at controlling the spread of nuclear weapons follows the evolution of technological and security situations. When separated and ordered, policy initiatives display a record of fairly timely response to security threats perceived from the spread of nuclear technology. The success or failure of policy, be it national or international in scope, is defined in the context of the technological and security challenges at which it was aimed. A process of learning can be observed in the application of policies against proliferation, although the success of a specific policy is qualified by the scope of the proliferation problem targeted. Equally important as a condition of success is the variation in national capabilities dedicated to implement international commitments.

The *international* non-proliferation regime has emphasized multilateral control of nuclear technology transfer. Since the Second World War, the continued evolution of arrangements to deal with the spread of technology has expanded to include both the range of technologies relevant to nuclear proliferation and the principal possessors of that technology in the form of nuclear suppliers. Although too late to deal with some threats of proliferation, the constellation of international institutions in the form of treaties and agreements currently restricts technology transfer.[1] As such, and to the degree that international commitments are imple-

---

1.   For the purpose of this discussion, the concept of proliferation includes numerous behaviors associated with the development of nuclear weapons. Among these behaviors are construction of unsafeguarded nuclear facilities, production of unsafeguarded special materials, research and development of nuclear weapons, testing and development of weapon components, additions to stockpiles of unsafeguarded weapon material, and research and development of delivery systems.

M. van Leeuwen (ed.), The Future of the International Nuclear Non-Proliferation Regime, 205-230.
© 1995 *Kluwer Academic Publishers. Printed in the Netherlands.*

mented by governments, international policy poses a considerable barrier to nuclear technology transfer for weapons purposes.

Parallel to international collaboration, *national* policies and export control instruments have also grown in response to rising threats posed by proliferation. Much of the change in national non-proliferation policy has followed commitments to international agreements, usually but not exclusively led by the US government. As part of its leadership, the US has taken the largest role in periodically defining a shared perception of threat. In addition, democratic governments have increasingly responded to public pressures and demands for action to limit national responsibility for the spread of weapons of mass destruction. When compared, there is wide variation in the approaches taken by governments. National policies must match domestic structure, which includes such factors as the distribution of constitutional authority, regulatory administrative law, business and economic structures, and popular sentiment.

Despite its central role in the defense policies of leading governments, the normative opposition to nuclear weapons can be argued to be widespread and longstanding. This seeming contradiction between nuclear-based national security and alliance strategies, on the one hand, and the policy of non-proliferation on the other, is a contradiction of the post-Second World War security system made practical by reliance on US-extended deterrence. Accordingly, multilateral progress in the control of nuclear technology is very dependent on the overall security environment. In particular, activity and progress in the arms control and disarmament field, or quiescent concerns over the viability of US extended deterrence, create conditions for the advance of the non-proliferation regime. It is therefore not surprising to observe the implementation of international controls during periods of comparative reduction in East-West tensions, when threats in other global regions gain prominence. The strides of the 1990s, for example, coincide with the end of Cold War rivalries.

International and national polices respond to the development of technology. The rapid growth of civilian nuclear power programs, coupled to the development of the attendant enrichment and reprocessing industries, led to successive needs to control and safeguard technology transfer. Safeguards have emerged as a principal mechanism in restricting such transfer, first applied narrowly to uranium, then to facilities holding "special nuclear materials," later to "specially design or prepared equipment," and, most recently, to "dual-use" materials and equipment. Controls over technology and know-how pose the next hurdle for international policy, made difficult by important differences in how national governments can regulate scientific and engineering knowledge.

Government policies also respond to specific perceived threats brought about by the spread of nuclear technology. This was initially obvious in early periods of East-West rivalry, when controls were aimed at preventing the spread of nuclear technology to the Eastern Bloc. Since the mid-1960s, the dangers posed by the spread of nuclear weapons in regional security contexts have dominated the threat posed by nuclear technology transfer. While the Middle East has been the main seat of conflict and proliferation threat, there have been periods when South Asian and, especially today, East Asian regional security have been endangered by the possible appearance of a new nuclear nation.

Taken together, the record of growth of international and national non-proliferation policies represent learning behavior, in the sense that there exists a pattern of continued response to the problems posed by the spread of technology and threat. The effectiveness of policies has been uneven, since they are reactive to threats or problems that have emerged, and this is to be expected. Nonetheless, governments have continued to address in bilateral and multilateral fora the problems of proliferation as they have arisen. It is by no means a perfect record of international problem solving, nor is there a government that can claim an unblemished record of action in stopping the spread of nuclear weapons. When progress and setbacks are weighed, there exists a record of continued sophistication in the implementation of control measures to safeguard against the spread of nuclear weapons.

The Evolution of an International Structure of Policy

URANIUM CONTROLS

Despite the generalization that technological development precedes policies of control, the international control of nuclear technology preceded the completion of the first atomic bomb. On August 19, 1943, the governments of the United States and United Kingdom, with the collaboration of Canada, agreed to a controlling monopoly of uranium.[2] The Quebec Agreement, although a wartime decision, anticipated post-war proliferation threats by focusing controls on the one essential requirement for nuclear weapons, natural uranium. If the Manhattan Project partners could control uranium supplies, then nuclear science and the understanding of weapon physics could advance in the confidence that outsiders would not have access to the feed materials necessary to pursue an enriched uranium or plutonium path to an atomic bomb.

The Quebec Agreement was put into practice by what can be identified as the first institutional element in the nuclear non-proliferation regime. The Combined Development Trust was created in 1944 as a joint supply agency, which gave the three North Atlantic Anglo-Saxon governments a monopoly over uranium. Until additional uranium supplies undermined its effectiveness in the 1950s, such an agreement had a measure of effectiveness. The agreement itself remained in force until 1961, when the abundance of material and the creation of the IAEA safe-guards' system rendered it obsolete.

In addition to the early approach to proliferation through monopoly over uranium, it is noteworthy that the issue of control of sensitive nuclear materials and technology was contemplated at the very outset of the nuclear era. In November 1945, US President Truman, UK Prime Minister Attlee, and Canadian Prime Minister Mackenzie King reached a tripartite agreement on proliferation controls for the three collaborating nuclear programs.[3] At this first international meeting devoted to the issue of controlling nuclear technology, the tripartite monopoly over uranium was reconfirmed.[4] More importantly, the three post-war leaders issued a declaration that recognized that the military and civilian applications of nuclear technology share many methods and processes, and that international commerce requires "effective, reciprocal, and enforceable safeguards." They further proposed that an international commission be set up at the United Nations, a proposal that was accepted by the Soviet Union and resulted in the creation of a UN Atomic Energy Committee, which went on to debate the US Baruch Plan the following year.

---

2. Governing Collaboration between the Authorities of the USA and the UK in the Matter of Tube Alloys.

3. Beginning with this meeting, however, cooperation between the three Anglo-Saxon governments began to wane, and was completely terminated in July 1946 by the US McMahon Act.

4. Bertrand Goldschmidt, *The atomic complex* (La Grange Park, Ill.: American Nuclear Society, 1982), pp. 70-71.

Although the normative opposition to the spread of nuclear weapons was articulated by all the participants in the discussions and postures taken during the debates on the Baruch Plan in the United Nations in 1946 and 1947, actions were already taken to undermine the control system managed by the Anglo-Saxon monopoly of uranium. The Canadian government's decision not to pursue an independent nuclear weapon program did nothing to mollify the perceived need for nuclear weapons by the United States, United Kingdom and Soviet Union.

The explicit emphasis to be placed on nuclear weapons by the United States armed forces, especially in the form of the US Air Force's doctrine of strategic bombardment, was inconsistent with the Baruch Plan's call for restraint and international authority to control nuclear weapons.[5] The exclusion of the United Kingdom from the US program in 1946 soon compelled the UK to undertake an independent weapon program, and in the looming shadow of East-West rivalry, it could not have been a surprise that the Soviet Union had a fully dedicated priority program to acquire the atomic bomb.[6] The detonation of a Soviet nuclear device in October 1949 showed that the monopoly on uranium had had limited effect. That the Soviet test was much sooner than anticipated in the US and UK further showed that a large country could achieve a nuclear-explosives' capability if it was able to devote sufficient resources and was able to find a source of uranium.[7]

The Soviet development of nuclear weapons confronted the US-UK security policy with the direct threat of an emergent nuclear rival. Control of uranium supplies was not an effective restraint, since uranium was discovered to be more abundant than previous recognized. Nations that did not pose a threat to US security interests also worked to undermine the uranium monopoly. In Europe, the French government strongly supported the growth and development of the Commission de l'Energie Atomique and the work of the pre-war pioneers in nuclear science led by Frederic Joliot-Currie.[8] French uranium supplies, heavy

---

5. For an overview of the contents of US strategic doctrines, see Lawrence Freedman, *The evolution of nuclear strategy* (London: Macmillan, 1981), pp. 22-33.

6. David Holloway, *The Soviet Union and the arms race* (New Haven, CT: Yale University Press, 1983), pp. 16-22.

7. Lawrence Freedman, *Intelligence and the Soviet strategic threat* (Princeton, NJ: Princeton University Press, 1977), pp. 63-5.

8. Bertrand Goldschmidt, *Atomic rivals* (New Brunswick, NJ: Rutgers University Press, 1990), pp. 288-99 and 325-37.

water and the reactors that used them were built and operated outside the Anglo-Saxon monopoly.

Other Europeans worked to develop nuclear energy, and their efforts pointed out the limitations of controls on uranium, since much smaller, industrially advanced nations began nuclear research programs.[9] The Norwegians exploited their heavy-water production through the construction of a heavy-water reactor. After they were denied British and French uranium, the Dutch stepped forward with a previously undisclosed stockpile of ten tonnes of uranium purchased before the war, and a new Dutch-Norwegian program could move forward. Likewise, the Swedish government was able to persuade the French government to process uranium mined in Sweden for the research reactor built outside Stockholm.

ATOMS FOR PEACE AND SAFEGUARDED MATERIAL

Nuclear politics gained a primacy in the politics of the 1950s that will probably never be repeated. In foreign policy, extended deterrence and the US nuclear umbrella was a cornerstone of alliance politics.[10] The threat posed from the Soviet Union's nuclear capabilities took on huge proportions by the end of the decade, when talk of a missile gap figured prominently in the 1960 US presidential election.[11] US defense policy came to rely on nuclear technology as the key to mission definition and performance. The US Air Force transformed the ambiguously effective Second World War strategic bombardment doctrines to "war-winning" doctrines of massive retaliation, and the US Army and US Navy sought nuclear missions for their forces. Each service competed to apply nuclear technology in a variety of explosive applications and propulsion for delivery systems, of which the nuclear-powered submarine became most important to deterrence strategy.

In a more narrow European context, the failure of the European Defense Community and the shift in reliance to the Western European Union and the NATO alliance coupled governments with a nuclear-based security policy.[12] The independent British program became closely tied to US nuclear and defense

---

9.   Goldschmidt, *The atomic complex*, pp. 249-52.
10. Freedman, *The evolution of nuclear strategy*, pp. 45-90.
11. Freedman, *Intelligence and the Soviet strategic threat*, pp. 77-80.
12. Catherine M. Kelleher, *Germany and the politics of nuclear weapons* (New York: Columbia University Press, 1975), pp. 33-59.

policies, eventually leading the French government to establish a European alternative through a series of decisions made by governments in the Fourth and Fifth Republics.[13] While sharing the perception of the threat posed by the Soviet Union, French positions challenged Anglo-Saxon leadership in strategy, as they bridled against the uranium monopoly.

Civilian applications advanced rapidly, since the potential use of nuclear technology in power production was a by-product of military development. With the advanced development of US military programs, US firms were ready to assume commercial leadership of a global market for nuclear power and fuelcycle services. President Eisenhower's Atoms for Peace speech at the United Nations in December 1953 was accompanied by changes in the US Atomic Energy Act to remove obstacles to trade and technology exchange. More importantly, in 1956, the US Congress passed legislation asserting requirements for verifications to be made for the export of nuclear materials. As part of the Quebec Agreement's responsibilities, this US bilateral safeguards' system obliged the UK and Canada to develop their own national system of safeguards.

In October 1956, final negotiations took place in New York over the Statute of the International Atomic Energy Agency.[14] The purpose of the institution was, and is, to accelerate and enlarge the use of atomic energy, while seeking to ensure that assistance is not used to further any military program. Its main task is to apply safeguards on peaceful nuclear activities. However, even the narrow focus of safeguards on nuclear materials was made controversial by governments already estranged from the Anglo-Saxon mainstream of international non-proliferation policy.[15] The Indians, with Soviet support, tried unsuccessfully to block safeguards on plutonium, arguing that the man-made isotope was of domestic origin. The French, with Indian support, successfully negotiated that natural uranium would remain unsafeguarded unless it is converted to a form suitable for enrichment or fabrication into fuel elements.[16] Differences between governments were sufficient to prevent agreement on the specifics of IAEA safeguards'

---

13. Michael Harrison, *The reluctant ally* (Baltimore, MD: John Hopkins Press, 1981), pp. 33-7 and 95-8.
14. Lawrence Scheinman, "IAEA: atomic condominium?," in: Robert W. Cox and Harold K. Jacobson (eds), *The anatomy of influence* (New Haven, CT: Yale University Press, 1974), pp. 216-62.
15. Safeguards are to be applied to uranium oxide (UO_2), but not yellowcake (U_3O_8).
16. Goldschmidt, *The atomic complex*, pp. 279-88.

agreements until 1963, when model agreements were reached for research reactors (INFCIRC/61) and fuel-cycle facilities (INFCIRC/66).

The Indian program stands as an example of a program that was not controlled by the system of safeguards created by the US in the mid-1950s and transferred to the IAEA in the early 1960s. Given its early beginnings, even before independence, the Indian program accumulated technology and capability that eventually led to the ability by the Indian government to decide to build and test a nuclear explosive device.[17] Even though the program was not as advanced as the leading military and civilian nuclear programs, the Indian government's position, beginning with Nehru, not to enter into discriminatory agreements allowed it to divert technology to weapons development, which resulted in the test of May 18, 1974.

Neither the Anglo-Saxon monopoly nor the IAEA system of safeguards stopped the transfer of French technology to Israel.[18] However, the Israeli weapon-oriented program stands in contrast to the Indian nuclear technology development effort. Whereas the Indians openly sought to acquire an extensive and expensive civilian nuclear power program to support national economic and technology development, Israel wanted a bomb. More importantly to a nation with much more limited capabilities, the assistance by the French beginning in June 1956 and culminating in the supply of a research reactor and reprocessing facility was critical. An equally, or more serious, collaboration took place between the Soviet Union and People's Republic of China.[19] While the Soviets terminated the collaboration in 1960, by that time much nuclear and engineering technology must have been transferred.

The limits of the IAEA safeguards on nuclear materials were known at the time of finalizing the Statute of the IAEA. The Indian, French and Soviet governments, outsiders to the Anglo-Saxon nuclear marketplace, posed the greatest obstacles to the formation of an effective safeguards' system. Further, the Soviet Union and France served as the sources of unsafeguarded nuclear technology to other programs, in seeming violation of the spirit, if not the letter, of their commitments to stop proliferation as articulated in their membership of the IAEA.

---

17. Rodney W. Jones, "India," in: Jozef Goldblat (ed.), *Non-proliferation* (London: Taylor and Francis, 1985), pp. 101-24.

18. Seymour M. Hersh, *The Samson option* (New York: Random House, 1991), pp. 33-46.

19. John Wilson Lewis and Xue Litai, *China builds the bomb* (Stanford, CA: Stanford University Press, 1988), pp. 60-72.

ARMS CONTROL AND NON-PROLIFERATION

The problems posed by the transfer of technology by the Soviet Union and France were partly solved by changes in the security environment, which served as a necessary preparation for the extension of non-proliferation policy to include the supply of sensitive materials and equipment to unsafeguarded facilities. In looking for the appearance of learning behavior, one can spot changes throughout the 1960s leading to the advance of non-proliferation policy in the form of the NPT. Reductions in East-West tensions helped create a potential for dialog that eventually led to a period of detente. Because it was drafted by the US and Soviet Union, the NPT became an instrumental building block in the arms control record that was to follow. For the US government, the NPT addressed several nagging foreign and security problems. In gaining Soviet adherence to non-proliferation goals, a potential source of technology transfer was stopped, although the Sino-Soviet split had previously taught the Soviet government the dangers of nuclear technology transfer.

The NPT's Article III.2 stipulation that safeguards be applied to exports of "equipment or material specially designed or prepared for the processing, use or production of special fissionable material" stands as a major addition to the breadth of coverage of activities relevant to nuclear weapons' programs.[20] Even if the safeguards are restricted to "special fissionable material," the requirement that *all* non-nuclear weapon-state facilities come under IAEA safeguards is a valuable extension of international controls. That the NPT Nuclear Exporters Committee (Zangger Committee) could, during the period from 1971 to 1974, agree to a set of export control principles and a "trigger list" of sensitive export items is evidence of further sophistication in the international export control regime.

The history of the Zangger Committee, and the Nuclear Suppliers Group (NSG) which followed in 1975, illustrates the process of international learning behavior.[21] Even though it is far from being an institution or even a treaty, the Zangger Committee has met annually in Vienna to review the record of export

---

20. Scheinman, "IAEA: atomic condominium?," pp. 223-4.
21. The Zangger Committee notifications appear as IAEA INFCIRC/209 and the NSG actions are distributed as IAEA INFCIRC/254. See *Nuclear energy agency: the regulation of the nuclear trade*, vol. I (Paris: Organization for Economic Cooperation and Development, 1989).

controls in light of proliferation and technology developments. Chief among its activities has been the periodic refinement of the "trigger list," in order to expand the coverage of sensitive equipment and materials and also to provide better definition of controlled items. Because it is not tied to the NPT, the NSG can address supplier issues that the limits of the NPT language prevent the Zangger Committee from becoming involved. The NSG's incorporation of additional members, most importantly France, and the addition of principles guiding controls over the transfer of technology, as opposed to just equipment, were equally emblematic of learning. India's 1974 nuclear test, combined with the problems posed by French and German sales of facilities to Brazil, Pakistan, and to a lesser extent Iran and Iraq, created a need for the further development of supplier agreements. By the early 1980s, nuclear weapon aspirants could not acquire *direct and open* foreign assistance from the traditional nuclear suppliers.

EXPORT CONTROLS ON DUAL-USE ITEMS

Between the 1978 Nuclear Non-proliferation Act and 1992, the United States stood as the only government controlling the export of dual-use equipment and material on non-proliferation grounds. Despite the desire to push ahead in this direction, the US government's accomplishment in the 1980s was the Missile Technology Control Regime (MTCR), which extended the international regime to include a nuclear delivery vehicle. Even though MTCR can be argued to have gained a life of its own and to have become something of a side show to the nuclear proliferation regime, the 1987 agreement between the G7 governments did include a dual-use annex that provided a "trigger list" of missile-related equipment and technology. The US government's decision to exclude the Soviet Union pointed out the MTCR's inconsistency with the non-proliferation agenda that had developed since the 1960s. Arms control is important to non-proliferation.

A key feature of the MTCR was its implementation of dual-use export controls, which did not produce as much diplomatic rancor as might have been expected. The diplomatic success of the MTCR dual-use annex controls served as a useful precedent when the full disclosure of Iraq's nuclear weapon program called attention to the need to expand the international export control effort to include *nuclear* dual-use equipment and material. The experience of 1991-1992, when negotiations at the April 1992 Warsaw NSG Plenary led to agreement on a

NSG Dual-Use Annex,[22] demonstrates not just a capability to learn from recent mistakes, but also the ability to do so quickly.

The principles guiding the NSG dual-use controls are also broader than in previous agreements. Parties to NSG should not transfer equipment, material, or related technology (1) for use in a nuclear explosive activity, or (2) for use in an unsafeguarded nuclear fuel-cycle activity, or (3) when there is an unacceptable risk of diversion, or (4) when contrary to the objective of averting proliferation. These last two principles go beyond NPT-based controls and provide a fairly open-ended or context-based area for judgment of exports to NPT and non-NPT non-nuclear-weapon states. The May 1993 Declaration of Full-scope Safeguards as a condition of supply for NSG trigger list items, plus the addition of uranium conversion and other enrichment technologies, shows that the NSG has become a dynamic and responsive engine for international collaboration in the control of nuclear trade.

The experience to date of the NSG dual-use export controls is good, but needs a longer period of evaluation. Thus far, information sharing on export license denials has moved ahead. The April 1994 NSG Plenary Meeting called attention to the need to share information about proliferation threats, and to find a "more expeditious means for circulating information among members."[23] Application of the 1993 NSG Declaration on Full-scope Safeguards by the member governments is too new to assess, but if applied literally, it will bring about a trigger-list embargo against non-NPT nations. However, the continued absence of China from both Zangger and NSG constitutes a major hole in the effectiveness of the supplier agreements.

INTERNATIONAL LEARNING BEHAVIOR

The record of multilateral and international non-proliferation policy is mixed. The successes of the post-war international structure of export control can be counted as the number of safeguarded nuclear facilities of the non-nuclear-weapon states that are party to the NPT. Each such facility can be scored in the win column. But it is the threat produced by the failure of policy that properly commands attention. From the perspective of the fitful evolution of the regime, failures must be defined

---

22. INFCIRC/254, Part II.
23. Press Statement, NSG Plenary Meeting, Madrid, April 12-14, 1994.

in the context of the institutional setting of the period. Accordingly, during a time when only materials were controlled through the IAEA safeguards' system, the transfer of turnkey fuel-cycle facilities cannot be judged a failure of the regime. They represent a fault of the system, but they were an omission of policy that was only compensated for later.

The role of US leadership in the development of the international array of institutions and agreements is important to evaluate. From a position of leadership through attempted domination and monopoly, the US government has come habitually to attempt to lead through organization of multilateral efforts. The tendency, or urge, to "call the shots" may still emerge from time to time. Nonetheless, the US government may have learned that it can accomplish more of its goals through inclusion and not exception.

The pattern of change also shows a shift of emphasis from reliance on safeguards to development of more sophisticated export controls. Safeguards are still important, but significant improvements in the IAEA safeguards' system have been hard to come by since the 1971 NPT Model Safeguards' Agreement (IAEA INFCIRC/153). During the last two years, *de facto* improvements have been made in the IAEA safeguards' system, although it is too early to tell whether the gains will be consolidated and institutionalized. In contrast, international refinement of the supplier agreements has picked up speed, partly due to the smaller number of governments, self-selected to cooperate on export controls. And, since the principal suppliers are working together on export controls, greater progress can be noted and should be expected. However, as the supplier agreements expand to include many new emerging suppliers, it may become much more difficult to negotiate changes.

There is room for institutional growth in support of the international structure of export control, and this is true of the United Nations, IAEA, NPT, and the existing supplier groups. Bilateral action has been effective in the past, and will remain a part of international policy. In addition, although EURATOM has found it difficult to push its way into direct authority in the export control area, its safeguards' responsibilities make it an important example for other regional efforts. The absence of a "commanding height" from which to coordinate the activities of governments and multilateral efforts in these institutions is noteworthy, but also represents a problem that presents no easy solution. It exists because today's international non-proliferation system is not a product of design or planning; it is, instead, a result of learning and incremental policy change.

The Domestic Structure of Export Control

In addition to the importance of international policies in coping with the threats of nuclear proliferation are the policies and actions taken by national governments to implement non-proliferation commitments. Except in the case of IAEA safeguards on special nuclear materials, none of the multilateral agreements dealing with the non-proliferation problem possess an enforcement mechanism.[24] And, even in the case of the IAEA safeguards' system, some measure of support by national governments is necessary for the success of the Agency. In the end, the significant components of the international structure are the national elements that bring it to life. Failures of the international system can usually be attributed to the inadequacies or deficiencies of national control efforts and policies.

ELEMENTS OF EXPORT CONTROL

Traditional presentations of the main features of national policy, characterized as export controls, include five elements. First, a government must make the important international commitments through participation in the leading international agreements. At minimum, IAEA and NPT membership are taken as a basic level of support. For governments of nations with significant nuclear supply potential, participation in the Zangger Committee and the Nuclear Suppliers Group is an important commitment to export control.

Second, a government must enact the necessary laws or executive procedures as the basis for legal action. Given the variation in constitutional foundations for modern government, there can be considerable differences in the requirements for national action. The experience of new governments is illustrative. In 1992, the Russian government provided the statutory basis of action for export controls by issuing a series of decrees establishing authority for these regulations and administrative coordination in the form of the Export Control Commission. This took place in the absence of a federal constitution or an atomic energy law. The Polish government, on the other hand, has yet to provide a constitutional basis for action, since the numerous attempts to pass an atomic energy law were missed when successive coalitions failed in office. Among older governments, variations are also great. The German government relies on the Foreign Trade Law,

---

24. Scheinman, "IAEA: atomic condominium?," p. 238.

supplemented by the Atomic Energy Law, while the US government bases statutory responsibilities on a myriad of legislation, including specialized non-proliferation acts and topical amendments to trade and defense legislation.[25]

Third, export controls require the establishment and training of an effective licensing or export review body. Exporting firms and organizations must be educated in the requirements for application, and government agencies must be equipped to evaluate the technical significance of commodities and services. Here again, national variations are considerable. The US government relies on numerous sources of technical review, intelligence community support, and the policy perspective of different agencies. The German government, on the other hand, relies primarily on a single export-licensing bureau to judge export applications. The French and Swedish governments, in managing relationships with a smaller number of supplier firms, rely on the exporting companies to keep them aware of prospective deals to gain the support of the government prior to contracts for sales. In addition, the French government can involve technical experts from its military nuclear program, and the Swedish government can employ expertise developed from the earlier discontinued Swedish nuclear program.

Fourth, enforcement is an essential element in non-proliferation policy. Border controls and customs authority are obvious necessities, without which the management of sensitive technologies is impossible. Weaknesses in this area are frequently recognized by brokers, who exploit these opportunities to make illegal shipments, serving to undermine the international non-proliferation regime. While border and customs regulations are important, a criminal justice system that allows for the punishment of violators of law is equally vital to enforcement.

Fifth, it is generally considered important for governments to share information on proliferation issues, and especially actions taken to deny exports of sensitive technology to countries of proliferation concern. While a good deal of this exchange can take place bilaterally, even through the process of *demarche*, the evolution of information sharing among supplier governments in the context of the annual Zangger Committee meetings, and now in the Nuclear Suppliers Group, has strengthened national export-control administration.

To these five commonly identified elements of export control, others perhaps equally important can be added. A sixth important element of export control is the

---

25. See *Nuclear energy agency: the regulation of the nuclear trade*, vol. II (Paris: Organization for Economic Cooperation and Development, 1989).

existence of cooperation by exporting firms with export control officials and law enforcement bodies. If a government can encourage and facilitate self-regulating behavior by firms and business groups, then export control is made much easier and less expensive. Such a relationship came naturally in centrally planned economies, and to a lesser extent when government ownership extends to the leading exporting companies. In a free-market environment, fostering cooperation is more difficult. If the "good will" of the government is important to profits, conditions exist for close business-government cooperation on export control. The threat of legal action might open doors of cooperation, but is more likely to create an adversarial relationship not conducive to business support for export control.

The seventh element noted here is the role of intelligence data. Because export control licensing requires judgments about the non-proliferation credentials of the recipient country and risk of diversion posed by the end user, access to intelligence data and analysis of foreign nuclear programs is an increasingly important element of export control. Following the export guidelines of the Zangger or NSG agreements, trigger-list export controls must be based on confidence about safeguarded facilities. The NSG dual-use export guideline, restricting the sale of goods if there is unacceptable risk of diversion, can only be implemented if relevant information is available to license reviewers.

The number of necessary or sufficient requirements implemented by governments in the pursuit of export control is not as important as their configuration and suitability to the domestic political structure that translates them into effective public policy. Weaknesses in one area, licensing authority for example, may be compensated for in other areas, such as cooperation with business or an effective criminal justice system. One government's configuration of institutions and statutory regulations is not likely to match that of another government, although history has given some governments similar traditions in law and public administration.

The factors affecting the successful implementation of export controls can be grouped into three areas or types of approaches.[26] If national export control

---

26. The following discussion about patterns of export control administration probably cannot be applied or extended to other areas of public administration. Other comparisons of national differences focus on regulatory laws and institutions, which tend to rest on differences in property rights and features of civil law. Public policy for export control, while part of the same systems of public administration, differs to the extent that rights and responsibilities in the area of international commerce are sometimes addressed specifically in national constitu-

systems were to be rated according to their relative emphasis on the seven variables listed above, the unique combinations of attributes for each nation would be too numerous to enable generalizations to be drawn. Instead, synthesizing the various elements of export control (and there are probably more than seven) into just three characteristic approaches allows for the examination of government patterns or models of export control. Although they are simplifications of the many specific procedures and practices of government and economy, it is possible to develop and judge the relative strengths and weaknesses of consensus, arbitration and collaboration models of export control.

THE CONSENSUS MODEL

A regulatory system requiring review of sensitive exports by numerous official agencies is one that must rely on consensus for controls. Since it is not the nature of governmental agencies to work together to achieve consensus, the importance of national legislation mandating the statutory responsibilities of component agencies and ministries is important to decision-making. Strong laws empower agencies to participate in the export control process. To succeed, mechanisms for dispute resolution must work to bring consensus on overall policy and its application to particular cases. The alternatives are gridlock and barriers to export.

Dispute resolution under these conditions requires the participants to base their judgments and present their cases to other agencies, backed by evidence and analysis to support their position. Data about the sensitivity of the item or technology under review, and the possible risk of diversion to military use, are the important facts that allow agency positions to prevail. Therefore, a consensus model of export control requires a close association with technical evaluation and an intelligence community for success. Failing an extensive use of technical and intelligence data, agency positions will tend to devolve to narrow bureaucratic self-interest, probably defined in budgetary terms.

The United States export control system might serve best to illustrate a consensus-based approach to regulating sensitive exports. Although several other legislative actions shape the requirements for export control, the 1978 Nuclear

---

tions as an issue of national security. Furthermore, the national legislative action is derived from specific foreign trade law (not domestic commerce regulation), export control statutes and regulation (to address national security concerns), and atomic energy laws (for the purpose of nuclear non-proliferation policy).

Non-Proliferation Act (NNPA) specifically mandated inter-agency review in dual-use export licensing. In this area of export control, the Department of Commerce, which serves as the licensing agency, refers all items on the Nuclear Referral List (a seventy-two item list of sensitive items) for inter-agency review. The Departments of Energy, State, and Defense, plus the Nuclear Regulatory Commission and the Arms Control and Disarmament Agency have the opportunity to comment on the case during a period chosen as suitable for review, but not jeopardizing the exporter's contract.

Disputes are first resolved in the Sub-group for Nuclear Export Coordination (SNEC), chaired by the Department of State with the Department of Energy serving as the secretariat. If issues are unresolved, the case is passed to a higher level of political authority with the same representation, the Advisory Committee on Export Policy (ACEP). An agency can choose to resist or block approval of an export, so in the absence of consensus, the issue can be passed to successively higher levels of authority, including the National Security Council, the Cabinet and the President.

Throughout the process in the United States, the various components of the intelligence community are called upon to analyze the potential risks of diversion of the item, while technical evaluations feed the debate. The history of US preoccupation with COCOM, as a mechanism to stop the flow of technology to the Eastern Bloc, illustrates the key role of intelligence to export control. Likewise, the identification of technology transfer with threat supported the political consensus necessary to reach agreement on limiting economic relations.

THE ARBITRATION MODEL

An export control system that places licensing responsibility in the hands of a single review authority or agency can be described as regulation through arbitration. In this model, the responsible government agency is given the task of judging the merits of the case and taking responsibility for its actions. It may solicit technical or expert analysis and ask for the opinions of other officials or agencies, but the positions of other agencies and ministries is advisory, and their approval is not necessary. Should differences exist between agencies or ministries, the non-licensing agency must make an issue of the policy or case at the highest level of authority, typically at a coalition level. An arbitration model might tend to emerge from the existence of a government ruled by a multi-party government coalition, wherein various ministries are held by different parties.

This need not generate differences in policies, but does foster a desire for the independence of administrative authority; put simply, bureaucratic fiefs.

For arbitration to succeed as the mode of export control, the existence of a strong licensing authority buttressed by an effective criminal justice system (including strong border controls) is necessary. Obviously, this model emphasizes the role of a single agency that is staffed and trained adequately to handle independently the review and analysis of license applications. Further, the criminal justice system must be able to conduct investigations that can find violators and bring convictions in the appropriate courts.

The revealed deficiencies of German export controls in the late 1980s point out the importance to export controls that are based on arbitration of both licensing authorities and criminal justice.[27] Since the spring of 1989, when failures in export control became a dominant domestic political issue, the German government has undertaken numerous reforms that not only address deficiencies in arbitration, but also move in directions to improve collaboration with firms and industrial groupings.

The licensing authority, the Federal Export Office (Bundesausfuhramt) of the Federal Economics Office (Bundesamt für Wirtschaft), which is in the Ministry of Economics, has been expanded in personnel and expertise and, perhaps more importantly, has been given greater autonomy in an agency otherwise devoted to export promotion. Equally important improvements have come in the criminal justice system, which now includes harsher penalties for violations and measures aimed at enabling successful prosecutions by local authorities. Furthermore, greater collaboration between investigative agencies will improve detection and enforcement activities. Finally, the implications of changes in border control brought about by the creation of the European Union have caused the Kohl government to push for EU-wide standardization of export controls in order to allow German border authorities to operate in an environment of at least minimum common standards.

---

27. Harald Müller, Matthias Dembinski, Alexander Kelle, and Annette Schaper, *From black sheep to white angel? The new German export control policy* (Frankfurt: Peace Research Institute Frankfurt, 1994).

THE COLLABORATION MODEL

If government relies on a close relationship with exporting businesses to review and discuss pending sales and contracts, then collaboration is a prominent component of export control. In this model, the value of the government's "good will" is sufficiently important to the exporting company to motivate it to self-police its sales activities. The value of "good will" is an obvious by-product of a centrally planned economy, when divergence from government policy based in a Politburo is risky from an economic and political point of view. The "good will" of the government is also important in economies where government is active in industrial policy, which can be defined as the public promotion of advanced exporting sectors. This is further amplified when there is much public ownership of enterprise.

In a collaborative model of export control, there is frequent and regular contact between government licensing officials and exporting firms. Firms that export controlled items often notify government officials prior to concluding contracts. The extent of collaboration may extend into areas of marketing strategies and promotion assistance.

Of the seven elements important to export control, it is readily apparent that positive business behavior is most important to a collaboration model. After all, the exporting firms are policing themselves. Government bureaucracies dedicated to licensing can remain small, yet still be in command of the flow of controlled exports. Likewise, because firms are a prominent part of the export control effort, the criminal justice system need not have many special provisions to seek out and prosecute violators. For most firms, the loss of the government's support and "good will" is punishment enough. In fact, such punishments will probably have greater monetary value to the firm's profitability than might be derived as a penalty from criminal prosecution.

Another important element of collaboration is the maintenance of international commitments to the non-proliferation regime. Demonstrable evidence that national policy requires business participation and support of export controls is important leverage that the government needs to induce collaboration. Governments must take these commitments seriously and agree to principles of behavior that can be offered to exporters as the rules of the road played at home, and by their competitors in other supplier countries.

The administrative procedures of Sweden's export control policy describe a collaborative model.[28] The Inspectorate General of Military Equipment (Krigsmaterielinspektionen, KMI) of the Foreign Trade Department in the Swedish Ministry of Foreign Affairs is staffed by only eight people, who handle license applications for all military-related sensitive exports at a rate of about 2,500 each year. The key to the Swedish system's success is the responsibilities placed on the firm. Exporting companies are expected to meet periodically with the KMI to discuss the market situation and to receive confidential assessments of the government's security concerns. Firms make quarterly reports of sales activities and equipment involved in contract negotiation. A firm must notify KMI four weeks prior to signing a contract for export. A written request for permission to export can be submitted, in addition to submission of a Declaration by End User by the purchasing country's defense authorities. It is only then that an export license application is made.

KMI coordinates the review throughout the period prior to license application. Political examination is initially conducted by the Political Department of the Ministry of Foreign Affairs and the Advisory Board on Exports of Military Equipment, which includes representatives of the political parties seated in parliament. KMI is further assisted in its technical review of exports by the Technical and Scientific Council, comprised of representatives from the leading government-sponsored research establishments, including the National Defense Research Institute, the Aeronautical Research Institute, the Academy of Engineering Sciences, and the Royal Institute of Technology. KMI can remain small because the system places the greater responsibility on the exporting firm. Furthermore, KMI can count on numerous governmental resources for technical evaluation. The prominent role of political parties and the Cabinet in the licensing process points out the importance of the political context of a firm's export behavior.

HYBRID MODELS

Three approaches to successful export control define three models, or characteristic types, based on national structures that emphasize each. This should not disguise the realization that combinations of important elements exist as a rule.

---

28. Sven Hirdman, *Sweden's policy on arms exports* (Stockholm: Utrikesdepartementet, 1989).

Governments undertake policies and programs to alter their location in the artificial three-dimensional conceptual space described here. For example, the US and German governments' outreach programs to industry are attempts to increase collaboration in an export control system that otherwise emphasizes consensus or arbitration. Indeed, as governments commit themselves more and more to the success of export controls, the role of multiple elements of export control increases.

Accordingly, the perfection of export control in an "ideal" model - excellence in consensus, arbitration, and collaboration - is just that, a goal to be pursued without expectation of perfection. In fact, it may be that trade-offs exist. For example, it is probably the case that success in arbitration precludes some level of effort in collaboration with industry.

Other hybrid models exist. Japan's export control system, which gives the Ministry of International Trade and Industry (MITI) a dominant role, represents a combination of arbitration and collaboration. MITI serves as the judge and jury, but its longstanding ties to leading firms through its execution of competition and industrial policy provides the opportunity to collaborate. The French government relies on its close relationship to vertically integrated exporting firms, many of which are owned by the state, to provide a strong collaborative element to export control. In addition, the office of the French President, with its separation of powers from government and parliament, requires that consensus be achieved through presidential leadership.

EMBRYONIC EXPORT CONTROL SYSTEMS

The former governments of the Soviet Bloc (Warsaw Pact or COMECON) have all experienced democratization and liberalization since 1989. In earlier times, these governments could effectively use a simple form of the collaboration model of export control. A small licensing bureau need only keep state monopolies in line with party-based political objectives. Total control of exports could be maintained with a minimum of licensing activity.

A. *The Problem of Russia.* The transition to free-market reforms in the Russian Federation has required a new system of export control. In the absence of a constitution and a legal framework upon which to base statutory authority in the export-control field, policies have been made through the practice of *Ukase*, or Presidential Decree. Through a series of such decrees, an export licensing system has been set up to provide the arbitration necessary for policy. A two-key system has bureaus at the Ministry of Foreign Economic Relations and the Ministry of Economics jointly agree to grant approval of export applications. A strong collaboration dimension is also present, since decisions have been taken to preserve the state's nuclear energy monopoly in the Ministry of Atomic Energy and Science (MINATOM). The extent to which MINATOM is able to control the components of the former Soviet nuclear civilian and military establishment is the extent to which collaboration contributes to export control.

The current weakness in Russian export control stems from the lag between capabilities and the design of the system. MINATOM cannot exert oversight or control over all facilities holding sensitive equipment and materials. During this period of liberalization, there is a semi-feudal structure of industry, signified by overlapping layers of hierarchical authority. In addition, there are independent brokers and agents created to exist outside the monopoly of MINATOM. The stakes for economic survival are high, and improvement may only come from an overall more stable economic situation.

The capabilities of the criminal justice system are also inadequate for supporting the export control system. Great doubts exist about border control. The frequent smuggling of radio-isotopes suggests serious deficiencies, but judgment should await a more detailed investigation of the problems. The quantities of materials seized by German authorities since May 1994 are small, and US or Canadian authorities would probably not detect similar shipments. Indeed, reporting suggests that the materials in question passed through numerous European borders. The problem is broader than just border control. A complete range of investigative activities is necessary to support the Russian export control system.

The prospect for the control of dual-use equipment and material is gloomy until border controls improve. In addition, the investigative capabilities to support criminal prosecutions may have been preserved from the Soviet system, but, for either economic or political reasons, customs and police forces do not seem to have been tested in the area of enforcement of export control regulations. If authorities are not capable of performing investigations, then a Russian system based on a combination of arbitration and collaboration is crippled. Too many exporters will lie outside the monopolies tied to the export control authorities, and few mechanisms will exist to police their activities.

B. *The Problem of Ukraine.* As the Russian Federation has required a new export control system, so has the new Republic of Ukraine. Although Ukraine does not possess the full range of technologies overseen by the NSG trigger list and dual-use annex, it is an industrially advanced economy with many fuel-cycle and nuclear facilities, leaving aside what degree of control exists over former Soviet nuclear warheads based in Ukraine. In short, there are obvious reasons for Ukraine to be a responsible government in the application of export controls.

The absence of export control is a possible position for government. The Ukrainian government has occasionally made positive statements in support of international non-proliferation policy, but the Ukraine is not a yet a party to the NPT[29] nor to the supplier agreements that occurred thereafter. Worse for the prospect of minimal export control, there is no legislative basis for action, and the current distribution of political authority in Kiev makes it difficult to forecast. It follows, then, that there is no central licensing authority nor provisions in the criminal justice system for enforcement of export controls. In the absence of a framework for export control, there is little opportunity to share information with other governments, who see Ukraine as part of the problem and not the solution.

LEARNING AND EXPORT CONTROL

The study of national export control systems shows that change is also common. Unlike international policy, change in administrative policies is constrained by the underlying constitutional and regulatory laws of the nation. The opportunity to "design" export control systems is possible through the overhaul or amendment of key legislation. But we know from government practice, that governments are reactive to problems and, therefore, change occurs as a product of difficulties or embarrassments. That the political stakes can be high is evidence that the issue of export control is close to the heart of security policy. Therefore, changes in political administration and governing coalitions can also change export control policies. In short, within the three-dimensional space described in this chapter, there is frequent movement towards and away from better consensus, arbitration, and collaboration.

Some changes can be mapped according to the models presented above. If there is a cross-national trend, it is because of the improvement of national

---

29. Editor's note: this chapter was submitted before Ukraine ratified the NPT in December 1994.

systems by combining more elements of export control to strengthen the overall effectiveness of policy. The international structure appears to support this trend, since information sharing supports the arbitration dimension by each government, and deepening international commitments support greater collaboration with business. While no government can achieve the ideal position of uniformly strong consensus, arbitration, and collaboration, most governments are improving their abilities in each dimension of export control.

Political Will and Export Control

Whether the focus is on national or international policy, the political will to deal with the problem of nuclear proliferation is essential. The threat to national security or economy may be real, imagined, or potential. Equally, the desire for new export control policy need not be shared by citizens, coalition partners, or foreign allies. Therefore, the decision to act is usually forced on governments that would otherwise devote economic and political resources to other aspects of public administration. When the political will is shared by many governments, progress is possible in advancing the international structure of non-proliferation policy. But even if a government is alone in wanting improvement, much can be done to improve the successful implementation of export controls.

The choice by government to commit itself to the international structure of non-proliferation and export control has been made easy. The development of international institutions and agreements means that a decision to commit to non-proliferation can result in rapid accession to the key international bodies with full participation. Witness the recent actions by the Argentine and South African governments in gaining access to main non-proliferation activities, and contrast this record with that of the Algerian and North Korean governments, whose ambiguous relationship to the NPT and IAEA safeguards' systems leaves room to question their credentials and motivations.

While the political will to perform well in the national administration of export controls is essential, it is not so easy to make progress. Depending on the state of government rule-making capabilities, the road to creation and implementation of even basic licensing measures may be long and tortuous. However, the existing level of performance among the NSG supplier nations is at a historical high point. New adherents will have to struggle to catch up.

The advancement of the international and national structures of export control has reached the point where the political will to curb proliferation can have meaningful results. Today, export controls can do more than slow the spread of technology and buy time for diplomacy and changing circumstances. Export control *is* diplomacy and it changes the circumstances under which technology spreads. The actions of government can stop many proliferation activities, but not all. If the past record reflects light on the future, then the governments engaged in non-proliferation will not learn to live with proliferation threats; they will continue to learn new ways to address new threats and deficiencies of export control.

William K. Domke

Table 1 Summary of dates of policy implementation

	U	SNM	EDP	D-U
Multilateral	1943	1956	1973	1992
International	1956	1965	1973	1992
United States	1943	1956	1973	1978
United Kingdom	1943	1956	1973	1992
USSR/Russia		1965	1973	1992
France	1965	1978	1992	
China		1971	1992	
Canada	1943	1956	1973	1992
Germany		1965	1973	1992
Italy		1965	1973	1992
Japan		1965	1973	1992
Sweden		1965	1973	1992
Argentina		1965	1993	1993
India		1965		
Israel		1965		
South Africa		1965	1993	
Ukraine		(1965)		

U   Uranium controls, dated to monopoly or application of safeguards

SNM   Special Nuclear Materials controls, dated to safeguards' requirements along the lines of INFCIRC/66, 1965

EDP   Especially Designed or Prepared equipment controls, dated to requirements for export licenses for export of items to facilities under IAEA safeguards, as in the Zangger Committee

D-U   Dual-use equipment and materials controls, dated to requirements for export licenses for export of dual-use items at risk for diversion, as in the NSG Dual Use Annex.

8 CTBT and NPT: An Essential Linkage?

Jan Th. Hoekema

Introduction

In the run-up to the Conference to review and extend the Nuclear Non-Proliferation Treaty in April 1995, the issue of a Comprehensive Test Ban Treaty has taken on special significance. Many nations, both parties and non-parties to the NPT, have for a long time already attached special importance to the idea of a comprehensive ban as a yardstick to measure "progress" towards the realization of the goals of the NPT, or at least those goals connected to nuclear disarmament (notably Article VI of the Treaty and the NPT preambular paragraph on changing the 1963 Partial Test Ban Treaty (PTBT) into a comprehensive ban). And so have many academic authors and commentators, especially those with a "left-wing" perspective (if that epithet is still applicable ...).[1]

In this brief paper I will analyze whether this special role for the CTBT in nuclear non-proliferation is still warranted. In doing so, I will concentrate mainly on two questions:

a) Is a comprehensive test ban essential to the chances of survival for the NPT? and

b) Is a comprehensive test ban an effective means against proliferation?

I will also pay some attention to a third question: will nuclear weapons' reductions by recognized nuclear powers make proliferation more attractive to some threshold countries? This last question is loosely connected to the first two, which in my view are at the core of the problem before us.

---

1. For a concise historical survey, see Jozef Goldblat, *Arms control: a guide to negotiations and agreements* (London: Sage for the International Peace Research Institute Oslo, 1994), pp. 40-52.

M. van Leeuwen (ed.), The Future of the International Nuclear Non-Proliferation Regime, 231-241.
© 1995 *Kluwer Academic Publishers. Printed in the Netherlands.*

THE TREATY AND THE TEST BAN

In answering the question whether a comprehensive ban is essential for the survival of the Non-Proliferation Treaty my thesis would be that it is not, as far as the *substance* of nuclear non-proliferation is concerned, but that it could be essential from the point of view of conference *tactics and strategy* in 1995 and possibly beyond. This arguments needs some elaboration.

The cessation of all nuclear tests in all environments and the conclusion of a CTBT have been longstanding wishes for a large part of the world community, not only to prevent radioactive contamination of the environment, but also to put a halt to, or to slow down, vertical proliferation, both quantitatively and qualitatively. This twofold goal was laid down as early as 1963, when the Partial Test Ban Treaty was concluded.

Over the years, the environmental and arms control benefits of a CTBT have been emphasized to varying degrees. With safety and environmental conditions of underground tests in the United States steadfastly improving, attention shifted to the French open air tests in the Pacific (France did not sign the Partial Test Ban Treaty), and later on the hazards of the more primitive and powerful tests in the former Soviet Union.

As far as the arms control aspects are concerned, the belief that a comprehensive test ban is the best means to end - to "suffocate" - the nuclear arms race was held for a long time, and is still held by many. A majority of states that are party to the Non-Proliferation Treaty, notably from the non-aligned group, and a number of vocal non-parties, have been pressing for an early conclusion of a CTBT as a means to assure the forced disappearance of nuclear weapons from the arsenals of the five nuclear-weapon states under the NPT. For the NPT parties another, politically motivated, argument played a role. A complete test ban would in their view signify as well an end to the discrimination between nuclear-weapon states and non-nuclear-weapon states, which has been embodied in the NPT and which has been seen as a fundamental flaw. In all honesty, it has to be acknowledged that this argument contains some political symbolism, because an end to testing is associated in a rather too direct way with nuclear disarmament and the addition of nuclear weapons. Nevertheless, the argument carried a lot of weight for a long time.

It is interesting to observe that these arguments have been forcefully used, irrespective, to some extent, of relevant developments in the area of nuclear arms control. These developments were, in essence, twofold. First of all, reductions of the nuclear arsenals of notably the - then - two superpowers formed part of the pattern of relationships between them, despite the Cold War. For more than two decades, long- and intermediate-range nuclear weapons (SALT, START, INF), as well as short-range nuclear weapons, were the subject of intensive negotiations, agreements and unilateral reduction measures by the United States and the Union of Soviet Socialist Republics. Assuming that international security trends continue in the same direction, it is not too bold to expect that at the end of the century only a minimum stock of nuclear weapons will be left as a sort of life insurance, possibly aimed at "rogue" states within the NPT fold or outside of it which have (nuclear) ambitions that broach the interests of Washington (and Moscow). It can be expected that these arsenals will remain at the disposal of the nuclear-weapon states; further into the future one could envisage the UN (Security Council) as the only legitimate possessor of these arsenals. Furthermore, other measures improving confidence and stability, like retargeting - admittedly politically motivated and reversible - nuclear warheads, have greatly lessened the role of nuclear weapons at the present time.

One could, therefore, argue that the CTBT, in its original role as a device to cap, limit and bring down nuclear weapons to (almost) zero, has been taken over by events, or more precisely, a managed decline of the nuclear stocks. However, it is necessary to point to the fact that the arsenals of the other three nuclear powers are not (yet) subject to negotiated reductions. A comprehensive ban to which the United Kingdom, France and China would adhere would therefore still have relevance in practice. China, especially, is a case in point; the country has a sizeable nuclear arsenal and continues to conduct tests, despite American, British, Russian and French moratoria on nuclear tests.[2] It is therefore no surprise that China, in particular, reacts warily to present efforts to reach a speedy conclusion of a Comprehensive Test Ban Treaty in Geneva via negotiations in the Ad Hoc Committee on a Nuclear Test Ban installed by the Conference on Disarmament (CD). In that forum it has presented several proposals that are controversial and which complicate the achievement of consensus, such as an insertion into the Treaty text of a no-first-use declaration by nuclear-weapon states, and the exclusion of "peaceful" nuclear explosions from the proposed ban.

---

2. It recently performed tests in October 1993, June 1994 and September 1994.

Tests and Simulations

A second, not so much political but practical, reason why, in my view, a CTBT has lost some, if not much, of its significance, is the fact that nuclear explosions can be simulated much better than in the past. Countries can either produce a nuclear bomb without, or almost without, testing (Israel, Pakistan), or maintain the reliability of their stockpile by computer-simulated explosions in laboratories. Furthermore, countries can credibly play with the nuclear option entirely without testing, but merely by hinting at a nuclear capacity (Iraq, Libya, North Korea). In the paragraphs below on the effectiveness of a CTBT as a non-proliferation tool, I will dwell further on this point because of its relevance to the question of how important a CTBT would be for the survival of the Non-Proliferation Treaty.

The CTBT as a Negotiations' Gambit

Starting from the differentiation between the "substantive" and "strategic" importance of a Comprehensive Test Ban Treaty for the survival of the Non-Proliferation Treaty, it can be argued that the test ban issue will continue to play a "strategic" role, as it will still be seen as a litmus test for the success of the NPT review conference(s). Only as late as 1990 the conference broke down on the CTBT issue, despite the fact that at that time the argument could already be made that nuclear reductions were obviating the need for a CTBT as a means to check the arms race. In 1995, as in 1990, the CTBT controversy may prove to be a stumbling block although, as far as the decision on extension is concerned, the conferences have very different rules of procedure. In 1990 the consensus rule was applicable. A single country could prevent the adoption of a final statement concluding a review conference. In 1995, however, the decision to extend the NPT can be taken by a majority of votes. Technically, therefore, no state has a veto right on extension. From a political point of view, however, an extension decision arrived at by consensus will be much more powerful and telling than a decision taken by majority vote in the face of opposition of important parties to the Treaty. Advocates of indefinite extension, therefore, have been trying hard to reach such a consensus. Much depends on conference diplomacy and personalities. It cannot be ruled out that the CTBT issue will be used as a political gambit at the review and extension conference - and beyond. Starting from the assumption that a Comprehensive Test Ban Treaty will not be finalized in the spring of

1995, even though the negotiations in the CD Ad Hoc Committee have made significant progress, it is possible that non-aligned, and even some "progressive" Western countries like the Scandinavians and Australia, will demand a comprehensive ban as a prerequisite for indefinite extension. To reverse the argument, some nuclear-weapon states, for instance the United Kingdom and France, have played with the thought to condition their support for a CTBT on a vote by the non-aligned and the "progressive Westerners" for an indefinite extension of the NPT.

Other countries advocating a CTBT will, in my view very reasonably, argue that there is now, for the first time, a real prospect that a Comprehensive Test Ban Treaty will be concluded. Only some years ago a ban seemed a long way off; the United States under President Bush wanted a CTBT only on certain specified conditions (related to the arms reduction process) and, at a later stage, kept open the option of a (limited) number of tests for safety and reliability purposes. Only President Clinton went ahead to install a moratorium on tests, depending on the behavior of the other nuclear-weapon states. The UK also suspended testing (its test sites being located in the United States), and French President Mitterrand followed suit in spite of strong opposition from political and military quarters. The Russian Federation, always a verbal proponent of a CTBT, was more or less forced to enunciate a moratorium after Kazakhstan - where the former Soviet Union's main test sites had been located - had become independent and raised objections to testing, also for environmental reasons. The great strides made in this field were demonstrated by the fact that for the first time in history, a resolution supporting multilateral negotiations on the conclusion of a Comprehensive Test Ban Treaty in an Ad Hoc Committee of the CD was adopted unanimously by the General Assembly in the fall of 1993. The consensus text was co-sponsored by 156 states and visibly demonstrated the dramatically changed scenery in the international arena, where in the past the CTBT resolutions in the United Nations General Assembly's plenary and in its First Committee gave rise to bitter dispute and strongly divided voting patterns (an overwhelming number of "yes" votes and a small but significant number of "no" votes of most of the nuclear-weapon states.) The political breakthrough of 1993 led to the start of negotiations on a CTBT in Geneva in 1994, some fifteen years after the earlier trilateral talks between the United States, the United Kingdom and the Soviet Union on a complete ban broke down, mostly for political reasons.

CTBT Negotiations in Geneva, 1994

In 1994, three negotiating sessions of the Ad Hoc Committee on a Nuclear Test Ban and its two Working Groups on Verification and Legal and Institutional Issues were held in Geneva. In September, when the third and last official CD session of the year was closed, a heavily bracketed rolling draft text presented by the Mexican chairman, Marin Bosch, illustrated the progress made and the difficulties still waiting ahead. Optimism prevailed about the eventual feasibility of a Treaty, but at the same time it had become increasingly unlikely that a Treaty could be reached before the NPT conference starts in April 1995.

First, disagreement had arisen on the scope of a ban, and the need for explicitly defining the "nuclear explosion" concept. Including a definition might well be counter-productive as it could indicate ways to evade the ban. Several questions were raised in this connection. What tests, if any, should still be allowed? The People's Republic of China wanted to exclude "peaceful" explosions from the Treaty - a point of view not supported except by some non-aligned countries. The United States, the United Kingdom, France and Russia wanted to exclude hydro-nuclear tests from a ban, arguing that such tests do not involve a detonation, although they do produce a nuclear yield. If hydro-nuclear tests were allowed, this would complicate verification of the Treaty, as such tests are difficult to distinguish from "ordinary," banned low-yield tests. Then, should computer simulations be counted as tests and brought under the Treaty? Various non-aligned states argued in favor while nuclear-weapon states opposed inclusion. Verification would in this case be virtually impossible.

Secondly, no agreement had been reached on the scope of an initial verification regime. All negotiating parties could agree that the verification system should be based on international seismic monitoring supported by on-site inspections, but application of various other techniques (radio-nuclide, infra-sound, hydro-acoustic and satellite) remained controversial with regard to their effectiveness in relation to their costliness.

Other remaining questions were: must test sites be dismantled, closed or monitored? The nuclear-weapon states argued against, the non-aligned countries were in favor. Must preparations for testing be explicitly included in a ban? The prevailing view was negative. Which organization should be made responsible for verification - the IAEA or a new agency? The United States, China and Australia argued in favor of a new agency. The prevailing view became that a new agency should be created, located in Vienna and loosely associated with the IAEA without being under its supervision. What should be the procedure for the Treaty's entry into force - should there be an explicit list implying a veto for a single or a few obstinate countries? Or should there be a less defined formula? How could especially significant countries, threshold countries, for instance, be included? Should there be a withdrawal clause and, if so, what conditions ought to govern withdrawal? To the surprise and concern of many others, the United States proposed a fairly easy withdrawal procedure after ten years.[3] There was wide agreement, however, that the duration of the Treaty should be indefinite.

The "Cut-Off" Concept

Recently, proposals to achieve a global cessation of the production of weapons-grade fissile material ("cut-off") have been put forward in tandem with proposals for a Comprehensive Test Ban Treaty. These proposals terminated a long period during which the "cut-off" concept was at best dormant, with Canada and the Netherlands tabling a United Nations General Assembly resolution asking for a study on the subject by the Geneva Conference on Disarmament. The CD did not take up the issue out of lack of consensus on the subject. The United States, especially, has during the past two years advocated a "cut-off" with renewed energy. Its bilateral talks with countries like Israel, India and Pakistan have not met with much success so far, but in the fall of 1993 the General Assembly of the United Nations welcomed President Clinton's "cut-off" proposal with great enthusiasm. The Assembly adopted a resolution by consensus to have the Committee on Disarmament prepare negotiations on a treaty that banned the production of fissile material for nuclear weapons or other nuclear explosive devices. The follow-up in the CD, however, has been much less propitious. The appointed Special Coordinator had to report after more than six months of efforts that diplomats proved unable even to formulate a generally acceptable negotiating mandate concerning a "cut-off." In particular, it proved to be very difficult to reach an agreement on whether the negotiations should include existing stockpiles as well as a prohibition on future production of fissile material.[4] The nuclear-weapon states opposed inclusion, while many other delegations felt that existing

---

3. This position has been attributed to controversies within the various US departments involved in preparations for the CD negotiations.
4. At the time of writing, no agreement had yet been reached.

stockpiles were at least as important as future ones. Several non-aligned countries wanted explicit reference to existing stockpiles. For obvious reasons concerning their uneasy relationship with nuclear-capable neighbors, Pakistan and Iran were especially adamant on this score. Others argued that the subject could be discussed during negotiations without it being formally included in the mandate.

Likely Effects on the 1995 Conference

In sum, with regard to the CTBT issue, the playing field of the 1995 NPT Review and Extension Conference could differ noticeably from the earlier battles between strong, unconditional proponents of a test ban at the earliest occasion and those, the United States first in line, pleading for a careful, balanced "step-by-step" approach, where a comprehensive ban fits into a more encompassing process of nuclear arms control and reductions. For now and the near future, the discussion is likely to concentrate, rather, on timing and modalities of the Convention. As to the first aspect, I have already indicated that it is unlikely that a Comprehensive Test Ban Treaty will be concluded by spring 1995, but the *perspective* for a Treaty by, for instance, 1996 (the date mentioned by President Clinton) could be maintained in a credible way. The question is: will the most uncompromising states allow themselves to be convinced to drop their maximalist demand of a CTBT as a condition for their positive decision on an indefinite extension of the NPT?

In weighing these factors, states will also bear in mind other related arms control aspects, such as the prospects for a "cut-off" in the production of fissile material for nuclear weapons' purposes mentioned earlier. Although negotiations on a "cut-off" have not yet really begun, the prospect of a negotiated "cut-off" treaty is there. Combined with a perspective on a CTBT in 1996/1997 (although one should not underestimate the difficulties entailed in defining the scope and exact parameters of the ban, the involvement of China and "difficult" non-aligned countries such as India and Pakistan) and the present state of nuclear reductions, one could be rather optimistic about the role the CTBT will play in the 1995 conference. Still, nations could, for whatever reason, decide that only the maximum (a negotiated complete ban) counts and/or that a CTBT should be used as a tool to arrive at more far-reaching goals which, from the point of view of the nuclear-weapon states would be even more objectionable than over-ambitious schemes concerning the timing of a test ban, such as a complete elimination of all nuclear weapons by the year 2000. For the conference itself this would complicate decision-making, in the sense that some might be attracted to only a brief extension and not an indefinite, unconditional extension, as forwarded by many Western countries.

A CTBT as a Non-Proliferation Instrument

The question of whether a CTBT is an effective means against proliferation has already been partially answered above. I should now qualify my implicit negative reply by pointing out the potential differences in this respect between vertical and horizontal proliferation. Until recently, a CTBT seemed rather effective to counter vertical proliferation, because nuclear tests were deemed necessary to improve existing weapons and to develop new, more modern nuclear weapons. Although the testing programs and results of the nuclear-weapon states are not publicly disclosed, it is to be assumed that both modernization and maintenance of warheads were for a long time heavily dependent upon testing of both nuclear and non-nuclear components. Now that simulations and laboratory tests are capable of doing the same thing, a CTBT looks both less relevant and at the same time more feasible. In my view, this paradox is the core of the CTBT issue before us in the 1990s.

A caveat is appropriate here: the techniques of simulation, etc., are best developed in the United States and to some extent in the Russian Federation. France is trying to come to grips with the latest techniques, which explains its somewhat reluctant position on the different test moratoria by the nuclear-weapon states; of course the political color of the present government - and President! - should also be taken into account.[5] China has its own particular point of view: first the other four, then us. The United Kingdom is dependent upon the technical facilities (test sites) in the United States and, therefore, its view (almost) entirely coincides with that of the US. In any case, France and China are the least enthusiastic for an early CTBT. These parameters may, however, be subject to change. The French presidential elections, after the NPT review conference, are a case in point; so is the offer made by the United States to China to transfer and assist in demolition techniques and materials.

---

5. Editor's note: this chapter was submitted in the fall of 1994.

Hence, the usefulness of a CTBT in halting *vertical* proliferation becomes more and more limited, a fact which deprives the test ban of at least part of its original meaning. To combat *horizontal* proliferation, the effectiveness of a CTBT has always been questionable at least. Only one proliferator (India) conducted a "peaceful nuclear explosion" (in 1974), leaving aside the famous, mysterious double flash over the South Atlantic Ocean in 1979. Threshold countries such as Israel, South Africa, Pakistan and North Korea have in all probability developed their nuclear weapons without staging tests.

Here, again, the point can be made that a CTBT will contribute more to positive political atmospherics than to effective non-proliferation. Other measures (political, technical, economic, export control) that are needed to fight the spread of nuclear weapons in practice are dealt with elsewhere in this publication. In sum, by concluding and agreeing on a Comprehensive Test Ban Treaty, the nuclear-weapon states would mainly signal that they, too, take seriously the concern of non-nuclear-weapon states for non-proliferation and nuclear arms reductions as combined and interrelated policy goals.

Will Nuclear Arms Reductions Stimulate Horizontal Proliferation?

Lastly, the question of whether nuclear-weapon reductions by the recognized (five) nuclear powers would make proliferation more attractive to some threshold countries. This question, I think, should be answered in the negative. This is especially the case in the present circumstances where the nuclear-weapon states still possess both sizeable nuclear arsenals and a wide array of (very precise!) means of delivery and, in more general terms, a deterrent capability, including modern smart conventional weapons (cruise missiles, for instance), which is well suited to the successful projection of military power far from the homeland.

In other words, threshold countries are not likely to be influenced in their decision "to go nuclear" or to create the - possibly ambiguous (North Korea!) - option of going nuclear by the level of reductions by the five. These countries will probably be more motivated by political and security considerations directly relevant to them, than by the vertical nuclear restraint of the nuclear-weapon states. This could possibly change over a longer period when reductions would approach zero and the deterrent capability would hereby be greatly damaged; combined with a zero level for tests and production of nuclear material (by a CTBT and a cut-off), a state might be lured into a security gamble by playing with the nuclear option. All in all I consider this option as improbable, because of the power projection/deterrent capability of the big powers, in which nuclear weapons anyway tend to play a lesser role than used to be the case. On top of that, missile defense will further decrease the attractiveness of nuclear attacks, at least in the traditional mode (for example, Israel versus Iraq in the Gulf War).

Conclusions

The CTBT has over the years taken on a highly political and symbolic significance as an unmet promise contained in the arms control Treaties of the 1960s (PTBT and NPT); at the same time its realization would effectively terminate a fifty-year period of nuclear testing and, by that, mark "the end of an era." While its effects on the quality and effectiveness of the remaining stockpile would be less substantial than in the past because of the great technological strides made by the nuclear member states and the US in particular, the coincidence of at least the perspective of a Treaty and the NPT Review and Extension Conference in 1995 could be extremely beneficial. If well played and negotiated, this could be a decisive factor in bringing together the true NPT believers on the Northern side and the more politically motivated other non-aligned countries; politically, because many of these latter countries also perceive the NPT's continuation to serve their security, but still find difficulty in accepting its indefinite extension. The NPT's discrimination between haves and have-nots is both essential for the Treaty and a barrier for truly wholehearted support by all of the international community. Nuclear weapons have by their nature a highly symbolic character. With reductions and a test ban well on their way, the pain of further acceptance of the two categories, nuclear-weapon states and non-nuclear-weapon states, could be greatly softened.

9   Security Guarantees and the Role of the UN Security Council

Mohamed I. Shaker

Introduction

For many years, and until the present time, a distinction has been made between two types of nuclear guarantees, namely positive and negative guarantees, the first meaning an offer for the protection against the use, or threat of use, of nuclear weapons, and the second meaning an undertaking not to use or threaten to use nuclear weapons.

The creation of the Nuclear Non-Proliferation Treaty sharpened the issue of nuclear guarantees in a manner not experienced in the pre-NPT negotiating phase. Non-nuclear-weapon states contemplating their adherence to the NPT were seriously worried about their own security in a world which had not yet banned nuclear weapons altogether. Twenty-five years after the NPT entered into force, nations are still struggling with the two types of guarantees, hoping that fair and credible guarantees could be agreed upon, an event which would bolster the non-proliferation regime and contribute to the longevity of the NPT.

The ongoing efforts seem to concentrate on the updating of Security Council Resolution 255 of 1968 and on an international convention banning the use or threat of use of nuclear weapons. This is unfortunate in that the division between positive and negative guarantees is a fictitious one, as they are two sides of the same coin, and therefore can both be addressed by means of one instrument, as will be explained later, I will first follow the traditional approach of differentiating between the so-called positive and negative guarantees. Security Council Resolution 255, which has so far been categorized as a positive guarantee, will be dealt with under the section on Security Council Guarantees in this chapter, with a view to investigating a possibility of transforming and not just updating Security Council Resolution 255 into a vehicle for all inclusive security guarantees whether positive or negative.

M. van Leeuwen (ed.), The Future of the International Nuclear Non-Proliferation Regime, 243-272.
© 1995 Kluwer Academic Publishers. Printed in the Netherlands.

Positive Guarantees

Several forms of positive guarantees have been contemplated. The main forms are alliance relationships, international multilateral agreements, formal undertakings in the NPT, and declarations.

FORMAL ALLIANCES

Joining an alliance such as NATO or the Warsaw Pact, or entering into a formal bilateral arrangement with a nuclear-weapon state, were possible alternatives for non-nuclear-weapon states wishing to guarantee their security whether in conjunction with the NPT or otherwise.

NATO, however, merely provides that if an attack occurs against one or more NATO parties, each of the parties will take, individually and in concert with other parties, "such action as it deems necessary, including the use of armed force, to restore and maintain the security of the North Atlantic area."[1] There is no explicit formal guarantee of a nuclear response.

In the case of the former members of the defunct Warsaw Pact and their recent affiliation with NATO, it is quite obvious that they also do not benefit from any explicit nuclear guarantee under NATO.

With regard to the neutral and the non-aligned states, we need not underline the well-known hostility of this category of states to any formal alliance links with a nuclear-weapon state.

Bilateral guarantees are particularly discarded by the non-aligned states. For them, nuclear disarmament is best for their security. For example, in the aftermath of China's first nuclear explosion in October 1964, even India opted for nuclear disarmament, after some indications that it might be interested in obtaining a joint guarantee from both the United States and the Soviet Union.[2] Ten years later, India openly exploded its only "peaceful nuclear device."

Another interesting case is that of Israel, which cooperates closely with the United States on strategic matters, a cooperation that by its very existence extends

---

1. Article 5 of the North Atlantic Treaty.
2. Shelton L. Williams, *The US, India and the bomb*, Studies in International Affairs, no. 12 (Baltimore, MD: Johns Hopkins University, 1969), p. 50.

some form of assurances to Israel in spite of the fact that Israel is known to have developed a nuclear-weapon option a long time ago.[3]

INTERNATIONAL MULTILATERAL AGREEMENTS

This form of guarantees was favored by the non-aligned states if the guarantees were offered by all the major nuclear powers in a way that would not affect their non-aligned status.[4] It was propagated at the Conference of Non-Nuclear-Weapon States held in Geneva a few weeks after the NPT was opened for signature on July 1, 1968, but with no avail.

AN NPT UNDERTAKING

Nigeria was the only state during NPT negotiations to have suggested a formal undertaking on positive guarantees in the text of the NPT. The guarantees were to be offered *on request* by any non-nuclear-weapon state that is party to the NPT and is threatened or attacked with nuclear weapons.[5] Nigeria then had no confidence in the Security Council as a guarantor against aggression with nuclear weapons.

The Nigerian proposal had a cool reception. On the one hand, the two superpowers seemed reluctant to commit themselves beyond the context of their alliances. On the other hand, the non-aligned states hesitated to accept any provision which would affect their non-aligned status in any way. Nigeria many years later put forward a major proposal prescribing an international agreement on non-use or threat of use of nuclear weapons, which we shall deal with shortly under the section on negative guarantees.

DECLARATIONS

Unilateral pledges made by US President Johnson during the early phases of NPT negotiations in 1966 left the impression that the United States might act individually on a world-wide scale as a guarantor of nuclear peace. However, it turned out

---

3. There is a rich literature on this aspect. One of the recent books on the subject is William E. Burrows and Robert Windrem, *Critical mass* (New York: Simon & Schuster, 1994).
4. UN Doc. A/6817, September 19, 1967, Aun. IV, pp. 7-9.
5. Doc. ENDC/202, November 2, 1967, Article II-A; and ENDC/220/Rev. 1, March 14, 1968.

to be a pledge that the United States was ready to undertake in concert with others and in the context of the United Nations to support a non-nuclear-weapon state threatened with the use of nuclear weapons.

The idea of pledges or declarations was followed up in later phases of NPT negotiations and served as a basis for the three declarations made by Depository Governments of the NPT, the United States, the United Kingdom and the Soviet Union (Russia) at the Security Council and in conjunction with Security Council Resolution 255 of 1968. They will be examined later in this chapter.

Another declaration of certain significance is the Trilateral Statement by the Presidents of the United States, Russia and Ukraine in Moscow on January 14, 1994, in which they reaffirmed their commitment to seek immediate UN Security Council action to provide assistance to Ukraine, as a non-nuclear-weapon state that is party to the NPT, if Ukraine should become victim of an act of aggression or object of a threat of aggression in which nuclear weapons are used.[6] It is clear that these positive security guarantees are drawn directly from security guarantees made by the three Depository Nuclear-Weapon States in 1968. The statements do not come into effect until Ukraine joins the NPT. Consultations had been held with the United Kingdom, which is prepared to offer the same security guarantees to Ukraine once it becomes a non-nuclear-weapon state that is party to the NPT.

Negative Guarantees

Several forms of negative guarantees have also been contemplated. The main forms are prohibition of use or threat of use of nuclear weapons by means of a convention or an international agreement, declarations, an article in the NPT or a protocol attached to it and denuclearization.

A CONVENTION OR AN INTERNATIONAL AGREEMENT

A convention as a means of prohibiting the use, or threat of use, of nuclear weapons had been promoted and supported by the former Soviet Union since the mid-1940s when the United States had the monopoly of nuclear weapons. Soviet

---

6. See Selected Documents from the US-Russian Summit, *Arms control today*, January/February 1994, p. 21, hereinafter referred to as Selected Documents.

interest in a convention continued even after its ascendancy to nuclear-weapon status in 1949.

The United States was then not willing to give up the right to use nuclear weapons at a time when the Soviet Union was preponderant in conventional weapons and enjoying great influence in Eastern and Central Europe.

The Non-Aligned Movement had adopted the concept of a convention since the Tenth Special Session of the UN General Assembly which in 1978 was devoted to disarmament. The Movement, through its members in the Conference on Disarmament in Geneva, continued to support it as the best means for the prohibition of the use of nuclear weapons. The 1993 and the 1994 Report of the Ad Hoc Committee on Effective International Arrangements to Assure Non-Nuclear-Weapon States Against the Use or Threat of Use of Nuclear Weapons of the Conference on Disarmament clearly indicated the preference of the non-aligned members of the Conference: the conclusion of negative security assurances in the form of a multilaterally negotiated Treaty.[7]

The Non-Aligned Ministerial Conference in Cairo, June 1994, urged the Conference on Disarmament to negotiate, as a matter of priority, an international convention prohibiting the use or threat of use of nuclear weapons under any circumstances.[8]

The most outstanding proposal for an international agreement was put forward by Nigeria at the fourth NPT Review Conference in 1990. According to Articles I and II of the proposed agreement, each nuclear-weapon state that is party to it would undertake not to use or threaten to use nuclear weapons against any non-nuclear-weapon state that is also party to the NPT and which does not belong to a military alliance and does not have other security arrangements providing for mutual defense with a nuclear-weapon state. The undertaking of non-use or threat of use would also benefit non-nuclear-weapon states party to the NPT which belong to a military alliance, or have other security arrangements providing for mutual defense, with a nuclear-weapon state but have no nuclear weapons stationed on their territories.[9] Nigeria had also called for the convening of a conference which would approve such an agreement.

---

7. Doc. CD/1219, August 25, 1993, p. 2, and Doc. CD/SA/CRP.26/Rev. 3, August 29, 1994, p. 3.
8. Final Document of the Eleventh Ministerial Conference of the Movement of the Non-Aligned Countries, May 31-June 3, 1994, Cairo, Egypt, NAC./M.11/Doc.1, para. 36.
9. Doc. NPT/CONF.IV/17, June 1, 1990.

The proposal has not been successful so far. It is, however, still on the table, as Nigeria continues to refer to it in the aforementioned Ad Hoc Committee on security assurances of the Conference on Disarmament.

The United States and some of its allies do not seem ready yet to accept such a sweeping undertaking in an international agreement, in spite of the dramatic changes that Europe has witnessed in the last few years which led to the dismantling of the Soviet Union and the request by East and Central European states to be affiliated with NATO.

The stalemate on a convention or agreement led me to suggest almost two years ago *an interim measure* which borrows from the safeguards' system applied by the International Atomic Energy Agency in accordance with Article III of the NPT. This article requires the non-nuclear-weapon states party to the Treaty to conclude safeguards' agreements with the IAEA to meet the requirements of the NPT, either individually or together with other states. In negotiating such agreements the Agency and the parties are guided by the document worked out by the IAEA which constitutes a model safeguards' agreement, later known as the "blue book."

With regard to negative security assurances, then, why should it not be possible to contemplate a model security guarantees' agreement to be negotiated by the parties to the NPT? It would serve the parties individually or collectively in guaranteeing for themselves security guarantees provided by the nuclear-weapon states party to the Treaty whether individually or collectively. As is the case with the safeguards' agreements, security assurances agreements based on the model could vary slightly with different countries, or groups of countries, without jeopardizing the uniformity generally needed to make such guarantees acceptable and credible. This idea would overcome the difficulties facing certain nuclear-weapon states, difficulties that prevent them, for the time being, from assuming a sweeping non-use obligation of a general nature, beneficial to all.[10]

The model agreement could be simple and straightforward. It could be negotiated within the Ad Hoc Committee on security assurances of the Conference on Disarmament and later sanctioned by the Security Council.

---

10. Mohamed I. Shaker, "The 1995 NPT Extension Conference: A rejoinder," *Security dialogue*, vol. 23, no. 4, December 1992, p. 35. The proposal will be further developed in the light of remarks and observations received.

DECLARATIONS

Because of the difficulties of reaching an agreement on negotiating a convention, all the five nuclear-weapon states have made separate unilateral declarations in which they undertake not to use or threaten to use nuclear weapons against certain states and in certain circumstances. No need to say that they vary in certain degrees.

China, on the occasion of its first nuclear explosion on October 16, 1964, was the first to solemnly declare that at no time and in no circumstances will it be the first to use nuclear weapons.[11] This declaration was reiterated on many occasions and in the Tenth Special Session of the UN General Assembly devoted to disarmament in 1978. At that session the other four nuclear-weapon states made their unilateral declarations, which more or less all remain as the main sources of negative guarantees by the nuclear-weapon states.

It would be useful to recall the 1978 declarations by the five nuclear-weapon states, as they would be instrumental in devising Security Council guarantees as we shall endeavor to explain later.

China, in reiterating its position never to be the first to use nuclear weapons, favored a non-use agreement. In April 1982 China added that "it undertakes unconditionally not to use or threaten to use nuclear weapons against non-nuclear countries and nuclear-free zones."

The Soviet Union declared that it would never use nuclear weapons against those countries where there were no such weapons at present and called upon the other nuclear powers to do the same. In June 1982, it added that it had assumed an obligation not to be the first to use nuclear weapons.

The United States undertook not to use nuclear weapons against any non-nuclear-weapon state that is party to the NPT or any comparable internationally binding commitment not to acquire nuclear explosive devices, except in the case of an attack on the United States, its territories or armed forces, or its allies, by such a state allied to a nuclear-weapon state or associated with a nuclear-weapon state in carrying out or sustaining the attack.

The United Kingdom made a similar declaration to that of the United States. It formally gave the assurance to non-nuclear-weapon states that were parties to the NPT or other internationally binding commitments not to manufacture or acquire

---

11. *Peking review*, vol. VIII, no. 43, October 23, 1966, p. 6.

nuclear explosive devices, that it would not use nuclear weapons against such states except in the case of an actual attack on the United Kingdom, its dependant territories, its armed forces or its allies by such a state in association or alliance with a nuclear-weapon state.

France's declaration precluded any use or threat of use of nuclear weapons against states that were part of nuclear-free zones. France was in favor of case-by-case guarantees rather than an all-inclusive declaration. In June 1982, France expanded its negative security guarantees and announced that "it will not use nuclear arms against a state that does not have them and that has pledged not to seek them, except if an act of aggression is carried out in association or alliance with a nuclear-weapon state against France or against a state with which France has a security commitment."[12]

On many occasions, the credibility of unilateral declarations was questioned by the non-nuclear-weapon states. The predominant view is that they do not constitute legally binding commitments. Unilateral declarations can be changed at the will of the guarantor state.

Before moving to the other forms of negative guarantees, I refer once more to the Trilateral Statement by the Presidents of the United States, Russia and Ukraine in Moscow on January 14, 1994, in which Presidents Clinton and Yeltsin reaffirmed, in the case of Ukraine, their commitment not to use nuclear weapons against any non-nuclear-weapon state that is party to the NPT, except in the case of an attack on themselves, their territories or dependant territories, their armed forces, or their allies, by such a state in association or alliance with a nuclear-weapon state. As mentioned earlier, consultations had been held with the United Kingdom, the third Depositary Government of the NPT, which is prepared to offer the same security guarantees to Ukraine once it becomes a non-nuclear-weapon state and party to the NPT.[13] The remarkable aspect about this agreement is that, as each of the nuclear-weapon states had a different formula in its unilateral declarations on negative guarantees, they are for the first time harmonized with regard to one country. Needless to say that the guarantees to Ukraine by the three nuclear-weapon states will not be in force until it adheres to the

---

12. *The United Nations disarmament year book*, vol. 3, 1978, pp. 164-5 and chapter XI; and *Nuclear issues on the agenda of the conference on disarmament* (New York: United Nations, 1991), UNIDIR/91/68, pp. 6-9.

13. Selected documents, *op. cit.*, p. 21.

NPT.[14] As noted by one analyst, Ukraine's guarantees are closest to what the United Kingdom put forward in 1978.[15]

Moreover, in the US and North Korean statement agreed in Geneva on August 13, 1994, the United States, in order to help achieve peace and security on a nuclear-free Korean Peninsula, pointed out that it is prepared to provide North Korea with assurances against the threat or use of nuclear weapons by the US. North Korea also pointed out that it remains prepared to implement the North-South Joint Declaration on the Denuclearization of the Korean Peninsula.

AN ARTICLE IN THE NPT OR A PROTOCOL ATTACHED TO IT

During the NPT negotiations in the 1960s at the Conference of the Eighteen-Nation Committee on Disarmament (ENDC), all attempts to include an article in the NPT on negative security guarantees failed. The three outstanding proposals in this regard were put forward by the Soviet Union (the Kosygin proposal), the United Arab Republic (Egypt) and Romania.

The Soviet and Egyptian proposals were almost identical, except that the latter was based on a widely supported UN General Assembly resolution in 1966. The guarantee offered was limited to parties to the NPT provided they had no nuclear weapons on their territory.

The Romanian proposal was to benefit non-nuclear-weapon states undertaking not to manufacture or acquire nuclear weapons. The proposal also included an undertaking by the states that are party to the NPT to establish an appropriate procedure through the Security Council to ensure that the guarantee would be fulfilled. It tried to meet the objections raised by the NATO allies with regard to the Kosygin proposal, which was generally looked upon as aiming at the Federal Republic of Germany which had nuclear weapons on its territory.

The United States's reluctance to include an article in the NPT was related to its general strategic conception and more particularly to its determination to retain its freedom of action in Europe. At the First NPT Review Conference in 1975, Romania did not give up its attempts to introduce negative guarantees but this time in the form of a protocol on non-use attached to the NPT. The United States

14. Editor's note: this chapter was submitted before Ukraine ratified the NPT in December 1994.
15. Jack Mendleson, Deputy Director of the Arms Control Association (Washington, DC), "Prospects for Ukranian denuclearization after the Moscow Trilateral Statement," *Arms control today*, vol. 24, no. 2, March 1994, p. 23.

and the United Kingdom objected to such an idea, which was in line with their objection to an article in the NPT.[16]

The idea of protocols attached to the NPT on that issue or others was later objected to by the Depository Governments of the NPT, on the basis that they would be tantamount to amendments to the Treaty, to be introduced through the complicated procedures prescribed by Article VIII of the NPT for amending the Treaty. However, the idea of a protocol on negative security guarantees attached to the NPT is re-emerging again at the Conference on Disarmament in Geneva, as an alternative to, or pending the conclusion of, an international convention. Some members of the Conference on Disarmament do not seem deterred by the procedural argument against their approach.

DENUCLEARIZATION

In the present circumstances, it seems to us that the best vehicle for the introduction of negative security guarantees would be through the establishment of nuclear-weapon-free zones, as demonstrated by the 1967 Treaty of Tlatelolco establishing a nuclear-weapon-free zone in Latin America. Additional Protocol II of that Treaty, whereby the five nuclear-weapon states undertook not to use or threaten to use nuclear weapons against the contracting parties of the Treaty, has inspired similar initiatives in other regions of the world.

Protocol II of the Treaty of Rarotonga, establishing a nuclear-weapon-free zone in the South Pacific, and Protocol I of the draft treaty on an African nuclear-weapon-free zone, which is not expected to be signed before 1995,[17] include similar undertakings to that of the Treaty of Tlatelolco, although it must be admitted that Protocol II of the Treaty of Rarotonga has not yet been signed by all the nuclear-weapon states.

The revitalized peace process in the Middle East offers a chance for the establishment of a nuclear-weapon-free zone or a zone free of weapons of mass destruction in the Middle East, which can provide security guarantees similar to those provided by the other zones referred to above. The 1990 UN study on a nuclear-weapon-free zone in the Middle East encouraged such an approach

---

16. For a detailed discussion of the different proposals on an article or a protocol, see Mohamed I. Shaker, *The Nuclear Non-Proliferation Treaty: origin and implementation* (Dobbs Ferry, NY: Oceana Publications, 1980), pp. 496-502.

17. See Organization of African Unity (OAU), doc. POL/IACPH/23/6.94.

without hesitation.[18] It is hoped that the working group on arms control and regional security of the multilateral track of the Middle East peace process will soon have a chance to discuss and examine thoroughly all aspects pertaining to the establishment of a nuclear-weapon-free zone in the Middle East. The Israelis seem reluctant so far to enter into such an exercise. They should be encouraged to open up on this issue.

Nations embarking on the establishment of other nuclear-weapon-free zones should learn from the experience of others in negotiating their treaties and attached protocols. They ought to avoid pitfalls such as the transit of nuclear weapons through their zones, the extension of territorial waters beyond reasonable limits and the presence of foreign defense bases. Statements made by some nuclear-weapon states upon signature of Additional Protocol II of the Treaty of Tlatelolco underlined the difficulties with such aspects.[19]

Potential breakthroughs with regard to new nuclear-weapon-free zones, which are the most feasible approach so far on negative security guarantees, should not preclude nations from contemplating a universal approach such as the one promoted by the Non-Aligned Movement for an international convention on non-use or a renewed UN Security Council resolution. A universal approach should mean that security guarantees must be uniform, unconditional and legally binding. This brings us to Security Council guarantees.

Security Council Guarantees

In the course of our analysis of negative security guarantees, it clearly appears that there are high expectations for a strengthened role to be played by the Security Council on non-proliferation issues, including the offering of not only so-called positive security guarantees, for which Security Council Resolution 255 has so far been dubbed, but also negative security guarantees.

The Security Council role has been asserted in the last few years as a guarantor of international peace and security, although not always successfully. With regard to non-proliferation, the Security Council record is not bad. It took a strong stand and a unanimous one against Israel's attack on the Iraqi's nuclear

---

18. UN Doc. A/45/435, October 10, 1990.
19. For examples, see UN Doc. A/9137, August 30, 1973 (China); and *SIPRI yearbook 1979*, pp. 618-9 (USSR).

facilities in June 1981. Again on Iraq, its Resolution 687 of 1990 on the dismantling of all weapons of mass destruction in Iraq through the United Nations Special Commission on Iraq (UNSCOM), and in collaboration with the IAEA, is another example of the resourceful potentials of the Security Council. In the case of NPT non-compliance by the Democratic People's Republic of Korea, the Council did not hesitate to deal with the crisis, although efforts exerted outside the Council by the United States to rectify the situation have also been going on and have been favored by the latter.

Most outstanding is the statement made by the President of the Security Council (United Kingdom Prime Minister John Major) on behalf of its members at the conclusion of the meeting held at the level of Heads of State and Government on January 31, 1992 in connection with "The responsibility of the Security Council in the maintenance of international peace and security." Under the title disarmament, arms control and weapons of mass destruction, the members of the Council considered that "the proliferation of all weapons of mass destruction constitutes a threat to international peace and security." The statement in this respect is of unprecedented value and should be read in the context of the whole statement, which aims at enhancing the role of the Security Council in the preservation of peace and security.[20]

With regard to security guarantees, Security Council Resolution 255 still stands, together with the declarations made in the Council by the three Depository Governments of the NPT in conjunction with the resolution, as the only guarantees provided by the Council. These are, as indicated earlier, usually dubbed as positive guarantees, although in my view they imply negative guarantees as well, as will be explained later.

Security Council Resolution 255 has not generated full confidence in its effectiveness and even its overall credibility. Proposals were put forward to update it and enhance its credibility, and even to transform it into an instrument for explicit and not implied negative guarantees. The two outstanding proposals in this respect are put forward by Egypt and two scholars and former American and Russian diplomats, George Bunn and Roland Timerbaev. But before embarking on an examination of their proposals, a brief analysis of Security Council Resolution 255 is required in order to appreciate the shortcomings of the Resolution and the remedies needed to render it effective and credible.

---

20. UN Doc. S/23500, January 31, 1992.

(1) Security Council Resolution 255 of 1968

THE GUARANTOR STATES

The guarantor states are the Depository Governments of the NPT, that is Russia, the United Kingdom and the United States, the three nuclear-weapon states which made identical declarations in the Security Council.[21] France abstained in the vote on the ground that nuclear disarmament was the only way to overcome the danger of nuclear weapons. In adhering to the NPT in 1992, France did not make a declaration in the Council in conjunction with Security Council Resolution 255 similar to those made by the Depository Governments. The People's Republic of China was not yet represented in the United Nations when Security Council Resolution 255 was adopted. Basically, the resolution was aimed at China, a fact which was deplored by many states at the UN General Assembly and the Security Council. Against this background, it was not expected that China, in adhering to the NPT in 1992, would make any declaration in conjunction with Security Council Resolution 255. We shall revert to this point later.

Each of the three declarations is made conditional on the others. It is virtually a joint or a collective guarantee. Although the political significance of the three states acting in concert should not be underestimated, the presupposition that the three would always have a common interest in acting together might be far-fetched. A veto by one of them, or by one of the other two permanent members of the Council, would paralyze any action by the Council, which in principle is the main guarantor of world peace and security.

THE GUARANTEED STATES

Although some of the provisions of the three Declarations and Security Council Resolution 255 appear as generally applicable to all states, regardless of their individual attitudes towards the NPT, the latter is the *raison d'être* of the Declarations and the Resolution, and therefore only parties to the NPT would qualify for Security Council guarantees. Objections were raised by some non-aligned states

---

21. The following brief analysis is based on Mohamed I. Shaker, *Nuclear Non-Proliferation Treaty*, chapter 8, pp. 527-52.

against the discriminating nature of the Declarations and the Resolution on the basis that the UN Charter and its Articles 1, 2, 24, 39 should apply to all.

STATES AGAINST WHOM SECURITY GUARANTEES COULD BE INVOLVED

As earlier indicated, the circumstances in which the Declarations were made and the Resolution was adopted left no doubt that they were mainly aimed at the People's Republic of China, which exploded its first nuclear device on October 16, 1964 and was not represented in the Security Council at that time.

However, we have to distinguish between three categories of states: the guarantor states themselves, that is, the Depository Governments, the other nuclear-weapon states that are members of the Security Council, China and France, and the potential nuclear-weapon powers.

With regard to the first category, it is quite obvious that the foundation of Security Council Resolution 255 would be seriously compromised if one of the guarantor states were to commit an act inconsistent with its obligations.

With regard to China and France, which are latecomers to the NPT, the focus was on China as a potential aggressor, a matter which was deplored by the non-aligned states. China vehemently attacked the Resolution even before it was adopted. France at the time stated that nuclear weapons were only for defense and that France did not intend to use them either to threaten or to attack anyone. It must be said, however, that since the Resolution's adoption, the relations between all the nuclear-weapon states have undergone tremendous changes, to the extent that it is safe to say that the Resolution has lost its validity with regard to China, if it had one from the beginning.

If there is any justification for Security Council Resolution 255 and the Declarations associated with it, it has to be with regard to potential nuclear powers. South Africa in the past, and India after its "peaceful explosion" of May 18, 1974, were mentioned as potential nuclear powers. Israel also figures in the statements of Arab states.

The Declarations and the Resolution could operate as a deterrent against states that were contemplating the acquisition of a nuclear-weapon capability. Such acquisition might, by itself, be considered as a threat justifying involving Security Council Resolution 255, whether the potential nuclear power is a party or not to the NPT. In this respect, it ought to be noted that in the case of the weapons of mass destruction found in Iraq in the aftermath of the Gulf War, and in the case of NPT non-compliance by the Democratic People's Republic of Korea, there were no references to Security Council Resolution 255 in the Security Council's Resolution 687 of 1991 on Iraq, or in the Security Council's Resolution 825 of 1993 and the statement made by the President of the Security Council on May 30, 1994 about the Democratic People's Republic of Korea.

Actions or Threats Against which Security Guarantees could be Invoked

The actions and threats against which Security Council guarantees could be invoked are only aggression with nuclear weapons and the threat of such aggression. It falls upon the Security Council to determine whether an aggression by nuclear weapons or the threat of such aggression occurred. This seems to be the preliminary conclusion that the Security Council would have to reach before taking an action, and this would not be an easy conclusion to reach, taking into consideration the difficulties encountered over the years at the UN in defining aggression. As to the threat of aggression with nuclear weapons, it seems that the threat has to be explicit in pointing out the possibility of using nuclear weapons.

THE RESPONSE

Security Council Resolution 255 envisages certain responses stated in its three operative paragraphs:

First, the Security Council recognizes that aggression with nuclear weapons or the threat of such aggression against a non-nuclear-weapon state would create a situation in which the Security Council, and above all its nuclear-weapon state permanent members, would have to act immediately in accordance with their obligations under the United Nations Charter.

The corresponding provisions in each of the three Declarations are more detailed. They describe the situation in which the Security Council would have to act as a qualitatively new situation.The immediate action would be through the Security Council, and its objective would be to take the necessary measures to counter or suppress such aggression, or to remove the threat of aggression, in accordance with the UN Charter from which provisions of Article 1, paragraph 1, calling for "effective collective measures" are quoted.

This type of response drew skepticism on the part of some states which had little or no confidence in the possibility of an immediate action by the Council.

The Security Council also welcomes the intention expressed by certain states that they will provide or support immediate assistance, in accordance with the Charter, to any non-nuclear-weapon state party to the NPT that is victim of an act, or an object of a threat of aggression, in which nuclear weapons are used. The corresponding provision in each of the three Declarations made by these "certain states," that is, the former Soviet Union, the United Kingdom and the United States, as permanent members of the Security Council, is more specific in indicating that it is Security Council action which will be sought immediately in order to provide assistance.

The second operative paragraph was criticized because of the ambiguity of the word "intention" in contrast with the legally binding obligation of the UN Charter to come to the assistance of a victim of aggression, in accordance with a decision of the Security Council. It is also criticized because it was not clear what kind of assistance was offered; whether it was instant nuclear retaliation, diplomatic pressure, or a series of warning resolutions. In the view of some, retaliatory measures should have clearly been defined for the purpose of the NPT.

Third, the Security Council moreover reaffirms in particular the inherent right, recognized under Article 51 of the Charter, of individual and collective self-defense if an armed attack occurs against a member of the United Nations, until the Security Council has taken the measures necessary to maintain international peace and security. The corresponding provision in each of the three Declarations is identical to that in the Security Council Resolution, except that the Declarations also mention nuclear attack, thus emphasizing an additional opening for the application of Article 51 that was not envisaged when the Charter was drafted.

Opinion was divided on the value of such a reaffirmation in relation to the use of nuclear weapons. Some states were skeptical about the adequacy of Article 51 in the nuclear age, especially as far as the right of individual self-defense was concerned.

If the three operative paragraphs are read together and in relation to the Declarations made by the three nuclear-weapon states, the general conclusion that can be reached is the following: in recognizing that aggression with nuclear weapons or the threat of such aggression would create a qualitatively new situation, the Resolution and the associated Declarations have tried in the first place to establish the bases of a future Security Council action if a non-nuclear-weapon state that is party to the NPT were to become victim of such an act of aggression or an object of such a threat of aggression. In such an eventuality, an immediate Security Council action to provide assistance would be sought. The reaffirmation of the inherent right, recognized under Article 51 of the Charter, of individual and collective self-defense has apparently been introduced to reassure members of alliances.

The response is only envisaged through the machinery of the Security Council. In the case of the inherent right of self-defense, the right is exercised, in principle, until the Security Council has taken measures necessary to maintain international peace and security.

According to the Security Council Resolution, recourse to the Council has apparently become an obligation and not merely an option. As far as timing is concerned, immediate action by the Council has to be sought. It follows that the response is not automatic.

With regard to the type of response or its degree, nothing in the Declarations made by the three nuclear-weapon states or in the Resolution indicates that response to a nuclear attack or the threat of a nuclear attack will have to be in kind, that is, by using nuclear weapons or the threat of such use. The type of immediate assistance is left to the discretion of the Security Council. It is possible, therefore, to envisage a Security Council action with the use of conventional weapons to *counter* a threat of use of nuclear weapons.

The Declarations do not in any way deal with what would happen if the procedures of the UN Charter fail. If the right of veto is used by one of the permanent members, no effective action by the Security Council can be taken. But apart from the fact that the reaffirmation of the inherent right of self-defense, recognized by Article 51 of the UN Charter, is apparently designed to reassure members of alliances which include a nuclear power, the right can also be exercised as a residual right if the Security Council were to fail to take immediate action. In such an eventuality, measures taken would still have to be reported immediately to the Security Council.

The implications of introducing Article 51 of the UN Charter in the context of security guarantees against aggression with nuclear weapons or the threat of such aggression is quite significant. Most important is that the Declarations and the Resolution can be read in the light of the broad interpretation of Article 51 which justifies the exercise of the right of self-defense in case of "acts preparatory to armed attack." One of the clearest cases of the broad interpretation of the article is the one invoked by proponents of this interpretation with respect to the possible use of nuclear weapons, an argument based on such *de facto* circumstances as greater rapidity and power with which an armed attack can be made with nuclear weapons.

On the one hand, the limitations of Security Council guarantees, as far as the establishment of perfect security was concerned, were admitted by the representatives of the two superpowers. In the US debate it was reaffirmed that the Security Council Resolution did not involve the United States in any new commitment beyond those it already had under existing treaties, and that it did not change the basic obligations which were written into the UN Charter. On the other hand, the advantages of the security guarantees were stressed by the two superpowers. The making of identical Declarations by three permanent members of the Security Council was considered a political event of considerable importance. The sponsorship of the Resolution by the three states was also considered as an introduction of a powerful element of deterrence against nuclear aggression or the threat of such aggression. Moreover, the Resolution was defended on the basis that it gave more substance to those provisions of the UN Charter concerning the actions of the UN in the interests of maintaining and strengthening peace, especially with regard to a threat of nuclear attack.

FINAL ANALYSIS OF SECURITY COUNCIL RESOLUTION 255 AND ITS SHORTCOMINGS

The guarantees are of a positive nature insofar as they are aiming at providing or supporting assistance to states that are victim of aggression or threat of aggression. But these positive security guarantees may also imply negative guarantees, such as the non-use of nuclear weapons or the threat of such use. They need to be made explicitly in the context of a new resolution and perhaps in declarations associated with it.

The guarantees are offered by only three nuclear-weapon states in their capacity as permanent members of the UN Security Council and through the Council's machinery. The Declarations made by the three states are not merely unilateral declarations of intention, as each of them is made in relation to the others, taking into consideration the fulfillment of certain conditions. They are tantamount to an unwritten agreement establishing multilateral security guarantees and sanctioned by the Security Council.

In order to redress the imbalance among the permanent members of the Council, the two other nuclear-weapon states that are members of the Security Council should join in a new resolution, and in making declarations associated with it, especially because they are now both signatories to the NPT since 1992.

France abstained in the vote on the 1968 Resolution, not being a party to the NPT, and China had then not yet occupied its seat in the Council. Moreover, the 1968 Resolution seemed then to be addressed against China. The veto power of the five still haunts us and may paralyze any action contemplated by the Council, especially if the culprit is a permanent member of the Council.

The guarantees are to the benefit of non-nuclear-weapon states that are party to the NPT. Thus, the link is established between the NPT and Security Council Resolution 255. However, approval of the NPT does not necessarily mean approval of the Resolution and the Declarations associated with it. It is hoped that the guarantees would also be extended to parties of comparable instruments of nuclear abstention, such as treaties establishing nuclear-weapon-free zones.

The states against whom the assurances could be invoked are not necessarily the other existing nuclear-weapon states but also potential nuclear-weapon states. The latter are the real danger. A new resolution on security guarantees ought to highlight and attend to this particular danger, and the resolution's deterrent value against such states should be enhanced.

The assurances are only operational in the case of use or threat of use of one type of weapon, that is, nuclear weapons. But the use of conventional weapons may possibly imply the threat of use of nuclear weapons, and, therefore, carry with it the danger of escalation. However, it should be quite clear that the guarantees are nuclear guarantees. Defining aggression or threats of aggression will always remain problematic.

But if the guarantees are nuclear with respect to the nature of the attack or the threat of attack, they are not necessarily nuclear with respect to the response. The response is through the Security Council and the application of UN Charter provisions. In this respect the security guarantees are virtually a reaffirmation of UN Charter provisions and more particularly the special responsibility of the permanent members of the Security Council. However, such reaffirmation has been done in a world situation that is different from that prevailing when the UN Charter was signed. In a world of five nuclear-weapon powers and where the danger of further proliferation of nuclear weapons persists, the reaffirmation of the UN Charter is not void of meaning. However, in view of the shortcomings of the UN's past experience in the field of peace and security preservation, the mere reaffirmation of Charter provisions appeared to many states as a meager solution to the problems of security in the nuclear age.

A new resolution on security guarantees should attend to this lack of confidence in Security Council action. The response by the Council should be made more clear and predictable. In this respect it is far-fetched to expect that the response would be in kind as to do so would legitimize the potential use of nuclear weapons, and the response should not take place without consulting the victim or upon his request. And if the Council were to fail to take action as a result of a veto by a permanent member, it is not clear what residual action the Council may take in the circumstances. However, this ought to be spelled out.

Before and after the adoption of the Security Council Resolution, several remedies were suggested either to render the security guarantees more credible or to supplement them with other measures, which brings us to specific proposals being put on the table at present.

(2) Two Proposals for Updating and Enhancing Security Council Guarantees

The shortcomings of Security Council Resolution 255, as referred to above, have affected the credibility of the Resolution, although it must be said that it has not yet been, and hopefully it will never be, put to a real test. However, the Security Council ought to be ready for the worst scenario in order to cope effectively and credibly with a nuclear threat.

In the working paper submitted by Egypt at the Fourth NPT Review Conference in 1990,[22] security guarantees figured as a first item in the paper. Egypt called upon the Security Council to adopt a new resolution on security guarantees, which would include credible guarantees beyond the provisions of Security Council Resolution 255. In particular it called for:

— A clear indication of the mandatory action to be adopted by the nuclear-weapon states and the Security Council;
— The obligation of states to provide *immediate* assistance to the victim;
— Support of the imposition of sanctions;
— The obligation to pay reparation or compensation to the victim.

In making these suggestions, Egypt reiterated the importance of a commitment by all states that are party to the NPT not to use or threaten to use nuclear weapons from their territories against any other state that is party to the NPT which does

---

22. Doc. NPT/Conf. IV/31, August 24, 1990.

not possess or place nuclear weapons on its territories. Egypt's motivation for putting forward those ideas were spelled out in its paper. In its view, existing peril emanates from the practice of certain nuclear-threshold countries of an undeclared and ambiguous nuclear policy against their regional neighbors, these states having refused to join the NPT and allow for verification measures under effective international control.[23]

The Egyptian paper generated great interest and support for its objective at the 1990 NPT Review Conference and at the Conference on Disarmament in Geneva in 1991. As a result, Egypt further developed its ideas on a new Security Council resolution in a separate paper presented to the Ad Hoc Committee of the Conference on Disarmament in 1991. It remains unchanged at the date of writing.[24]

The second paper had a closer look at Resolution 255 and revealed the following with regard to the three operative paragraphs of the Resolution:

The opening operative paragraph of Resolution 255 was drafted without proper consideration to the gravity of the actual use or threat of use of nuclear weapons. Consequently, Resolution 255 lacks an explicit and unequivocal reference to this situation as one that would threaten international peace and security in conformity with the provisions of Article 39 of the Charter. The Resolution also did not contain a stipulation to deter states from using or threatening to use nuclear weapons, nor does it contain assurances that the Council shall embark on effective and immediate measures to respond to such a grave situation in accordance with the letter and spirit of the relevant articles of Chapter 7.

The second paragraph of Resolution 255 welcomes, in a rather superficial manner, the intention expressed by certain states that they will provide and support immediate assistance in accordance with the Charter to any non-nuclear-weapon state that is party to the Treaty that is a victim of an act or an object of a threat of aggression in which nuclear weapons are used. What is lacking is a clear-cut commitment from the nuclear-weapon states to take effective measures such as the application of sanctions. Furthermore, Resolution 255 did not clearly indicate the extent and definition of "assistance." As a result, any up-dating of Resolution 255 should entail a comprehensive definition of assistance so as to include technical, scientific, financial and humanitarian assistance.

---

23. *Ibid.*, p. 2.
24. The Egyptian paper is reproduced and attached as Annex I.

The third operative paragraph of Resolution 255, which reaffirmed the inherent right recognized under Article 51 of the Charter of individual and collective self-defense, did not contain, or bring about, any new addition to what has already been enshrined in the Charter.

For all the above-mentioned considerations, it has become imperative to update Security Council Resolution 255 by adopting a new resolution that would contain credible guarantees and would build upon the provisions originally contained in Resolution 255 of 1968.

The Egyptian paper stopped at that without suggesting a text for a draft resolution, leaving the task of negotiating a text to the nuclear-weapon states, which would inform parties to the NPT of any progress on appropriate action by the Security Council that may result from these efforts. However, a text for a draft Security Council resolution and a draft declaration associated with it has been worked out by two scholars and former US and Soviet diplomats.[25] The draft resolution and the declaration seem to be inspired by the Egyptian initiative for a new Security Council resolution and the need to overcome the difficulties in introducing negative security guarantees. The draft resolution and the declaration are, in fact, novelties as they attend to both positive and negative security guarantees at the same time. They may not have responded fully to the concerns and aspirations of many parties to the NPT, including the Egyptian requirements for a new Security Council resolution, but they are certainly a step forward in the right direction. A close look at the draft resolution and the declaration would reveal great subtleties and improvements but also shortcomings which would not be difficult to remedy.

Following the same pattern of analysis of Security Council Resolution 255 and the three Declarations associated with it, the guarantors in the new draft resolution and declaration are the Security Council and its permanent members, without naming them as nuclear-weapon states. The declaration is a single declaration made by all the permanent members of the Council instead of the three separate declarations made in conjunction with Security Council Resolution 255, thus indicating that the permanent members will act in unison and as one. Using the term "permanent members" was meant to highlight their special role in the

---

25. George Bunn and Roland M Timerbaev, "Security assurances to non-nuclear-weapon states," *The non-proliferation review*, vol. 1, no. 1, fall 1993, pp. 11-20. The draft resolution and the declaration are reproduced and attached as Annex II.

preservation of peace and security under the UN Charter and to de-emphasize their nuclear-weapon status.

With regard to the guaranteed states, the new texts speak of states accepting and observing an international obligation not to acquire nuclear weapons or other nuclear explosive devices. They are called the protected states. This is a great improvement to the 1968 texts, as, for example, a non-NPT member would benefit from such guarantees if it is a member of a nuclear-weapon-free zone.

All members of the United Nations would benefit from the provision of Article 51 of the UN Charter if an armed attack (including the use of nuclear weapons) occurs. The five permanent members, in moving together, would dissipate the unfair connotation that Security Council Resolution 255 was original-ly aimed at China. Moreover, the five, in providing negative and positive security guarantees, should at the same time should in principle eliminate the possibility that any of the five would be an aggressor. In acting together, the five would in essence aim at deterring potential nuclear powers. The new texts would enhance the deterrent effect against states that are contemplating the acquisition of a nuclear-weapon capability.

As to actions or threats against which security guarantees could be involved, the new texts differ from the 1968 texts in that they speak of the *use* of nuclear weapons or the *threat* of such use instead of the *aggression* with nuclear weapons or the threat of such *aggression*. The term aggression and its definition generated a lot of controversy in the past. Those drafting the new texts seem to have responded to those who have preferred the terms "use" or "attack," although the term "aggression" appears to be stronger and wider. With regard to the reaffirma-tion of the inherent right, recognized under Article 51 of the Charter, of individu-al and collective self-defense, the new texts speak of an armed attack (including one using nuclear weapons).

There are two sets of obligations in the new text, or in other words two sets of guarantees. With regard to negative guarantees, the draft resolution merely welcomes the declaration by the permanent members that they will not threaten to use or use nuclear weapons against any state observing an international obligation not to acquire nuclear weapons or other nuclear explosive devices. I believe that the Security Council should take stronger action than merely welcoming a declaration on negative security guarantees. Rather, the Council ought to sanction a stronger commitment on the part of the permanent members, such as a model agreement as earlier suggested under the section on negative security guarantees.

With regard to positive guarantees the new texts contain the following:

— A condemnation of the threat or use of nuclear weapons against any state observing an international obligation not to acquire nuclear weapons or other nuclear explosive devices. Such a threat or use of nuclear weapons would constitute a grave threat to international peace and security;
— The Security Council would act immediately in case of a threat or use of nuclear weapons in accordance with the Council's primary responsibility under the Charter for the maintenance of peace and security;
— In accordance with the UN Charter, the permanent members will provide assistance to any state that is the object of a threat or use of nuclear weapons;
— A reaffirmation of Article 51 of the UN Charter if an armed attack (including one using nuclear weapons) occurs against a member of the United Nations, until the Security Council has taken the measures necessary to maintain international peace and security. Moreover, the declaration recognizes that if the Security Council fails to take action, a right of individual and collective self-defense will exist. This is a clear improvement on the previous Declarations of 1968.

Despite the great subtlety, innovations and improvements brought about by the new texts, they still fall short of remedying the weaknesses of the 1968 texts. For example, there is no mention of Chapter 7 of the Charter. The types of assistance rendered to the victim, or sanctions imposed on the aggressor, are not defined. What about reparations or compensation?

However, one may finally ask, is it not better for the credibility and deterrent value of a new resolution not to try to overload it with so many elements and details? The fear is that we might end up with a strait jacket. Some ambiguity and uncertainty are not necessarily bad, indeed they may be valuable qualities for better deterrence against the use or threat of use of nuclear weapons by potential proliferators.

In Conclusion

Security Guarantees, whether positive or negative, can only be enhanced by a multiple approach in an atmosphere of detente and relaxation. On the one hand, improvement of the UN's peace-keeping machinery should continue to receive the utmost attention in order to produce some prompt and tangible results. On the other hand, just solutions should be found for protracted conflicts that are threatening world peace and security. Moreover, efforts should continue towards reaching a general prohibition of the use or threat of use of nuclear weapons. The declarations made by the nuclear-weapon states on non-use should be made in a more formal and binding instrument, preferably through the Security Council, and until the drive towards the conclusion of an international convention on non-use bears fruit. Lastly, nuclear disarmament should be pursued with greater vigor and perseverance. We have a long way to go but the obstacles are not insurmountable.

Annex 1

Working Paper submitted by Egypt to the Conference on Disarmament Ad Hoc Committee on Effective International Arrangements to Assure Non-Nuclear-Weapon States against the Use of Threat of Use of Nuclear Weapons - 1991

Ad Hoc Committee on Effective International Arrangements to Assure Non-Nuclear-Weapon States against the Use or Threat of Use of Nuclear Weapons.

EGYPT

Egypt attaches great importance to the issue of effective international arrangements to assure non-nuclear weapons States against the use or threat of use of nuclear weapons and believes that the most effective guarantee against the use or threat of use of nuclear weapons is nuclear disarmament under effective international control. Pending the attainment of this goal, security assurances are an important measure in this regard.

Egypt also believes that the non-proliferation Treaty, which is the cornerstone of the Non-Proliferation regime, should provide adequate security for all its parties.

On the basis of this understanding Egypt presented to the IV Review Conference of the Non-Proliferation Treaty which convened in Geneva in the summer of 1990, a proposal to this effect. Since then several important developments took place.

On December 19, 1990 the General Assembly adopted a resolution (A/RES/45/54) on the issue of effective international arrangements to assure non-nuclear-weapon States against the use or threat of use of nuclear weapons. The resolution contained in operative paragraph 5 a recommendation that:

> The Conference on Disarmament should actively continue intensive negotiations with a view to reaching early agreement and concluding effective international arrangements to assure non-nuclear-weapon States against the use or threat of use of nuclear weapons, taking into account the widespread support for the conclusion of an international convention and giving consideration to *any other proposals designed to secure the same objective*."

On January 24, 1991 the Conference on Disarmament decided to re-establish for the duration of its 1991 session, an Ad Hoc Committee to continue to negotiate with a view to reaching agreement on effective international *arrangements* to assure non-nuclear-weapon States against the use or threat of use of nuclear weapons.

In the course of the deliberations of the A.H.C. its chairman, Ambassador Kralik of the Czech and Slovak Federal Republic made many references to the Egyptian proposal and included it in the Chairman's papers. The debate also demonstrated wide support for the Egyptian proposal. One delegation expressed the conviction that while some may argue that the discussion of the so-called positive security assurances falls outside the purview of this committee, this delegation believed that the general objective of the Egyptian proposal is compatible with the thrust of this committee's deliberation. Additionally, a group coordinator stated on behalf of his group that they took note with interest of the intention of the Egyptian delegation to table a new proposal on this issue.

The Egyptian proposal stems from the conviction underlined by the United Nations Charter that the primary objective of the United Nations is to maintain international peace and security and to take collective effective measures for the prevention and removal of threats to the peace through a collective effective measures for the prevention and removal of threats to the peace through a collective security system. This guided the Security Council to adopt its resolution 255 of June 19, 1968 entitled "Question relating to measures to safeguard non-nuclear-weapon States parties to the Treaty on the non-proliferation of nuclear weapons."

This resolution which was adopted by the Security Council with five abstentions and without the participation of China culminated a process in which efforts exerted at the ENDC to incorporate clause covering this issue in the test of the NPT, failed.

Consequently, and when the General Assembly was considering the adoption of the NPT in the course of its resumed session in May 1968, many delegations emphasized the necessity and importance of incorporating provisions for security assurances for non-nuclear-weapons States in the text of the NPT. This demand was, regrettably, not looked upon with favour by the nuclear-weapon States, and as a result the NPT did not contain a clause providing for security assurances. Instead the Security Council adopted resolution 255 which stated:

1. Recognizes that aggression with nuclear weapons or the threat of such aggression against a non-nuclear-weapons State would create a situation in which the Security Council, and above all its nuclear-weapons State permanent members would have to act immediately in accordance with their obligation under the United Nations Charter;

2. Welcomes the intention expressed by certain States that they will provide or support immediate assistance, in accordance with the Charter, to any non-nuclear-weapon State Party to the Treaty on the non-proliferation of Nuclear Weapons that is a victim of an act or an object of a threat of aggression in which nuclear weapons are used;

3. Reaffirms in particular the inherent right, recognised under article 51 of the Charter, of individual and collective self-defense if an armed attack occurs against a member of the United Nations, until the Security Council has taken measures necessary to maintain international peace and security.

A closer look at 255 would reveal the following:

The *first* operative paragraph of 255 was drafted without proper consideration to the gravity of the actual use or threat of use of nuclear weapons. In fact what the resolution stipulates is that such an aggression or threat, would create a situation in which the Security Council would have to act immediately. Consequently, resolution 255 lacks an explicit and unequivocal reference to this situation as one that would threaten international peace and security in conformity with the provisions of article 39 of the Charter. The resolution also did not contain a stipulation to deter States from using or threatening to use nuclear weapons nor does it contain assurances that the Council shall embark on effective and immediate measures to respond to such a grave situation in accordance with the letter and spirit of the relevant articles of Chapter 7.

The *second* paragraph of resolution 255 welcomes, in a rather superficial manner, the intention expressed by certain States that they will provide and support immediate assistance in accordance with the Charter to any non-nuclear weapon State Party to the Treaty that is a victim of an act or an object of the threat of aggression in which nuclear weapons are used. What is lacking is a clear cut commitment from the nuclear-weapons States to take effective measures such as the application of sanctions. Furthermore, resolution 255 did not clearly indicate the extent and definition of "assistance." As a result any up-dating of resolution 255 should entail a comprehensive definition of assistance so as to include technical, scientific, financial and humanitarian assistance.

The *third* operative paragraph of resolution 255 which reaffirmed the inherent right recognized under article 51 of the Charter, of individual and collective self-defense did not contain, or bring about, any new addition to what has already been enshrined in the Charter.

For all the above-mentioned considerations it has become imperative to update Security Council resolution 255 by adopting a new resolution that would contain credible assurances and would build upon the provisions originally contained in resolution 255 of 1968.

The delegation in Egypt considers that a first step is necessary to initiate a process whereby nuclear-weapon State Party to the NPT would conduct consultations collectively or individually with the nuclear-weapon States not currently party to the Treaty on security assurances taking into account United Nations Security Council resolution 255 of 1968 and to inform other States parties to the treaty of any progress on appropriate action by the Security Council that may result from these efforts.

Annex II

DRAFT UN SECURITY COUNCIL RESOLUTION ON SECURITY ASSURANCES FOR STATES THAT FORSWEAR NUCLEAR WEAPONS

The Security Council,

— *recalling* its Declaration of January 31, 1992 that the proliferation of nuclear and other weapons of mass destruction "constitutes a threat to international peace and security;"
— *recognizing* that nuclear weapons are the most devastating weapons of mass destruction;
— *welcoming* the observance of international obligations not to acquire nuclear weapons by over one hundred fifty five (155) states and the commitments by some of the states that have nuclear weapons to cut their arsenals sharply;
— *recognizing* the desires of many non-nuclear-weapons states for security arrangements to assure that there shall be no threat or use of nuclear weapons against them:

1. *Condemns* the threat or use of nuclear weapons against any state observing an international obligation not to acquire nuclear weapons or other nuclear explosive devices;
2. *Recognizes* that such a threat or use of nuclear weapons would constitute a grave threat to international peace and security;
3. *Resolves* that such a threat or use of nuclear weapons would require the Council to act immediately in accordance with the Council's primary responsibility under the Charter for the maintenance of international peace and security;
4. *Welcomes* the Declaration by the permanent members that they will not threaten to use or use nuclear weapons against any state observing an international obligation not to acquire nuclear weapons or other nuclear explosive devices, and that, in accordance with the Charter, they will provide assistance to any such state that is the object of a threat or use of nuclear weapons;
5. *Reaffirms* the inherent right, recognized by Article 51 of the Charter, of individual and collective self-defense if an armed attack (including one using nuclear weapons) occurs against a member of the United Nations, until the Security Council has taken measures necessary to maintain international peace and security.

DRAFT DECLARATION BY PERMANENT MEMBERS OF THE SECURITY COUNCIL ON NUCLEAR
SECURITY ASSURANCES FOR STATES THAT FORSWEAR NUCLEAR WEAPONS

The Permanent Members of the Council appreciate the concern of some states that
renunciation of nuclear weapons could place them at a permanent military disadvantage or
make them vulnerable to nuclear blackmail.

The Permanent Members declare that they will not use or threaten to use nuclear
weapons against any state that has accepted and is observing an international obligation not
to acquire nuclear weapons or other nuclear explosive devices, hereafter called a "protected state."

The use of nuclear weapons, or the threat of such use, against such a protected state
would require immediate action by the Council in exercise of its primary responsibility for
the maintenance of international peace and security under Article 24 of the UN Charter.

As permanent members of the Security Council, the declarants promise to seek
immediate Council action to provide assistance, in accordance with the Charter, to any
protected state that is the object of a threat of use of nuclear weapons or the victim of such
a use.

The declarants reaffirm the inherent right, recognized under Article 51 of the Charter,
of individual and collective self-defense if an armed attack occurs against a member of the
United Nations, until the Security Council has taken measures necessary to maintain
international peace and security. The declarants recognize that if the Council is convened
to deal with a use of nuclear weapons against a protected state and the Council fails to take
action, a right of individual and collective self-defense will exist.

Any state or subnational group considering a use of nuclear weapons against a
protected state is hereby warned that its actions will be countered by collective or
individual responses taken in accordance with the UN Charter.

10 The NPT and the Post-1995 Non-Proliferation Agenda

Harald Müller

Introduction

We are approaching the end of an era in nuclear non-proliferation, and this end is marked by the NPT Extension Conference. Bolstered by recent improvements in the NPT regime concerning verification, export control, universalization and enforcement, the regime will - or so we expect - receive its final consolidation by a substantive extension in 1995. Some, and certainly many in the nuclear-weapon states, may hope that this puts an end to all discussions about the regime. Some parties may press hard for a majority vote for indefinite extension and, in order to put the seal on the non-proliferation regime, now and for ever, may try to push that vote through, even over the strong objections of quite a number of parties.[1]

I concur firmly that indefinite extension would be the preferable solution. The simple reason is that I cannot foresee a security environment where German, European, and world security would be enhanced by the absence rather than the existence of the NPT. If the NPT is to be replaced by a more comprehensive instrument - as foreseen in Article VI - then the parties are fully in a position to put an end to the NPT, even if its duration were indefinite, as spelled out in the Vienna Convention on the Law of the Treaties. If a party or a group of parties had really good reasons to leave the Treaty because its supreme interests were endangered, they can do so under the procedure laid out in Article X.1. And, finally, on the supposed "leverage" *vis-à-vis* the nuclear-weapon states that a

---

1. "The Nuclear Non-Proliferation Treaty (NPT): A twenty-five year success story," statement by Thomas Graham, Jr, Acting Deputy Director, US Arms Control and Disarmament Agency, before the International Conference on the Renewal of the Nuclear Non-Proliferation Treaty, sponsored by the Fondazione Alcide De Gasperi, Rome, Italy, July 2-3, 1994.

M. van Leeuwen (ed.), The Future of the International Nuclear Non-Proliferation Regime, 273-290.
© 1995 *Kluwer Academic Publishers. Printed in the Netherlands.*

limited period allegedly provides, I will elaborate further in the following section on "disarmament."

However, despite my support for indefinite extension I think the hard-nosed "push it to a vote and roll over objectors" is mistaken and will hurt the Treaty. A global regime must be based on as universal a consensus as possible, if not absolutely universal. Deep divisions between the faithful parties about such a fundamental issue as the duration of the NPT would be very destabilizing for the regime as a whole, and would give the very few countries who mischievously try to undermine it an ideal opening to pursue their objectives. And, most of all, I believe that any prognosis of "closing the issue" is completely illusory. If 1995 will end an era of heavy disputes, it will open a new era that will be equally characterized by difficult and often divisive discussions.

With the consolidation of the regime by an NPT extension, the door will be wide open for the nagging questions about the regime and its components, some of which are already being addressed today. But the questions are bound to grow because of changing international circumstances, new roles for different states and group of states and technological development. These questions will shape the non-proliferation agenda after 1995. In this chapter these issues will be discussed one by one, in each case reviewing what role an extended NPT will play in shaping, solving and approaching the underlying problem.

Hierarchy, Participation, and Export Controls

The first question is one of the hierarchy between states within the non-proliferation regime, the different levels of authority and participation, and the division of responsibilities. It is here that the often-heard myth that non-proliferation is a "North-South problem"[2] has its real roots. It is not, because proliferation is not a phenomenon where the North confronts a proliferating South; rather, faithful and committed adherents to the non-proliferation regime from both the developed and the developing world have to cope with a handful of non-adherents, pariahs and/or cheaters that do not abide by the rules. Non-proliferation is thus an

---

2. See, for example, Peter van Ham, *Managing nuclear non-proliferation regimes in the 1990s* (London: Pinter, 1993), pp. 4 and 22-23.

objective in which the overwhelming majority of both the industrialized and the developing world share a common interest. Nevertheless, regime activities, notably successful ones, rest very much with the industrialized countries. After the revelations of the second Gulf War, the improvements in IAEA verification methods were pushed through, sometimes with the support and sometimes against visible headaches of non-aligned countries, by delegations from the industrialized world in the IAEA Board of Governors. On the use of intelligence data and on the scope of "special inspection" authority, there is still much uneasiness, if not disagreement, below the surface of the Board's February 1992 agreement, as reported by the then Chairman.[3] In verification, enforcement and, most visibly, in export controls, the North sings the tune, and the developing countries, which make up for the vast majority of regime membership, are reduced to nodding or - as in export controls - to hapless bystanding.[4] This division is a grave danger to regime stability. Two resolutions during the last session of the UN General Assembly - on the elimination of export controls as soon as the Chemical Weapons Convention enters into force (sponsored by Iran) and on a critical study of existing non-proliferation regimes (sponsored by Mexico) - received more than 100 supportive votes from the developing world and were opposed by the industrialized countries.[5] This is a warning that should be heeded. The question is of how to co-opt leading developing countries into regime leadership.

The more the non-aligned countries perceive their lack of substantive participation in international nuclear decision-making as collective discrimination, the more difficult will be the task of isolating possible "evil-doers." If the United Nations has to resolve to impose sanctions, perhaps even military measures, against proliferators, then the overwhelming majority of the international community, including the developing countries, must agree to this course of action.

For the survival/continuation of the regime, new mechanisms of participation are a must. Non-proliferation should be adjusted to the members of the regime and, if possible, to those who are absolutely trustworthy. And participation should be representative. Universal bodies like the UN General Assembly, UNCTAD or

---

3. David Fischer, *Towards 1995: the prospects for ending the proliferation of nuclear weapons* (Aldershot, UK: Dartmouth, 1993), pp. 64-9 and 71-9; Eric Chauvistré, "The future of nuclear inspections," *Arms control today*, vol. 16, no. 2, fall 1993, pp. 23-64.

4. Harald Müller, "Reform of the system of nuclear export controls," *Nuclear export controls and supply-side restraints: options for reform*, PPNN Study 4 (Southampton), pp. 1-19.

5. *Disarmament times*, vol. 16, no. 7, p. 1.

even the IAEA General Conference have important tasks but they cannot be charged with more tasks and expectations - the United Nations Conference on the Promotion of International Cooperation in the Peaceful Uses of Nuclear Energy in 1987 definitely proved this.

Some of the smaller developing countries do not feel directly threatened by the proliferation of nuclear weapons, nor do they have interests in the peaceful use of nuclear technology. It is significant to win the active support for the regime of the opinion-leading non-nuclear-weapon states from the developing world if we wish to convince the majority of small states to follow suit. The one-sidedness of the current reform of the regime is therefore detrimental. We need no differentiation between the North and the South, but an unambiguous demarcation between the would-be nuclear-weapon states and the community of regime participants. The most important step is the regular involvement of countries like Egypt, Jordan, Morocco, Indonesia, Bangladesh, Thailand, Sri Lanka, South Korea, Venezuela, Peru, Mexico, Nigeria, Kenya and Zimbabwe in consultations about questions of non-proliferation. This must take place within the regular diplomatic relations of these countries. Furthermore, it is worth considering whether a special forum should be established for such a dialogue.

The NPT provides the framework for this understanding of the regime. It puts the issue of export controls (Article III.2) squarely within the context of civilian nuclear cooperation, with particular emphasis on developing countries (Article IV). On this basis, supplier cartels can only be a temporary stopgap measure. While supplier coordination remains crucial for any export control system to be effective, the NPT context suggests that it must be supplemented by dialogue with recipients, notably from the developing world. Finally, the NPT, by virtue of its membership, draws clear borders around the group of countries that will participate in the dialogue (leaders of the community of NPT parties) and those that will not (the outsiders).

The Future of the Nuclear Industry, Custody of Fissile Materials

The second question concerns the future of the nuclear industry and rules to deal with weapons-usable fissile material. The latter point currently threatens us with an undesirable rehearsal of the debate initiated by American President Carter in the second half of the 1970s, with all the consequences of embittered controversy among close friends that we know so well from that period.[6]

The end of the strategic rivalry between the United States and the former Soviet Union has motivated suggestions to revive the Baruch Plan of 1945, which failed at the beginning of the atomic age because of American-Soviet distrust. The Baruch Plan was based on the idea of transferring property and physical control of the complete nuclear industry (including all the fission material, i.e. from uranium mining to the final disposal of nuclear waste) to an international authority.[7] Some observers now see the chance to end the proliferation problem with a new Baruch Plan, bringing all nuclear-weapon states under the auspices of such an authority.[8] At first sight this project seems fascinating. But there are such serious objections to it that its materialization appears to be nearly impossible.

a) The core of the plan is the concept of merging property and control. The implementation, however, would be confronted by complex property relations in today's international nuclear industry. Ministries and state committees act as owner and management; state-owned firms and companies in centralized and in federal states meet entirely private-owned business. In some countries the utility sector is integrated into the nuclear industry, in others both are separated. In some countries nuclear research is entirely state-run, in others it is completely private. This complex structure means almost unsolvable legal and political problems for the concurrent nationalization and internationalization. In addition, there is the question of how to deal with compensation and who would have to pay the costs.

The ownership of European fissile material by EURATOM demonstrates that a mere nominal subordination under public ownership does not mean a lot. It is significant that the safeguard function of the European authority is much more important than its property right.[9]

---

6. *Nuclear fuel*, vol. 18, no. 19, September 13, 1993, pp. 5-6; vol. 19, no. 15, July 16, 1994, pp. 4-5; vol. 19, no. 16, August 1, 1994, pp. 15-16; Fabrizio Caccia Dominioni and Wilhelm Gmelin, "Euratom und USA: Probleme und Perspektiven der Zusammenarbeit," in Erwin Häckel, (ed.), *Probleme der nuklearen Nichtverbreitungspolitik: Beiträge zur internationalen Diskussion* (Bonn: Europa-Union Verlag, 1994), pp. 101-17.

7. Joseph Liebermann, *The scorpion and the tarantula: the struggle to control atomic weapons, 1949-1949* (Boston: 1970).

8. Christoph Bertram, *Die Zeit*, February 1992; Gerard Smith, "Take nuclear weapons into custody," *Bulletin of the atomic scientists*, vol. 46, no. 10, 1990, pp. 12-13.

9. Darryl A. Howlett, *EURATOM and nuclear safeguards* (Basingstoke: Macmillan, 1990).

b) The developing authority would be an organization with its own huge bureaucracy and - surely - all the symptoms of Parkinson's disease. Its dimensions would surpass the organizational structures of the biggest multinational companies. It remains unclear how such an organization could be effectively controlled and supervised.

Taking responsibility for the economic efficiency of the nuclear industries, the authority would develop owner's interests which run counter to its supervising tasks. This would not only affect the safeguarding but at the same time the physical protection of the fissile material and the safety of the facilities. These functions are separate in the present system. The management's responsibility for physical security and safety currently face control by state agencies (frequently distinguishing between those responsible for technical and radiological safety, physical security, and material accountancy) and the verification activities of international organizations. This separation of functions prevents pure economic interests harming verification and other control missions. Yet, even under these organizational conditions EURATOM and the IAEA are occasionally blamed for emphasizing the promotion of nuclear energy too much compared with its controlling tasks. Perhaps these suspicions would be quite justified of an authority in which all these tasks (and interests) are merged. It can be explained historically why these problems were neglected in 1946: then, all the governments were still under the impression of centralized wartime economies. Under regular circumstances, the principle of separating functions should be given preference, in particular to guarantee supervision and control.

c) One of the unsettled problems is the question of on whose territory different types of facilities would be sited. Assignment under an international authority veils the fact that there would be differences in proliferation risks (as today), because sensitive facilities and weapons-grade material - though under international auspices - would be located on the territories of various states which would then have a privileged proliferation opportunity. Of course the ensuing taboo, the forced overcoming of the authority's safeguards, would be harder to break than the present taboo, breach of contract and deceit of the inspectors. This advantage, though, would be a gradual and not a fundamental one.

d) Furthermore, the international ownership of "official" facilities and fissile materials does not eliminate the main problem of the present regime: the danger of secret facilities and undeclared fissile material for military purposes.

In summary, it can be said that the revival of the Baruch Plan would have the advantage of reducing the present discrimination and marginally strengthening the taboo which a proliferator would have to break. But there are serious disadvantages for property rights and of an organizational and financial nature, while on the whole the problem would be shifted but not solved. Under these circumstances, the results are not worth the effort.

If we can agree that the nuclear industry will remain heterogeneous and decentralized, then the basic rules laid down in the NPT retain their unique importance. The obligation to accept IAEA safeguards on all fissile material is the basis for all add-ons, reforms and improvements that the civil use of these materials may undergo in the future. Without that obligation, there would simply be no political (not to speak of legal) basis to ask for special inspections, environmental monitoring, facility-related measures or special rules applying to weapons-usable material, that is, all the various proposals to strengthen international verification that will be elaborated and implemented after 1995.

Most observers agree that the presence of weapons-usable fissile material and associated equipment and facilities in the civilian fuel-cycle presents an extra risk that must be approached with the greatest caution. However, previous efforts to eliminate such civilian use by external pressure have failed and are likely to fail in the future. We must thus assume that some countries will continue, or may even start anew, with the recycling of plutonium in their commercial nuclear industries.

A priority task is to devise a system of rules that obliges the users to observe strict criteria in their national energy plans, to increase transparency, to rely on "just-in-time" procedures with a view to avoid suspect stockpiling of materials, and to admit at least legitimate questions concerning their practices. The regime should provide for enhanced measures of accountancy and physical security, including peer reviews or even obligatory checks on how these measures are applied in practice. To arrive at such an arrangement, we have not only to overcome the apparently insuperable drive of certain US quarters to impose rules, but the equally obstinate insistence of pro-nuclear zealots in plutonium-using states who insist on complete national sovereignty over "their" fissile material without due regard to the standards of accountability that have risen in recent years.

If weapons-usable material is present in the civilian fuel cycle, the inspection effort must be stronger than in the absence of such material. The increase in cost of such safeguards is a factor that must be reflected in national fuel-cycle policies, even though safeguards' costs are borne by the entire community of IAEA member states. This international impact of (legitimate) national energy policy decisions implies that national decisions on fuel-cycle policy cannot be shielded from external considerations by the mere claim to national sovereignty. The use of highly enriched uranium and separated plutonium, both statistically and objectively, enhances the risk of diversion and thereby the shared costs of verification. Countries with a complete fuel cycle hence bear a particular responsibility and accountability towards the community of NPT parties. In particular, we must ask ourselves time and again how we can restrict the use of sensitive materials to a limited number of sites.

This does not mean, however, as some American voices will have it, that the civilian use of these materials is completely ruled out if and when economy of use is not guaranteed. Cost-efficiency is certainly an important factor, especially as far as large-scale use is concerned, but the need to develop currently uneconomical technology for later deployment at a time when the economics may have changed is also an argument that is not without its merits. It may actually justify the use of sensitive materials, if on a far smaller scale. Major plutonium users have repeatedly revised energy plans originally drawn up in the 1970s, when energy data and expectations were vastly different. This duty to show flexibility and readiness to reconsider remains important.[10]

As the accountability of civilian users is recognized, which surpasses the obligations derived from Article III.1 in combination with Article IV of the NPT, we have all the more right to insist on commensurate commitments on the part of the nuclear-weapon states to whom the NPT has accorded a lavish, and eventually harmful, lack of obligation to provide for transparency and accountability for their own nuclear material. The disastrous consequences are now being demonstrated by the deteriorating security of fissile materials in the former Soviet Union; the recent appearance of weapons-grade plutonium smuggled into Germany, if in a subcritical quantity, is a deeply alarming event.[11] Accountability for weapons-usable material is thus a principle that must apply across the board, to civilian and to military use.

---

10. For a Japanese view on this see Yasutaka Moriguchi, "International management of plutonium," *Plutonium*, no. 6, summer 1994, pp. 16-19.
11. *Der Spiegel*, 29, July 18, 1994, pp. 18-21; Mark Hibbs, "Russian weapons plutonium storage termed unsafe by Minatom official," *Nucleonics week*, vol. 35, no. 17 (April 28, 1994), pp. 1 and 7.

Global versus Regional Approaches

The third question is the relation between global and regional approaches, and this falls into two parts. First, one has to find the most effective arrangement for the mutual complementarity of the NPT and IAEA safeguards and regional agreements and organizations. If done correctly, it can help the IAEA focus resources on the most troublesome regions. If done badly, it may lead to unnecessary duplication or even competition.[12]

Second, the relationship between regional and global regimes requires attention and harmonization. For instance, the General Conference of parties to the Tlatelolco Treaty is authorized to determine non-compliance and to inform the UN Security Council, the UN General Assembly, the Organization of American States and the IAEA accordingly (Article 20). Theoretically, such a finding by a regional organization could collide with activities and decisions taken by either the IAEA or the UN Security Council; similar discrepancies could arise in other regimes if and when - as we might expect - regional disarmament becomes a more common feature of world politics.[13] Such discrepancies would detract from the efficiency of compliance-finding procedures and would engender an inter-organizational conflict that would be detrimental to the credibility and, eventually, the legitimacy of both the global and the regional regimes. While this issue may seem to be a largely academic issue at present, it would be prudent to provide for procedural steps to eliminate all possibility of such confrontation.

Third, we have to find ways to deal with regions that are, for the time being, intractable for the instruments of the global regime, without, however, creating precedences in regional arrangements or in global approaches aimed at the crisis regions, and without compromising the rules and norms of the universal regime. The cut-off is a case in point: it is very useful for capping nuclear arsenals in the Middle East and South Asia, but if done neglectfully, it can lead to the legitimation of unsafeguarded fissile material stocks and thus counteract the principles on which the NPT is founded. The dilemma posed by the North Korean challenge is another case in point: the "lost son" principle that suggests particular incentives to bring Pyongyang back into the regime and end the nuclear destabilization in the region, is at odds with the "bad example" principle that tells us that too many

---

12. Fischer, *Towards 1995*, pp. 69-71 and 79-80.
13. Jayantha Dhanapala (ed.), *Regional approaches to disarmament, security and stability* (Aldershot, UK: Dartmouth for UNIDIR, 1993).

carrots may cause more "sons" to get "lost," in order to attract comparable remuneration. The tight-rope walk that is involved in weighing regional against universal considerations is very much subject to a case-by-case rather than a generalized approach, but one must be aware of the repercussions to the regime in trying to defuse regional crises.

Whatever the detailed relation between global and regional regimes, in general it is, again, firmly rooted in the NPT framework. Article VII foresees the smooth working of regional arrangements in parallel with the Treaty. The NPT safeguards' system serves as the standard that might be enhanced by special regional agreement, but never undercut.

Global versus Functional Organizations

Another emerging issue is the relation between global and functional organization in the non-proliferation area. Before the end of the century, we are likely to have four functional arms control organizations, the IAEA, the OPCW (Organization for the Prevention of Chemical Weapons), the BWCOrg (Biological Weapons Convention Organization), and, possibly, a CTBTO (Comprehensive Test Ban Treaty Organization). The Conventional Weapons Register (CWR) may evolve into an organization, or else the UN Center for Disarmament Affairs may assume more and more the role of a CWR Secretariat. Even the Missile Technology Control Regime (MTCR) may finally become an international treaty, with organizational consequences. This development cries out for strong efforts at coordination, leading to the idea of fusing these regimes, to develop a gigantic, worldwide COCOM and to establish the adequate organizational structure for the verification of non-proliferation and the corresponding export practices.[14]

Ideas like these underestimate the characteristics resulting from the regimes' "stock," grown over the years, which correlate with the technological-political inner laws of the corresponding political fields. The nuclear industry, for instance, is under constant legitimation challenges from the anti-nuclear movement. Green criticism against the chemical industry is directed against certain aspects

---

14. Derek Paul *et al.*, (eds), *Disarmament's missing dimension: a UN agency to administer multilateral treaty* (Toronto: Canadian Papers in Peace Studies 1, 1990); Leonard S. Spector and Virginia Foran, *Preventing weapons proliferation: should the regimes be combined?* (Muscatine, IA: The Stanley Foundation, 1992).

and practices, but not against the very existence of the industry. Biotechnology takes the middle. This different state of legitimacy of the civilian twin of military technology demands different regime structures.

The nuclear non-proliferation regime (Article IV NPT, IAEA Statute) contains promises of cooperation; the Convention on Chemical Weapons is vaguer; the Convention on Biological Weapons even more. The MTCR is a pure regime of denial. It is completely unclear how a conventional weapons' system should be connected.

The technical prerequisites are also different. In the nuclear field it is crucial to supervise the flow of a controlled amount of fissile materials. In the chemical industry the number of substances subject to control and their manifold applications are much higher. The biological industry stands out because of the self-reproduction of its incriminated substances, which makes quantitative fixings obsolete, in contrast to the nuclear and - with restrictions - the chemical field. But if prohibition rules and the corresponding verification measures inevitably have to be based on different principles, what sense could a union of the regimes make? The doubts mentioned above against the revival of the Baruch Plan apply here too: the bureaucratization of the non-proliferation that the creation of a super-non-proliferation authority would engender, would be a mistake. Who could effectively control such an organization? Who would meet the costs? How could the emergence of a bureaucratic competition be avoided, as happens with the armed services of all developed countries, the rivalry between the air force, navy and army being mirrored by the competition between the nuclear, chemical and biological (and possibly the missile and conventional) inspectorate, at higher costs and technical doublings of course? Adding several layers of top bureaucracy does little but to empower people with no grasp of detail but big salaries.

The merging of the different non-proliferation regimes violates their technological, political and normative inner laws and autonomy, increases the costs, and the danger of bureaucratic idleness decreases the flexibility of the different regimes. The only calculable gain is probably the concentration of information about the activities of different states; such information would permit an assessment as to what degree world peace is currently threatened, or how regional stability is affected by proliferation events. But this goal can be achieved in less bureaucratic and less costly ways. What is needed is a procedure to pool information that is collected by the individual regimes, to facilitate their mutual cooperation, and to enhance the capabilities of the UN Secretariat to prepare political evaluation of such pooled information at the Security Council level.

Another popular proposal in the United States is to revoke authority for nuclear verification measures away from the IAEA and commit them to an agency which should be directly assigned to the UN Security Council or the Secretary General.[15] At the bottom of this, there is the fundamental criticism that the IAEA is combining two incompatible tasks, the promotion of nuclear technology and the political control of non-proliferation.

In the wake of the Iraq conflict the IAEA was blamed for having failed its tasks. These reproaches are not absolutely unjustified, but basically they reveal a serious misunderstanding of the role and function of international organizations.

International organizations can only perform what their members allow, they can only use those instruments their members concede to them. They hardly meet the ideal of a perfectly effective bureaucracy. Far more than a national administration they have to comply with political conditions, directions and restrictions which are opposed to their actual organizational function.

This also applies to the IAEA.[16] Its safeguard system was created to detect the diversion of fissile material from the civilian nuclear industries in the industrialized non-nuclear-weapon states, the main object of proliferation efforts when the NPT was negotiated, in particular in Japan and in the Federal Republic of Germany. The system was limited in favor of the nuclear industries, because the non-nuclear-weapon states had succeeded in getting the limitations through during the negotiations of the NPT and the safeguards' document INFCIRC/153;[17] that is, the constrained access rights of the inspectors to "strategic points" in declared facilities, the limitation to information provided by the state inspected.[18]

Under pressure from its members the IAEA inspectorate had developed a bureaucratic "work-to-rule" mentality, which is unhealthy for their watchdog task. This occasionally disturbed the UN Special Commission. It would be wrong to forget the genesis of this mentality and to blame the task and function of the IAEA (safeguards and promotion of nuclear technology) for it. This reproach is grotesque considering the "promotion" actually carried out by the IAEA; to a

15. Paul Leventhal, "Why bother plugging export leaks?," *Orbis*, vol. 36, no. 2, spring 1992, pp. 167-80.
16. Lawrence Scheinman, *The International Atomic Energy Agency and world nuclear order* (Washington, DC: Resources of the Future, 1987).
17. Fischer, *Towards 1995*, pp. 55-8.
18. David Fischer, *Stopping the spread of nuclear weapons: the past and the prospects* (London: Routledge, 1992), pp. 124-8.

high degree it limits its efforts to the use of nuclear technology in agriculture, medicine, materials testing and basic research.

The arguments for removing the IAEA are not convincing, but the consequences of this step are much less desirable. Under the non-proliferation regime, the organization offers the only place where nuclear-technological cooperation, which is part of the NPT "nuclear bargain," can take place. The coexistence of safeguards and the IAEA's modest program of technical aid makes the regime more acceptable for member states from the developing world and soothes their uneasiness about discrimination. To disintegrate these connections would mean to broaden the room for the reproach of discrimination.[19]

In addition, the IAEA offers an approved form of participation to the developing countries. Of course, they still want more. But nevertheless the IAEA is a forum to debate sensitive issues like safeguards and the detection of a "proliferation case" in the North-South dialogue without the special position of the superpowers having too much effect. Shifting the non-proliferation policy from this context to the more hierarchical Security Council would mean making the problem a "Northern" one, shifting it into a private affair of the five permanent members (faced with the right of veto and their geopolitical interests this would not necessarily be an advantage, as the North Korean issue has revealed).[20]

Furthermore, the outcome for the Security Council/the Secretariat would not be favorable. The Security Council is a political body and should remain one. Verification tasks of the regular type are mostly of technical nature. It is unreasonable to charge the Security Council with these tasks. They don't fit into its assignment and could only absorb energies. In addition, technical questions always include controversial points of assessment, of which the Security Council should remain free.

It is therefore recommendable to leave the current separation of tasks unchanged. Efforts to shift the *esprit de corps* of the IAEA towards a stronger "watchdog awareness" would be sensible. This would need a different attitude by the member states in particular. A further question is whether a change of middle management of the organization or an enlargement of the inspection team by

---

19. Fischer, *Towards 1995*, chapter 7.
20. Paul Bracken, "Nuclear weapons and state survival in North Korea," *Survival*, vol. 35, no. 3, fall 1993, pp. 137-53; "Beijing cites pact with Pyongyang," *International Herald Tribune*, July 9-10, 1994, p. 2; McGeorge Bundy and Gordon M. Goldstein, "North Korea: prepare for high-voltage power politics," *International Herald Tribune*, July 6, 1994, p. 6.

personnel who are free of the previous philosophy of the organization would not be helpful.[21]

In a way, the continuation of the NPT would help to keep the IAEA in the game for two reasons. First, the NPT nominates the IAEA as the guardian of the verification system. If the Agency changes statute and character, this would presumably force an amendment to the NPT, a road few people would be anxious to pursue. Second, the NPT combines (in Articles III and IV) exactly the same two aspects embodied in the Agency: safeguards and nuclear cooperation. It would be somewhat illogical to have a unified legal instrument for non-proliferation, but to enact a divorce of these two functions in the administrative body meant to guard the Treaty.

Treaty Enforcement and the UN Security Council

This immediately invokes the fifth point, Treaty enforcement and the role of the UN Security Council therein. The North Korean case has brought all the difficulties of the enforcement process to the fore, not the least the absolute necessity to solicit the cooperation of the incriminated government's neighbors and, conversely, to heed those neighbors' advice on how to deal with the matter. Enforcement procedures are not well developed, and much remains to be done: creation of a greater arsenal of enforcement options, and a clearer understanding of which option applies under which circumstances.

The right to impose mandatory sanctions, including military actions, is unequivocally located with the United Nations Security Council. In accordance with Chapter VII of the UN Charter the Security Council can make use of all sanctions, reaching from economic boycott to the use of violent measures if a country threatens "peace or international security." Within the NPT regime the discovery of a diversion is reported by the IAEA Board of Governors to the Security Council, and the Security Council must be fully informed of the reasons for a withdrawal from the NPT. Before 1991 the Security Council did not connect proliferation and disturbance of peace. The second Gulf War changed this: the armistice Resolution 687 demands Iraq to reveal its nuclear potential, to open it

---

21. Such an effort is planned in the context of the "93 plus 2 program" for safeguards' reform currently discussed in the IAEA.

for international inspection, to destroy the entire nuclear weapons' potential and to place all its nuclear technological activities permanently under international surveillance. In July 1991, the IAEA Board of Governors stated that Iraq had violated its obligations towards the IAEA. In its Resolution 617 it decided upon a long-term destruction and surveillance program for Iraqi nuclear activities: the rights to unlimited development of civilian nuclear technology from Article IV of the NPT are refused to Iraq; enrichment, reprocessing, the possession of weapons-grade material are forbidden for the long term.[22]

Iraq lost a war. Therefore these sanctions cannot be applied to other situations without difficulties. In its decision of January 31, 1992, the Security Council made clear that the proliferation of weapons of mass destruction is to be seen as a threat against peace and international security.[23] There is thus the option of actions in accordance with Chapter VII of the UN Charter. After the statement of the Security Council on January 31, 1992, no would-be nuclear-weapon state can rely on the UN ignoring its activities. It will finally all depend on how the members of the Security Council judge the particular case.

The case of Iraq highlighted the crucial problem of the non-proliferation regime: what happens if a country breaks its obligations or if the international community perceives an intolerable threat in an act of proliferation? Until 1991, the interpretation prevailed that the UN Charter Article 51 applies to such a case, which deals with the option of self-help for the threatened countries. But already the Israeli attack on the Iraqi Osirak reactor had caused world-wide uneasiness. Unilateral acts to maintain an international regime are not satisfactory solutions.[24] Therefore the procedure for such a case has to be settled.

The question of which sanctions should be imposed in which cases cannot be fully answered. As military actions cannot be excluded, no member of the Security Council will be prepared to give a *carte blanche* without examining the

---

22. Serge Sur, *Security Council Resolution 687 of April 3, 1991 in the Gulf affair: problems of restoring and safeguarding peace* (New York: United Nations, UNIDIR Research Paper 12, 1992); Eric Chauvistré, *The implications of IAEA inspections under Security Council Resolution 687* (New York: United Nations, UNIDIR Research Paper 11, 1992).

23. *UN Security Council declaration on disarmament, arms control and weapons of mass destruction*, PPNN Newsbrief, no. 17, spring 1992, p. 15.

24. Mark D. Mandeles, "Between a rock and a hard place: implications for the US of Third World nuclear weapons and ballistic missile proliferation," *Strategic studies*, vol. 1, no. 2, winter 1991, pp. 235-69, and 242-5.

situation. On the other hand, the possibility of military sanctions - for instance to destroy military nuclear-weapon facilities or to seize fissile materials - may not be ruled out. The deterrent impact of such a possibility would be used optimally if the Military Committee of the Security Council was charged with the task of exploring options for this case. Additionally, the Security Council could request an investigation, carried out by the Secretary-General, to find out which opportunities are available for the Council if the decision of January 31, 1992 had to be applied. After 1995, it will be most important to establish the deterrent impact of sanctions through launching and maintaining a sanctions debate, if there are no concrete operations in place (it is to be hoped for lack of opportunity).

The threat of sanctions cannot be directed against NPT parties alone; it must equally concern the threshold states that stubbornly stay out of an international regime to which the vast majority of UN members have now subscribed. Limiting UN Security Council action to NPT violations, but turning a blind eye towards the outsiders, would mean discrimination to the disadvantage of members of the regime, and such discrimination would undermine the regime. In this respect, it is favorable that the Security Council's declaration speaks about the proliferation of weapons of mass destruction in general and mentions violations of the NPT only as a special case.

Whichever option for "military non-proliferation policy" is taken into consideration, the risks involved are high, the decision alternatives present a moral dilemma. Only in a desperate situation will the international community decide on the "*ultima ratio*," the use of military force. And only the observance of the legitimate decision procedures in the UN Security Council will prevent the international community from breaking asunder under the impression of such an action.[25] Once more this refers to the priority of a preventive non-proliferation policy.

Nuclear Disarmament

The last, most substantive as well as controversial issue is nuclear disarmament. Since the end of the Cold War, questions about the reasons to keep nuclear arms

---

25. Matthias Dembinski, Alexander Kelle and Harald Müller, *NATO and non-proliferation: a critical appraisal* (Frankfurt: PRIF Reports 33, 1994), pp. 33-48.

have gained new legitimacy and are bound to become more, and louder, in the coming years.[26] A few years ago nuclear disarmament was the Utopia of peace-pipe dreamers. But more recently strategists and military men unsuspected of pacifist drives, such as Paul Nitze and Air Force General Horner, think aloud as to whether it would not be in the US and global security interest to move towards nuclear disarmament.[27]

For many reasons, not all of which reside in the stubbornness or ill will of the nuclear-weapon states, nuclear disarmament is far from easy to realize. To consider the opportunities, conditions and requirements of a non-nuclear world, while arms reductions, transparency measures, and various constraints are negotiated and implemented, however, is an endeavor that the "nuclear haves" cannot refute without provoking serious concerns about the long-term viability of the non-proliferation regime.[28]

To start with, nuclear-weapon states should subject themselves to a reciprocal commitment of transparency. This should include the civilian fuel cycle in these countries as well as the supervision of a cut-off to the production of fissile materials for explosive purposes. Moreover, nuclear-weapon states should at least offer general data on the number of nuclear weapons and on the total fissile material circulating in their military fuel cycle. Annual changes should be reported. This would be a valuable addition to the regime, even if international verification could not initially be introduced. The German suggestion of establishing a nuclear weapons' register is thus fully justified and timely. The strong rejection of this idea by some nuclear-weapon states should not lead to resignation, particularly since in the United States, under the leadership of the Department of Energy, valuable steps are being taken towards more transparency, and first agreements have been achieved with Russia in this respect. As a final measure, a convention on the physical protection of fissile material in the military fuel cycle could complement the system of rules that place obligations on the nuclear-weapon states.

---

26. See my considerations in Harald Müller, David Fischer and Wolfgang Kötter, *Nuclear non-proliferation and global order* (Oxford: Oxford University Press, 1994), chapter 9.
27. Paul H. Nitze, "Replace the nuclear umbrella," *International Herald Tribune*, January 19, 1994, p. 7; "Scrap nuclear weapons, a General says," *International Herald Tribune*, July 16-17, 1994, p. 2.
28. Regina Gowan-Karp (ed.), *Security without nuclear weapons?* (Oxford: Oxford University Press, 1993).

The meaning of the NPT in this context is that it is the one and only valid international instrument that obliges nuclear-weapon states to embark on the road to nuclear disarmament.[29] If the NPT is abandoned, the obligation would fall away. The nuclear-weapon states could then take the position that their arsenals were legitimate means of self-defense under Article 51 of the UN Charter. Since the global norm that is gradually emerging against this assumption - that nuclear weapons have no legitimate use - is to a large degree based on the NPT, again, this norm would also weaken. The non-nuclear-weapon states are thus in the paradoxical situation where the purported "leverage" to force disarmament upon the reticent "haves" - scrapping the NPT - means "threatening" the destruction of the very legal tool that keeps them faithful to disarmament. And worse, if the NPT disappears, the voices in the nuclear-weapon states that argue for a renewal of the build-up in order to caution against the newly emerging multiple proliferation threats would no doubt gain strength.

Conclusions

Two conclusions derive from this analysis. First, the NPT, by and in itself, will not be able to solve the new questions coming after 1995. It needs to be supplemented by additional instruments, institutions, and practices. Second, without the NPT, such instruments, institutions and practices are unlikely to emerge. The NPT will remain the core of the nuclear non-proliferation regime unless and until it is replaced by a treaty for nuclear disarmament, and the termination of the Treaty without a substitute will most likely mean an erosion of all elements of the regime that would initially remain.

---

29. Fischer, *Towards 1995*, chapter 9.

11 NPT Extension, International Security, and the End of the Cold War

Brad Roberts

With 163 states as party to it, the NPT is the most widely subscribed to international treaty of any kind. The steady accumulation of new adherents in recent years, including a number of especially important states from the perspective of nuclear proliferation (such as China, France, and South Africa), only adds to its apparent vitality. From this perspective, posing questions about whether or not it should be extended, and under what conditions, appears to be an exercise in simple intellectual fatuousness. However, in fact, the NPT may not be extended. Or it may be extended only for a short period or with tough conditions attached. Or it may survive in form but not in actual substance, as more parties violate the Treaty while remaining signatories and the Treaty itself grow increasingly impaired in dealing with such non-compliance. Taking for granted the certainty of NPT extension under favorable terms may in fact contribute to just the opposite outcome. Panicking that its collapse is imminent is equally ill advised.

What sort of global nuclear control regime remains desirable or possible in today's world? Working 25 years ago, the architects of the NPT could hardly have imagined how large and interesting a question this would become by the time of the extension conference. The transformation of the superpower nuclear competition into a process of "safe and secure dismantlement" and far-ranging arms control in nuclear and other dimensions are but the most potent symbols of the changing circumstances; so too is the uncertainty about Russia's current ability and future willingness to remain as a partner in this process. Arms control itself has grown far more sophisticated, with the emergence of rigorous control regimes that operate at the bilateral, regional, and global levels, backed by comprehensive verification and compliance mechanisms and various unilateral measures. The nuclear proliferation problem has taken on distinctive regional attributes, with a pattern of partial nuclearization evident in some parts of the world, deproliferation in others, and an absence of interest in yet others. The democratic revolution in Latin America, Asia, and Africa has changed the way in

M. van Leeuwen (ed.), The Future of the International Nuclear Non-Proliferation Regime, 291-310.
© 1995 *Kluwer Academic Publishers. Printed in the Netherlands.*

which many countries think about problems of national security. And the emergence of a global trading and energy system has propelled the widespread diffusion of militarily significant technology, while at the same time increasing the economic leverage of states over each other.

This chapter offers eight propositions about the future nuclear control regime and the place of the NPT within it.

(1) *Over the Past 24 Years, the NPT has worked neither as badly as its Detractors, nor as well as its Most Passionate Supporters, would claim; it has, essentially, worked well enough.* The NPT has been the target of much criticism in recent years. Discoveries of violations by Iraq and North Korea have deepened doubts about the effectiveness of the NPT regime in detecting and responding to cheating. Doubts about the efficacy of the regime also have their roots in a number of suspected programs in other countries, such as Iran, the emergence of a new tier of suppliers of nuclear technologies, the possibility of nuclear proliferation following the breakup of the Soviet Union, and the general fear of instability wrought by the end of the bipolar international order. Surveying these problems, critics of the NPT have dismissed the Treaty as an irrelevant or at least waning instrument of international security.

NPT supporters have often made a similar but opposite mistake: they protect the Treaty too readily, sometimes sounding naive in defending a regime that has suffered some glaring failures, as in pre-war Iraq. In dealing with specific cases of nuclear proliferation, it is fair to argue that the NPT has worked about as well as the major powers have wanted. Where the NPT has worked less than well, is largely as a result of the absence of consensus among these states about the issues at stake or their allegiances in time of conflict.

In general, the NPT has been valuable, primarily because of the political norm it embodies and nourishes against the nuclearization of national security policy, whether through the acquisition or use of nuclear weapons. This norm has been critical in establishing the expectations of many states (Germany and Japan are two prominent examples) about their long-term nuclear interests and orientations. It has thus helped to build confidence among states, thereby reinforcing the norm. Consequently, the NPT has been the foundation for a broad international effort to constrain weapons' proliferation and the diffusion of militarily relevant technology generally, without which the expanding set of global negotiated measures (such as the conventions on chemical and biological weapons) and export-coordinating mechanisms (for example, the Australia Group, the Missile Technology Control Regime) would have been much less likely or effective.

This is a perspective that looks at the nuclear crises in the former Soviet Union, Iraq, and North Korea not as failures of the NPT but as challenges and opportunities for the regime, as reminders of the stakes involved, of the instabilities attendant to nuclearization, and of the necessity for cooperative international responses to such problems - and of the importance of resolving these crises in ways that sustain the non-nuclear norm in international affairs. For example, the ability to marshal collective responses to both the Iraqi and Korean problems hinges primarily on both states being signatories to the NPT; if such a legal framework were absent, the international politics of diplomacy that are necessary to confront these challenges would be played out with much less success. In future efforts by the United Nations Security Council to deal with proliferation where it is a threat to international security, as foreshadowed in the January 1992 statement S25000, this framework and the consensus it embodies will prove to be essential foundations of sustained international support.

The NPT is basically a tool of policy, to be used in conjunction with other tools (such as other treaty regimes, the UN, military action, export controls, etc.). With meaningful political commitment these tools can be used to reduce proliferation. Used badly or not at all, they can make the problem worse. That the NPT is not perfectly verifiable or universally subscribed to is not quite the point; whether it is adequately verifiable or broad enough in its adherents is in the eye of the beholder. Non-proliferation is a means to an end - a more secure international environment - and not an end in itself.

How important is an imperfect regime? To cite Lawrence Scheinman:

> "If a country believes that its vital security interests or national integrity require the acquisition of nuclear weapons, it will make that decision. What is more interesting is the extent to which its evaluation of all the political, economic, diplomatic, and security considerations that enter such decisions are shaped, influenced, and tempered by the more general environment and especially by its normative content. The argument presented here is that the impact is more than we might be ready to admit, but less than we might dare to hope. Neither the NPT medium, nor its normative message alone, can prevent a determined nation from acquiring nuclear weapons. In no case has it been, nor is it in the future likely to be, the decisive factor. But as part of the environment in which states operate, to which decision-makers respond, and in which decisions ultimately are taken, it plays an unquantifiable but meaningful role. It tints the lenses through which the world, both its opportunities and its restraints, are seen. In this sense, at least, the NPT has made a

difference, and its demise would be felt far more profoundly than some of its critics would like to think."[1]

There is a related question: why has the regime worked as well as it has? Much of the answer derives from the structure of the international system that has prevailed during the life of the NPT. The West's strategy of containment, the engagement of both superpowers in the security affairs of regional allies, and the joint fear of cataclysmic nuclear war arising from uncontrollable regional conflicts have all served to constrain narrowly the tendencies towards proliferation, except where superpower security assurances were not taken as credible or sufficient, as in the case of Israel, or where the international community had little leverage, as in the case of India. In this broad context, the NPT was a political undertaking not easily abrogated by developing countries with client relations to the North, and the International Atomic Energy Agency was simply given the task of monitoring the declared activities of states. Non-proliferation outcomes in the international system consequently depended heavily on the nature of the system. Non-proliferation policy tools were employed only at the margins where major powers had no sharply conflicting interests, as in South Africa.

The passing of the bipolar order thus raises basic questions about the new proliferation environment. Politically, the guarantees and strictures of the past are gone. Technologically, the diffusion of nuclear technologies, materials, and competence has put nuclear weapons within the reach of many new states. But the role of global factors and the structure of the international system in shaping the proliferation problem and the NPT debate should not be overemphasized. Regional factors have played an increasingly important role in recent years in the politics of the NPT and as determinants of proliferation behavior. The future of the nuclear non-proliferation regime will be determined to a very significant degree by how states respond to the exigencies and opportunities of their local security environment, although the repercussions of the end of the Cold War on regions around the world and on the future roles of the major powers will be felt for years to come.

(2) *Whatever the Past Utility of the NPT, the Debate about its Extension should revolve around its Utility for Future Challenges.* That the NPT has worked in one

---

1.   Lawrence Scheinman, "Does the NPT matter?," in Joseph F. Pilat and Robert E. Pendley, (eds), *Beyond 1995: the future of the NPT regime* (New York: Plenum Press, 1990), p. 62.

particular fashion in the past is no guarantee that it will work in the same fashion in the future. There are reasons to hope that it might function even more effectively (as the safeguards' systems are strengthened, broader membership is achieved, and the major powers take a renewed interest in its success). But there are also reasons to believe that it will not work better - or even as well as it has. The problems of old have not gone away and they threaten to grow even less manageable in an era of global instability and technology diffusion.

Because the important successes of the NPT are political, it seems logical to conclude that the NPT will survive as an effective instrument of international security policy only if the non-nuclear norm remains germane and sustainable. Will it?

Among the founders and long-time supporters of the NPT, the Treaty's continued value as an international public good is an established fact. A commitment to non-proliferation is perceived essentially as an attribute of good global citizenship. The inability of these NPT supporters to project the past relevance of the NPT into the future, and to argue credibly for ways in which the non-nuclear norm is helpful for the specific security problems faced today and tomorrow by states contemplating nuclear acquisition, works against indefinite and unconditional NPT extension.

For what sorts of general problems of post-Cold War international security do the non-nuclear norm and the NPT remain useful? The NPT makes a tangible contribution to slowing, halting, and reversing the proliferation of nuclear weapons and to the national security of many states. It also gives expression to international will aimed at preventing destabilizing changes, creating and enforcing agreed norms of behavior, reinforcing international standards of statecraft, demonstrating the possibility and efficacy of negotiated measures that bridge international divisions, and laying the basis for states in the fluid post-Cold War world to work together and take risks in pursuit of larger goals. More specifically, for relations among the advanced countries, the NPT remains a bulwark of their commitment to a set of relations in which war is a virtual impossibility. It provides some stability in terms of a fixed set of rules, expectations, and procedures of special relevance during a time of sweeping global change. It imposes significant constraints on aspiring nuclear powers, leaving them only compelling national interest as an incentive to pursue weapons and acquire capabilities that remain "in the basement." It imposes obligations on the nuclear-weapon states to accept constraints to their power, and, by raising the stakes of nuclear use, it pressures the nuclear-weapon states to adopt doctrines and strategies that limit such use to cases of last resort. Of course, not all countries will always perceive these utilities as relevant or desirable, or perceive their values in the same ways.

However, might abandonment of the non-nuclear norm and the NPT also serve some international security interests in the post-Cold War era? In the views of NPT opponents are to be found the seeds of a possible future nuclear order, one in which the non-nuclear norm has been abandoned and nuclear arsenals have diffused widely to states of all capability and rank. How well might such an outcome serve international order?

In such a system, many states would enjoy the ability to veto the actions of others or at least to raise the perceived risks and actual costs of interventionary action to a very considerable extent. Speculation about how such a unit veto system might function has focused both on its potentially stabilizing effects, that is preventing imperialist or hegemonic states from manipulating others, to its destabilizing ones, such as undermining the collective security principle and establishing zones where ruthless dictators might be free to annihilate hated enemies or pursue fantasies of social engineering.

However well (or not) such a system might function, it would not immediately emerge with abandonment of the NPT. In the short term at least, disincentives of an economic, political, and security nature will continue to constrain nuclearization. Some of these may remain operative for a long period of time. Besides, not all states seek security through nuclear means: a more competitive regional nuclearization would probably bring some of the most harmful aspects of arms races and crisis instability, of the sort that threatened the US-Soviet nuclear relationship. Weapons would also undoubtedly fall into the hands of leaders bent on using them for purposes of aggression, blackmail, or aggrandizement, probably thereby increasing the likelihood of a nuclear confrontation with nations committed to collective security actions. All of this would have negative and possibly far-reaching security repercussions, not just for the existing nuclear powers but also for many non-nuclear states, including even those who have not been signatories to the Treaty.[2] At the very least, the demise of existing international forums to deal with nuclear proliferation would force management of the problem ever more into unilateral, bilateral, and other multilateral channels.

---

2. See Lewis A. Dunn, "The collapse of the NPT - what if?," and Joseph F. Pilat, "A world without the NPT?," in: Pilat and Pendley (eds), *Beyond 1995*, pp. 27-40 and 151-63.

Given the many possible deleterious effects of widespread nuclear proliferation, even critics of the NPT and challengers to the international *status quo* are not actively agitating for a universal pro-nuclear norm. The case against nuclear non-proliferation made by countries like India, Iran and China is based much more on narrow national self-interest than on the global good. Thus many of these states walk a careful line between opposing the Treaty strongly enough to serve their perceived national needs, but not so strong as to threaten the collapse of a major element of global order.

If there is little certainty about the future effectiveness of the NPT, there is even less certainty about the nature of the world order towards which we are moving. Basic questions are today unanswered. What will be the roles of the great powers in the international system? Do the large industrial powers have any special roles in an international system of nearly 180 states that is marked by growing regionalization, a diffusion of high-leverage military capability, and the differentiation of economic and political power? Will the United States seek continued international leadership or return to more isolated or at least insular ways? Will Russia and China achieve solid membership of the international community as supporters of existing international mechanisms and norms, or will they seek to obstruct the functioning of those mechanisms while also generating conflicts around their periphery? What continuing roles do the United Kingdom and France desire, or can they sustain, and are India, Brazil, or others ready to join them as states taking a special responsibility for dealing with common problems of international security? Will the United Nations and the collective security principle emerge rejuvenated or eviscerated from the post-Cold War decade? Will inequities of wealth and welfare erupt into militarized North-South confrontation? Will a global system marked by sharply different types of regional structures (for example, a liberal political one in Latin America, an economic one in East Asia) generate order or disorder? Will transnational issues related to the environment, population growth, and resource planning sow the seeds of great global cooperation or sharper conflict? Will the Chemical Weapons Convention (CWC) and an amended Biological Weapons Convention (BWC) emerge as serviceable adjuncts to the NPT? What type of nuclear order will emerge among the nuclear-weapon states? All of these factors will have a major impact on the fate of the non-nuclear norm.

This points to the near impossibility of securing agreement among the community of nations that the non-nuclear norm is something that serves common interests in perpetuity. However, agreement that the non-nuclear norm continues to serve common interests for the foreseeable future may be easier to secure.

Even this may prove elusive, however, for a simple reason: with the passing of the Cold War, the bargain between the nuclear-weapon states of the mid-1960s and the remainder of the international community is not sustainable forever on its own terms. This does not perhaps mean that some new basis cannot be found for an international consensus in support of an unequal allocation of nuclear rights and responsibilities. But there is little evidence that the advocates of NPT extension among the nuclear-weapon states have sought to think through or make this case.

Thus, the answer to the question posed above (will the NPT survive?) is, "it depends." It cannot be argued with certainty that the nuclear order embodied in the NPT can, will, or should be sustained in perpetuity or even indefinitely. The non-nuclear norm may well be more durable than the particular embodiment of it in the NPT. However, it can surely be asserted that abandonment of the NPT in 1995 would bring with it a new degree of uncertainty and new pressures for proliferation that would be more immediate and tangible than the benefits of extension.

(3) *The Nuclear-Weapon States are not Ready to Relinquish their Nuclear Weapons, but this does not Preclude Substantial Future Progress in Implementing their NPT Commitments.* None of the nuclear-weapon states is any more willing today than in 1968 to abandon the nuclear status enshrined in the NPT. For Russia, the United Kingdom, France, and China, nuclear weapons are a basic element of the claim to Great Power status, a prominent feature of their global diplomatic and political roles, and a perceived stabilizing feature in their international security environments. Of the nuclear-weapon states, only the United States has pressed for the delegitimization of such weapons. In the case of the United States, nuclear weapons remain a fundamental aspect of national identity and self-confidence, and, as they did in the years immediately after the Second World War, they continue to underpin what remains of a US willingness to assume international obligations.

On the other hand, at the April 1995 review conference the erstwhile superpowers will have a strong case to make that they have made progress in stepping back from the nuclear brink, with the implementation of a broad array of arms control agreements and the program of safe and secure dismantlement of nuclear weapons. The United States, for example, is currently destroying nuclear weapons as fast as it can, at a rate of about 2,000 warheads per year. They can also point to the expected future reductions in nuclear weapons following implementation of the Strategic Arms Reduction Treaty (START) 2 agreement.

Looking to the future, further progress in honoring NPT commitments will be required of the nuclear-weapon states. Will this be possible? With the rapid contraction of the superpowers' nuclear arsenals, the other nuclear-weapon states emerge as more significant in the global nuclear order. As yet, neither the United Kingdom, France, nor China appears willing to shrink its nuclear arsenals, accept new limitations on their use, or move towards the future elimination of nuclear weapons. They would argue that arms reductions are both unnecessary, because they did not indulge in the huge buildup of the Cold War years, and unwise, because they would threaten essential forces in contrast to the largely superfluous excesses of the superpowers.

But assuming the successful implementation of START 2 and the absence of any major new state armed with a militarily significant stockpile of weapons of mass destruction and long-range delivery systems, the nuclear-weapon states will face mounting pressures, of both a political and economic nature, to step even further back from nuclear weapons. Indeed, even modest arsenals with no apparent purpose other than the defense of national stature will face sharp public scrutiny. It is not unreasonable in these circumstances to anticipate a future Treaty that would provide a kind of nuclear order among the nuclear-weapon states. Such a Treaty might follow on from the START reduction process and incorporate all of the recognized nuclear-weapon states into a structure of balanced forces at lower levels. It is also reasonable to expect efforts to integrate such an instrument formally into the larger global nuclear order.

As an interim or substitute measure, some constraints on the ability of the nuclear-weapon states to enjoy ready recourse to their nuclear weapons may be considered, what might be called "nuclear neutralization,"[3] whereby there is a progressive shrinkage, partial dismantlement, and international supervision of the nuclear assets of the nuclear-weapon states. Related efforts aimed at formalizing a

---

3. Lewis A. Dunn, "Fifty years since Stagg Field: nuclear non-proliferation challenges and opportunities," prepared for a symposium at the University of Chicago, November 24, 1992, p. 35; Jonathan Dean, "The final stage of nuclear arms control," *The Washington Quarterly*, vol. 17, no. 4, fall 1994, pp. 31-52. See also George H. Quester and Victor A. Utgoff, "Toward an international nuclear security policy," *The Washington Quarterly*, vol. 17, no. 4, fall 1994, pp. 5-18.

commitment to consult at the UN Security Council prior to making first use of a nuclear weapon might also have a positive effect in establishing in the minds of nuclear proliferants that any nuclear use against a nuclear-weapon state would automatically entail a concerted international response and not just a solitary one by the targeted state. Such measures appear non-negotiable today, but might prove more palatable a decade or two hence if deep reductions by the erstwhile superpowers have led to improved stability and if nuclear proliferation has been held in check. However, major nuclear reductions will not be extracted from the nuclear-weapon states without some equally significant concessions by others, perhaps in the form of greater support for non-proliferation enforcement actions by the Security Council.

It is important to note that abandonment of the NPT prior to the establishment of any substantial global successor regime would probably have the effect of reversing tendencies towards nuclear cuts, de-emphasis, and neutralization among the nuclear-weapon states. Indeed, the expectation that the nuclear non-proliferation regime will function even better than in the past is a foundation for all such proposals.

(4) *The Emergence of New Nuclear Powers does not require Abandonment or Amendment of the NPT; Other Complementary Approaches offer Promise as Interim Measures for Restraining these Programs.* The challenge of finding a legal status within the Treaty for the new nuclear states (such as India, Israel and Pakistan) has bedeviled diplomats for years. Of the proposed remedies (such as expanding the formal nuclear club or creating a new category of states), none would strengthen the NPT because each suggests that the proliferator nations will easily cross legally from a non-nuclear to another status. Rather, supporters of the non-nuclear norm should look for regional adjuncts to the global regime that establish controls over new nuclear arsenals without also diluting the NPT. The emergence of a separate control regime in Latin America with the Treaty of Tlatelolco should be the forerunner of regional measures elsewhere, and these should preferably be formal, negotiated measures that provide clear benchmarks of compliance and should be backed by some type of international authority. During the next few years nuclear-weapon-free zones are likely to be established in Africa and expanded in the South Pacific; a weapons-of-mass-destruction free zone has emerged as a long-term possibility in the Middle East. Meanwhile, where formal control regimes appear impossible at this time, interim measures that are focused on confidence-building and transparency are being pursued, as in

South Asia and East Asia. These should be welcomed as instruments supportive of the non-proliferation aspiration, even if they provide partial legitimization of weapons' programs. *Ad hoc* arrangements also ought to be acceptable on an interim basis.

Regional measures can be strengthened by extension into these regions of new global mechanisms, such as a Comprehensive Test Ban Treaty or a ban on weapons grade fissile fuel production. Perhaps a Treaty among these new nuclear-weapon states might also be considered, one that defines acceptable constraints and formalized commitments to goals that are short of full nuclearization.

Assuming such regional measures are successfully implemented over a sustained period, it may prove feasible to integrate them into the global nuclear control regime. Again the case of Latin America is instructive: the bilateral, multilateral, and regional nuclear arms control measures that have developed there in recent decades are increasingly converging with the NPT, such that the principal near-nuclear powers appear ready to join the NPT.

(5) *There may be Other Ways to craft an International Treaty that accomplish shared Aspirations to control Nuclear Weapons, but there is now no Alternative to Extending the NPT.* It is conceivable that a replacement instrument might be crafted that would incorporate the various bilateral and multilateral nuclear arms control measures, the relevant national policies already in place, and tighten constraints on the nuclear-weapon states and the near-nuclear states. But it is difficult to conceive that such a new measure would go substantially beyond existing obligations at this time, and it is impossible to conceive that such an instrument could be ready by April 1995. The best, in the sense of an ideal, comprehensive Treaty, could very likely prove to be the enemy of the good - the preservation of the non-nuclear norm. Advocates of the ideal must recognize that the next significant steps in global nuclear arms control await regional outcomes that are as yet not certain. There are great doubts about the fate of post-Soviet reform and the inherited Soviet nuclear arsenal, the future attitudes of the nuclear-weapon states towards their nuclear weapons, the peace process in the Middle East, the South Asian balance, and the efforts to prevent nuclearization in Iraq and North Korea. Until positive outcomes are achieved on most of these, the NPT remains the only possible global nuclear measure.

Moreover, even if another treaty could quickly be negotiated, it could not quickly be brought into force or, when brought into force, achieve legal status with anything near 163 participants. Parliamentary approval would be required again; in the case of the NPT, 19 years were required for all of the 94 original signatories to complete the ratification process.

The NPT has always been understood as a bridge to something else, although the goal has been understood differently by different states, some defining it as nuclear de-emphasis and others as nuclear disarmament. In this new era, that bridging function is more important than ever. The NPT must be sustained in 1995 because of what it makes possible later. It is a means to begin and focus the discussion about the nature of the post-Cold War international security dynamic and the place of nuclear weapons therein. A serious weakening or abandonment of the NPT in 1995 would probably work against the international cooperation necessary to keep the bridge sturdy.

(6) *Making Incremental Fixes to the Nuclear Non-Proliferation Regime is a Necessary but not Sufficient Condition for the Achievement of Future Nuclear Non-Proliferation; the Basic Political Bargain in the NPT must be reinvigorated.* A host of measures have been proposed to strengthen the nuclear non-proliferation regime, largely with regard to the safeguards' system and more universal membership. Some steps may prove helpful; others may not. As a whole, however, such fixes are not a substitute for the political task of rejuvenating an international bargain on nuclear weapons, one that is perceived as valid and is believed to be sustainable in the post-Cold War era. Failure to do so may not preclude NPT extension in 1995, but it would contribute to the perception of the NPT as a hollow, dated instrument, largely sustained in the service of Great Power military superiority.

The old bargain entailed commitments by some states to forswear nuclear weapons in exchange for negative and positive security assurances and the promise of assistance to develop nuclear technologies for peaceful applications. It was a bargain legitimized by a Cold War in which nuclear weapons were widely seen as preventing "Hot War," even as the nuclear buildup raised the stakes. It was also a bargain that conspicuously granted nuclear status to the victors of a major international war five decades ago.

It is politically untenable that the NPT be seen as a tool for projecting into the future a global order rooted in a world now half a century past. The diffusion of nuclear technologies, materials, and expertise makes that political reality of paramount importance, because opponents of the current distribution of nuclear assets are empowered to upset the balance.

The key question is whether a discriminatory regime - that is, one that allocates rights unevenly - can find a workable consensus in the new strategic environment. As a point of departure, it is important to recognize that a broad international consensus already exists on this point: most states do not oppose such discrimination, indeed some welcome it as a way of securing the benefits of credible guarantees from a powerful state. A political scientist might also note that a completely non-discriminatory regime that establishes equality among states is simply unrealistic: all states should be equal before the law, but their inheritances of geography, culture, and political economy, and their recognizable differences of power and assumed international obligation, also require that international agreements be crafted to exploit these differences for common purposes. Yet opposition to the discriminatory nuclear regime exists, and it is vocal. Indeed, in some key nuclear-capable states, such as Indonesia, the NPT is dismissed as having failed to achieve its "fundamental objectives."

In order to rejuvenate the international bargain on nuclear weapons, the nuclear-weapon states must take the lead in articulating and pursuing a vision of international politics and of an allocation of nuclear rights and responsibilities that is politically sustainable in the period ahead, for another ten or twenty-five years. The extent to which the nuclear powers can make a persuasive case that their retention of nuclear weapons as the sole nuclear-weapon states, under some system of checks and balances, remains relevant to the solution of new, post-Cold War problems of international security, provides some basis for the sustenance of a continued inequality of obligations.

Around what basic principles might such a new bargain be built, or at least discussed?

One element must be what Lewis Dunn has labeled "nuclear de-emphasis ... a strategy aimed at reducing the role of nuclear weapons in regional and global politics to the absolute practical minimum."[4]

A second element must be nuclear stewardship. To the degree that the nuclear-weapon states have begun to articulate a new vision of their nuclear responsibilities, they tend to define their role as one of safe custodianship - ensuring that the build-down phase is unthreatening to others, promotes international stability, contributes to non-proliferation, and is carried out in an environmentally sensitive fashion. This is a minimalist agenda, to the extent that it

---

4.   Dunn, "Fifty years since Stagg Field," p. 35.

defends nuclear retention as being an unavoidable inheritance and one that must be managed so that it is unthreatening to others. But a more ambitious agenda seems necessary if international consensus is to be sustained, one that looks beyond safe custodianship to effective stewardship, that defends nuclear-weapon status as something held in trust for the larger international community. Stewardship involves national restraint and international obligation.

Stewardship also involves tying nuclear retention to the management of new challenges. For what post-Cold War problems of international security are a discriminatory regime relevant and necessary? Finding answers to this question will involve thinking through the role that nuclear weapons play in the relationships of the nuclear-weapon states (and in limiting war among them), in sustaining the confidence and power of states that have assumed significant international treaty and enforcement obligations (as have members of the Security Council), in deterring the aggressive ambitions of states intent on conquering neighbors or capturing international economic assets, and in weakening the incentives of states to acquire other unconventional weapons, especially biological ones. The old answer that nuclear weapons are important for deterring East or West is no longer legitimate. But it is possible that there are new answers that might be widely accepted as legitimate.

It seems unlikely that answers to these questions will come quickly, or that their implications for national force structures and doctrines will be easily implemented. Politically, it seems unnecessary that such answers be found prior to the 1995 NPT conference. But failure even to begin this discussion, or to recognize that it is necessary, will mean that the nuclear-weapon states have made too little effort to sustain the political reality that gives the legal instrument its operational force.

As the nuclear-weapon state with the most far-flung international obligations and entanglements (and as the first and only state to use a nuclear weapon), the United States has chief responsibility for articulating such a vision. In order to achieve a new global bargain on nuclear weapons, the United States would be well advised to demonstrate to the world its willingness to take steps to harness its power more firmly to collective goals, rather than advertise its efforts to preserve its military advantages in perpetuity. Americans (and many of their allies) fear that this implies abandoning a significant proportion of those advantages; it need not. Although such advantages are not politically sustainable at a global level on their own terms, meaningful military superiority may be preserved for a long time if the United States rearticulates the purposes of American power - and especially its nuclear weapons - in the changed global context.

Until the United States takes on this challenge, the accusations that it is an essentially conservative, *status quo*-oriented power that holds on to its nuclear preponderance in order to perpetuate its moment of pre-eminence after the Second World War will continue to find their mark. This will have a direct impact on the effort to extend and strengthen global controls on weapons of mass destruction and to make the most of the new opportunities for the UN. For many developing countries, as for many developed ones, these treaties and institutions are essentially security instruments embodying an agreed allocation of rights, responsibilities, and power in the world. They are reluctant to codify a set of rules for a new era without some revitalized consensus about the nature of the international security agenda now that the Cold War is over, and of the utility of those instruments for new purposes. The United States makes achieving a new consensus more difficult by turning a deaf ear to the concerns of other states about its own uncertain role, thereby reinforcing their fears that the United States really has little or no idea of how to use its power on behalf of the larger international community.

This is not to argue that the nuclear powers confront a strong and distinct negotiating adversary in the so-called South. Quite to the contrary, there is a wide variety of orientations and ambitions among states in this group. The Non-Aligned Movement continues as something of a factor in the post-Cold War era, but with diminished force. China wants to lead the group of "aspiring powers" on global issues but has to date not pursued the kind of diplomatic strategy that would make this possible. Iran, India, and Pakistan, among others, purport to lead a "Southern camp" opposed to existing non-proliferation approaches, but the depth of their support among developing countries appears scant. The problem confronting the advocates of NPT extension arises precisely from the disparate and volatile nature of these political forces and the possibility that they will coalesce around a few key issues of broad importance. At the moment, only a very few developing countries are likely to want to abandon the structures now available - the NPT, the BWC, the UN, etc. - in an effort to upset a stable international security environment, but others will join their cause if through mismanaging the proliferation problem the United States helps turn it into a confrontation between states fearful of change and states resentful of US power.

(7) *Some Compromise appears likely between those who desire Indefinite Extension and those who prefer a Shorter Term; There are Many Obvious but no Easy Points of Compromise.* The ideal outcome of the NPT conference in April 1995 would be one that sustains the commitment of the international community to the non-nuclear norm and, given the circumstances, to the NPT-based expression of this norm. The case for indefinite extension is strong. Widespread nuclear proliferation is unlikely ever to be perceived as something desirable for all states. Moreover, companion regimes controlling biological and chemical weapons (the BWC and CWC) are both permanent Treaties that specify no end-date. The worst outcome would be abandonment of an almost global regime because of the strong opposition of a few key states. Of course, many of them will not be represented officially at the conference because they are not parties to the NPT, although their views are certainly being felt in the lead-up to the review. Only slightly less undesirable would be abandonment of the NPT for the utopian project of recreating it in different form at a later time.

Also desirable would be an outcome that respects the contingent character of many of the factors determining the long-term commitment of states to the non-nuclear norm. If things go well in the coming decade or two for START, for regional security, for international cooperation generally, new possibilities for global nuclear control may well come into focus, and the NPT may well be succeeded by something else. If they go badly, the non-nuclear norm is likely to be but one of many casualties.

Unfortunately, the specific provisions of the NPT provide no easy way to achieve both extension and contingency. Without amending the Treaty, parties face a simple choice: extension or not, and if so, for how long. Extension on anything other than a permanent basis would signal the beginning of the end of the NPT, as its expiration is confirmed by a certain date. Opting for another review conference after extension would also require amendment; so too would tying extension to specific actions by parties beyond those required in the Treaty (for example, implementation of a comprehensive test ban). Successful and timely NPT amendment is virtually impossible, requiring as it would parliamentary review, which would at the least weaken if not cripple the Treaty. These factors account in significant measure for the United States' commitment to seek permanent extension.

The United States government believes that it is well supported in this view, despite the debates about discrimination and limited extension, if not by all parties to the NPT, then at least by a majority (the threshold necessary under NPT provisions to secure extension). It correctly observes that the most vocal opponents of unequal nuclear rights are few in number and generally not states that are party to the Treaty.

But if a significant minority objects to extension, the disgruntlement of the minority may become manifest in a willingness to cheat or an unwillingness to support efforts to secure compliance by others. Dismissing such states as malefactors denigrates too easily the modest leverage they seek to maintain over the nuclear policies and arsenals of the nuclear-weapon states - which they would lose with permanent extension. It also dismisses too easily their desire to narrow the ability of the nuclear-weapon states to exploit nuclear advantages for narrow national purposes - a sentiment widely shared by the public of the nuclear-weapon states and among NPT signatories.

At the time of writing, some compromise appears inevitable, not least because the nuclear-weapon states have done so poor a job of establishing broad international legitimacy for their nuclear advantages and paying heed to the fears created by the end of the Cold War.

Short-term extensions offer the fewest benefits for sustaining belief in the durability of the non-nuclear norm. A one- or two-year extension pegged to implementation of a Comprehensive Test Ban Treaty could actually stimulate nuclear programs in states that fear the advantage regional adversaries might seek to gain with a crash program. (Moreover, advocates of such short-term extension have not made the case that the amendments necessary to make this work are feasible within this time frame, or even at all.)

A seven- or ten-year extension tied to conclusion of START 2 implementation would have more logic, but could have a similar effect in generating nuclear programs as counterbalances. (The importance of looking beyond START 2 in an NPT context is underscored by the fact that as planned, US and Russian nuclear force levels after START 2 implementation will remain well above those in place at the time that the NPT entered into force.) But a delay of this length might also coalesce with other forces at work in international politics to undermine the NPT. It is not difficult to conjecture, for example, that Germany and Japan, facing uncertain NPT prospects and worsening strategic relationships with a nuclear-armed Ukraine,[5] North Korea or China might move towards near-nuclear status

---

5.   Editor's note: this chapter was submitted before the achievement of the US-DPRK Agreed Framework and Ukraine's ratification of the NPT.

through the accumulation of the necessary ingredients of a "virtual arsenal." Nuclearization by both Germany and Japan appears highly unlikely at this time, but such a risk would certainly be heightened in a deteriorating international environment defined in part by minimal expectations of NPT extension.

Of the limited extension options, a 25-year extension makes the most sense, parallel as it is to the current 25-year phase. The incipient pressures for nucleari-zation it might generate would be modest. The pressures it would generate on supporters of the non-nuclear norm, and especially on the nuclear-weapon states, to set in place foundations for a successor nuclear order could well be construc-tive.

But in an era of global uncertainty and strategic drift among the nuclear-weapon states, these possible benefits of extension for a fixed but long term may well be outweighed by the benefits to be gained from doing something now to set in place a major building block of global order and long-term predictability. This points to the possibility of some consensus on a decision to extend the NPT for fixed periods of 25 years each, subject to a decision by NPT parties at the conclusion of any 25-year period to abandon the treaty.[6]

The conference may make use of an alternative mechanism to secure both conditionality and extension: a suspended review, whereby final closure of the conference is held in abeyance for as long as a year or two until achievement of a Comprehensive Test Ban. Many Treaty supporters deem such an outcome undesirable because it would raise questions about whether extension might ever be achieved. It also seems an unlikely outcome given the strong backing to the Treaty and to indefinite and unconditional extension by most major states and leading international institutions. But it may prove preferable to forcing an end to the April 1995 conference by abandoning the consensus-based process of the past for a formal vote on extension, which would probably result in a majority decision to extend the Treaty but also a weakening of that consensus among those opposing the vote.

---

6.   David Fischer, *Towards 1995: the prospect for ending the proliferation of nuclear weapons* (Aldershot, UK: Dartmouth for UNIDIR, 1993), see chapters 13 and 14.

(8) *Non-Proliferation cannot be Successful if Pursued in the Absence of a Larger Strategy for North-South Relations that redresses Basic Grievances and shares Common Resources to address Basic Problems of Governance and Development.* The diffusion of the defense industrial base, more so than of weapons themselves, has changed the very nature of the proliferation problem. It is proving increasingly difficult on the basis of denial strategies alone to prevent states from acquiring the weapons they desire *in extremis*. This compels the non-proliferation community to focus increasingly on the will to acquire weapons, and not just the ability to do so.

But dealing with the will of proliferator states to acquire weapons requires more than just rejuvenation of the discriminatory NPT bargain. It also requires some effort to deepen the stakes held by such states in the international system, by tying the system more closely to their political and developmental aspirations. It is difficult to conceive of a circumstance in which poor countries would forswear high-leverage military instruments if they understood that rich countries took little interest in their well-being and security. The general problem with export controls and strategies of technology denial is that they suggest that the rich are interested in keeping the rest of the world both weak and poor.

Failure to deal with this perception will reinforce North-South tensions on a broad array of issues while fueling possible conflict between states desirous of change and *status quo* powers fearful of it. Extending the North-South agenda to a broad set of issues, and identifying non-proliferation as a means towards a common end, rather than an obstacle to it, will reinforce the benefits of cooperation with global non-proliferation norms.

If the diffusion of weapons and weapons' technologies is thus to be constrained or reversed, a comprehensive strategy must be pursued that incorporates the various elements (arms control, export controls, military instruments and collective security, as well as a joint commitment to the prosperity of the developing nations as well as the modernization of their political lives) into a coherent whole, enjoying the strong backing of most members of the international community and especially of its most influential members.

To single out the proliferation problem as the major or sole theme of North-South relations would only accentuate the problem. It would give states of the South reason to believe that the North understands or cares little about their security problems, and would also give them reason to fear a punitive Northern attack, thus giving rise to armaments and rhetoric in the South that would have the effect in the North of generating fears and rationales that would sustain large and modernized nuclear weapon stockpiles for purposes of possible North-South conflict. If over-accentuating the proliferation theme might have these effects, too little attention might well convey lack of interest, with the result that newly emboldened states might seek to acquire or use arms to test the limits of will of the North.

Similarly, to single out the security issue as the sole focus of concern of Northern states may accentuate the alienation of states from the South. Security is important not as an end in itself but for what it makes possible for national development. If the North can only be a partner for the task of creating global enforcement mechanisms or regional alliances, it may well find little partnership from Southern states that desire a stronger international community that supports their economic and political aspirations - and in some cases a more prominent role in leading that community.

Non-proliferation successes will thus depend not just on the skillful application of traditional non-proliferation mechanisms. A broader international strategy that strengthens collective security mechanisms, that strengthens and deepens the global trading system, and that nurtures the shared norms and political values that define international society must be cooperatively elaborated and pursued by both North and South. Such cooperation will not be possible without leadership by a few key states with the vision to define so comprehensive an agenda and the propensity to work with multilateral mechanisms and in a spirit of collaboration. The 1990s will prove the test of this leadership.

12 A Summary of Main Conclusions[1]

The purpose of this book is to describe and analyze nuclear proliferation problems as well as real and potential instruments to counter the spread of nuclear weapons in the future. First, policies and capabilities of proliferating countries have been covered as they are at the heart of the matter, with a strong emphasis on the regional security context. Next, export controls, safeguards and verification have been scrutinized. Then, the issues involved in negotiating a Comprehensive Test Ban and security guarantees by nuclear-weapon states to non-nuclear weapon states have been addressed. To conclude, two generic contributions shed light on the future of the international nuclear non-proliferation regime.

This summary follows the structure of the book.

Regional Issues (Mack, Foran, Van Leeuwen, Potter)

Under the circumstances, the "Agreed Framework" between the United States and North Korea of October 1994 offers the best feasible solution. To all appearances, the agreement has neutralized the threat of rapid proliferation by North Korea, and the risk of reactive proliferation by neighboring states has, as a consequence, been strongly reduced too. The weakness of the accord, however, is in the verification and control arrangements. North Korea will not have to submit to full-scope safeguards for a few years yet, so this means that in the meantime it may still obtain enough fissile material for a small number of nuclear explosives.

---

1. This summary, produced by the editor, is based on the authors' written contributions and the workshop debates held at Clingendael in September 1994. Author's names are given in italics at the top of each paragraph.

M. van Leeuwen (ed.), The Future of the International Nuclear Non-Proliferation Regime, 311-317.
© *1995 Kluwer Academic Publishers. Printed in the Netherlands.*

In addition, it cannot be ruled out that unreported installations in North Korea continue to function in a secret weaponization program: in the past the North Korean regime has consistently demonstrated its unreliability, and there is no reason to believe that its attitude on international relations will change until the political system of the country is fundamentally altered. It should be noted, on the other hand, that the October Agreement contains instruments that offer continued mutual leverage to both contracting parties.

It is unlikely that India and Pakistan will abandon their nuclear options in the foreseeable future. Indian relations with China have improved over the past few years, and as a consequence, India's motivations for maintaining a military nuclear capability have arguably been reduced. Major sources of conflict, however, continue to exist between India and Pakistan. Powerful political forces in Pakistan favor nuclearization, and in India, too, the influential radical Hindu party BJP strongly supports nuclear weapons. Governments in both countries have to take this domestic factor into account. On the other hand, post-Cold War fears that India and Pakistan would officially announce their nuclear weapons' capability have not been justified so far. Domestic and international economic and financial factors may be credited with having exercised a restrictive influence in the past. They may continue to do so. Whenever possible, international organizations (including non-governmental ones) and major states like the United States must try to help improve Indian-Pakistani relations. In their attempts to move India and Pakistan away from the nuclear threshold the United States (and others) must preferably use carrots (such as economic incentives) and switch to sticks only as a means of last resort. They must take into account, however, that too pronounced and single-minded a focus on non-proliferation aims in their dealings with India and Pakistan may have the adverse effect of stimulating domestic pro-nuclear forces or making the nuclear option more interesting as a bargaining object.

The Arab-Israeli peace process opens opportunities to reduce some regional proliferation risks, in particular a freeze and phased reduction of Israel's nuclear capabilities. Such a "cut-off" and freeze could at the very least be interpreted as a confidence-building measure. Full denuclearization should not be expected of Israel as long as Iran, Iraq and Libya - the other three regional powers allegedly fostering nuclear ambitions - remain outside the peace process. A Middle East nuclear-weapon-free zone only stands a chance of being realized if these three countries, too, renounce the acquisition (through purchase or indigenous production) of weapons of mass destruction. A real breakthrough will depend on domestic political developments in Iran, Iraq and Libya, and on a lasting improvement in the relationship between Iran and Iraq. In the meantime, an international policy of great caution and selective restrictions in selling relevant technologies or hardware to these countries, which are all largely dependent on outside help for realizing their nuclear options, will at least help to slow down proliferation, and full-scope safeguards should be applied to them with particular severity. As much as possible, outside powers should help to redress regional conflicts and alleviate tensions.

None of the Soviet successor republics, including Ukraine, has even seriously aimed at permanent status as a nuclear-weapon state. They have used the nuclear systems on their soil as bargaining chips in negotiations, in order to obtain more generous compensations and security guarantees in exchange for parting with the missiles on their territories. The real proliferation risks, however, are caused, particularly outside Russia, by the terrible deficiencies in fissile material accountancy, physical protection of relevant stocks and buildings, export regulation and its implementation, in the lack of proper control at Russia's borders with the other successor states, and, apart from that, by the fact that in the entire area there is a strongly felt need for hard currency. In this case, too, it is true that solutions cannot be imposed from the outside. But foreign powers - the United States and Europe especially - must offer financial and technical support in fighting the deficiencies mentioned. In this context, they should pay much more attention to the non-Russian successor states; they must see to it that promises of help are implemented expediently; apart from that, they must show with greater credibility that they themselves are living by the non-proliferation rules they want the former Soviet countries to respect (this argument is very much true in the Indian case as well).

Safeguards and Export Control (Harry, Domke)

The details of Iraq's illegal nuclear weapons' program have caused serious reconsideration, on various national and international levels, of the effectiveness of export controls and safeguards, and have led to the definition of improvements.

As far as export controls are concerned, attention was focused on including dual-use hardware and technology. As to safeguards, improvements in the regime are sought, especially in the performance of special inspections, the use of national intelligence data, and the further development of environmental monitoring. These measures can be supplemented. Natural uranium ore concentrate, for instance, should be brought under safeguards so that illegal uranium enrichment programs may be detected more easily, especially in combination with environmental monitoring. The IAEA must be granted the financial means to adjust to its more and more demanding safeguarding tasks. Meanwhile, automation of safeguarding functions can be useful and economical, but it should not lead to an irresponsible reduction in human inspections.

As more and more weapon-grade fissile material becomes accessible as a result of the arms reductions' programs of the former Soviet Union and the United States, internationally binding agreements should be made on the physical protection of such materials to prevent theft. Arguably, the most effective and economically sound way to dispose of highly enriched uranium and plutonium is to reintroduce them in the civil nuclear fuel cycle. From this point of view, the present campaign against reprocessing is counterproductive. Reprocessing and enrichment should be organized in international consortia (see *Müller* on internationalization of the civil cycle in general), and the International Plutonium Storage concept may serve as an example, especially with regard to its proposed safeguards' arrangements. The nuclear-weapon states should submit all the nuclear material from their dismantled weapons, but also their civil nuclear cycle, to full-scope safeguards.

Political decision-making is the key both to the spread of nuclear weapons' capabilities and the fight against that spread. A state bent on obtaining a nuclear option is likely to succeed in the end. International non-proliferation instruments (measures to detect and slow down proliferation while also aiming to reduce the motivations leading to proliferation) can only be applied successfully if national authorities are convinced of their necessity and are willing to invest energy, attention and means in them.

Non-Proliferation Incentives: CTBT, Security Guarantees, and "Cut-Off" Proposals (Hoekema, Shaker)

Chances that a Comprehensive Test Ban Treaty will be drafted and adopted have increased since the end of the Cold War and the dramatic acceleration of nuclear arms' reductions. At the same time, the technical relevance that such a Treaty would have has decreased further, as the United States and Russia can satisfy future testing needs by computer simulation. The United States, in particular, has since 1993 abandoned its resistance to a CTBT, taking along the Russians and up to a point the British. The other nuclear-weapon states maintain their reserve towards the conclusion of a CTBT in the short term. As a technical means against horizontal proliferation, the concept of a full ban on nuclear testing has never been relevant, but its political and symbolical importance remains as strong as ever. Many developing countries continue to see a ban as an equalizer between non-nuclear-weapon states and nuclear-weapon states, and as concrete evidence of good behavior by the latter. In 1994, negotiations on a CTBT held under the auspices of the Conference on Disarmament in Geneva made relatively good progress, but offered no prospect for the realization of a Treaty before the NPT review and extension conference in April 1995. Attempts also made in Geneva to start negotiations on the cessation of the production of weapon-grade fissile material, however, failed completely. The question then became prominent of how participants in the NPT conference would evaluate the uneven progress made, and especially whether they would deem it sufficient to vote for indefinite extension.

During the Cold War, questions of international security were dominated by the deep distrust between the two power blocks, and as a consequence it proved impossible in a treaty to enshrine collective positive and negative security guarantees protecting non-nuclear-weapon states that were party to the NPT against the use or threat of use of nuclear weapons. The end of the Cold War opens up new opportunities.

A combination of negative and positive security guarantees laid down by the United Nations Security Council would be the best option. Appeals for guarantees should be directed to the Council, which should also monitor implementation. Negative guarantees should be offered not only to non-nuclear-weapon states that are party to the NPT, but also to others if they are part of a nuclear-weapon-free zone. The relevant Security Council resolution should be explicit about its aim to deter the use or threat of use of nuclear weapons by threshold countries. It should also provide some indications - though not in too much detail - of the range of instruments at its disposal, and it should state the right of victims to humanitarian and technical aid and reparations. By way of an interim solution, a model guarantees' agreement could be formulated following the example of the model safeguards' agreement of the NPT, to serve as the core of arrangements drafted in bilateral negotiations between "protectors" and would-be "protected."

The Future of the International Non-Proliferation Regime (Müller, Roberts)

The Non-Proliferation Treaty by itself is not sufficient to counter proliferation. On the other hand, it has shown its value as the legal basis for a variety of complementary rules and measures. This is one important reason why the NPT should not be allowed to lapse.

Support for the Treaty can best be maintained by redressing discriminatory characteristics of the international regime as much as possible. Leading developing countries must be invited to participate actively in the decision-making concerning export controls. Apart from that, leading industrialized countries should be explicitly prepared to support the economies of developing countries and their global integration. Internationalization of the civil nuclear cycle would be impracticable because of the complexity of questions of ownership and control (compare with *Harry*). In any case it would not be an effective means to prevent illegal programs. Prohibition of the application of sensitive technologies, especially reprocessing, is likely to fail. It is better to try to concentrate the utilization of sensitive materials at a limited number of places (again, see *Harry*), and countries using sensitive technologies or materials in their civil cycle should accept particularly stringent IAEA safeguards. Nuclear-weapon states must accept full-scope safeguards on their civil cycle. In addition, they must provide transparency concerning the number and types of nuclear weapons and the amounts and other characteristics of weapon-grade fissile material in their possession. A convention should be set up on the physical protection of nuclear material used for military purposes.

Regional non-proliferation systems should be fine-tuned to the international system and the NPT as much as possible. Such systems should not inadvertently legitimize nuclear options. (As *Roberts* poses, regional systems are useful because they encapsulate threshold countries that are not willing to ratify the NPT for the time being.) Combining all verification and control systems aimed at halting the spread of weapons of mass destruction (nuclear, chemical, biological, and missile technology) would produce an inefficient and extremely expensive bureaucratic monster. However, well-structured exchanges of relevant technologies and data would be a much better alternative. The IAEA may not have performed perfectly in the past and it must reinvigorate its alertness, but on the other hand, some of the accusations raised against it have been unfair. The IAEA should remain the safeguarding organization for the NPT, although it is high time that a re-evaluation takes place of decision-making procedures in cases of suspected proliferation, as well as possible sanctions and means of enforcement within the international non-proliferation regime. Moreover, offenders outside the NPT should not be allowed to escape such measures. There exists a legal justification for steps against all proliferating countries now that the UN Security Council has resolved that weapons of mass destruction are a threat to international security and peace.

On the basis of the wide international support the NPT has enjoyed during recent decades, it may be concluded that most states considered non-proliferation to be in the interest of their national security and accepted the discrimination between the five nuclear-weapon states recognized by the NPT and the rest of the world in the bargain, or even felt comfortable with it. The end of the Cold War and the concomitant end to bipolarity ought to raise the question of whether so many countries will continue to accept the distinction as meeting their own interests. It must be presumed that the five nuclear-weapon states will not agree to full nuclear disarmament in the foreseeable future. There may well be convincing arguments in favor of continuing the discrimination, but this issue has yet to be seriously discussed. Ignoring it may well undermine the international non-proliferation norm unnecessarily. The United States, as the only remaining nuclear armed superpower, should put the debate on the international agenda.

With regard to the important changes in the international security system and the increased global spread of relevant technologies, is it justified to ask whether the Non-Proliferation Treaty will remain the best legal anchorage for the international non-proliferation regime. The lapse of the NPT before an ameliorated, widely and vigorously supported successor treaty is in place, however, would endanger the international non-proliferation norm and might also induce nuclear-weapon states to reconsider their arms reduction programs. The Non-Proliferation Treaty must be extended in order to make possible the creation of improved norms and rules in the future.

Index

About the Authors

Dr. William K. Domke is a senior researcher at the Lawrence Livermore National Laboratory, University of California, USA.

Virginia I. Foran is research director of the security assurances study and assistant director of the nuclear non-proliferation program at the Carnegie Endowment for International Peace in Washington, D.C., and a Ph. D. candidate, government and politics, at the University of Maryland, College Park, USA.

R. Jörn S. Harry, M. Sc. is project co-ordinator safeguards research at the Netherlands Energy research Foundation ECN in Petten, and fellow of the European Safeguards Research and Development Association (ESARDA).

Jan Th. Hoekema, M.A. is a member of the Dutch parliament and former director of political and UN affairs at the Netherlands Ministry of Foreign Affairs. He was president of the first preparatory committee for the 1995 NPT conference.

Dr. Marianne van Leeuwen is a senior researcher at the Netherlands Institute of International Relations "Clingendael" in The Hague.

Dr. Andrew Mack is professor of political science at the Australian National University, Canberra.

Dr. Harald Müller is director of international programs at the Peace Research Institute Frankfurt.

Dr. William C. Potter is a professor and director of the Center for Russian and Eurasian Studies at the Monterey Institute of International Studies, Monterey CA, USA.

Brad Roberts is editor of the Washington Quarterly.

Dr. Mohamed I. Shaker is ambassador of the Arab Republic of Egypt to the United Kingdom. He was president of the 1985 Review Conference of the NPT.

Clingendael Publications

Books

The United Nations and NATO in Former Yugoslavia, by D.A. Leurdijk, Tulp bv: Zwolle, 1994, 106 p. Price: Dfl 19,95 ISBN 90 73329 04 3

Restructuring Armed Forces in East and West, Jan G. Siccama & Theo van den Doel (eds), Westview Press: Boulder, 1994, 141 p. Price: Dfl 40,- ISBN 0 8133 2476 9

Central Europe: The New Allies? The Road from Visegrad to Brussels, by Theo van den Doel, Westview Press: Boulder, 1993, 126 p. Price: Dfl 40,- ISBN 0 8133 8844 9

Americans and the Palestinian Question; The US public debate on Palestinian nationhood, 1973-1988, by M. van Leeuwen, Rodopi: Amsterdam, 1993, 545 p. Price: Dfl 165,- ISBN 90 5183 533 7 (CIP)

The Disintegration of Yugoslavia, Yearbook of European Studies 5, M. van den Heuvel and J.G. Siccama (eds), Rodopi: Amsterdam, 1992, 218 p. Price: Dfl 35,- ISBN 90 5183 353 9 (paper)

Anerkannt als Minderheit. Vergangenheit und Zukunft der Deutschen in Polen, Hans van der Meulen (Hrsg.), Nomos Verlagsgesellschaft: Baden-Baden, 1994, 256 p. Price: Dfl 77,50 ISBN 3 7890 3634 X

Deutschland im Superwahljahr 1994; Beobachtungen aus deutscher, niederländischer und französischer Sicht, Friso Wielenga, Harald Fühner (Hrsg.), Van Gorcum: Assen, August 1994, 70 p. Price: Dfl 20,- ISBN 90 5031 039 7

Im historischen Würgegriff. Die Beziehungen zwischen Ungarn und der Slowakei in der Vergangenheit, Gegenwart und Zukunft, Robert Aspeslagh, Hans Renner, Hans van der Meulen (Hrsg.), Nomos Verlagsgesellschaft: Baden-Baden, 1994, 180 p. Price: Dfl 45,- ISBN 3 7890 3290 5

Bekannt und unbeliebt. Das Bild von Deutschland und Deutschen unter Jugendlichen von fünfzehn bis neunzehn Jahren, by Lútzen B. Jansen, March 1993, 100 p. Price: Dfl 8,-

Clingendael Papers

Adversaries All Around? (Re)Nationalization of Security and Defence Policies in Central and Eastern Europe, by Pál Dunay, January 1994, 69 p. Price: Dfl 10,- ISBN 90 5031 037 0 (Research Paper)

Through the backdoor; PLO-US contacts, 1974-1988, by Marianne van Leeuwen, August 1992, 40 p. Price: Dfl 10,- ISBN 90 5031 028 1 (Research Paper)

The political debate over a bill of rights for South Africa, by Henk Botha, August 1992, 54 p. Price: Dfl 10,- ISBN 90 5031 029 (Policy Paper)

Nationalism and political change in post-communist Europe, by André W.M. Gerrits, April 1992, 44 p. Price: Dfl 10,- (Research Paper)

The Break-up of Yugoslavia: Threats and Challenges, by Radovan Vukadinonic, February 1992, 39 p. Price: Dfl 10,-

Changing Hearts? The Bush administration, American public opinion, and the Arab-Israeli conflict, by Marianne van Leeuwen, November 1991, 40 p. Price: Dfl 10,- (Research Paper)

Occasional Papers

Decision-making by the Security Council: The Case of Rwanda, 1993-1994. A review of resolutions, by D.A. Leurdijk and L. van Zandbrink, 1994, 16 p. Price: Dfl 10,-

Decision-making by the Security Council: The Case of Haiti, 1993-1994. A review of resolutions, by D.A. Leurdijk and L. van Zandbrink, 1994, 19 p. Price: Dfl 10,-

Decision-making by the Security Council: The Case of Former Yugoslavia, 1991-1994. A review of resolutions, by D.A. Leurdijk and L. van Zandbrink, 1994, 42 p. Price: Dfl 10,-

Report of the Round Table on the Transatlantic Relationships in the Field of Security and Economics, The Hague, September 15-16, 1994, H.H.J. Labohm (ed.), 1994, 65 p. Price: Dfl 10,-

Redefining the Security Interests of Russia in the post-Soviet Era, Conference Report of the International Seminar February 17-19, 1994, 24 p. Price: Dfl 7,50

Case-Studies in Second Generation United Nations Peacekeeping, Januari 1994, 65 p. Price: Dfl 10,-

Developing Romania's Energy Resources: The Prospects for Cooperation between the European Community and Romania, by I. Daduianu-Vasilescu, 1993, 56 p. Price: Dfl 10,-

G-7 Economic Summits: A View from the Lowlands, by Hans H.J. Labohm, Februari 1993, 40 p. Price: Dfl 10,-

Around NATO's new strategy, Report of a seminar for experts in the field of defence strategy, September 17-18, 1992, December 1992, 87 p. Price: Dfl 10,-

Continuity and change in post-communist Europe, by Jadwiga Staniszkis, June 1992, 37 p. Price: Dfl 10,-

A short guide to Diplomatic Training, by P.W. Meerts, August 1991, 32 p. Price: Dfl 10,-

Clingendael Publications can be ordered at:
The Netherlands Institute of International Relations "Clingendael"
Research Department
Clingendael 7
P.O. Box 93080
2509 AB The Hague
Telephone 31-70-3245384
Telefax 31-70-3282002

The International Law of Nuclear Energy
Basic Documents

edited by
Mohamed M. ElBaradei
Edwin I. Nwogugu
John M. Rames

This book provides, for the first time in a single publication, a collection of basic documents relating to the international law of nuclear energy. The series of introductions facilitate the understanding of the documents and their context. They embrace the four concerns associated with the safe and peaceful use of nuclear energy, i.e. to ensure: that nuclear energy is used in conformity with basic safety standards; that nuclear material and nuclear facilities are protected against theft and sabotage; that nuclear facilities are not subject to attack during armed conflict; and that nuclear material and facilities are not used for military purposes.

The book is an invaluable reference work for all those working in the field of international nuclear law and the regulation of the use of nuclear energy as well as for teachers and students of law.

1993, 2148 pp.
ISBN 0-7923-1747-5
Hardbound NLG 795.00 / USD 485.00 / GBP 315.00

Kluwer
academic
publishers

P.O. Box 322, 3300 AH Dordrecht, The Netherlands
P.O. Box 358, Accord Station, Hingham, MA 02018-0358, U.S.A.